Opening

C000072335

Contents

Preface

In the summer of 2013 Christine Hickman-Smith, then County Chairman, asked if I would write a book for the Centenary to celebrate the work of the Worcestershire Federation of WIs since 1980. Being a good WI member, I said I would and went away to think about its format. Money was earmarked by the Board of Trustees for its printing and they approved my suggestion of a book in two parts, the first part chronicling what had happened in the Federation and illustrated by photographs and other memorabilia; the second to be comprised of a page for each of the County's WIs, thus capturing both their similarities and diversities, as the pages would be written in their words.

So began the work of four and a half years, this too falling into two parts as I undertook the research and writing of part one and the superintending and editing of part two.

The project was introduced at the ACM in October 2013, a flyer asking WIs to nominate a representative for their page was sent out and an email address, dedicated to the book, was set up to receive communications. Once a nominee had contacted me, I sent out details for the requirements for a WI page in the way of word number, font size and picture quality but wrote "You will have complete freedom to show off your WI and what it has achieved and meant to its members since 1980. Of course, there will have to be editorial discretion to make sure that the whole book reads well."

Meanwhile, a start had been made on the research. The proceedings of the Federation are to be found in a variety of documents and every one had to be read. Minutes are taken of all Board and Sub-committee meetings along with those of special committees called ad hoc committees which are those set up for a particular event. Financial details are also kept. There are also minutes from the annual Council and half yearly meetings, whilst Annual Reports, the County News, the Yearly Handbook and Federation scrapbooks all contained information.

I took notes and photographs from all of the sources mentioned above. Some of these sources are kept in WI House, the rest being housed in the County Council's Record Office at The Hive, Worcester. Most of the latter was uncatalogued, so the numerous boxes comprising the WI archive had first to be inspected to ascertain their contents. In this I had the invaluable help of Mary Davis, then WI Archivist, who had consigned most of the deposits to the Hive and had a record of what had been sent. Contrary to what might be supposed, we spent many happy days at the Hive sorting out just what was what! Here I must thank the very patient and helpful staff of the Hive for their part in achieving what, at times, felt like the impossible.

In both writing and in interviews, the Past County Chairmen and many others provided their memories, photographs and memorabilia from their time serving the Federation. Their contributions are used throughout the book and I thank them all for providing the extra dimension that cannot be gleaned from the official words, for the time they have so willingly given and for the pleasure these contacts brought. Nothing was too much for some of them who went to great lengths to secure information or even one detail for me. Mary Wehner, chasing an elusive name for a photograph, emailed two weeks before her sudden death "I've got it ! I've really, really got it !! .... is the lady's name."

Fiona Leighton and Trudi Tayloe have been appealed to so many times for information, lists and a myriad other things. They have provided them all so promptly and so kindly that I feel blessed by their being in charge of the WI office.

Many of the illustrations are taken from old and, sometimes, poor quality sources. Many have had to be scanned or photographed and almost every one of the illustrations has been enhanced or adjusted digitally. Some, however, remain inferior to the hoped-for standard. The 395 used in Part One represent only a portion of the ones collected. There are a further 222 in Part Two.

I have done my best to make all the facts as accurate as possible but inevitably some things may not chime with the reader's recollections. There has been some unavoidable repetition where things were relevant in more than one section. I wished to include the names of all who have served on committees for about at least a year. This proved no easy task and was made more difficult as those early sources which did contain names, did not usually record first names. Thank you so much to the many members with the longest memories who have very willingly spent time filling in the gaps. One hundred percent was not achieved and so, those which have eluded us are styled with their surname plus Mrs or Miss in the lists. Some names were given with different spellings, from which I have chosen one and some of you may be named twice because of name changes. I apologise now if anyone has been overlooked. A further observation is necessary regarding dates. As these were not always clear, I decided that, to give continuity, a date would be recorded as that given in the yearly handbook when it was not obvious from the other sources. Lastly, the name changes of County committees, positions and documents could have resulted in confusion and so, in general, the subject is referred to by the name it held at the chronological time unless it is more sensible to use the current appellation.

In my original outline to the Board of Trustees, I said that the pre-printing preparation of the book was not in my remit. Well, it soon became obvious that it would have to be for when the WI pages came in they needed formatting there and then. So, after consultation with my husband and the agreement of the Board, this was taken on too for the whole of the book. I reported at the 2016 ACM that many WIs had kindly commented on my expertise in re-formatting their entries but felt I had to come clean, that I was not the computer whizz they thought me. It was my husband, Richard, who worked that magic and for this he has my deepest thanks.

My heartfelt thanks also go to David Hickman-Smith for proofreading the whole of the document and to Mary Davis, Christine Hickman-Smith and Sue Stone for reading the draft of the Federation section, though of course the ultimate responsibility is mine.

I have been asked several times if I regretted taking on such a large undertaking, for after all I had limited experience in authorship, though a long history in researching data. The answer is that I loved every minute of discovering and writing about this organisation. The more I did, the more amazed I became at the energy, inventiveness and kindness of the members of this Federation. It made me even more proud to be a member and it has been such a pleasure to put the activities of the Worcestershire Federation 1980-2018 into print.

Sylvia Beardshaw   December 2017

From the County Chairman, Sue Stone

Almost the first task I was asked to undertake as the newly elected Chairman of WFWI was to write a forward to this book. Of course, I said yes, but first had to read the text.

This book is a gem. It is full of names, past and present. Some you will know, others you might not recognize, but all have played their part in this story. It tells of experiences, some exciting like the train trips on the Raspberry Ripple, meeting Prince Charles and the celebration dinner held at Severn Hall Malvern but also some devastating, the wrath of anti-hunt lobbyists, no heating or catering at an ACM and the speaker not turning up. (We know that one!) Most of all it tells of how WFWI dealt with both the good and the not so good and will continue to do so.

Please read this book. It does not have to be read cover to cover. It is written in such a way that you can dip in and out of headings and sub-headings and it will make sense however you chose to do it.

Congratulations to Sylvia and all those who helped with the WI pages. It is a memoire of the greatest value to us all, members and non-members alike.

Sue

From the Chairman of the Centenary Committee, Christine Hickman-Smith

In 2015, I was asked by the Board of Trustees if I would Chair an Ad Hoc Committee to plan WFWI Centenary in 2018. What a journey and a privilege this has been.

Knowing that we had 'our history' from 1918 - 1980 written in a publication entitled Madam President Fellow Members, a book I had read when training to be a WI Adviser, I thought it would be good to have our story updated for our centenary.

I knew just the friend and WI member to ask to consider taking on the task for us, Sylvia Beardshaw. Sylvia, a member of Chaddesley Corbett WI, has published other books on local history and a beautiful guide and history of our village church, St Cassian's.

I was delighted when Sylvia agreed, and so the work of this book 'Opening Doors' began.

Many emails, conversations, much research and much writing, over thousands of hours, have taken place. On behalf of all our members, my sincere thanks to Sylvia for the huge amount of time, expertise and dedication she has given to this publication. Our sincere thanks also to her husband, Richard, who has formatted all the pages and has been so supportive.

As WI members, we seek to Inspire Women and this is the work of an Inspiring Woman.

Thank you, Sylvia for this wonderful book which brings our story to life.

Christine

Opening Doors

A Centenary Celebration

The Worcestershire Federation of WIs
From the Diamond Jubilee Celebrations to 2018

Welcome to this celebration of the WI in Worcestershire. If you are a member then you will be justly proud of the achievements of our movement in the County since we celebrated our Diamond Jubilee. If you are not a member then it is hoped that the recollections in this book inspire you to join, though you must of course be a Woman!

This book charts the years from 1980 and is in two parts. The first part covers the activities of the Worcestershire Federation of WIs – WFWI. The second part covers the activities of the individual WIs who belong to the Federation. Each has been given the opportunity to tell its story over the same period. There are currently 125 WIs with over 4000 members. The WI in Worcestershire at its Centenary, is a slimmer version of its Diamond Jubilee self. It continues, despite the fact that so many women work and have less time to devote to hobbies, despite the many financial changes that have occurred during the period and despite the Jam and Jerusalem image so beloved of the uninitiated.

It continues because its members know just how much can be gained from it, not only from the educational aspects which have characterised WI from the beginning, but from the friendship, fellowship, opportunity and just downright enjoyment that it offers.

It also continues in Worcestershire, at both local and county level, because of the enormous commitment from those members who volunteer to run its affairs.

They do this because of their belief in what the movement has to offer women at any stage in life. They are willing to give their time and talents to further these ends, whatever other calls are made on them, and in doing so, often enrich their own lives in a way that they could not imagine on first joining. *It has indeed opened doors for so many.*

Part One

The Worcestershire Federation of WIs

Introduction

The first part of the book recounts the activities of the Federation and of those WI members who have volunteered to serve at County level. Some members served for many years, others for a much shorter time, but all added to the rich tapestry which makes up the events chronicled here. Involvement has sometimes changed the course of a member's life and it is often the case that being a member of a County committee gave back more to the volunteer than she could have envisaged. Several such instances were encountered during the research for this book and are alluded to throughout the text. Gwen Bullas, retiring from the Executive Committee in 1986, said "So many doors have been opened to me since I joined this committee. I am so grateful for the opportunities that have been offered." It is most striking that on joining, little did she know just how many doors existed, and this has been the experience of many women throughout the years.

In 1919 the National Executive had stated the aims of the fledgling movement in its new magazine 'For Home and Country.' "WI offers women the opportunity of sharing friendship and education to help widen their horizons and influence local, national and international affairs. It aims to improve and develop the quality of life for women and their families, advance the education of women and enable them to work together to put into practice the ideals for which the organisation stands."

Today's members will know that these aims have not changed in nearly a century and the Federation committees direct their energies towards furthering them.

This observation from a new member was quoted at the 1992 Annual Council Meeting or ACM. "I have lived in the same street for twenty-two years but, since I joined the WI a year ago, I have made more friends than I did in the previous twenty-one." At the 2004 ACM Clarissa Dixon Wright stated that the WI was "An oasis of calm in a mad world."

County badge pre 2011

Greta Mitchell said in 1995 "I have gained a lot from WI. Like many of us, when I first joined I was totally lacking in confidence. I was a mouse. I have learnt so much in many areas, flower arranging is now a hobby and my cooking has improved. There are so many facets available which can help us to become more fulfilled and, let's face it, a more interesting person." She could have mentioned too that through WI she gained so much confidence that she became an Adviser, a chairman of sub-committees and County Chairman!

1980, where this account begins, was a very good year for Worcestershire Federation of WIs. The successful diamond jubilee celebrations, devised by an ad hoc committee, had been enjoyed by 7,500 members in 177 individual WIs, the length and breadth of this large County. Positive publicity both in press and on radio had been joyfully received and, to cap it all, a healthy financial situation had been created.

The Federation affairs were, at that time, run by an Executive Committee composed of 15 elected members. They made appointments yearly to six sub-committees, each of these responsible for one of the WI's areas of interest, but not to the Organisation, now Advisers, Committee. The appointment of members to this committee, although approved by Worcestershire, falls to the National Federation of Women's Institutes or NFWI.

All of these committees had been involved in the celebrations, not only creating special events for the year but also putting on their usual activities and making them extra special. For instance, the Home Economics and Craft Committee's Rally was so popular that a second had to be arranged. The publicity machine worked wonderfully with lots of coverage in the County's newspapers. Very much appreciated too was the almost monthly air time given by the BBC which enabled Executive members to publicise the forthcoming events on the radio programme, Time Off. All the interviews were pre-recorded but the last, in November, was transmitted live, quite a nail biting event for the three ladies who spoke.

The packed programme was very varied, showing the very best of WI achievement. The events started in April with a thanksgiving service in Worcester Cathedral. Over 2000 members attended. There was a large choir composed of WI members and the floral decorations were also the work of members. The Cathedral authorities were so impressed by the flowers that the Federation was asked to join the prestigious flower rota and WI members have contributed the flower arrangements for one week a year ever since. During the service two books were blessed by the Bishop, the original Minute Book from 1917 and 'Madam President: Fellow Members,' the story of the Federation to its 60th Birthday. The latter was written by Dorothy Williams and illustrated by Janet Wooldridge.

Members were able to snap up the Royal Worcester dishes and the pairs of prints specially made as Jubilee souvenirs and, as the summer progressed, visit Derbyshire Well Dressings and Chatsworth House. Demand for places on this outing was so great that a second visit was arranged. A Sports Day, with many different pursuits on offer, was followed by a week-long Drama Festival culminating at the Theatre Royal, Redditch. In July a County Ball was held, and in September more than 500 guests enjoyed a family Barbecue at Broadclose Farm, Inkberrow. November saw two sittings of 90 members each at the Shoppers lunches in WI House.

November also saw the staging of Jubilee Jems at the Malvern Theatre, produced by Peggy Cox and featuring members from eighteen WIs. The decades' themed show began dramatically with ultra violet light picking out the letters WI. The letters were formed by the white dresses amongst the black of the massed choir. It was a wonderfully received performance; the theatre management saying that many compliments were heard. If anyone noticed that the member singing 'Waltzing in the Clouds' had broken the heel of her shoe, then they kept quiet. On entering the venue in the dark she had inadvertently fallen down some steps and landed under the piano!

The 1980 Jubilee Celebrations

Pair of Commemorative Prints

The Jubilee Committee[1]

Order of Service at Worcester Cathedral

Below – Blessing of the first Minute Book and the Jubilee Book.

Opening scene from Jubilee Jems, picking out 'WI' in white

Above - Shoppers Lunch at WI House
Below – The Family BBQ

Royal Worcester Jubilee Dish

---

[1] L-R: Leonie Rimmer, Valerie Freeman, Grace Adkins, Raley Clifton-chairman, Daphne Hopkins, Lorna Matthews.

The first prize in the Diamond Jubilee Draw, a diamond and gold necklet, was received by a delighted Phyllis Cooper during the interval.

There was however one mistake made in this year, for 1980 was not the Federation's sixtieth birthday but its sixty second! Now the odd time span of this publication is explained.

Dorothy Williams' research into the Federation's past showed that the long held belief in a 1920 foundation for the Federation was false[2]. It had become a Federation two years earlier. Too late to halt the celebrations, they went ahead. When and how this misapprehension occurred is not known but it had been held for many years. Indeed, the handbook and the Honours Board at WI house have shown the first Federation Chairman as Lucy Hingley in 1920. In fact, the first Chairman was the Countess of Plymouth in 1918.

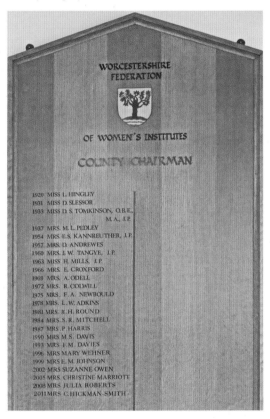

She had chaired the preceding Conference of Worcestershire WIs since its inception in 1917. The record was set to rights for the 75th Anniversary whilst the handbook was amended in 2017 to include Lady Plymouth in time for the Centenary. The Honours Board awaits an update.

Dorothy Williams' closing sentence in the Diamond Jubilee book, 'Madam President: Fellow Members' posed the question "What will the WI be like in 38 years' time?" This is echoed by a similar sentiment found in a special newspaper, the Jubilee News edited by Diana Farmiloe, which recorded all the events. In that publication Grace Adkins, the County Chairman, ended her overview of the successful year by writing "Dear Fellow Members, ... I wonder what the next Jubilee will bring. In these uncertain times it is difficult to forecast the future but it is my fervent hope that the enthusiasm of our Diamond Year will turn to optimism and determination, that we will be spurred on to greater achievements and experiences, so there will be even more to celebrate when Worcestershire Federation of Women's Institutes Centenary comes along."

---

[2] 'Madam President: Fellow Members' published in 1980 (ISBN 0 9506868 0 8) is an excellent account of WFWI's first 62 years.

Well, here we are at that Centenary, so how has WFWI done?

Grace Adkins words certainly held a note of trepidation along with the strong streak of hopefulness.

The trepidation may have resulted from two trends prevailing at the time; a decline in WI membership which in Worcestershire had seen a fall from the 60's high of over 10,000 to 7,500 in Jubilee year, and the circumstances prevailing in the country at that time.

The 'Winter of Discontent,' had occurred in 1979 and through the early 1980's the country continued in recession, with inflation reaching 20% plus. High unemployment, many strikes and the threat of terrorism were also ever present. Against this backdrop the WI was an ageing movement. Those stalwarts of the First and, more numerously, of the Second World Wars were thinning out and younger women were less attracted to what they perceived as their Grannies' preserve. Women also had greater job opportunities. The introduction of maternity leave in 1975 had allowed many to continue their work after starting a family. Rising costs and house prices made this income a necessity in many homes. County committees met during the day and the minutes are dotted with resignations due to increased work commitments.

For what leisure time was left, the WI found itself competing with newer organisations. The Housewives Register, set up in 1960 and which often met in the evening, appealed to young mums who wished to join a female group. The U3A which sprang up in the early 1980's aimed to attract the retired women at the other end of the age spectrum. It offered a wide range of locally based courses which were tutored, mainly, by fellow members and it was also open to men, which meant that couples could share the same club.

Despite these circumstances and those which have influenced the country over the intervening years, it is the hopefulness expressed in Grace's speech that has triumphed. The County Federation's part in this success, for of course the members of individual WIs have also played their part, is due to the efforts of the 502 women, volunteers all, who have run the County's affairs during this period. Between them they have held 848 posts. What these dedicated ladies have offered the wider membership since 1980 is astonishing. By the end of 2017, 3,382 separate events, some days or even a week long, have been organised, averaging 89 per year. The workload taken on to accomplish this has been enormous. What it has meant in personal development is incalculable but so many of those who have served the Federation say how much it has meant to them. This part of the book is a testament to their achievements and to them the Federation owes its success.

Some might think that it would not have mattered if WFWI did not exist. That idea is to misunderstand the WI as a movement. It exists to help women develop themselves. The myriad opportunities that have been offered to members by the Federation could not be provided in individual WIs because of the costs involved. The Federation is also one of the 69 County Federations which together make up the National Federation of WIs. NFWI would find it impossible to cater for some 200,000 members without a regional structure.

A short look at the origins of our Federation highlights this interdependence.

WFWI is older than all but a handful of the WIs within the County. It started as the Conference of Worcestershire Women's Institutes on 3rd November, 1917 at the Shire Hall, one of only six of the incipient County Federations in existence by the end of 1917[3].To understand why the WI, as the Women's Institute movement is now usually called, is a movement that is at once national, regional and very local requires acquaintance with its foundation. It was introduced into this country in 1915, from its Canadian birthplace, by Mrs Madge Watt who, by 1917, held the imposing title of 'Imperial Organiser'. At first shunned by those she approached, she eventually gained support from some members of the influential Agricultural Organisation Society which was promoting increased food production during the First World War. She held the first meeting in Wales at Llanfairpwll, Anglesey[4], being asked to do so by the local aristocracy. [5]

So, at the beginning, local WIs owed their formation to persons of influence in the community. These early leaders got together on a County basis. This resulted in the setting up of Conferences, as happened in Worcestershire, where the fledgling WIs could hold discussions on policy. As things began to develop, the Conferences in turn wished to hold joint discussions and sent representatives to a Central Committee based in London. This committee devised the structure and constitution which, with some alterations, still governs the movement today. So the hierarchy, familiar to all WI members, evolved right at the start.

Mrs Watt spoke at the inaugural Conference of Worcestershire Women's Institutes in 1917 and the first Executive Committee in Worcestershire was composed of many leading names in the county. Their involvement probably allowed the movement to thrive. Women meeting, learning and discussing together was a novel idea and was viewed with suspicion in some quarters. However, if the 'lady of the manor' was involved, well, perhaps that was alright.

Worcestershire's first Chairman was the Countess of Plymouth but it was Lady Isabel Margesson who seems to have been the prime mover. She was a Suffragette and, like many of the other women founders of WI, had learned much of her organising ability in that movement. She lived in Barnt Green where, in 1916, she established the first WI in Worcestershire. She was elected to the inaugural Central Committee of Management, the precursor of The National Federation, at its first National meeting in London in October 1917.

On the 11th June 1918 the Worcestershire Conference became a County Federation and on the 21st November 1918, ten days after the end of World War One, it was affiliated to the National Federation which was by then gaining its independence from the Board of Agriculture, The Countess of Plymouth remaining as County Chairman. At this point, as there was no money for paid organisers, two Voluntary County Organisers or VCOs, now

---

[3] J W Robertson Scott – 'The Story of the Women's Institute in England and Wales and Scotland,' 1925

[4] Ruth Burton, a Barnt Green member born in 1901, wrote in 2000 that the head teacher of her school in Bangor attended this meeting and told the girls of it next morning.

[5] Jane Robinson – 'A Force to be Reckoned With' 2011 tells the story of NFWI

known as WI Advisers or WIAs, were trained by Mrs Watt to undertake the formation of WIs nationally. Lady Isabel Margesson was one of the two. Worcestershire has been at the very centre of the WI from the beginning.

With hindsight, the story of WFWI really does change in character around 1980 where 'Madam President: Fellow Members' ends and this book begins. The Diamond Jubilee book covering the first sixty-two years shows the joy of a new organisation exploring the way forward and forging new opportunities for women. It also deals with its maturing self when expanded membership and familiarity had given it a comfortable presence in the Nation's identity.

This book covering the following thirty-eight years from 1980 has to deal with a gradual decline in WFWI's fortunes when compared with the early years. It is a period characterised by both external and internal changes which constantly meant that the Executive had to face up to and deal with many challenges. These changes in circumstance needed to be addressed successfully if the doors of opportunity were to continue opening for members. With some slight hiccups, WFWI has been outstandingly successful in facing and overcoming the challenges posed.

This is down to the leadership of the successive Executive Committees, later, Boards of Trustees, and the dedication and determination of those who have served on this and the other county committees. All that they have faced, overcome and achieved is now to be examined.

To understand just what these women have achieved, an explanation of the way the Federation is run is required. Just what sort of organisation does a member join on venturing 'upwards' from the grass roots? It is highly likely that such a member, new to the running of the Federation, may not know much about what she is taking on, despite the talents she may bring.

In whatever the capacity a member serves, it is of the first importance to emphasise its voluntary nature. The only reimbursement which can be received, apart from honorariums for Chairman and Treasurer, is for travel to meetings or for expenditure incurred when furthering the activities of the Federation. Betty Johnson wrote about this service in the Annual Report for 1999 saying "Reading through past annual reports I have always been amazed at the huge range of activities, abilities and concerns demonstrated by your Executive and supporting committees especially when one reflects they are all accomplished quite voluntarily."

In 2017 a look at the makeup of the country's sixty-nine Federations, as listed by NFWI, shows that Worcestershire had the seventeenth greatest number of WIs and twenty-third highest total membership. Devon has the greatest number of WIs with 218 compared to Worcestershire's 125 whilst Cheshire and Essex both top the members list with 9,183 members compared to Worcestershire's 3,917 (NFWI figure; WFWI latest count is 4,139). Gwynedd Meirionnydd, the smallest Federation, has 14 WIs and 320 members.

WFWI officers have always regarded Worcestershire as progressive and go ahead within the family of Federations and this has proved invaluable in the years since 1980.

The Board of Trustees, formerly the Executive Committee

The responsibility for all the decisions, the administration and the financial health of the Federation is undertaken by this committee whose proceedings are governed by standing orders and terms of reference and its members have the ultimate legal responsibility for everything the Federation does.

It is important to know that the Federation, like the National Organisation, has been a charity, number 228994, throughout the whole period covered by this book and so has to adhere to the laws governing charities. This factor influences many of the decisions taken by the Board.

Called the Executive Committee until December 2009, it then received its present name, the Board of Trustees (BoT). The name Board of Trustees is a more accurate description of the role played by this committee as its members had acted as trustees since at least 1990 when the Federation rejected incorporation.

The members of this committee are voted in every two years by the WIs. There were fifteen elected places in 1980 but this has gradually been reduced, first by one in 1987 then by two in both 2004 and 2011 finally reaching a minimum of eight in 2016. Throughout the period until 2016 the co-option of up to four more members on a yearly basis has always been available but then it increased to six. From 1980 to 2017, 105 ladies have served on this committee. The longest serving, giving nineteen years, is Ann Canham.

BoT members hold a ballot to choose the County Chairman from their number. This person usually serves for a maximum of three years, being re-elected annually. Since 1980 there have been fourteen Chairmen. There have also been eight County Treasurers whose appointment is also made annually.

The ladies who undertake these two roles are the most prominent members of the BoT and indeed are very important in the guidance of the Federation. This is particularly so in the case of the Chairman, as hers is the role of leader. However, as befits this democratic organisation, the Board as a whole has the final vote.

1991 Executive Meeting in WI House Committee Room[6]

Other members are appointed yearly to specific jobs. There are two vice chairmen and an assistant treasurer. The rest take on roles which are devised in response to the standing orders and terms of reference of the BoT. The type of role has changed over the years with the changing needs of the Federation but all of them are recorded here.

Members have taken responsibility for the Federation's interest in: The Associated Country Women of the World - ACWW, Broadcasting, Denman College, Holidays, the WI Magazine, Liaison with WI Markets, Press and Publicity, Promotion, Publications, Resolutions, Test Certificates and as a Voluntary Education Co-ordinator (VEC). Each year too, a member is assigned the responsibility for a sub-committee, in the early years as chairman, later as a member. Besides all these responsibilities, representation on outside bodies has been required and this means regular attendance at these meetings for the member involved. There were fourteen of these posts in 1980, although, as is seen later, the number diminished as the years passed. Some of these responsibilities have, as will also be seen, devolved elsewhere, mainly to the sub-committees. It must be noted here that, in this early part of the text, reference will be made to various facets of the organisation without explaining what it is. This explanation will be found later in the text when the facet is dealt with in detail.

Whatever official posts were held, the minutes show that Executive and later BoT, turned their hand to all the myriad jobs demanded by the events of the time. These include attending Council Meetings, giving reports, delivering post by hand, producing any number of cakes for any number of events, providing supper for the Worcester Disabled from 1980 to 1987, stewarding at Denman, donating raffle prizes, doing the stock-taking at WI House, helping with WFWI mailing, meeting members at membership events, promotional work especially at promotional events, including modelling the WFWI range of clothing at the 1989 half yearly council meeting, looking after an old sampler, taking part in the Malvern

---

[6] Clockwise from top - Mary Davis, Brenda Spragg, Liz Osborn, Shirley Noble, Grace Richardson, Beryl Bubb, Eileen Chapman, Diana Cartmel, Rosemary Roberts, Margaret Deakin, Betty Luxton, Patsy Anderson, Gwyn Wilmore.

Well Dressing activities, responding to the BSE crisis, writing a job description, completing a medical form, being attached to a Group, running the Talbot Room, continuing to make cakes, be involved in the sale and purchase of WI House, clearing the house and holding yard sales of unwanted goods, demonstrating against excess packaging, completing a skills audit, making more cakes, visiting the nearly completed Bull Ring Centre in Birmingham, visiting the NFWI headquarters in London, offering help in the County Flooding

Above - Bull Ring visit 2007
Left - 2005 Executive Committee's Promotional Walk for NFWI's 90@90 initiative[7]

emergency, taking part in physical activities especially walking, loading the van for the annual meetings and making more cakes. In 2001 there was total disruption of the planned activities and much reorganisation was required when Foot and Mouth struck. Appeals were made to help those affected and Worcestershire Federation responded magnificently, giving nearly £5,000 in goods and money. The appreciation can be seen in the letter on the next page from the Worcestershire Rural Stress Support Network.

This very long list of activities undertaken by the Federation Committee over the years illustrates only part of the work done. It shows that Committee members can and do turn their hand to anything they are asked, over and above the position they have accepted in the Committee.

Holding Trustees

The Board has invited women with an intimate knowledge of the running of WFWI to fill these posts. Usually three in number they are responsible for WI House and the scrutinising of the Board's work, especially latterly, the financial aspects. There have been ten ladies serving - Olive Odell, Sheila Walker, Ruth

Olive Odell   Sheila Walker   Ruth Palmer   Jean Newbould

---

[7] L-R Back - Sheila Bishop, Chris Marriott, Christine Hickman-Smith, Ann Canham, Sylvia Beardshaw, Sue Arnold
Front - Julia Roberts, Suzanne Owen, Freda Davies.

Palmer, Mary Glaze, Jean Newbould, Mary Davis, Greta Mitchell, Pat Harris, Suzanne Owen and Christine Hickman-Smith, all past Federation Chairmen or Treasurers. Those not pictured as Chairman or Treasurer are shown on the previous page. In 2006 the minutes stated that they no longer needed to be appointed annually and from 2010 they have received the minutes of all meetings and have a standing invitation to any Board meeting.

WORCESTERSHIRE RURAL STRESS SUPPORT NETWORK
HELPLINE 01905 381818

24th August, 2001

FROM THE CO-ORDINATOR; Roderick B. Waugh
Roseville Cottage, Ash Lane,
Martin Hussingtree,
Worcestershire
WR3 8TB

Mrs Betty Johnson
Chair Worcestershire WI
W.I. House,
Worcester

Dear Betty,

Now that it seems the spectacular response of W.I. Members to the groceries for Farmers Appeal has finally ended I just felt it important to write to you to express my personal, and the networks thanks, for all that you and your members were able to do during the Foot and Mouth Crisis. From the figures below you can see just how spectacularly your members did respond.

I would however particularly like to feature in my thanks Cynthia and Margaret and the others who, from time to time, work in the Office. I have written separately to Cynthia on that point and enclose a copy of that letter for your files. Their cheerfulness and willingness to respond was marvellous and certainly helped to keep me going throughout the crisis.

We estimate that the total of groceries collated has been in excess of £2900 (that, I am told, is the equivalent of over 40 monthly shopping trips for an average family). Their willing labours to carry that into storage and then into my car is not only very appreciated but represents a huge physical effort amongst their already busy schedule. Monies collected were £1889. 32 making a grand total of £4792. 32 passing through our funds. The other good news is that that will all be match funded by the Countryside Agency making your members effort therefore twice as fruitful.

The response from those receiving the parcels of groceries has been overwhelming thanks and relief that one worry has at least been dealt with by your members kindness. The crisis is by no means over yet and Worcestershire Rural Stress Support Network continues to support Rural Families as much as resources allow us. Buying fodder for next winter and helping Mothers with groceries, holiday breaks and school clothes for next term are all part of how the money is being spent.

Can I extend my thanks to you personally for bearing this extra work as Chair so cheerfully, your willingness and co-operation was always very much appreciated. I hope we will have the chance to work together again sometime but in the meanwhile I send my best wishes and grateful thanks to you and to all your members.

Yours with regards,

Roderick B. Waugh

30 AUG 2001

Prior to then they attended two meetings per annum with food being served at a social gathering afterwards.

It is at the Board meetings that most of the decisions affecting the County are discussed and action voted upon so a look is now taken at how they are conducted and what is discussed.

Since 2011 the Board has conducted its business at eight monthly meetings, each held on the first Wednesday. Previously, it met every month except August. These regular meetings total 408 to the end of 2017. Reports are given on each facet of the organisation including the National Federation and County WIs. Letters and requests from outside are also dealt with. Usually, the agenda is lengthy.

Minutes are taken by the Administrator. Whatever is agreed is then implemented by the relevant officer or committee and communicated to the WIs. This is done by letter or email or whenever possible in the County News (Letter) - CNL. It is reiterated again at the Annual or Half yearly Council meetings.

In 1980 the mood at County business meetings was still very formal. Everyone was addressed as Mrs or Miss, both in speech and in the minutes, the latter making it difficult to trace the first names of some of the early members. All of the meetings took place during the day and the members could expect a six hour sitting, although there was a lunch break. The business was run by the Chairman and all speakers directed their comments via the chair. Gradually relaxing in tone and length over the years, much of the verbal content of the business has been replaced by written minutes and reports which can be studied by members before the meeting. A private session, held when necessary, immediately before the main meeting and not attended by the Federation Administrator, became more frequent from 2002.

The day to day working of the committee has been described above but there were many issues which had to be addressed by its members, either on a yearly or occasional basis, especially those proposed by NFWI. Since 1980 NFWI has set out proposals to change the Constitution of WI not once but three times. The first came in 1989 when the financially ailing NFWI announced a big shake up.

WI votes for charity status to meet challenge of new century

1990 Newspaper headline on the changes to the WI Constitution

Its wish to take charity status and become incorporated as a company limited by guarantee was the most contentious part. This caused great consternation in Worcestershire. Meetings were held around the county and after much heart searching by members it was decided that Worcestershire would oppose the measure. County Chairman, Pat Harris, held talks with other Federation chairmen and there was a lot of discussion at National Council, but the changes were voted in by 81% at the National AGM of 1990 just after Pat left office. Worcestershire voted against the motion.

Many Federations followed National's lead and became incorporated. Worcestershire was not one of them, a decision upheld by subsequent committees. This is the current

13

position, the Federation's legal status being governed by its Trust Deed and decisions being made in accordance with the Standing Orders and Terms of Reference pertaining at the time.

Ten years later and despite the assurances that the constitution would not be altered for many a year, NFWI revamped it again, provoking many objections from Worcestershire members at the two meetings held in the County. These were to no avail, as the changes went through. A third new constitution was approved in 2013. It was in the Financial Report of 2001, just after the second changes, that the members of Executive were first called Trustees.

The BoT sets its own budget and must approve those submitted by the other county committees. As the years went on it also gave much thought to forward planning. This aspect came to the fore in 1991 when WFWI held meetings on the subject with a consultant. Policies and Decisions data has always been kept and this was updated by Doreen Jeeves in 2015 and subsequently annually.

It appoints the members of the sub-committees biennially. Each of these committees is responsible for a particular area of interest. As with the Board, a limited number of extra helpers can be co-opted each year. All the decisions taken by a sub-committee are agreed by the Board before implementation.

The Board recommends to National candidates for training as Advisers and, until about 2008, Judges.

It appoints ad hoc committees to administer special projects or events and these also must submit their recommendations to the Board. This type of committee ceases when the event is concluded. At least fifty ad hoc committees are noted in the minutes as having been set up by Executive. Any large undertaking is entrusted to this smaller group whose members are chosen from Executive, sub-committees and the general membership according to the skills required. They usually meet over two years, the number of meetings varying according to the subject. They take their own notes and the chairman reports to the Board. Anniversaries, fashion shows, County events, promotion, NFWI shows and exhibitions, Denman bedroom refurbishment, the Three Counties Show, train outings and Jubilees are some of the events for which ad hoc committees were set up.

It is now time to look at the roles of the main officers: - the County Chairman, the County Treasurer and their assistants.

County Chairmen

Since 1980 there have been fourteen County Chairmen: - Grace Adkins, Jeanne Round, Greta Mitchell, Pat Harris, Mary Davis, Freda Davies, Mary Wehner, Elizabeth (Betty) Johnson, Suzanne Owen, Chris Marriott, Julia Roberts, Christine Hickman-Smith and Marjorie Whiting, and each has brought her own ideas to the running of the Federation, has had a strong influence on the direction it has taken and generally has dedicated three years of her life to the job; the fourteenth, Sue Stone, took up the reins in October 2017.

All have felt it a privilege to hold the position and have taken great pride in doing so.

They also report having enjoyed their time in office, particularly in meeting so many of the County's membership. They have all appreciated the help and support given by the Board members but especially the Vice Chairmen who help in whatever way is required and who carry out the Chairman's duties if she is unavailable. Several would have liked to have served on the National Federation Committee but only two have been successful. Olive Odell was elected prior to 1980 and completed her work as Vice Chairman of the National Executive in 1983. Julia Roberts joined the National Board in 2011 and has served as National Treasurer since 2013.

Grace Adkins *[8]

Pat Harris *

Mary Wehner *

Betty Johnson *

2014 Standing L-R Freda Davies, Chris Marriott, Greta Mitchell, Mary Davis. Seated L-R Suzanne Owen, Jeanne Round, Marjorie Whiting, Christine Hickman-Smith.

Julia Roberts

Sue Stone

They have, between them, prepared for and chaired most of the 408 regular Committee meetings, the rest being taken by a Vice Chairman, as well as the extra meetings which are needed when circumstances dictate, such as during the Foot and Mouth Crisis in 2001 and the sale of Pierpoint Street in 2005. They also chair two council meetings a year and attend to the day to day queries which arise from the membership. Many of the Chairmen worked but usually their job gave enough flexibility for the demanding role of Chairman. It was Mary Wehner's opinion that one needs certain attributes to succeed as Chairman "A reliable car, good health, an insatiable curiosity and a most supportive husband."

Other attributes are needed too. There are the many thank you letters for all the enjoyable occasions for which Chairmen receive invitations as well as the formal and business letters which fall to the Chairman's lot. One must enjoy meeting people and be prepared to take on board their various ideas about WI in general and the Federation in particular. It is not always plain sailing. At the end of her chairmanship Chris Marriott recorded it as "a challenging three years as much change has gone on and the organization

---

[8] *Died - Grace Adkins 2001, Pat Harris 2008, Betty Johnson 2016, Mary Wehner 2017

is moving with the times. It has however got much involved with the community in the last year with the great milk debate, let's cook and eco teams bringing the work of WI more publicity and with it new members."

Several have kept scrap books and the contents show the many WI events to which they are invited. The logs of the last two incumbents show the amount of time and effort put in by a County Chairman.

Christine Hickman-Smith's record of her engagements from March 28th to November 24th 2011 includes 177 separate events and meetings, of which 63 were to do work for the Federation, 40 were committee meetings and 79 were of a social nature both in and out of the County. Almost all the engagements were during the week. In this period there were 139 weekdays and Christine did something for the Federation on most of them as 132 days of her time were taken up by County affairs in this eight month period.

1991 Executive Committee at Pierpoint Street[9]

1996 Mary Wehner and the Executive Committee at a social event[10]

Marjorie Whiting kept a log of all her commitments through her three-year tenure. During the summer of her first year she had a major operation which curtailed her activities for two months but the amount of time devoted to the Federation is again impressive. From November 2014 to October 2017 she had 385 engagements. 129 were events or work for the Federation, 152 were committee meetings and 104 were of a social

---

[9] L-R   Back - Greta Lawrie, Eileen Chapman, Gwyn Wilmore, Grace Richardson, Shirley Noble, Junay England, Patsy Anderson, Beryl Bubb, Liz Osborn, Brenda Spragg.   Front - Diana Cartmel, Freda Davies, Mary Davis, Rosemary Roberts, Margaret Deakin.   Not shown - Nora Henderson, Anne Hingley, Beth Milsom.

[10] L-R   Joy Peers, Margaret Deakin, Gwyn Wilmore, Anne Ballard, Mary Wehner, Jackie Green, Anne Quiney, Patricia Waddington, Ann Canham, Jill Hammonds, Betty Johnson, Anne Nicholas.
Not shown - Eileen Chapman and Junay England

nature. The figures include visits to WIs and Groups as well as outside organisations. These were spread over 310 days and on eight of these occasions she was away from home for at least one night.

2012 Christine Hickman-Smith representing WFWI at the City reception for the Queen

County Chairmen have been invited to represent the Federation at many prestigious County events. Some were put on by the High Sherriff of Worcestershire such as those recorded by Jeanne Round. Betty Johnson attended a City Reception for the Queen and Prince Philip in 2001 whilst Christine Hickman-Smith was honoured to represent WFWI at the Guildhall for the Queen's visit to Worcester in her 60th Jubilee year. She also "Felt it a privilege to be invited to and take part in The Opening of the Life After Stroke Centre, lunching with the Duke of Kent and attending a forum and debate at Hindlip Hall with guest Shami Chakrabati."

Worcester Cathedral hosted many special services at which the Chairman represented WFWI but it is the Federation's own celebrations there that are best remembered. Julia Roberts considered "The crowning glory of our 90th Birthday year celebrations was walking down the aisle in November accompanied by National Chairman, Fay Mansell and Suzanne Owen. The Cathedral was completely packed. We had no idea exactly how many would come as we had only invited WI Presidents to join us for tea after the service and some had doubted a good attendance, so it was thrilling to see so many there." Betty Johnson, in her final Chairman's letter in the CNL, chose two memorable moments. "In January 2000 Bob and I were invited to the Forest Group special Millennium Service at Rock church. This church is blessed with a wonderful organist and after the service he played 'Land of Hope and Glory' very gently. The congregation began to hum the tune and gradually began to sing the words almost reverentially. Spell binding. After the Gala Dinner of 2000 Anne Quiney, Brenda and I left the hall, when a Redditch member started the spontaneous, unaccompanied singing of Jerusalem. Everyone joined in and I can honestly say this rendition was equally as wonderful as when the hymn is sung in the Albert Hall."

1998 Mary Wehner on a glider trip

Less reverential events are attended too, such as Mary Wehner taking a glider trip and Pat Harris being invited to join the Red Nose Day party at BBC's Pebble Mill.

County Chairmen have often been sought out by the local media for comment or participation. Suzanne Owen recalls "In 2004 we were involved in the 'Save Our Streets Campaign' which was set up by English Heritage and the National Federation of WIs to declutter our streets by reducing unnecessary signage. It involved speaking on local radio and television from the High Street when the project was launched in Worcester. We were televised again, at the Worcester Beer Festival, when we were introduced as virgin beer drinkers and asked for our opinions on three different types of beer."

In different years Freda Davies and Suzanne Owen were chosen in the NFWI County Chairmen's ballot to attend a Buckingham Palace Garden Party, whilst Marjorie Whiting had tea there with the Royal Guests at NFWI's own Garden Party in 2015. This was held to mark the 100th Birthday of WI in this country and she was "Lucky enough to have a conversation with Camilla, Duchess of Cornwall." Marjorie was selected to attend another Palace Garden Party in May 2017 along with seven other lucky Federation Chairmen.

Chairmen attend every Federation event possible and usually have to prepare a speech suitable for the occasion. Chris Marriott was handed a very big assignment. "The national annual general meeting was held in Cardiff in June 2006. I was asked by the general secretary Jana Osborne to give the vote of thanks to Faye Mansell our National Chairman at the end of the meeting. This I did although it was a very nerve racking experience in front of 5,000 women."

2017 Marjorie Whiting attending a Palace Garden party

This is how Chris Marriott gave the thanks:

We've journeyed here, From far and near,
From Durham, Kent and Worcestershire,
From Hayward's Heath and Heckmondwyke,
The Isle of Man, the Isle of Wight,
From Bodmin, Basingstoke and Bedford,
To the land of the Eisteddfod.
"Oh, dear, you say, There's nothing worse
Than hearing votes of thanks in verse."
But here in Wales, that is the law,
So please relax – There's plenty more!

It's wonderful to come together.
We're different birds, but all one feather,
We come from every walk in life
From working mum to Prince's wife,
We are the Women's Institute,
We're courteous, dignified, astute,
Non-sectarian, non-political
With minds both sharp and analytical,
Making valued contributions
As we air our resolutions:

Sport for all, or solar panel,
Wind farms in the English Channel.
Denman College which is our pride
To be refurbished by a cycle ride.

And so, our thanks I must convey
To Mrs Mansell: Thank you, Faye.
You've done a really splendid job
Controlling such a lively mob.
And Jana Osbourn we applaud:
Our every word she did record.

And may I add my warmest thanks
To someone from the noble ranks
Of Tony Blair's front-bench artillery
Dear Mr Benn, not Tony, Hilary.
So now, with energy renewed,
We make for home in buoyant mood.

Safe journey is my wish sincere
We all look forward to next year.

The Chairman can be a key holder for WI House and might be summoned to any out of hours incident.

Each Chairman spends at least a day a week in the office to sort out business with the staff, and letters of all kinds must be sent and answered.

Suzanne Owen remembers "One of my first tasks as Chairman was to reply to a questionnaire from NFWI as to where we in Worcestershire saw the future of the WI in 10 years' time - and part of our reply was, to ensure that the WI enters the 21st century with a growing and vital membership dedicated to exerting a stabilising influence in an unsettled world. Surely never more true than today."

Julia Roberts says that "I was delighted when I was elected as Chairman of Worcestershire. My name led to some fun press comparison with a certain film star. I felt especially privileged to be in that role as we celebrated our 90th anniversary. My particular memories relate to that special year in 2008 which featured the celebration dinner with Eve Pollard at the Three Counties Showground, the Mad Hatters tea party at Great Witley with David Barby as well as the celebration in the cathedral."

Many of the Chairmen have had to deal with negative responses from both members and the media, especially when there is change or modernisation under discussion, or when adverse publicity over falling membership and financial reforms is encountered. Most of these are dealt with elsewhere in the text although a 1984 ACM press release is included here.

The Chairman and Treasurer represent the

No easy ride for chairman

THE annual council meeting at Malvern this month marks the end of Mrs Jeanne Round's term as chairman of Worcestershire Federation, after three years in office.

It has not been an easy ride for this popular lady.

It fell to Mrs Round's lot to be chairman during the most challenging period in the history of the WI. It was a time when it was determined that the public should be made aware that WI has a firm place in modern society.

It has been Mrs Round's task to lead and encourage her members to show themselves off and to stimulate others' interests in their affairs.

She and her fellow committee members and the VCOs have had to explain and encourage a national promotion which, it is fair to say, has not always found favour with members.

Through it all she has met comments and criticism with charm and courtesy and almost invariably has won the support of her audiences.

A measure of the success of Mrs Round and her loyal band of helpers in the heartening information that four new WIs have been formed during the past 12 months, one at Upton Snodsbury and three in the Redditch area. The very latest, Kingfisher WI opened only this month.

There are hopes, too, for the possibility in the near future of opening two more WIs in the Kidderminster area.

Mrs Round has worked very hard, travelled many miles and spent nights from home on behalf of her fellow members and we are very sorry to lose her as chairman. She is due for a well-earned rest.

Like her predecessor, Mrs Grace Adkins, Mrs Round will continue her work as a VCO.

The new county chairman and the new executive committee will be introduced to members at the council meeting.

The two guest speakers at this meeting will be Mrs Sally Diplock, Press and Public Relations Officer of the National Federation and Susan Swanton who will speak on "The Power of the Spoken Word."

The result of the Mary Pedley Award music composition will also be made known and the winning entry performed.

The county art exhibition opens at Worcester Art Gallery on Saturday and will remain on view until March 17.

DIANA FARMILOE

1984 ACM press release

Federation at the yearly National Council Meeting weekend held currently at the Wyboston Lakes hotel in Bedfordshire. Prior to 2003 these were a twice-yearly occurrence and between 1980and 1982 the weekends also had a different nature in both content and venue. Jeanne Round recalls staying at the YWCA with Mary Glaze whilst attending one conference. The fire alarm went off in the middle of the night and there they both were, in their nighties, shivering on a London pavement.

The WI celebrates its 90th birthday

Members of the Worcestershire Federation of Women's Institutes gathered at the Three Counties Showground earlier this summer for a gala dinner to celebrate the 90th birthday of the WI in the county. The guest of honour was Eve Pollard, novelist, broadcaster and former national newspaper editor, who regaled guests with tales of her career in a male-dominated industry.

PICTURES AND CAPTIONS: STUART PURFIELD

Chris Marriott and Julia Roberts.

Angie McCarthy, Pat Bond, Margaret Burbery and Beryl Evan

Di Jakeman and Joan Lane.

Eleanor Barrett, Barbara Harris, June Buchanan, Joyce Roberts, Pam Cobourne, Yvonne Kelson, Jackie Docker and Val Everton.

Pat McDonagh, Michael Jeeves, Doreen Jeeves and Sue McLean.

Judy Forrester, Barbara Jones and Pat Jude.

Doreen Cope, Hazel Spires, Molly Groom, Wendy Sanger-Davies and Christine Powell.

Chris Pugh, Beryl Berry, Alan Bamber, Jane Powe Peter Pugh, Pauline Bamber, Tom Chitty and Pat Chitt

Suzanne Owen, Eve Pollard and Julia Roberts.

Jenny Jenkins, Patricia Evans and Sandra Charlton.

Sue Quibell, Trixie Brown, Betty Padmor Barbara Evans and Beryl Morr

Eve Pollard

2008 WFWI 90th Birthday Dinner as reported in Worcestershire Life

Successive Chairmen have all worn the County Badge. This was given to the Federation by Miss Kate Mainwaring. It is made from silver gilt, can be worn as a necklace or brooch and has been in constant use since 1970. It succeeded a star shaped badge given in 1923 by Lucy Hingley. Each Chairman has it in her charge and several tell of the 'adventures' the badge has had. Greta Mitchell hid the badge so successfully when she went on holiday that she couldn't find it on her return. Mary Wehner was on the way to Badsey WI's 70th Birthday when the badge went missing. She first dropped off her husband, who was to walk with the German exchange group and took the opportunity to chat to them. Getting back into the car she realised the badge was not attached to her. In panic she searched the car and finding nothing, opened the door to retrace her steps. There was the badge in the gravel by the car door. Freda Davies was noticed by Prince Charles at the Buckingham Palace Garden Party she attended. "Who are you?" he asked as he prodded his finger at the badge on her bosom, "This is a splendiferous badge." "Yes," was the reply, "we are very lucky in Worcestershire, I have never seen one to equal it."

In 1997, at a dinner celebrating 100 years of WI internationally, the past County Chairmen were presented with a commemorative badge which subsequent Chairmen have also received. A list of all the County Chairmen can be found on the book's inside back cover.

Sometimes Worcestershire members do not recognise the badge. Several Chairmen, when attending WI functions such as fetes, have been asked if they would consider joining the WI, whilst one was charged entry as a visitor despite the fact that she was to speak that night. She did meekly say that as she was speaking she didn't need to pay. "Oh no, you're not the speaker, she has already arrived" was the reply, so she duly paid up.

When not wearing the badge many Chairmen have been told how well the Worcestershire Federation arranges its annual meetings, how well they flow and how interesting and enjoyable they are. Basking in this praise of one of the most important events of her year the Chairman has been deflated by the question, "Were you there?"

1997 Past County Chairmen receive their badge from Mary Wehner, on right
L-R   Olive Odell, Helen Mills, Phyllis Colwill, Jean Newbould, Grace Adkins,
Jeanne Round, Greta Mitchell, Pat Harris, Mary Davis, Freda Davies

County Treasurers and Finance

Every WI member pays a yearly subscription. This was £2.25 in 1980 and has risen to £41 for 2018. The resultant money is divided unequally between NFWI, WFWI and the WIs. The WIs have received an increasing share of the whole over the 38 years and it is now about half. WFWI has always had the smallest portion. The amount garnered from the subscription, £5,500 in 1980 rising by roughly £5,000 per decade, is minuted as never being sufficient to pay for the running of the Federation.

A statement which details the Federation's finances is sent to WIs each year, a copy of which must be kept at WI House for 7 years. The financial statement is formally adopted at the ACM where the Treasurer gives a verbal report. She also makes an interim statement at the half yearly Council Meeting.

The required method for the presentation of the financial statement has changed over the years. In the early eighties it was a single sheet with a list of income and expenditure. The current statement has a much different structure, being set out according to current accountancy practices, thus making comparison of yearly finance very difficult.

However, these statements show that the income of the Federation has come consistently from the following sources. Subscriptions, dividends and interest on money held, any surplus on the events held, advertising revenue from the various publications and inserts, money generated by letting part of WI House, and from the hire of rooms in the house by outside bodies and some individual WIs. Yearly expenditure was required for the house, office expenses, staff remuneration, professional advice, insurance, the events put on by the Federation, committee expenses, reimbursement of committee members' expenditure, training and Denman bursaries.

The charity status and unincorporated nature of WFWI also impacts on the way the finances must be run as does the administration of VAT. The minutes show that the last seems to have been a headache for successive County Treasurers.

The constant battle to keep the finances of the Federation in good heart and the many events and activities which have been devised and implemented to make this goal a reality, has taken up much of the Board's time and energy. It has fallen to successive County Treasurers to advise on and deal with the financial aspects of these decisions.

In the first two years, 14 members served on the long-standing Finance Sub-Committee, two as chairman and four solely on this committee. The three Holding Trustees attended frequently. Advising Executive on financial policy, it met three times a year to scrutinise expenditure, the county and sub-committee budgets and the fund-raising strategy. It also advised on staff appointments and office arrangements. A small finance group was set up in 2011, meeting at first weekly and subsequently eight times a year.

Mary Glaze
1980-85

Shirley Noble
1985-87

Mary Davis
1987-90

Freda Davies
1990-93

Ann Canham
1993-2004

Julia Roberts
2004-08

Monica Smith
2008-11

Sue Chilton
2011-present

Eight Treasurers: - Mary Glaze, Shirley Noble, Mary Davis - and the following five who have worn the Treasurer's Badge given by Mary Davis - Freda Davies, Ann Canham, Julia Roberts, Monica Smith and Sue Chilton, have taken on the task of guiding the Federation. They receive a commemorative badge on retirement, this being inaugurated in 2007. Each has had an assistant (two between 2006-8) who shares the work, especially the day to day transactions and who has usually become the next incumbent. Marion Hawkes is currently Assistant Treasurer.

Monica Smith was the first treasurer to have an accountancy qualification, as does Sue Chilton. The others either had book keeping or business experience.

The Treasurer has always had a room in WI House. It was quite a small one in Pierpoint Street with only one cupboard but that at Hallow is more commodious. There, usually one day a week, the Treasurer often aided by the Assistant Treasurer, deals with the money, logging all the payments received by the office staff and signing cheques. She also goes to any large event to oversee the money.

The accounts have to be prepared for the year end and these were done by hand in the early period. Freda Davies recalls that it was a great rush just before Christmas and that a stiff whisky was required after balancing. The whole job became easier after Ann Canham computerised the accounts in 1996 and even better when the Sage accounting scheme was introduced in 2000, although training in its use was necessary. The statement was then sent to be scrutinised professionally. Julia Roberts remembers first meeting Ann at this time as the newly appointed assistant. "I was very nervous but we soon discovered a shared love of Jane Austen and cats. We had happy times for many years poring over the accounts, paying invoices, inputting Sage and encountering HMRC. We continue to be the best of friends and see each other regularly." Ann, the longest serving incumbent, was a great help in putting 'flesh' on the bones of financial minutes for this section.

Marion Hawkes
Assistant
Treasurer
2013-present

Preparing the Federation budget for the next year was also time consuming for all Treasurers, requiring quite a bit of thought and maybe some crystal ball gazing.

The Treasurer also invested excess money, with Federation approval, taking advice from the accountants. This includes bequests and collections made in memory of members such as that to honour Mary Pedley. This money, collected in the late 50's, helped finance a Denman Bursary. The bequests which from time to time are made to the Federation are usually in memory of a past member. Sometimes there is a stipulation as to the use, otherwise the Board allocates it. The first was recorded in 1980 when a lectern was purchased using a legacy commemorating Mrs Delany. A 1981 legacy of £500, in memory of Margaret Delahay, was used to convert the first floor library into a kitchen and the 1982 Pat Merry legacy of £200 bought a table. In 1987 the downstairs store room was refurbished and renamed the Talbot Room after the donor who made it possible. A £500 legacy received in 2001 from Miss Plummer provided a hand rail for the second staircase in WI House. The 2008 Catherine Guest bequest of £26,000 was used in the Denman bedroom refurbishment and to fund a yearly Denman bursary whose recipient is chosen from those nominated by each WI. Four bequests were received in 2009. The £6,000 in memory of Anne Fellingham also funds a bursary to Denman as does the £500 donated in memory of Diana Farmiloe and a further anonymous donation of £1,000. A picture was commissioned for Worcestershire's Denman bedroom from Bea Woodfield's £1,000 legacy. In 2013 a best in show trophy was purchased with £500 from the family of Margaret Mills and £500 was received from Julia Roger's family in 2015 which purchased three bed quilts for the Worcestershire bedroom at Denman, thus honouring her role as Denman Representative.

| Margaret Delahay | Catherine Guest | Bea Woodfield | Diana Farmiloe | Anne Fellingham | Margaret Mills | Julia Rogers |

All of the county's activities and WI House required insurance which the Treasurer arranged at the most advantageous rate. In 1987 one comprehensive policy was taken out and all WIs joined this scheme. A year later there was a big increase in the amount of the provision for public liability and therefore the cost and in 1993 extra insurance was taken out to cover possible terrorist activities. The cost of insuring WFWI and the WIs was just over £3,000 in 2017.

The festivities of the Diamond Jubilee left the Federation enjoying a spectacular surplus of between £3,000 and £4,600, so well had the members supported the activities. Alas, the next year there was a deficit as the recession of the 1980's began to bite. Cost savings were needed in this hard economic climate.

Reducing the number of sub-committee meetings and a county draw were the answer but by 1986 budget cuts were needed again, this time brought about by the rapidly rising prices in the British economy, the decrease in affiliation fees as membership reduced, by the increased expenditure of the sub-committees, the doubling of the salary bill since 1980 and most importantly, the spiralling cost of maintaining the house. The situation was described in the minutes as very serious and difficult, an extra worry being how to pay the VAT bill. Strong measures were needed. Sub-committees pruned their costs and charged more realistically for courses and events, the Organisation Committee was to reduce its meetings by one, car parking reimbursement was withdrawn, only one Denman bursary per sub-committee was allowed and the Voluntary Market County Organiser or VMCO's offered to pay for their own expenses and training. Investment money was moved into higher interest accounts as inflation roared away. The big saviour, however, was the formation of the Fund-raising ad hoc committee. The accounts were back in the black the next year and Mr Simmonds, the long serving auditor, retired. Rabjohns were appointed to take over.

1998 Ann Canham and assistant Betty Johnson at work in the treasurer's room, Pierpoint Street

The next ten years were fairly stable, the major loss occurring in 1991 when the roof of WI House was replaced. During these years, a three year plan was adopted, a deed of appointment drawn up for the holding trustees, and the financial separation from WI Markets was accomplished.

As the Millennium approached, a period of alternating profit and loss took place. Salaries had doubled again and a back payment of nearly £2,000 for income tax for the cleaner was required. Matters improved in 2000 but 2001 was an awful year, the Foot and Mouth epidemic wiping out most of the programme. It was in this year too that pension provision for the Federation Secretary was begun and WI House was refurbished. Money saving strategies were introduced again, with each sub-committee having to submit a more detailed yearly budget. However, by 2004 expenditure had risen again and fund-raising income was disappointing. Luckily, participation at the Evesham Fishing weekend produced welcome extra funds for the next six years and good revenues were coming from holidays and the sale of County items. Fund-raising generally improved but more good housekeeping was required beyond the tightening of expenditure. The decision was taken to sell the Pierpoint Street house which, as well as a drain on finances, was becoming increasingly difficult to maintain. The balance of money from its sale and the purchase of the Hallow property was invested along with the refunded VAT. Despite these difficulties, Worcestershire was reported as doing relatively well - other Federations were having worse problems. At this time too risk assessments were introduced for every Federation activity as a protection against possible claims.

Changes came thick and fast in 2005 and 2006. There was an update on what could be claimed as expenses by Executive and sub-committees, and itemised expenses claims had to be submitted. Honorariums for County Chairmen and Treasurers were withdrawn, but were reinstated in 2015. A move to internet banking was made in 2006 though disquiet was minuted because only one signature could be used. The Federation initially acquired a debit card which was not used. Insurance payments were reduced, especially for the house contents and for public liability. On the debit side Lloyds could no longer discount on bank charges. New SORP (statement of recommended practice for accounting standards) regulations came in requiring more detail in the Trustees' report and Federations were informed that there was no legal need to prepare for or seek approval from members for a budget. At this time too, a box was added to all event application forms regarding data protection.

After 2006 the Federation suffered from the global financial crisis and its income took a severe hit. The high interest rates of the Nineties were replaced by much lower ones which have become even lower as the years roll on. From 2008 members felt less secure financially and numbers attending events, including both annual and half-yearly meetings, fell, whilst event costs increased, mainly because hall hire charges rose sharply. Professional charges also increased, in particular, Rabjohns which rose by 11% in 2008. In this year the salary bill had risen by over £10,000 to a peak of £31,500. The money saving strategies used in the past were implemented again along with some new initiatives. Non-members attending WI events were to be charged more than members whilst the loss making Home Economics and Crafts spring rally was incorporated into the ACM and Rabjohns was replaced by Mr Yelland who specialised in Charity accounts. The Supporters Club was resurrected, later becoming Worcestershire Winners as a result of NFWI concerns about rules of the Charity Commission regarding gambling. It was disbanded in 2013 through lack of support. In 2010 it was announced that cheques were to be phased out. It is considered that if this had come to pass the Federation would have struggled even more. In fact the number of cheques handled by the Federation in 2015 tripled as both the number of events and the number of attendees saw a significant increase.

Sue Chilton at the ACM 2015

In 2011 very big savings were made. £10,000 was cut from the salary bill by reducing office hours whilst the pension payment was reduced from eight to five percent. There were reductions in Advisers' meetings, the Board was reduced to ten members, Judges training could no longer be afforded, savings on postage and stationery were made by using email and sub-committees had tighter rules when organising events, being allowed only one advertising flyer per year. Indeed fewer, larger events were to be the norm. A bright point was the net increase in membership by 120. A small finance group, which included the Chairman, Assistant Treasurer and two other Board members as well as the Treasurer, kept a close watch on expenditure at this time, and investment strategies were overhauled. An indemnity insurance policy of half a million pounds was taken out to cover the Board. It was difficult to find a bank as most, including building societies, would not take charity accounts. The Co-op would accept such accounts and also did not charge for banking cheques so the business was transferred to it whilst much of the day to day banking is done through the local post office.

In 2012 the NFWI instigated a successful claim for the repayment of VAT on subscription payments. This helped the situation and by 2013 the Federation was able to report a healthy financial situation. The first five-year plan, initiated in 2009, had worked and the second was put into action in 2014. Since then there has been a very healthy surplus each year, nearly £17,000 in 2016, this total being achieved by the £9,000 boost to funds from the 2015 Three Counties Show. The Board began working on the third plan in 2017.

In 2016 Mr Yelland retired and Rob Richards of The Richards Sandy Partnership began acting as auditor to the Federation from 2017.

When asked to remember anecdotes about her time as County Treasurer, Sue Chilton, after many months had passed, said apologetically "I really can't think of anything at all which is either amusing or interesting about my time as Treasurer!"

The successive Treasurers, whilst dealing with the Federation's finances, have also advised and guided WIs with their financial affairs. The Treasurer is present at all the Treasurers' courses put on by the Federation, gives advice through the newsletter and sends information on changing requirements. In 1980 NFWI advised that any WI with an income of more than £15 per annum from property such as its own hall or from investments must register with the Charity Commission. The Treasurer gave information in the County News as to how to proceed in the matter. In 1982 WIs were urged to make their own insurance arrangements and this continued until 1987. In that year there were VAT changes. Any event put on by WFWI or an individual WI attracted VAT but certain parts were exempt. For instance, meals incurred VAT, coaches were zero rated and this had to be made clear in the returns.

> ■ I M P O R T A N T INFORMATION ON GIFT AID
> The Charity Commission has made additional restrictions on claiming Gift Aid. If members of the WI Gift Aid Scheme attend classes/events which are offered to non-members at a higher charge (eg Denman Courses/ some Federation events), the difference must be regarded as a 'benefit' and taken into account when entering names on the R68 schedules. This is a legal requirement, and full explanatory notes are included in the Federation's March mailing. Any concerns should be directed to Doreen Jeeves on

2013 Treasurers' Course:
Sue Chilton centre

In 1990 NFWI voted to become a private charitable company. The subscription now had VAT levied on the National and County Federation portions but not on that of the WIs. In 1992 a list of all WIs having a gross income of £1,000 or more had to be sent to National as they too had to become registered charities, thus the 1993 Charities Act had a big effect on the nature of WI fund-raising, for there were strict rules to follow and only fund-raising for inside the WI or for very local causes was allowed. The Treasurer offered advice to all WIs on this thorny subject. An independent adviser was now required for the accounts. This eventually gave rise to the training of IFEs, Independent Financial Examiners, nine becoming operative in 2011. Since then all new WIs are recommended to use their services; 45% of all WIs taking up this service in 2016. Some of the original IFEs have retired but more have trained making eighteen in 2017 plus Julia Roberts who remains an IFE trainer. There was also training for WI treasurers in the early 2000's to enable gift aid to be applied to the yearly subscriptions and in 2010 the Treasurer had to explain the impact of differing charges for non-members on this benefit. In 2003 VAT could be reclaimed on fund-raising activities.

The Responsibilities of the Board

The Board has many other responsibilities besides those undertaken by the Chairman and Treasurer because its main purpose is to facilitate education and training for the Federation's membership plus liaising with the National Federation. This being so it has been, over the period covered by this text, an employer, an owner of property, a landlord, an organiser of events, a fund-raiser, a publisher, a holiday provider, Denman supporter, a promoter and publicist, a supporter of outside bodies and of course it looks to the smooth running of the Federation by providing training and fostering links with the wider movement. In the roles mentioned above the Board has undertaken responsibility for about 407 events, many of which were very large. Each successive Board had to grapple with the thorny issue of a steadily declining membership and the reduction of income this entailed and many of the above named responsibilities have the twin value of addressing these problems. These various and very varied facets are now to be explored.

The Board as an Employer

2017 Fiona Layton-Federation Administrator, right, and Trudi Tayloe-Assistant Federation Administrator will greet members who contact the County Office at Hallow

The interaction between WFWI with both its member WIs and NFWI requires a very large input of time and almost immediately after its foundation the Federation realised it needed a paid secretary to keep things functioning and a place for her to work. Thus it became an employer.

The total number of staff has always been small but the Federation could not function without them. Since 1980, nine ladies have filled the role of Secretary and each has had an assistant with ten ladies filling this role, two of whom became County Secretary. Four more ladies have supplied additional help, mainly as a part time book-keeper and two of these served briefly as assistant. There has almost always been a cleaner and the five ladies who have kept the house in good order are named in the WI House section.

The Federation Administrators, who before 2004 were known as County Secretaries, and their Assistant Federation Administrators, prior to 2004 Assistant County Secretaries, ensure continuity, as one County Chairmen succeeds another. The staff know all the workings of the organisation and the Federation could not function without them. Most, though not all, have been WI members. One of the assistants, a non-member, found that she had never laughed so much in a job before, decided there must be something in this organisation and duly found a WI to join.

Goodbye jam and Jerusalem . . .

. . . hello to a bright new image

CALLING all women in their thirties. Your Women's Institute needs you.

"We miss out on that age group completely," said county secretary Margaret Mills.

"It's extraordinary, but we don't seem to be attracting 30 year olds. We have a few in their twenties — member's daughters I think, but when they start getting into their jobs and young families, we don't seem to get them.

"But that's the most innovative age. It's the time to have new ideas, try new things. The time when we have so much to offer them — and we offer it much cheaper than anyone else.

"I'm convinced there must be dozens of women in their thirties who just don't realize that we can offer them almost any skill they want to learn, at a knock-down price. That's what we want to get across."

The Federation of Women's Institutes has the same problem as Elsie Tanner. They're stuck with an image. Just as she can't get away from sex and the middle-aged swinger, they can't duck out of jam and Jerusalem.

☐ ☐

With their new, middle of the road WI pop song, they're trying to give would-be members the idea that whatever you

"We're fed up with it," said one member crossly. "It's not that we want to change of image, we just want a complete image."

Since last week's annual conference the WI locally and nationally is shedding its jam and Jerusalem image.

want to do, you'll do it better with the WI.

Looking through their last annual report is rather like looking through a What's On magazine. You name it they've got a sub-committee for it . . . aerobics, art, bowls, tennis, 22 choirs, public speaking, bridge, geology, overseas groups, agriculture, drama festivals, drama workshops, poetry competitions, art exhibitons (all our own work), numerous crafts,

the list is endless . . . and that's just in Worcestershire.

Their new song says: At the WI there's a guaranteed greeting. For different ideas at every meeting. At work or leisure, got it together, Knowing we're growing and going on forever. Their trouble is, getting everybody to believe them.

☐

• Margaret Mills, county WI county secretary . . . calling all women in their thirties.

● Susan Lunn, the new County WI secretary.

L to R:

Dorothy Smith
1980-82

Carole Graham
1984-85

Susan Lunn
1985-87

Above: Margaret Mills
1982-84

Below: Brenda Spragg(R)
1987-2000 with
Greta Lawrie

L to R:

Cynthia Mortimer
2000-02

Heather Jeffries
2002-11

Fiona Layton
2012 to present

Front Office Pierpoint Street

Inner Office Pierpoint Street

These employees needed somewhere to work and WFWI has had an office almost from the outset. The working hours in this office have varied with circumstance and cost. Until 2012 the Administrator almost always worked full time but in that year the working week was reduced to four days, Monday to Thursday. There has always been an August closure. The time of office opening has also varied, with members' visits and phone calls being restricted, partly or fully on some days,

Brenda Spragg, at her desk in WI House, Worcester.

to allow staff time to catch up with their work without interruption. The current access is four mornings per week. The trial opening on four Saturdays in 1994 to help working members failed as there were too few visitors and has not been repeated.

In 1980 the office was on the first floor of Pierpoint Street in Worcester, today it is situated on the ground floor at Hallow. At both, a member would be greeted by the Assistant Administrator ensconced behind a counter. The Administrator is in the background, indeed she was in a separate inner office in Worcester, and only appears to deal with the more complex situations.

Greta Lawrie behind reception at Pierpoint St.

Dorothy Smith, whose assistant was Joan Taylor, retired in 1982. Margaret Mills the new County Secretary, featured in many of the newspaper articles promoting WI. She, in 1983, was the only one in this role invited to attend a Buckingham Palace garden party. Updating of the office began when a desk calculator and printout machine were purchased, soon to be followed by a second hand copier and stencil scanner. In 1983

1982 Dorothy Smith's Retirement Party[11]

---

[11] L-R Back - Cynthia Cooksey, Grace Adkins, Nan Gardner.   Middle - Pat Ogle, Anne Green, Mary Fynn, Raley Clifton, Bridget Lewis, Diana Farmiloe, Edna Pugh, Greta Mitchell, Betty Hudson, Catherine Guest, June Garvey, Gwen Bullas, Nan Turner, Margaret Crowther. Front - Jeanne Round, Dorothy Smith, Mary Glaze.

Helping the needy

● *WI chief Brenda Spragg thanks Parcel Force men Steve Peet (left), the assistant depot manager, and driver postman Mike Jacob.*

Brenda Spragg began her seventeen years in the office starting as Margaret's Assistant, whilst Renee Wilkes, for a short time, worked one day a week helping with the typing. Carole Graham began in 1984 but suffered ill health and Margaret Mills returned temporarily until Susan Lunn was appointed. Eileen Chapman worked in the office from 1985 to 1988 and was assistant for a short time. New electric typewriters were purchased at this time. Brenda Spragg became County Secretary in 1987, Greta Lawrie filled her Assistant's roll in 1988 and Betty Tong came to be Book-keeper, remaining until her death in 1997. To save money, Executive members began to deputise when any of the staff were absent or on holiday, a practice that still continues. In 2015 six 'office angels' were mentioned performing this role but it has since reverted to present or past BoT members.

The following account draws on the reminiscences of Brenda and Greta and outlines the work done by a County Secretary and her assistant. Much of what they say still applies today.

Committee meeting days were always very busy and, in preparation, there was at least one weekly meeting with the County Chairman. There were also meetings with sub-committee chairmen as she was secretary to all standing committees and also for the twice yearly Group Leaders meetings but not ad hoc committees, although she did type the minutes for all of them. The minutes were sent out to members along with the agenda for the next meeting. All the work necessary to implement a committee's decisions such

as informing WIs of a visit by an Adviser or the details of an event was in her hands. She was also responsible for arranging the things which facilitated the event and might include booking coaches and halls; sourcing, booking and looking after speakers; providing equipment and the organisation of catering. Coaches for the Federation ACMs and for National AGMs were organised and this was sometimes quite terrifying so complicated were the arrangements. Vivid in Brenda's memory

Off to the National AGM in the early 1980's

is her last AGM when one lady was missing after the meeting at the Albert Hall. A worried group fanned out to look for her but with no success, so reluctantly, Brenda telephoned the lady's husband. He was adamant that they could not leave an old lady alone in London but, with many others to consider, the coaches finally departed. The old lady got home first! She had looked briefly for her coach then caught the train.

The organisation of the Federation ACM was a huge yearly task for the office. Once the Board had made the decisions the Secretary put them into practice. The venue was visited, invitations dispatched, seating plans made, display areas decided on. All the necessary equipment including the lectern and tablecloth, all the paperwork and all the stationery had to be organised for the meeting, packed into a van and transported to the venue. Catering and flowers, usually done by WIs, had to be arranged. On the day the smooth running of the meeting was her responsibility and of course minutes of the proceedings had to be taken. Once over everything had to be cleared away, packed up and taken back to the House.

New Speakers' Evenings were arranged for those desirous of talking at WI events and meetings and once a speaker was accepted the details were added to the yearly handbook. This of course also contains Federation contacts which are well known for containing data that is not entirely current. This has happened because of the mismatch of dates between printing and WI annual meetings and, though improved, is still not perfect.

The County News was also put together by the Administrator. Submissions were typed, a draft copy sent to the printer and the proof agreed. Originally monthly, except in August when WI takes a holiday, it is now produced nine times a year.

Brenda was often contacted by the media, especially Radio Hereford and Worcester, and one time she found herself doing a live broadcast, with no preparation, from a radio car at 7 am on the morning of a council meeting. A nerve racking start to a really long day.

During her time as County Secretary more health and safety rules came in, so 'EU approved' typist chairs and desks were purchased whilst plants were added to counteract the fumes from the copier. Computerisation came in 1995, along with some training, and the workings of a fax machine, franking machine and laminator had to be assimilated around the same time. Despite all these aids the office became overloaded with work. This was particularly so when a big event such as a pantomime or a celebration such as the Federation's

WI Flower arrangement in the House

75th birthday was being planned. The Executive took steps to reduce the workload, especially in 1989, when too many visitors and interruptions were taking a toll on staff efficiency, but work overload was reported again in 1991 and yet again in 2001 when there was a huge increase in sub-committee work.

Greta Lawrie saw an advert for someone who could type and get on with people. She got the job despite being the oldest applicant and began in 1988 as Assistant Secretary. The work conditions were not quite what she had been used to. The first shock was being asked to copy the enclosures for the mailing. Down to the cellar she went and there found an elderly Gestetner. This was far removed from the state of the art copier she had used previously. The ominous rustling of furry creatures amongst the crammed area did not help either. The facilities gradually improved which was just as well as Greta copied everything the Federation sent out. This included such things as programmes for carol services and music and drama festivals, on top of the Federation information and the paperwork for all events.

As well as being receptionist, she opened all correspondence, dealt with bookings, answered phone enquiries and sold WI stationery and other goods. She spent a day filling envelopes for the monthly WI mailing, weighed them and then bought the correct stamps, though the later use of Landers Printers franking machine saved a lot of time and licking. Late inclusions, often from National, were accepted if the envelopes were still unsealed. There was often so much mail that the postmen collected from the house in huge grey sacks.

Each day Greta banked the money which had come to the Federation. Security resulted in her varying the route and carrying a whistle. She used a hand calculator when totalling the amount, the handle of which kept falling off. Ann Canham was 'looking after the pennies' so a rubber band was enlisted to keep it in place.

A record was kept of anything that was hired from the house and requests were sent to WIs when it was their turn on the house flower rota. The flowers were always a lovely addition and beautifully arranged. Other examples appear in photos elsewhere as well as opposite.

Greta and Brenda had some rather more unusual tasks too. Brenda was the first out of hours contact once the burglar alarm was installed and she had to respond several times. This often meant getting out of bed. Once at about 1 am she was parking in Pierpoint Street in response to such a call when she noticed a police car gliding down the street and halting at WI House. Jumping out quickly she pressed down the lock of her car door only to see, too late, that her keys were still in the ignition. She rushed to the House only to find that it was a false alarm. The police took pity on her when they realised her predicament and took her to a taxi rank so that she could go home, get the spare set of keys and return to retrieve the car. At other times when there had been a break in she had been greeted by an awful mess.

On top of this, as well as attending to dead pigeons in the sitting room chimney there was once a litter of three tiny kittens in the cellar to look after. Alerted by a strange mewing sound, they were discovered on an inside window ledge but without a mother. How they arrived there was never worked out but they were given diluted milk and tucked up in a box until taken away by the RSPCA and found good homes. Brenda, a cat lover, had to be dissuaded from adopting all three.

Unlike the kittens and other wildlife, the police applied for permission to use the premises so that two CID officers could mount a drugs watch on Southfield Street which was opposite WI House. They installed themselves in Brenda's office and for several days nothing happened. Then the phone call came after one of the officers had left. Greta and Brenda listened eagerly, something had happened at last. "Oh, a cheese sandwich please," was the disappointing gist of the conversation.

Post and parcels were delivered daily but one visit resulted in a court appearance for Brenda, Greta and Mary Wehner in 2000. An incident had occurred in 1996 when a parcel deliveryman with a very heavy sack had, climbing eight steps of the staircase, caught his arm in the banister and fallen backwards. This resulted in a chronic back injury. Four years later he brought a claim against WFWI but the Federation was exonerated of any responsibility by the court. His employer was found liable.

2001 Social Gathering - Executive Committee and Holding Trustees with Greta and Brenda[12]

Injured worker in £36,000 payout

A WORCESTER postal worker crippled for life is urging former colleagues not to lift heavy packages – even if it means disobeying orders.

Graham Stanton, aged 58, suffered severe back injuries while trying to deliver a heavy parcel to first-floor offices in Worcester.

He was medically retired against his wishes from his job with Parcelforce Worldwide, the parcel delivery arm of the Post Office.

Mr Stanton, from Ronkswood, cannot work and is unable to walk for any distance. Last week he was awarded £36,000 in an out-of-court settlement.

"I was determined to do my job but now I've learnt my lesson and I urge anyone in the same position not to lift very heavy packages – even if it means disobeying orders," he said.

"I've no future and my wife has been forced to go out to work to help pay our living expenses."

Mr Stanton, who gets a disability living allowance and another for industrial injury, claims he told supervisors that the parcel he was delivering to the Worcestershire Federation of Women's Institute in Pierpoint Street appeared to be overweight at about 40 kilograms.

But he claims they replied, "just deliver it".

"I feel I've been very badly treated and I'm pleased with the settlement, but it should never have come to a court case," said Mr Stanton.

"I've been advised that my future

Crippled after trying to deliver heavy parcel

by SARA PAWSEY

Evening News

employment prospects are limited. Perhaps I should've refused to deliver the parcel but I never shirked a job, just did as I was told. For that my life has been ruined."

Mr Stanton said he managed to struggle up eight steps before catching his hand on the banister and tumbling backwards to the ground floor, where he fell heavily.

He went on to deliver the parcel and later made other deliveries in Worcester.

The following morning he was suffering back pain but went to work for another four weeks before seeking medical advice. It was later discovered he had displaced four spinal discs.

Mr Stanton, supported by the Communication Workers' Union, sued his former employers at Birmingham County Court for damages arising out of the accident in April 1996.

The case against Parcelforce hinged on Post Office regulations which say the maximum parcel weight is 30kgs.

CWU claims managers at Parcelforce

▲ Former Parcelforce employee Graham Stanton who was injured at work.

are forced to cut corners and say overweight parcels are routinely accepted.

"This was an unfortunate incident," said a Parcelforce spokesman.

"If there are suggestions that the weight regulations are being ignored they should be raised with the management."

2000 WFWI exonerated from damages claim

---

[12] L-R Back - Betty Rooney, Rosemary Adams, Eleanor Barett, Mary Davis, Mary Wehner, Ann Canham, Margaret Norris, Mary Glaze, Pat Harris, Greta Mitchell, Liz Davies, Jean Newbould, Beryl Village, Betty Johnson, Olga Glaze, Anne Quiney, Joy Peers, Suzanne Owen. Front - Greta Lawrie, Brenda Spragg, Freda Davies.

Greta retired in 1998 and was followed by Cynthia Mortimer who could use a computer. Anti-glare screens and regular eye tests were now required for secretaries. Cynthia followed Brenda as Administrator in 2000 and saw the Federation connected to the Internet. Margaret Powell filled in as Assistant on Sue Millington's departure, seeing with Cynthia an explosion of work for the office, hard for them but representing a thriving Federation. A pension payment was made to Cynthia when she left in 2002 and Heather Jefferies as Administrator and Jacki Clark, as Assistant, became the next incumbents. It was at this time that staff assessments were started and written job descriptions introduced. The MCS, Membership Communication System, was initiated in 2004 with the Administrator receiving training in its use. This was a very big task and it was considered fortunate that a computer virus attack had occurred a year earlier and not after its installation. The cost of office time was factored into the price of events for the first time and Heather was appointed Health and Safety Officer on the move to Hallow. She joined a group of Federation Administrators to swop ideas in 2007 and official documents became paperless the same year. The use of computers became indispensable to the work of the office and during the whole time these and other office aids including copiers, printers and franking machines, were constantly updated.

Rosemary Thom succeeded Jacki as Assistant Administrator in 2009 followed shortly by Trudi Tayloe. Heather took redundancy in 2011 when the hours were reduced. Jane Sherwin briefly became Administrator followed by Fiona Layton in 2012. At this point pensions became a legal requirement, although Heather Jefferies had been in receipt of one before then, and since 2016 have been necessary for all employees. Throughout the years, office life has changed little and so it continues with Fiona and Trudi's tenure. They have few incidents to report but once Trudi disappeared for a long time. Eventually Fiona noticed her protracted absence, and began a search. She was trapped in the toilet as the inside lock had failed. She was easily released from the outside and swiftly a better mechanism was fitted.

Another type of furry animal caused an uproar in this house. The alarm went off and Doreen Jeeves, the then key holder, arrived to find a bat had set off the alarm. Having an aversion to bats there was much screaming. She retreated to safety, gave a call and both the bat and Doreen were rescued with no damage done to either.

The Board as Property Owner

WFWI had premises in Worcester almost since its inauguration. At first rented but, from 1945, a house which it owned in Pierpoint Street.

After World War Two, housing was in short supply, as were building materials, so it was a triumph for the Federation to win approval from the authorities to purchase 11, Pierpoint Street in central Worcester. Success was achieved as the Executive, led by County Chairman Mrs Pedley, explained that the house would provide an educational centre accessible to more than 10,000 women, employment for staff and a flat for a caretaker and all of these were being eagerly sought by the new, post war government. The premises, consisting of Mulberry House and Mulberry Cottage with the latter having its door in Sansome Walk, has deeds dating from 1745 and is a Grade Two listed building. Until its purchase it had been a small commercial hotel and was in very poor condition.

The purchase price was £2,500 and a further £1,000 was needed for repairs and alterations. To secure this money, Worcestershire Federation of WI House Ltd was set up and the money raised by offering £1 shares to WIs and individuals. The final cost rose to about £5,000 but it was paid off and the trust wound up in 1960. This was to be home, office and headquarters for the next 60 years. Worcestershire seems to have been the first County to own its own premises. Certainly a letter came from Devon Federation in 1948 asking how to do it!

1946 Lady Albemarle, NFWI Chairman opens WI House. Front R-L Mary Pedley, Miss D Tomkinson, Mrs H Walker

WI House has been administered in several ways since 1980. Firstly there was a House sub-committee on which fifteen people have served, two as chairman and twelve on this committee only. Replaced in 1990 by a Housekeeper appointed from within Executive, this was quickly abandoned and the Board has taken direct responsibility ever since. Twice, in 2002 and 2014, a small House group, drawn from the Federation Committee, was appointed to advise. To the present time 38 events or activities are recorded associated with the House. These include four structural changes, twenty-one decorations or repairs, whilst four large clearances have been overseen. Its 50th birthday in 1995 was celebrated with a weeklong display of flowers and crafts.

Served on House Committee
Diana Boorn
Dorothy Bucknall
Muriel Carmichael
Raley Clifton*
G Day
June Green
Catherine Guest
Daphne Hopkins
C Jones
Sheila Morris
Betty Padmore*
Catherine Paterson
Helen Perks
Betty Tuffin
Mary Wells
* = Chairman

Ten events held to raise funds for these renovations are recorded. These have included coffee mornings and open house days or weeks, but the most successful and enjoyable, though demanding the hardest work from those involved, have been the lunches. Suzanne Owen remembers that "In an effort to boost our finances, in 2002 we held some Christmas lunches at WI House which was still in Pierpoint Street. These proved to be very popular, in fact we had to have several sittings, but although it was hard work to provide three course lunches in a house which was not very convenient, it was lovely to have the house full of members."

These lunches, variously called Shoppers, Harvest or Christmas lunches, have been prepared and served by the Executive or House committee. Visitors were always encouraged to come to the house at any time and the Federation was pleased to welcome those from outside the County such as the London Welsh WI in 1981.

The Pierpoint Street building had four floors plus cellars, WFWI occupying only the two middle floors for most of this period. By 1980, to help pay the bills, the flat on the top floor was rented out and the ground floor, except for one room, was let as offices. The use of the interior had undergone several rearrangements since purchase but change came again in 1981 when the first floor library was converted to a kitchen using the Margaret Delahay bequest. She had been a County Vice Chairman until her death in 1979. The mini kitchen,

2002 Serving Christmas lunches in the Committee Room. Eleanor Barrett at front

used for demonstrations in the second-floor conference room, was installed in 1987, one of the first floor sitting rooms became the Treasurer's room and the downstairs store room was refurbished and renamed the Talbot Room after the donor who made it possible. This was manned, for the sale of County items, from 2001 by WIs and then from 2002 by members of Executive.

An old building is usually expensive to maintain and so Pierpoint Street proved for WI. Its upkeep was a constant worry to successive Committees and the formation of a Fund-raising Committee in 1987 was partly driven by the escalating cost of the house. Its running costs were £3,500 in 1980 and, despite every attempt to reduce the figure it had risen to a high of £8,291 in 2001. Costs then fell marginally and were reduced to £5,938 in its last full year.

Every year there were things to do to keep the house up to standard. The forecourt was refurbished in 1983 when the wrought ironwork was installed. The central heating was updated at least twice, men's toilets had to be provided, the exterior was repainted several times, carpets and curtains were renewed as they wore out and rooms were decorated regularly, the biggest refurbishment being in 2001, achieved with the help of £2,600 in donations from WIs, £1,000 from the National raffle and the work of Monica Carden and family. Regular inspection by the fire brigade and the implementation of their suggestions kept the building safe and many members will remember the regular fire drills which took place from 1985 onwards. Some of the introductions were however viewed with trepidation. There were two staircases but evacuation of the second-floor conference room became an issue, so a trap door was cut into the floor to provide an extra exit. Most people avoided sitting in the chair placed on it if they could.

However, it was the unforeseen that always caused difficulties and also meant extra, unbudgeted expense. Many things were stored in the two cellars where the injudicious placing of some items led to the second outbreak of dry rot during the 1980's. Woodworm was found in various parts of the building and there was a constant battle with 'furry friends', a major mice infestation being noted in 2000. A flood in the cellars in 1985 damaged some of the paperwork stored there and leaks elsewhere, mostly from central heating and the kitchens, caused problems. The building was checked for asbestos in 2004.

The most daunting undertaking came in 1990. The whole roof needed repair at a cost of £17,855 plus VAT. As a charity and because of the listed building status, grants totalling 40% of the total were received from English Heritage and Worcester City Council, although offset against this was the £1,500 lost in revenue during the work period. The Lakeland chimney pot, still displayed in the Hallow house, was found at this time.

Sometimes work on the premises was not done to standard. The company who refurbished the forecourt managed to fill the drains with concrete. A solicitor's advice was needed in 1989 to resolve the dispute over the poor fitting of the mini kitchen when the original contractor was asked to remove his work and a new contractor, Hatt, redid the job. In 1995, some of the external windows were in a bad state. Replacements were too

*The first WI House Pierpoint Street Worcester
2016 photo*

2001 Sitting Room

*Display and
Lakeland Chimney
Pot in 2001*

1990 Replacement of WI House Roof

*1981 Grace Adkins
in the new kitchen*

Sansome Walk(L) and Pierpoint St entrances in 2001

2001 Committee Room with mini kitchen on left

Top floor flat in 2001 – Sitting room and bedroom

expensive, partly because of the rules governing replacement in a conservation area, so they were mended and secondary glazing was installed. The company made a shoddy job of the refurbishment but when the Executive tried for redress they found that it had closed down and the owner had left area.

The rent paid by the tenants occupying most of the downstairs was crucial in offsetting the running costs, though it did mean that access to the WI rooms had to be via stairs. The various firms - Jones & Philips, who were taken over by Sheldons Insurance Brokers, rented for forty years to 2001. Hyde East Tickner and lastly Worcester Senior Citizens Advocacy who changed their name to Onside Independent Advocacy, followed and all proved good tenants. Their premises were upgraded along with those of the WI portion. It seems that rates and services were included in the rent, but in 1985 it was found that both parties had been paying water rates. This was soon rectified! In 2003, as costs rose, the commercial tenants agreed to pay a quarter of the heating and insurance bills.

The flat on the other hand seemed to pose more problems although its occupancy meant there was always someone on the premises. It required constant updating in its furnishings and décor and, like the rest of the building, it had to conform to the increasingly demanding fire regulations. This was difficult given its top floor situation. Exit in case of fire required agility for it was by rope harness, through a window down to Pierpoint Street.

The incumbent in 1980 was a man who gave the Executive a difficult time. He did some unauthorised and inferior work on the flat and fell more and more behind with his rental payments. Eventually a solicitor was called in who, in court in 1984, successfully pursued a repossession order and won the recovery of the back rental. From then on all but one of the tenants were ladies. One complained that the heating bills were too high, another wanted better white goods but the nicest request was for permission to use the piano in the conference room which was gladly given.

In 1996 the decision was taken not to re-let the flat. A lot of money needed spending on it to bring it up to standard and a tenant had not been forthcoming, but there were also security fears by then for anyone alone in the building. The rooms were given over to storage for the Performing Arts wardrobe and documents.

The issue of security was always present. In 1982 there was a series of break-ins at the downstairs offices, and a theft from the WI office was reported in 1984 but the cheques were recovered. Further break-ins and vandalism, by youths setting off a fire extinguisher in the hall in 1985, led to worries over staff and tenant safety and the fitting of a voice lock on the main entrance in Pierpoint Street. This increased staff duties as each caller had to be verified and let in by pressing the release mechanism situated in reception. Incidents became more frequent in the 90's, despite the upgrading of security on the advice of specialists. All of the contents were photographed and marked, bars were put on the downstairs toilet window and better locks put on the doors. An alarm system was installed, a CCTV camera was erected on the wrought iron WI sign on the corner of the building and sliding mesh doors and windows were put in place in Sansome Walk. This last round of security cost £2,000. All of this did have the unintended consequence of locking a lady in the premises after a meeting in 2005. It also meant the burglars became more creative, coming in through a roof fanlight and damaging the interior. A later theft, through the strengthened front door, took computers and china, and did quite a bit more damage. One burglar was less competent. He locked himself in between the two Pierpoint Street entry doors. Several of these break-ins took place during Mary Wehner's chairmanship and her response each time was to take the office staff, Brenda and Greta, to The Postal Order pub up the road for a restorative gin and tonic. There were also many false alarms. In 1998 keyholder Brenda Spragg was called out twice in one night only to find the culprit was the wind. By 2000 the Marrs Bar nightclub next door was also giving cause for concern.

The first minute regarding the sale of Pierpoint Street was in 1983, when it was proposed by Elmley Castle WI. Despite its central position, close to the railway station in Worcester, it was felt to be unsuitable as it had no parking and no easy access to the first-floor office. A questionnaire to the membership reinforced Elmley Castle's view but the Executive felt it could neither afford to move nor relocate downstairs as that would cut off the rental income. In 1988 the Executive set up an ad hoc committee to explore the possible purchase of the NFU's Worcester premises but this came to nothing. Nine years later a lift for WI house was considered but proved too expensive at £6,218 plus VAT as well as posing installation difficulties. So lots of money was still required to make WI House friendly and accessible to all. However, if the improvements were carried out the Executive was uncertain that members would use the house because the major problem of car parking could not be overcome despite the renting of a few spaces close by.

This sparked a second questionnaire but the replies were not helpful, many WIs saying they rarely used the house. The solicitor's opinion, given at the time, suggested that if there was to be a sale then 25% of the WIs must be present at a special meeting and 75% must vote for the resolution to sell.

A legacy from Miss Plummer provided a hand rail for the Mulberry Cottage stairs in 2002 but in that year more stringent Health and Safety regulations came into force and an informal House committee was formed to identify and implement the necessary changes. It was realised too that legislation was to come into force requiring the provision of disabled access to public buildings. This would pose real problems because of the internal configuration and listed status of the building. A letter was sent to the Council asking for clarification and the reply stated that WI House was not considered a public building but every attempt had to be made to make it user friendly and accessible to all. Suzanne Owen remembers "The future of WI House was frequently discussed at meetings and it was while I was chairman that we started to seriously think about selling Pierpoint Street and also to think about moving out of Worcester to modern offices with some parking but it was a little while before our plans came to fruition." Chris Marriott continues "My very first executive meeting involved the selling of WI house. The decision had already been made that we purchase a smaller property. Finding a new building took some time as properties both in the city and further afield were explored."

So by 2005 the sale of Pierpoint Street was again on the agenda. The ground floor tenants had been given notice as an increase in rental could not be agreed, but other factors combined to bring things to a head. They included the restricted access for members, the poor state of the electrics which would cost over £2,000 to put right, the large drain on finances the house represented, the high quotes for external window cleaning due to the new safety rules, the need to erect scaffolding for any external repairs, and the valuation of £300,000 which was a great bonus! All WIs received a letter explaining the situation. A decision was then made to sell and a search was made for a new WI House.

This was found at Hallow, a fairly new office building on a small rural trading estate and, after some negotiation, £190,000 was the agreed purchase price. Its purchase necessitated many changes. Dot Coles, the cleaner, knew of the proposed move but felt the travelling was too much to continue. The new premises could not hold all the items from the old one so an inventory was made and a decision taken on what to keep. Many items had been donated by WIs or individuals and efforts were made to 'repatriate' those for which space could not be found. Once this was done the better quality items were sold at auction, inferior ones went into a yard sale or to car boot sales and the like and from these £1,250 was raised. All the Federation documents had been stored at Pierpoint Street but there was far less room for them at Hallow. The minutes were examined and most of the early ones, along with other memorabilia and items from closed WIs, were deposited at the County Council's Record Office. The Performing Arts wardrobe and manuscripts were to be sold or disposed of and the cellars cleared. The cellar clearance took many days of Executive and sub-committee time. Dot Coles must have been a thorough cleaner as, amongst

Modern move in WI HQ sale

IT IS the end of an era as after 60 years the Worcester home of the County Federation of Women's Institutes, WI House is up for sale.

The Georgian property in Pierpoint Street is on the market for £310,000 and the WI is hoping to buy a more suitable new up-to-date home.

Priorities will be access for the disabled, plenty of all-day parking space and a manageable size, including offices and meeting rooms.

"It is exciting. It will mean a new start for us," said county chairman Chris Marriott.

"The WI bought this building with great foresight 60 years ago and we have been very happy here, but it is just too big for us."

Formerly two houses, the listed building covers 2,500sq ft, including ground floor offices that have been standing empty since the last tenants left.

▲ County chairman Chris Marriott outside WI House, which is being sold after 60 years. 29668001

"We have been advertising the office since February and it has meant a big drop in income," said Mrs Marriott.

"If we could find purpose built offices somewhere else in Worcester, that would be wonderful, but it is very unlikely that we shall be able to afford to stay in the city."

Although the Worcester park-and-ride service had been an "absolute godsend" to WI members, Mrs Marriott said for courses often had to bring equipment that was difficult to carry on public transport.

Before buying WI House, the federation had rented offices in various parts of the centre, including St Nicholas Street, Mealcheapen Street, High Street and Broad Street.

From December 2005 WFWI's new house, Hallow

the items discarded were five worn out vacuum cleaners. A large lorry was piled with the rejects from the cellar but the old saying "one man's junk is another's treasure" held true. Suzanne Owen remembers her husband's amazement when a passer-by swiftly extracted some old mannequins from his lorry.

All the contents moving to 7, Elgar Business Centre on the outskirts of Hallow or destined for the Worcestershire bedroom at Denman were packed up and the removal took place in December 2005 although only after a last minute scare over the Pierpoint Street sale. Julia Roberts comments "My background in mortgage work stood me in good stead and the officers, as a team worked well together, each bringing different skills. I well remember the joyous occasion when Chris Marriott and I were at Denman on our respective Chairman and Treasurer courses and we heard that the contracts were exchanged."

The sale price was £310,000 and the new property purchase price was £190,000. The expenses included estate agents' fee of £3,100, removal charges of £6,500 and accountant's fee of £2,250, all plus VAT. After spending about £19,000 to remodel and furnish the interior of the new WI House and paying and finally reclaiming £30,000 VAT on the transaction, there was a net £86,000 surplus to invest. After the remodelling, the new House had an office downstairs with a kitchen and two cloakrooms, and an upstairs which was sub-divided into a conference room with large storage cupboards, a kitchen and a Treasurer's office. There were three parking spaces immediately outside the front door and five allocated in the general car park, although there was no alternative transport which made access difficult for some members. Rates, at £1,700, were cheaper compared to the £4,300 for Pierpoint Street. Also, as WFWI has charity status, rates attracted an 80% reduction at both properties. The Health and Safety and Fire inspections were completed successfully and a cap of thirty people in the house at any one time was imposed. The old wrought iron sign, given by Chaddesley Corbett WI, was brought from the old premises after investigations into the attached CCTV camera's ownership had been resolved.

Since 2007 the running costs of WI House have pretty well halved, though these years have not been uneventful. In 2012 bats were found in the building necessitating the purchase of a bat box, a stair lift was purchased, members being invited to contribute 40 pence each, an application to develop the car park was fought, being lost on the second

2016 Looking from reception to the back of the office[13]

2016 View from Administrator Fiona Layton's desk to Assistant Trudi Tayloe's reception area

---

[13] L-R Patience Broad, Fiona Layton, Sue Chilton, Marjorie Whiting, Trudi Tayloe

application, and PAT testing of the electrical appliances arrived. The House was redecorated in 2009 when some furniture, including a small sofa, was relocated to the Denman bedroom and a clock, fortuitously spotted on e-bay, was purchased for £400 and sited in the conference room. This clock had been the gift of Isabel Margesson to Barnt Green WI.

2015 The Centenary Ad Hoc Committee at work in the upstairs Conference Room Hallow[14]

The biggest expenditure has been on heating. On one occasion the oil ran out despite being monitored by a company. Then in 2013 there were two oil thefts from the tank which was situated behind the building. Each of these events left the building unheated. Staff were given a bonus to compensate for the cold conditions and the decision was taken to install new insulation and air source heating at a cost of £9,000. A yearly risk assessment was introduced in 2015 but smart water marking of the contents was deemed too expensive. A fire proof safe was installed and most records other than minutes were backed up in 'The Cloud' as well as elsewhere. It was minuted that a £50 deposit was now required for borrowing equipment as previously some had been damaged on return.

A hearing loop was installed in the committee room in 2016 and a mobile loop was purchased at the same time. In 2017 a loop was installed downstairs at a cost of £903.

Both Pierpoint Street and Hallow have been used throughout the period for most of the purposes originally envisaged in 1945. Anything pertaining to the Federation is housed there, as are the effects of suspended WIs. The latter are now sent to the County Council's Record Office at the Hive if, after three years, the WI is officially closed. Periodically, Federation records join them there as storage space has been more limited since 2006 and this is considered best practice by archivists and historians.

Display boards and cabinets have been used in both houses to showcase members' activities and arts and crafts. WIs have taken it in turn, on a voluntary basis, to provide flowers to beautify the premises, especially at Pierpoint Street. Pictures of both are elsewhere in the book. Many rehearsals have taken place and visiting members, both local and from other Federations, have been entertained there. Many open days have been held and members have always been encouraged to use the house and, especially when it was in Worcester, as a place of respite during shopping expeditions

Some WIs such as Worcester Central and Barbourne paid a fee to hold their meetings in the Worcester House. So did some outside organisations such as CPRE. It held its branch meetings there though it was sometimes tardy in paying its dues. Until 1995 WI Markets had a room in the house but this could not continue for free once they became a separate

---

[14] L-R Christine Hickman-Smith - chair, Sue Chilton, Pat Gale, Suzanne Owen, Joy Gammon, Marion Cumella plus the coats of Janet Murphy, Sylvia Beardshaw

entity. Legal agreement was reached for the continued use of WI House as their registered address and meeting place, but meetings there ceased in 2014/15.

As many courses and meetings as possible have always been held at the house although in 1994 it was noted that there was pressure on the space for classes. WIs were asked to say what facilities were available to them and many country halls and town venues have been used as a result. This is still the case as the Hallow building has a limit of 30 people. Also, there are no facilities for cookery demonstrations in the small kitchen.

All of this activity meant employing a cleaner was a must. Mrs Williams tendered her notice in 1983 and was followed by Mrs Rosemary James whilst Mrs Patterson is mentioned as watering plants in the summer. Mrs Dot Coles was in position by 1986 and continued until Pierpoint Street was sold. Jacki Clarke took on the cleaning at Hallow followed in 2009 by Catherine Cooper-Berghausen but since then it has been done by a private company at weekends.

2013 Art class in the conference room at WI House Hallow

1988 Mastering Australian Cross stitch in the committee room Pierpoint Street. Tutor, Roma Punt standing

The Board as a Fund-Raiser

Of all the items considered by succeeding Committees, two have constantly featured in the minutes and have given the most concern. They are the falling membership and the financial position of the Federation.

In 1980 there were 7,300 members in 177 WIs. By the end of 2017 there were 4,139 members in 125 WIs.

To attract new members, retain the existing ones and raise funds, whilst seeking publicity and promotion, have been the over-riding aims of the Federation throughout the years. This has meant that the Board has taken direct responsibility for many fund-raising and promotional activities. However, on most occasions the participation and help of at least one sub-committee was required. A committee dedicated to fund-raising was established in 1987 but despite this, the minutes record 407 Board-led events some requiring enormous input from those involved in the delivery. The fun and educational aspects were not forgotten in these endeavours for many have remarked how much they had learned and how much enjoyment there was in participating in these schemes despite the hard work involved.

So the next few pages take a look at some of the events the Executive Committee/Board has undertaken in this respect over the 38 years.

Train Outings

This event is a very good illustration all of the factors mentioned above. For ten years, from 1981, train outings were organised by ad hoc committees. These outings began in the mid 70's. The one in 1979 had proved very popular and so they recommenced after the Diamond Jubilee year. The destinations were Exeter, Winchester, Plymouth, York, Portsmouth twice, Brighton, Lincoln, Salisbury and Liverpool and at each of these the visitors were hosted by the local Federation. For the most part a hugely successful fund-raiser, this annual event is remembered very fondly by members, despite its many hiccoughs and problems, and they have reminisced about it often because of all the fun they had. There were very few complaints, even when sub-standard rolling stock or catering service from British Rail marred the journey.

The train was a special, hired from British Rail and known to the ad hoc committees, says Gwen Bullas, as the Raspberry Ripple because of the red stripe on its cream coachwork. At its height the event attracted up to 1,000 passengers, these numbers necessitating two trains, one beginning in Birmingham in addition to the original which started in Malvern. The organisation of these outings took a lot of detailed planning and preparation. There would be a reconnaissance visit to the destination, to make sure there was enough to do and to make the arrangements for the welcome, the provision of tea, and sometimes lunch, with the host County Federation. Many negotiations were held with British Rail and with the supermarkets involved in the provision of food, as coffee and biscuits were served on the outward journey, an evening tray meal on the return journey and buffet service was available throughout. Each successful applicant was issued with detailed instructions: a train schedule, their carriage's and steward's designated letter, a seat number, a BR ticket and a pass for refreshment at the destination.

Despite all this planning things could and did go wrong. Diana Farmiloe's recollections, written in the early 90's and found in the archive, along with anecdotes by others, bring alive these unforeseen events. There were several pick up points in the county and the precise way in which seats were allocated always caused a few problems, especially where platforms were too short for the train, for it was necessary to fill the front coaches first. Then the driver could move up the track allowing access to the rear coaches. "Utter chaos occurred one year at Worcester when the train arrived with the coaches in reverse order from that planned. Before we could do anything, a well-intentioned helper had crammed passengers into the wrong seats at the far end of the train. Quite a lively journey ensued!"

Some members will remember the ill-fated Lincoln trip. All those gathered on the platform for the return journey were startled to hear an announcement over the tannoy from BR that it had mislaid one of the trains. Mary Davis remembers the announcement "We are sorry for the delay but we have lost one of the trains! The whole platform erupted in laughter." What else does one do having endured torrential rain all day, one woman remarking that she was wet right down to her knickers! "It was quite a while before this second train appeared."

What was more, the day had also started with complete disorganisation. Diana wrote "Two trains of different capacity were each picking up their largest contingents at Droitwich. The previous night I had prepared two large, clear placards, Blue - First Train, Yellow - Second Train, the colours referring to the tickets. The trains arrived late, Yellow first and then Blue. I threw away my placards."

Catering too had its moments. "There was the occasion when British Rail was catering for us. The food was fresh and good but we watched in dismay as the first generous portions gave way to smaller and smaller helpings as it became evident there was a serious shortage. Some helpers went hungry that day. What really flummoxed us was the grumble from the catering gentleman that he had been given the wrong number of orders. Correct. But we had fewer passengers travelling than anticipated, not more!"

1982 Worcestershire members on the Train Outing to Winchester watch Jeanne Round receiving greetings from the Hampshire chairman

On most trips though the catering was done in house, mainly by volunteers from both the ad hoc committee and Home Economics and Crafts committee who passed up and down the train on both outward and homeward journeys carrying trays of the relevant refreshments. Beth Milson recalls that bringing the food to the tables was both a joy and a surprise, for members became increasingly inventive in the decoration of their tables, some bringing along candelabra and wine to add class to this part of their day.

Mary Davis remembers that the prepared supper from M&S did not arrive at the Worcester station before the train left. The train was stopped on its journey and the food, having caught up, was passed over barriers to the waiting committee. Diane mentions the astonishment on one trip when "just beyond Hereford, the train pulled up and bread rolls suddenly came flying through the air. Looking out we saw a number of people with piles of rolls in baskets (luckily all wrapped) which they were hurling in the general direction of the guards van. Another branch of our forgetful supermarket had come to the rescue."

York though went well. "We ate all day long. Coffee and biscuits on the train, a civic lunch, no less, in York, then out to country WIs for splendid teas. I had strawberry tarts at Castle Howard. Then back on the train for a tray supper going home." Worcestershire members were regarded as 'rainmakers' in the city as their arrival coincided with a cloudburst breaking a spell of drought. The 'rainmakers' were not quite so pleased.

Returning from Portsmouth, "We were mystified by the lone lady whom no-one seemed to know. Hardly surprising, really, as we discovered she belonged to the Shropshire Federation and had got on the wrong train!"

On an earlier occasion, Portsmouth featured again when three people had to be left behind. Although they were only ten minutes late returning from the Isle of Wight, the scheduled train could not miss its departure slot.

There was always a raffle. Mary Davis mentioned that this took up all of the outward journey time, whilst Freda Davies always says she walked to Lincoln whilst selling them, though both really enjoyed this aspect, as they could chat with so many members.

Liverpool was the last destination. By 1990 the hire train had received the attentions of the many football fans it carried and was in a very poor state. The hire costs had risen greatly so a much reduced profit could be expected. Members were writing to say it was too expensive, they could go by bus to

NEARLY 600 Women's Institute members from Worcestershire — some pictured here on their arrival — turned rain makers in York today.

They arrived on a chartered train for a day's outing — two hours before the heavens opened.

It rained for the first time for 23 days and in rural parts of the Vale of York there was sleet and hail.

"The dry spell broke with a vengeance," said a weather watcher at Royal Air Force Linton-on-Ouse.

In weather terms, 15 days without rain is considered a drought.

Gardeners and sportsmen welcomed the cloudburst — but their joy was not shared by the visitors from the Worcestershire Federation.

Arrival in York of the rainmakers

They were met at the station by Mrs Betsy Walkington, chairman of the North Yorkshire East Federation of Women's Institutes, the vice-chairman, Mrs Pat Reader, and Mrs Kathleen Greensit, and other executive members.

The party was hosted for afternoon tea at the Assembly Rooms by their York colleagues and on the journey home they were provided with individual meals by British Rail.

Liverpool for a third of the £17.50 cost. Only about 400 travelled, the outing returned no profit and so, to the regret of many, the yearly train outing was shunted into the siding.

It was revived for WFWI's 75th Anniversary by the Fund-raising committee. Members were very keen to go and the outing was oversubscribed resulting in an allocation being made to participating WIs. A comment in the 1992-93 Annual Report hints that not all aspects had been harmonious. "The train outing to Cambridge, although having many problems, gave a great amount of pleasure to a large number of members, and this committee appreciate the many messages received from members who had spent a most enjoyable day." No further train outings were organised so this really was the end of the line.

Worcestershire, in its turn, received visits from Federations on their train outings. Derbyshire Federation took a blossom tour with tea in 1981, 360 ladies visited from Devon in 1982 and the same year Hampshire Federation was also entertained. In 1983 visitors from Norfolk enjoyed the Worcestershire countryside from twelve coaches as they travelled to their tea destinations, these provided by local WIs.

In June 1985 a welcoming committee waited to greet 540 Yorkshire East Federation guests at Worcester's Foregate Street station but when the train arrived not one of the visitors got off. Were the 540 three course lunches, prepared by the Home Economics and Craft sub-committee, to go uneaten? The 540 Yorkshire ladies were also waiting. They were wondering where the welcoming committee was and, in its absence, what to do next. A puzzled Greta Mitchell contacted the station staff. Worcester has two stations and the visitors had been disembarked at Shrub Hill. BR sprang into action, got the missing ladies into carriages and somewhat belatedly delivered them to the right station. Heaving a sigh of relief that all was well, the Worcestershire ladies entertained the Yorkshire ladies to a walking tour of Worcester and a most enjoyable lunch at the Guildhall. The comments on this event in the Home Economics and Craft sub-committee's minutes read, "Enjoyable, but hard work". Somewhat of an understatement as it involved making, then serving in three sittings, a three course lunch to nearly 600 guests, from kitchens which were three floors down from the dining area. They decided that the meal would be a plated up first course with no choice of pudding if it was done again. It wasn't.

Three Counties Show and other major events

Worcestershire has long been associated with the Three Counties Show which takes place each June on the permanent showground at Malvern. The Federations of the three counties involved, Worcestershire, Herefordshire and Gloucestershire, in turn provide a refreshment tent at the three day event. As well as being a catering venue it provides a showcase for WI and is a great help in boosting Federation funds, for there is always a large attendance. Even in 2009, at a time when the nation was tightening its belt, 92,000 people were recorded over the three days as passing through the gates, but it did have an effect on the Federation takings for 2009 and 2012. However 2015 showed a handsome surplus of £9,000.

Worcestershire has hosted twelve Three Counties Shows since 1980, the first being in 1982. Each had an ad hoc committee and all but three were chaired by the immediate past County Chairman, the exceptions being Evelyn Rose in 1982, Beth Milsom then Roma Punt in 1985 and Joy Peers in 2003. The committee is appointed and begins work about two years before the event. In 1982 the committee had eight members and held ten meetings plus a wind up. In 2015 there were five meetings and an average of six members but the workload was much the same. It was not until 2003 that a file was written on how to run this show.

Activity is theme of WI's ambitious exhibition at show

ACTIVITY is the key word to the Worcestershire Women's Institute exhibit at the Three Counties Show this year. Not just a static display, but a living, moving hive of activity, from 10 a.m. each day to 6.30 in the evening, for the three days of the show's duration (June 15, 16 and 17).

The Worcestershire Federation is harnessing all that is best from its vast range of talents and expertise to get over to the public every aspect of WI life. With four demonstration stands, and a programme geared to the interests of women — and men — everywhere, the WI will be making, cooking, sewing, growing and showing the talents for which it is justly famous.

The list of crafts is formidable — not just crochet and tatting, macrame and machine knitting, but silk flowers, soft toys, lace making, spinning, cracker making, fabric boxes, paper crafts, smocking and patchwork — and how does glass engraving grab you? Or what about fly tying and smoking your own trout once you have caught it? And how would you like to paint a portrait? And what on earth is Pot et Fleur?

DELICIOUS

In addition to all this there will be a continuous delicious aroma as the cooks get down to cooking with yeast and herbs, making mouth watering summer puddings and savouries or icing that special cake that we all have to make at least once in a lifetime. And as a bonus in the cookery section, the Worcestershire Federation have just produced their very own sweet making booklet, written by Olive Odell of Hartlebury and Mary Williams of Blakedown. Recipes from this booklet will be made at the show to assail the nostrils and tempt the appetite.

As a background to all this bustle, the four seasons will be depicted and an overall theme will be "Hands and Feet" — hands around the world with ACWW (Associated Countrywomen of the World) — hands to make and cook with, hands to clap with and hands to welcome you in.

So the Worcestershire Federation are expecting that thousands of feet will be walking their way to see what they have to show — a present for the Royal Baby no less, an exhibition of needlework pictures illustrating "My Countryside," a full range of WI books and publications and last but by no means least, the food for which WI is renowned.

Fresh salads and sandwiches, home made cakes, fruit and piping hot tea and coffee will be there in abundance, served with a smile and a chat if you are in the mood.

The Three Counties ad hoc committee, under the chairmanship of farmer's wife Mrs Evelyn Rose of Belbroughton, has been working for twelve months to make this year's WI tent the most successful of all time.

Members of the committee will be working at the showground during the weekend before the show and also on Monday, June 14 to make sure that everything goes without a hitch on the opening day, and stewards will be in attendance throughout the show to give information and to assist the public.

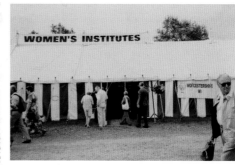

The WI marquee at the Three Counties Show

2015 Catering area in the marquee

1994 Freda Davies, centre, interviewed by Ed Douglas at the Three Counties Show

Advance publicity for WI at the 1982 Three Counties Show

2015 Display area inside the marquee
Foreground - Jules Evans, Patience Broad

1994 As usual catering was busy all day

The first thing the committee must ascertain is the size of the marquee, so one person takes on this responsibility. Once done the area inside the tent is divided up between the catering facility and the display area. Occasionally the allotted space in the catering section has been too small resulting in lost custom. In 1982 the main tent measured 105ft by 30ft plus a 24ft by 12ft kitchen. Linked to this was a 12ft by 12ft space for WI Markets where they sold their goods and produce. The size of the marquee has changed and the shape altered over time and the space for Markets has varied. Until its separation from the WI in 1995 Markets had a big presence. Now, they no longer use the WI marquee.

The person organising the marquee also takes on other responsibilities. The catering area must be sub-divided for preparation, serving and consumption of refreshments. Furniture has to be hired both for these areas and the display space. In 2015 the 120 chairs and 40 tables allowed 60-80 covers in the marquee for food and sufficient tables and seats for the display area. Water and electrical points, tills, sinks, cookers and their calor gas, water heaters, fridges, milk dispensers, chiller cabinets and duckboards to name the most prominent items, have also to

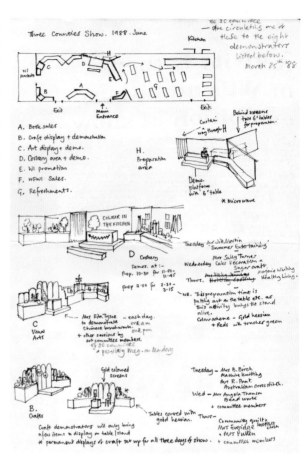

1988 Three Counties Show Diana Cope's design for the display area

1988 How the visual arts display was staged

be sourced, either by hiring or by donation. All of these must be transported to and from the show and set up. So must items for display and these join the catering equipment which has been gathered for transport by van from WI House.

An area is set aside as a rest and store room and this is usually manned by volunteer WI stewards. Coats and other belongings are put here. In 2012 the weight of the rain soaked garments broke the clothes rail!

Just before the show begins the grass has to be cut in the tent and, nowadays, the risk assessment completed.

A second person is responsible for the overall design and realisation of the display space in the marquee. She in turn has her own team which forms a sub-committee. A theme is chosen and there are many meetings needed to bring it to fruition. Di Cope's plans for the 1988 show are pictured and help show the planning which goes into making the idea a reality. The two centrepiece pictures from 1991 and 1994 show the high standard of execution. Appropriate milestones in WI history have been celebrated such as in 1997, the Centenary of WI's birth in Canada. Sometimes a theme could be recycled, as in 2009 when the previous year's anniversary display for NFWI's 90th birthday was used. The theme for 1991 was Home and Country and the eight strong committee decided to hold a competition for a garden design. It was staged as one of the classes at the Home Economics and Crafts Rally in 1991. There were sixty-three entries. The judges, Frank Hardy of Pershore College and John Gunsell manager of Webbs, were so impressed by the standard achieved that they awarded more prizes than originally intended. Powyke WI won and Webbs Garden Centre constructed their design as the centrepiece of the marquee. More publicity was gained when all the designs were displayed at Webbs. In 1994 Pershore College students helped dress the Family Occasion themed area whilst plants and other help were often given by local firms including Grange Farm Nurseries. In 2006 the marquee won a gold award for a trade stand.

As the display area is planned to show off and promote WFWI all the sub-committees are invited to man an area which they organise themselves with the main theme in mind. They employ a static display, demonstrations or interactive activities. County items and publications have

1991 Powyke WI's winning entry for the central display in the marquee

1994 central display in marquee

At the Three Counties Show this was the centrepiece in the W.I Marquee. It was organised by the Worcestershire Federation of W.I's and sponsored by Webbs of Wychbold to the theme of "Family Occasions". It is the work of;
Beth Milsom - Pershore W.I.
Joan Green - Ekington W.I.
Anna Yelland - Drakes Broughton W.I.
All three members have their own businesses and Beth was runner up in this years competition for Worcestershire Business Woman of the Year. She was sponsored by W.F.W.I. Nemesia Confetti is a new introduction from Webbs of Wychbold and is available from our Shrub Department price £4.99 each.

1994 Three Counties

1994 Junay England, in pink in middle, organised the catering

2012 Marquee kitchen Mary Lou Lockyer, Suzanne Owen and helpers

2015 The Farmers' Bar

always sold very well whilst selling haberdashery was a success in 2015. Staging is done prior to the show's Friday opening day, latterly on the Thursday. Attention to safety is very important and an increasing number of tests have to be undertaken. There was a cautionary note in the 1988 round up minutes from the organiser "Any platforms should be tested for the weight of the general public standing on the front. On my first test the see-saw effect would have sent our demonstrator off into a double somersault."

Once completed the tent and its contents needed insurance and to be guarded through the rest of the week. In 1994 the Hanley Sea Scouts are mentioned as doing this but more recently the on-site security team have been employed.

To facilitate further security there has been at least one caravan behind the marquee. This is used during the show by the committee chairman and at least one other, both usually staying overnight for the show period. Pat Harris went for a shower early on one of the mornings only to find she was sharing the facility with a goat. This was also being prepared for the day ahead.

The caravan is especially useful for the County Treasurer who attends each day and deals with the money. At first using a portable safe, then the on-site Lloyds bank, she has since 2009 used the facility on the Thomas Cook stand.

At first members' caravans were used but in 1992 a caravan was gifted to WFWI. This was stored by Mrs Tomkins at Earls Croome, added to the insurance and guidelines for its use were drawn up. It was borrowed by the other Federations for use at the showground but by the early 2000's it was quite old and, as Mrs Tomkins had stored it, WFWI gave her ownership. Since then caravans have again been borrowed from members.

A third committee member takes charge of the volunteer rota. The majority of these volunteers work in the catering section, fewer are needed in the body of the marquee where the sub-committee members often man their own stalls. There were 150 day passes, 13 wristbands, 23 vehicle passes and 14 other badges required for the 2009 show though these numbers are fewer than the 250 passes required in 1994. Volunteers need to be fit. They were required to work for five and a half hours a day in 2015. When the lists come in from the WIs an imbalance is sometimes found. In some years too many wish to serve resulting in disappointment for those not chosen, whilst in other years too few offer. Added to this is the variability of the daily numbers, too many volunteers on one day, too few on another. Balancing the numbers is always a headache but much preferable to the years when there are too few to man the three days, as happened in 2012. That year the required number for every session was thirteen stewards in the marquee, six in the Farmers' Bar and two in the Leadon Suite. The early shift starts at 6 am. Letters are sent to the individuals with instructions and a later letter conveys thanks. It was noted in the 2012 roundup minutes that it was beneficial to have someone available to instruct new volunteers.

Some weeks before the event the person handling publicity issues a press handout and in most years there is very good coverage.

It has to be said that the WI teas and lunches are the main attraction of the marquee and also the main fund-raiser, so whoever organises the refreshments must be very competent and a very hard worker. In 2009 the Show Committee asked WI to cater at two other outlets, The Farmers' Bar and the Leadon Suite in the Worcester Pavilion. This has continued ever since despite the difficulties of moving food between the three venues. The name Farmers' Bar does lead to dashed expectations however. Many are those who are disappointed by not finding their favourite tipple.

Sourcing all the food and equipment for the catering is a mammoth task in itself. Some of those who have taken on this post have their own utensils and these items must also be transported to and from the site to join those brought by van from WI House. A list compiled by Suzanne Owen in 2012 shows that she and Vicky Coghlan amassed forty and forty-eight different food and non-food items respectively to use at the show, most in multiple numbers. These included such various items as micro wave ovens, hand mixers, buckets, bowls and storage containers including a large white trunk, chopping boards, collapsible waste bins, plastic table cloths, 24 kilograms of ham, 200 bacon baps, 36 lettuce, five litres of mayonnaise and eleven and a half kilos of bacon. The Federation is unable to store all of the equipment required to service such large undertakings, especially since the move to Hallow, so it hires or buys quite a lot each time, selling off some items at the end.

All of the necessary items have to be set up in the kitchen and preparation areas of the marquee and also in the serving section where WI banners are often displayed. A soak away must be dug for the sinks and refuse neatly binned. One year the dustmen offered more black plastic bags if the volunteers would do a 'Calendar Girls.'

The two newer outlets have been reported as needing some hours cleaning. The party investigating the Farmers' Bar in 2009 were surprised to find a used rubber item amongst the debris from the party held the night before. Worse still the urns were not there, and didn't work when they did arrive.

The officials from Environmental Health inspect regularly. In 1988 they attended each day. Food hygiene certificates are required for the lead personnel, and the volunteers have to adhere to strict rules. For catering staff this includes the removal of rings and nail varnish.

1991 Chairman's Reception

2007 Chris Marriott hidden left meeting Prince Charles

Chris Marriott cooling off in 2009

The volunteers are usually asked to wear black and white over which many don green tabards. These were made partly by the Three Counties display committee and partly by the Worcester Group for the 1994 show, financed by Lloyds Bank sponsorship. These have mostly replaced the pinkish ones made early in the 1980's and have been augmented by new green check aprons bought in 2000 and by white ones bought from National. Volunteers are detailed to a specific area, the serving counter, the tills, the preparation area, the washing up or the cleaning of tables according to requirements.

The type of food has varied over time and much is freshly prepared on site. The huge volume of ingredients, sourced prior to the event, is delivered or fetched daily. Salads, ploughman's, filled rolls, sandwiches, desserts, fruit and cream and of course cakes have usually featured, whilst beverages include tea, coffee and soft drinks. Ripple cups have been introduced and were well received but those asking for soya milk are yet to be accommodated. In 1997 the Three Counties committee asked WI to sell bacon baps early in the morning especially for the show's judges and people manning or showing that day who have to arrive early. This service has been well received. Later, vouchers issued by the Three Counties committee were introduced to stop abuse of this now enhanced breakfast service but some people still turned up without one.

The amount of food required is large and financing it is always challenging. The 1997 minutes show some of the quantities of food for the catering area. Mentioned are 75 tubs of margarine donated by Stork and 234 cakes donated by WIs. The WIs also gave £650.50 for cake ingredients. Donations instead of cakes have continued and much of the baking is now done by the volunteers and committee. Despite sponsorship, the expenditure has continued to rise and the 1997 committee recommended that the next ad hoc committee should hold fund-raising events to deal with this. In 2009 sponsorship was sought from Waitrose and Taylors Tea, and from Silver Spoon who donated sugar. In 2015 Waitrose gave a cash donation.

The chairman of the WI Three Counties ad hoc committee entertains guests and a list of invitees is made. In 1997 the guest list for the evening reception was limited to 110. As costs have risen the hospitality has been pared back and for the last three events a lunch has been given for eight to ten people, the catering being done by a third party. Dignitaries open the show and they usually visit the marquee. Chris Marriott had this experience: "Another unusual event during my time as chairman was meeting Prince Charles and the Duchess of Cornwall at the Three Counties Show in 2007. Herefordshire were the host WI and the chairmen of Gloucestershire and Worcestershire were invited to attend a special presentation to mark the 50th anniversary of the Three Counties Show. The daughter of the Gloucestershire representative worked at Highgrove, Prince Charles's home, and was well known to Prince Charles and the Duchess of Cornwall. So we had a few minutes together with them and some lovely photographs taken."

However good the organisation, the weather cannot be managed and some chairmen have had to deal with extremes. It was so hot in 2009 that after her exertions Show Chairman Chris Marriot was grateful to soak her feet in a bucket. Three years later there was a deluge. Christine Hickman-Smith recalls that "True WI spirit was challenged as we waded through the

2012 Making the best of a very wet year

Judy Neale, Marjorie Whiting

L-R Christine Hickman-Smith, Fiona Layton, Anne Smith. Christine's outfit was judged third best for Ladies Day

wettest June weekend in the show's history" with all the helpers living in wellies for the four days of the show. A small river ran through the kitchen, the roof leaked too and the situation was made worse as the water from an adjacent pool was emptied each night in the marquee's direction. However much straw and bark was put down it could not stop the interior resembling the Glastonbury Festival mud and many helpers skated about on the kitchen duckboards whatever was done to reduce their slipperiness.

WFWI has been invited to many other shows and similar events and has attended these when possible for the publicity and promotion and in the hope of generating income from County items and publications. Each demands the same degree of organisation as that detailed above for the Three Counties Show.

The organisers of the Three Counties Show have diversified their activities. Other types of shows and events have resulted in which WFWI has been invited to take a part.

In 1986 they introduced their yearly Malvern Spring Show. WFWI agreed to have a stall and WI Markets shared the pitch. This continued until about 2010. Each time there was a need for a design idea for the stall and for its staging, both of which entailed a large amount of work and volunteers. Eventually the minutes note that it was difficult to recruit stewards. A similar presence at the Malvern Autumn Show first staged in 1995, lasted only a few years as the results were much poorer. In 1992 Federation members joined the cast of the Archers Radio Serial when they became Borsetshire WI at the Three Counties Ambridge Festival.

'Countrytastic', a show aimed at children and held at the Three Counties Showground, invited WFWI to attend in 2009. Participation continued until 2015 and the stand featured cooking and biscuit and box making.

A minute book of an NFWI catering committee for the Royal Show at Stoneleigh is in the WFWI archive. Joan Smith, Jeanne Round and Di Cope all sat on this committee. This Show was bigger than the Three Counties and the arrangements reflect this. The manning of the marquee there seems to have been on a rotational basis among the Counties neighbouring the showground near Warwick. Worcestershire undertook this in 1984 and 1985 and many members of the Federation Executive Committee were involved in the two resultant ad hoc committees. Ann Garman of the Home Economics & Craft committee was responsible for designing the NFWI exhibit at the show in 1984 and they, along with the Art committee, made major contributions in both years. 200 stewards were needed over the period of a show and they were transported by coach every day, each clutching the two unfilled sponge cakes they had been asked to bring. The decorative panels produced by Worcestershire's artists were much admired and the whole was a great success except for the slimmers' lunches which were offered. There were some mishaps. Some cakes were "Not up to scratch," and sugar sachets were pilfered but this was not as serious as the incident when the caravan was broken into and money taken from handbags.

No such problems occurred at the 1987 two day Heart of the County show at Grafton Flyford but poor attendance meant that only £200 was raised. As 1983 was the Community First year, WFWI agreed to be the sole caterer at Brintons Carpets' Bi-centenary Gala Day in Kidderminster where they providing tea and cakes for the 6-10,000 attendees. Other smaller events were supported. In 1989 sandwiches for one hundred were produced and served at Madresfield Court in aid of the Cathedral Appeal. So much catering was being done by the Federation that a Catering Committee was set up in 1994 but it was disbanded within the year as the six team members were overworked.

Twenty years elapsed before County Chairman Suzanne Owen floated another large-scale project like the Brintons' tea party. In 2003 WFWI was asked to provide cakes and tea at the Evesham Fishing Festival over the August Bank Holiday weekend, an event which attracted between 10-20,000 people. Again, with promotion and profit in mind agreement was reached, cakes and donations requested from the membership and in 2004 the first foray into this particular fund-raiser was undertaken. The site and facilities were not the best. In the first year the volunteers had to depend on a hosepipe as the only source of water, the tent was badly furnished and it was shared with the beer counter. However, year on year improvements were made and WFWI was very pleased with the annual boost of the £2-3,000 the Federation received from this event. In 2008 the site was very muddy but "Helpers looked resplendent with green rosettes on black and white, then came the wellies." In 2009 however, the money was down and, to make matters worse, the health inspector's report was not as favourable as in the past. It said there was no written record of procedure and that there should be a training day held before any catering event. Their later report on items removed from Evesham showed that one was not up to expected standard. This, as well as the increased charges from the new organisers, finally rang death knell of the Fishing Weekend and the last participation was in 2009.

2004 Catering at Evesham Fishing Event

Between 2005 and 2007, lunch was provided at the Magistrate's Court in Worcester when, each year they hosted the Schools Mock Trials day.

There is, however, much more to fund-raising than attendance at shows and the Federation was alive to any project which would raise money, promote WFWI and of course provide interesting events for members.

The 1983 Caravan Weekend which took place at Malvern Show Ground really sparked the imagination. Roma Punt remembers that no sooner had she suggested the idea than County Chairman Jeanne Round, who had never been in a caravan, had booked the event and Roma was heading its ad hoc committee. Believed to be the first WI caravan event, it attracted 99 units at £8 each, eighteen of which came from ten other Counties. The rest came from thirty-nine Worcestershire WIs. The National Chairman, Anne Harris, came and was very impressed by both the attendance and by the programme of events, most of which were put on by the sub-committees. 320 people visited despite the very wet weather paying £3 each and the only criticism heard throughout the weekend was that there was too much to do.

Some big sales of work and craft fairs were organised by the Federation often designated as County Events. The success of these relied heavily on the Home Economics and Craft sub-committee and members. The 1987 Autumn Bargains, a fund-raising event at the Guildhall, Worcester was WFWI organised but the more numerous type involved taking a pitch at outside events. These have included the 1988 Worcestershire Craft Festival, which lacked organisation and punters, the 1992 Malvern Hills Well Dressing, the 1993 City Christmas Fayre where the choir also sang and the City's Strawberry Fairs from 2008 to 2011. Fashion Shows were always well attended. Executive members modelled Country Casuals clothes in 1983 and further shows are reported in 1986, 2004 and 2012.

As a response to the recession of the 21st century, the BoT again took on the co-ordination of major fund-raising. The first to be organised in 2010, was a day of activities at the National Trust's Croome Court Estate for which each County sub-committee devised one or more attractions. 800 members enjoyed the fashion show, craft displays, teas, and treasure hunt. 2011 saw several hundred attend a Mary Berry Day at Sixways Stadium, Worcester. Five coaches took members to tour the London Olympics Site and a full house enjoyed the repeat of the 2010 half yearly meeting evening talk on the Staffordshire Hoard. In 2012 there was a visit to a recording of Countdown in Manchester. The 2013 'A Grand Day Out in London,' for which each sub-committee devised various activities in the capital, was somewhat ambitious in its complexity, especially as Oxford was also offered as a destination on the same trip, but the 2015 lunch for 500 at Sixways Stadium with Michael Portillo proved a resounding hit. County Chairman Marjorie Whiting found this a particularly memorable day although one hiccough did occur. Whilst escorting the guest speaker into the venue she called him David, having just spoken to David the catering manager, and continued to do so in her introduction. Throughout his talk he referred to Marjorie as Margaret.

● Members of the Worcestershire Federation of Women's Institutes and their friends wander through the showground (above) while (right) Mrs Jeanne Round, county chairman, Mrs Anne Harris, national federation chairman, and county secretary Mrs Margaret Mills take a well-earned rest. (Below): A section of the car driving test.

County campers smile on through

THE weekend's wind and rain did not stop Worcestershire WI's first-ever caravan and camping rally being a great success.

Over 230 WI members, their families and friends from as far as Devon, spent two days at the Three Counties Showground taking part in a wide range of activities.

As part of the Federation's newer and younger image, a disco was even arranged for Friday night.

Tots took a twirl at about 5.30 p.m. to be followed by their elders, who danced the night away.

the more energetic walked the Malvern Hills, with regular parties being organised throughout the weekend.

National chairman Mrs Anne Harris even joined the party.

Helped by Gloucestershire's chairman, Mrs Margaret Mills and Herefordshire's Mrs Jame Maoreton, she judged the fancy dress show on Saturday.

Four-year-old George Hammond, from Suckley won the children's section, dressed as Phil Drabble from 'One Man and his Dog.'

Mr Dennis Barrett, from Stone, was the adult winner.

The 43 dogs that accompanied the caravanners were not for-

gotten, with a special dog show arranged during the weekend.

Intrepid drivers were given a chance to show their talent.

Lower Broadheath's Mr F. R. Charge won the car rally event.

WI spokeswoman Mrs Diana Farmiloe said: "It was such a success that we have been asked to do it again next year. But I do not know about that yet."

● Making a giant kite (above) is Mrs Denise Cotterill of Martin Hussingtree, with her children David and Lynne, while (left) Suckley WI's Mrs Jill Hammonds and Mrs Betty Hudson, from Hanley Castle, find

58

Farm visits, including that to Henson's farm in 2011, and walks were popular. In 1982, 262 members strolled around Betty Hudson's farm and this was the start of many walking events both long and short. The promotional entry in the Race for Life and walks to celebrate the 90th birthday are illustrative of this but

1979 Walk at Evelyn Rose's farm   *2011 Henson's farm visit*

perhaps the most interesting was the 1995 NFWI Best Foot Forward initiative aimed at aiding members health and wellbeing. Chairman Freda Davies decided to take up the challenge. She would walk round the County. It would also be a good PR exercise and a chance to raise money for the Federation and Denman. WIs in all areas along the 134 mile route provided coffee stops, lunch, afternoon tea and more importantly, a nightly bed in a member's home. Drivers and minders were needed each day whilst members, sometimes numbering more than twenty, turned out daily to accompany Freda when the route passed through their area. Concluding at Hallow Village Hall, many members also turned out to witness the finish.

National then entered Freda's Best Foot Forward project into the 1996 Health Alliance Awards and it won its category, jointly with Pauline Linley who had walked Offa's Dyke.

*1995 Best Foot Forward Health
Alliance Award
Freda Davies second left*

2004 Helping at Flog It, Worcester Guild Hall[15]

---

[15] Pictured - Anne Smith, Suzanne Owen, Mary Lou Lockyer, Trish Waddington, Julia Rogers and three Malvern members

Events which involved entertainment included the 1987 visit to the Denman Flower Festival when 159 members went in three coaches and the 1999 Federation Day at the Swan Theatre, Worcester on Aspects of Worcestershire. This raised £2,300, was Mary Wehner's swan song as Chairman and received such a demand for tickets that Henry Sandon kindly reprised his part for those who had been disappointed. The 2002 Queen's Jubilee Revue, also staged at the Swan by the Performing Arts sub-committee, raised £4,600 for the Federation. In 2004 the Guildhall in Worcester was the venue for a recording of the TV programme 'Flog It' and WFWI happily answered the call to help steward the potential 'customers' and keep things running smoothly. The volunteers enjoyed it immensely and said Suzanne Owen "spent much of the time talking about the WI while keeping everyone supplied with cold water on a very hot day."

1999 Mary Wehner's 'Swan Song' L-R Joy Peers, Ann Canham, Henry Sandon, Anne Ballard, Mary Wehner

2004 Race for Life Competitors[16]

2002 Queens Jubilee Revue Choir

2002 Queen's Jubilee Revue Cast

---

[16] L-R Mary Lou Lockyer, Heather Jefferies, Vicky Coghlan, Rosie Styles, Suzanne Owen, Jacki Clark, Jill Hammonds, Christine Hickman-Smith, Janet Clemas, Gerry Cooper, Rosemary Edwards, Trish Waddington, Julia Roberts, Margaret Coward

Various books have been published, two entirely by WFWI. The 1980 'Madam President: Fellow Members', though successful, did cause some anxiety. The publisher did not follow the author's instructions, the most glaring mistake being the additional 'e' on Madam in the title. The pages had to be reprinted so that the full stops inserted by the printers in between the letters of words such as W.F.W.I. were removed, the title was over stamped on the cover and the dust jacket redone but WFWI members seemed to have been employed in inking out the offending 'e' on the spine of each copy. Legal exchanges followed as the Federation felt the publisher should bear the cost of the rectification. The printer, who didn't view the matter in the same way, eventually conceded but the book was delivered six months late in the Diamond Jubilee Year. The 'Favourite Tastes from Worcestershire', containing members' recipes, produced for the 75th Anniversary by the Fund-raising committee had a happier birth and all the 2000 copies were sold.

 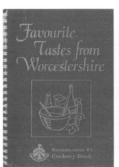  

Two other books were produced after an approach by a publisher. First came 'The Worcestershire Village Book' of 1988, co-ordinated by Betty Hudson for which WIs researched the history of their village. This was followed in 1995 by 'Worcestershire Within Living Memory' co-ordinated by Eileen Chapman, for which WI members submitted facts about their Worcestershire past.

Smaller in-house pamphlets have also been produced for sale. In 1981 a magazine called 'The Rondel' was produced by Executive. This brought together reports on both WI and WFWI activities. The 1981 minutes record "Well done Mrs (Catherine) Guest," who was the editor, for all 300 were sold at 15p each and a further 100 were printed. The 1982 edition also sold 350 at 20p but the following year printing had to be abandoned because of changes to the office staff. It appeared for the last time in 1984. In 1987 a pamphlet called Snippets, produced by Margaret Taylor, brought together the WFWI items published in Home and Country the year before. A smaller scale publication of 1982 was the successful sweet making recipe leaflet.

Other Activities

There are far more aspects of WI though than raising funds and promoting the Federation.

In 1983 members knitted squares in the studio at BBC Pebble Mill for Children in Need. In 1992 a survey of working and childcare was undertaken for Hereford and Worcester Council but the 2003 Hospital Questionnaire was undertaken in response to members' fears about the lack of car parking facilities at the new Worcester Royal Hospital. Over 1,400 members' replies were processed and analysed. Supported financially by the South Worcestershire PCT it became the Federation's Community Challenge project, the results being shown at Denman. The findings resulted in better bus services to the Hospital and some parking changes, especially free parking for volunteer drivers. In 2006 Worcestershire Federation's Eco Team was one of eight in the NFWI pilot scheme and went on to be one of the subjects in a Leeds University study of Women's Volunteering. In the same year the County's Let's Cook initiative began and Chris Marriott reported on the diversity of activity in the Federation, as shown opposite in her letter in the CNL.

2004 Hospital Questionnaire
Suzanne Owen, Sylvia Beardshaw

2009 Ashton Underhill WI Let's Cook Course

2006 NFWI Eco Team
L-R Laura Dyson, Joy Evans, Sylvia Beardshaw,
Elizabeth Mountford, Sue Arnold. Not pictured
Christine Hickman-Smith, Margaret Norris

2006 Chris Marriott's Chairman's Letter in the CNL

Federation Holidays

Many hundreds of members and their partners have enjoyed the holidays arranged since 1980 by the Federation which has greatly appreciated the surplus some of these events have generated. Visiting 125 destinations, this has been a much valued part of the County's programme. It has been especially appreciated by those who wished to travel with like-minded companions and with an escorted group. Nine holiday organisers have been appointed over the period, all but two being Board members. Each organiser liaised with a tour operator, who sometimes offered free places according to numbers involved.

IT WAS a bright and early start for the Worcestershire Federation of the WI as members and their husbands, making a grand total of 72 people, set off for the romantic city of Paris.

The mammoth group set off sharp at 8.15am from Merstow Green in the hope to arrive in Paris by the afternoon.

Pictured are all 72 members before they embarked on their journey.(N556B)

1991 Holiday

Having agreed the content of the trip she then contacted those members on the list who had shown an interest as well as advertising the holiday. Once numbers were confirmed she apprised those travelling with the details and provided the documentation. When the journey was underway she was on hand to help throughout the tour, making this an arduous but rewarding job.

Marjorie Plummer was in charge in 1980, arranging one tour a year for about 45 people. France in 1981 and the Black Forest in Germany in 1982 were the first destinations but a weekend trip to London in March 1982 received little support and was cancelled. It was the weekend of Mothering Sunday.

When Marjorie retired in 1982 a small committee took over, headed by Pam Morton, but in 1983 the organisation reverted to one person, Cynthia Cooksey, who now made arrangements via the office staff. Day tours were offered for a time whilst short breaks in Britain and trips to Europe continued. By 2017, sixty-one European holidays of varying length had been enjoyed including seven Christmas market trips, whilst there were fifty-two holidays in all corners of the British Isles. Not all of the holidays proposed found sufficient takers and there were, from time to time, problems with the tour operators. In 1986 Cynthia Cooksey found out by chance that the operator had ceased trading, the cheque was stopped immediately and the

2001 Lake District Holiday

2003 Heidelberg

2008 South Africa

WI tour Normandy and Paris

MALVERN GAZETTE 4·6·81.

OVER 40 members, husbands and friends of Women's Institutes throughout Worcestershire returned last week from a tour of Normandy and Paris.

They arrived at Le Havre in time to take a short walk around the new Basin and its beautiful new all-metal footbridge. The architecture of this suspension bridge and the rebuilt town has not been without its critics, as it is largely concrete, but seemed to us (writes a WI member) quite pleasing and in French style.

In Rouen members walked down the pedestrianised Rue de la Grosse-Horloge where the tiny "Big Ben Pub" nestles beneath the Grand Clock. The Eglise Jeanne D'Arc martyr was impressive, the theme being marine, the slated roof like an upturned boat, and inside the timbers as the ribs of a ship. In addition to the stained glass windows, some lower ones were fish shaped plain glass to let in light.

There was a whole day in Chartres, visiting the great cathedral, for centuries a pilgrimage centre, and the Saturday was spent in Paris, with a coach tour of the city, shopping and a cruise in the evening followed by a visit to Montmartre.

Sunday was spent quietly at Lagny-sur-Marne, visiting the Town Hall, in what was the abbey, and the adjoining church, entered through a dull facade which gave no clue to the glory inside, with a beautiful amethyst mist of light above the aisle and rainbow shafts of light from the clerestory windows.

Monday saw a visit to the Chateau of Vauz-le-Vicomte with its richly painted ceilings and silk furnishings: impressive, a smaller forerunner of Versailles and Fontainebleau.

A sunny Tuesday was spent at Rheims for last-minute shopping and a visit to the cathedral.

The party drove through the vineyards of the Marne valley to Epernay, to sample the champagne after visiting the labyrinth of man-made caves stretching for many miles under the famous Champagne factory.

All-too-soon came last Wednesday, and the return home with many memories of an interesting and enjoyable week. It will be repeated for other WI members, husbands and friends at the end of September. And there are vacancies for anyone who is interested.

1981 Report of WFWI holiday

2015 Harrogate for NFWI Craft Show

business transferred elsewhere, whilst Margaret Taylor and Grace Richardson, taking over in 1988, had to arrange the delivery of tickets by hand, courtesy of members of the Executive, to the 114 participants when a postal strike prevented the usual route.

By the late 80's an increasing number and type of destination was being offered. The first of the three visits to The Oberammergau Passion Play took place in 1990 and during the journey the 75th Anniversary of WI in Britain was celebrated with cake and speeches at the side of a German autobahn. Christmas visits such as Tinsel and Turkey weekends in the UK commenced, continuing for ten years and theatre weekends, especially in London, were very popular

Junay England took on the organisation in 1992, continuing until 1999 and these years saw a continued increase in the number of tours. A highlight for many was the visit to Llanfair.pg for the WI Centenary year of 1997, whilst Mary Wehner represented the County in Canada for this anniversary.

2009 Ireland

2017 Weekend at Sheffield and Chatsworth RHS Flower Show

Freda Davies, the next organiser, was the first to introduce both holidays by air and destinations outside Europe, twelve in all by 2017. At this time too, continental Christmas Market tours took over from the UK Tinsel and Turkey trips. The laughter, gluhwein and chips form a memorable part of the Christmas Market holidays. Like other organisers, Freda had to deal with medical emergencies, lost luggage, changes of tour provider, unforeseen price increases, occasional struggles to fill sufficient places and the myriad other incidents both during day and night which crop up on holiday. It was ensured that the Federation insurance fully covered the organiser because of these responsibilities. New challenges appeared; an outbreak of SARS threatened a holiday to Canada and the 2001 Foot and Mouth outbreak could have scuppered a walking holiday on the Isle of Wight, but didn't.

A 2005 cruise to the Caribbean, though enjoyed, did not provide the group atmosphere which characterised the Federation holidays and especially missed was the happy hour experience on coach journeys when everyone poured out their favourite tipple. It was during the cruise that a member was hospitalised on land with Freda accompanying. This was not as taxing linguistically as another night-time hospital visit in Italy. Fortunately

Freda was accompanied by a member's doctor husband who acted as translator. He had an 'O' level in Italian.

The holidays were very successful, offering many and varied types of experiences for members, whilst boosting the Federation's finances. Betty Johnson reported in the County News in 2001 that on the Federation holiday to New Zealand. "Mary Wehner had promised to do a special bungee jump for us and.....she didn't."

However, in 2005 the accountants pointed out that the Federation was at risk of contravening its charity status because of the amount of money going through the books from the holidays. The recommendation was that the Board should set up a trading company but the decision was against this. Instead holidays were limited to three a year and, with Barbara Maskell as organiser, came under the auspices of the Fund-raising committee. This continued for four years until 2010 with two or three trips per year being offered. The Board's Finance Committee then took on the organisation until 2014 when Christine Hickman-Smith assumed the role as a member of Leisure and Pleasure sub-committee. Weekends in Harrogate and at the 2017 inaugural Chatsworth Flower Show and a visit to Canada have been much enjoyed.

The Federation and Denman College

One of the yearly appointments is that of Denman Representative, known from 2012 as Denman Ambassador, whose responsibility it is to keep abreast of activity at Denman College, keep members informed and encourage them to use it. Anne Smith, Ambassador in 2017, writes regular updates in the County News apprising members of vacancies and courses and says that

Denman College in 2014

usually about twenty members each year advise her of their independent visits though she thinks the true number is higher. To facilitate its use the Federation offers bursaries and assistance with travel costs, funded in part by the legacies left by former members and detailed in the finance section.

As can be seen from the frequent mentions in their own pages, individual WIs also offer bursaries and visits. A notable first occurred in 1994 when Worcestershire's German exchange group became Denman's first overseas visitors.

Until 1991 members seem to have attended independently but at that date there is the first mention of a formal Federation visit organised by the representative. These have continued at intervals becoming more regular from 2001 and 21 have taken place to 2017. Thirteen have been of two or three nights' duration, with five or six courses being offered. The Federation always aims to fill the college so that Worcestershire members can enjoy each other's exclusive company. Eight one-day visits have also been organised, the first in

1993 and a taster day in 2009 saw 170 members at the college, but members do continue to go independently, one and sometimes two benefitting yearly from the Denman dip introduced at the ACM in 1999. All are encouraged to inform the ambassador of their trips.

Purchased by NFWI in 1946 and opened in 1948 as a national education and training centre for members, Denman is regarded by many as the jewel in WI's crown. Its situation in the small Oxfordshire village of Marcham near Abingdon makes it fairly central for the Movement.

It is primarily a residential college although it does run day courses and it offers a very wide range of topics in its yearly programme. It is a centre for conferences and seminars on WI activities and also a centre for training. Advisers, Financial Examiners, WI judges all attend courses there and there are many other training sessions for those serving the Federation.

In 1948 some Federations agreed to be responsible for the upkeep and furnishing of a bedroom. Worcestershire agreed to share a large, four bedded room with Warwickshire. This was on the first floor of the main building and was the only one to have an en-suite bathroom. This was the arrangement in place in 1980.

Several refurbishments of the room have taken place. Jeanne Round liaised with Warwickshire for the 1982 makeover which cost Worcestershire £12,680 plus VAT. This was entirely covered by WI donations and many gifts were also made by WIs to help beautify the room. All WIs who gave donations were thanked by letter and the expenditure explained. However, in 1989 there were complaints about the bedroom, some calling it dowdy, others complaining about the beds. It was agreed with Warwickshire that it did need an update but agreement on the refurbishment did not go smoothly. Three years later Denman announced a building programme which would provide mostly single, en-suite accommodation. Warwickshire opted to take one of these rooms and so the big room on the first floor, with its lovely views of the gardens, became the Worcestershire bedroom. Although the new arrangements would take some years to realise, an ad hoc committee was set up to facilitate the change and further refurbishment. Agreement had to be reached about reimbursing Warwickshire for fixtures and fittings and of course they took away their Federation property. The road to separation was not smooth, but eventually even the impasse over chandeliers was worked out and Worcestershire took sole charge in 1997.

The room was refurbished again. WIs were invited to sponsor items and did contribute £2,340 to the £3,600 cost, but times were changing and there were several complaints over these 'demands'. Despite a sewing team being recruited to make the soft furnishings and fund-raising events taking place, the scheme was not completed on budget.

2006 saw the need for another upgrade. A local company, County Furnishings Ltd, advised the Federation ad hoc committee on style and content and this time the finance was raised from Catherine Guest's legacy, from fund-raising including a garden party at Chris Marriott's home, and by means of a new raffle held at the ACM called the Denman Dip. Winners received cash towards a course at the College. The three beds became two, plus an occasional third and the bathroom was re-fitted. Costing £7,650, over a hundred members saw the results when they attended the WFWI 90th birthday celebrations.

The Worcestershire Bedroom

Clockwise from top left
-1950's
-1982
-1997
-2014
-The Bathroom upgraded in 2006

Clockwise from above left

-2014 Visit: Members in the dining room
-2011 Visit: Cookery Course
*   Pat Jewkes, Jane Baker*
-1998: 80th birthday wall hanging
-2007 Visit: Preserves Course participants
-1997 Visit: Two views of Social Time

Two years later Denman took over the upkeep of all bathrooms which naturally led the Board to wish they had stayed the refurbishment of Worcestershire's very large one.

More craft items were made for the room including the three pears wall hanging for WFWI's 80th Birthday, made by Diana Chester at a cost of £430. In 2011 the Mary Pedley wall hanging was cleaned and installed along with refurbished furniture from WI House. In 2012, a painting for the room was commissioned from Antony Bridge with money from the legacy of Bee Woodfield who was an ardent Denman supporter.

The survival of Denman College has been in doubt several times over the period. In 1985 Greta Mitchell attended a NFWI meeting in London to discuss the future of the college as it had become a drain on National's finances. Following this, Greta and Shirley Noble stood for its committee. Worcestershire voted 2:1 in favour of saving Denman and an ad hoc committee arranged fundraising events. A Severn Valley Railway trip, a cheese and wine party, and the 'Easter Eggstravaganza' craft fair, as well as members' donations, helped to send £10,000 to the college. National agreed that the building would be repaired and upgraded to meet fire regulations and was guaranteed safe for three years.

In 1992, to support the college further, National set out to raise a million pounds by members buying £1 'bricks.' This Buy a Brick scheme was enthusiastically supported by the WFWI membership. In 1995 part of the funds raised by Freda Davies's County walk went to Denman

By 2016 Denman's fate was again in the balance but a member-led appeal is raising funds to cover the upkeep of the building and it was announced in early 2017 that Denman is secure. By the end of 2017 Worcestershire Federation and its WIs had sent £8237 towards this from fund-raising activities.

2016 Members enjoy a day visit to Denman

Promoting the WI in Worcestershire

Ever since its inauguration WFWI has promoted and publicised itself as does the wider movement. As much coverage as possible has always been sought in every media. The very large scrap books stored at WI House, a good source of illustrations for this book, are testament to this, but it is good to keep in mind a quote from Joy Peers who considered "The best hunting grounds for the promotion of WFWI and for attracting new members were the school gates, supermarkets and the bus stop."

Responsibility for one or more of the aspects have been handled both by sub-committees and by individuals.

Press and Publicity

The position in 1980 was that a member of Executive was elected as publicity officer but promotion and recruitment had no formal representative. That is not to say that they were not actively sought for they were, with several promotional drives attesting to this. They were also covered incidentally in all the events open to the public that WFWI put on, and through publicity.

1983 Letter in CNL re 'Ban the Bomb' confusion

The position of Publicity officer continued well into the next century, the job being to obtain as much coverage as possible from any media available by informing them of WI events and initiatives. The local press, radio and TV were most helpful in this aim although national media have also given coverage. The media, in turn, often ask WI for its help or opinion which is then incorporated into the programme or article.

There is the odd incidence of bad publicity noted in the records. In 1982 members were asked not to take cuttings and plants on garden visits after adverse comments were sent to the Federation.

In 1983 letters had to be sent by Executive to the press refuting the claims that the NFWI was going to campaign against Nuclear Disarmament. Similar letters were sent to all Worcestershire Presidents as this leak had resulted in great misunderstanding among members nationally. The content of the letter was reiterated at the Resolutions Meetings. In 1987 Jill Hammonds penned a spirited response, shown opposite, to the adverse comments about WI in an article printed by Berrows Journal.

In the early days much local newspaper space was given to Annual Council Meetings - ACMs, the Home Economics and Craft Rallies, Federation holiday destinations and the like whilst Berrows Journal printed its first Federation column in 1983. As time went on newspapers generally showed more interest in the more unusual things such as the inadvertent mislaying of 540 Yorkshire visitors, a new WFWI publication, the results of the Hospital Questionnaire and the demonstration at the ACM by the Hunting Ban Lobby when staunch hunt supporter Clarissa Dixon Wright spoke. However, the summer tea parties of 2005 were given good coverage in the Worcester Evening News. In 2007 the first Federation column called Jam and Jerusalem appeared in Worcestershire Life and, over the next few years, the publication gave good, up to date coverage on many Federation activities. Several of these pages are reproduced in this book.

**News
and
Information**

March 7th 1987.

Dear Mr. Chapman,
          I was very disappointed with your article in the March 6th
edition of Berrows Journal. You claim "The WI movement in Worcestershire
is struggling because county women are staying away from meetings".
          I assure you that Worcestershire WI is thriving. We are by far the
biggest womens organisation in this county having a total of 173 WIs
some with memberships of over 100 and others with waiting lists. Because
of being such a large and continually changing group we do sometimes have
to close a WI such as Malvern Wells. Others are newly formed such as
Heronswood and Foley Park.
          We provide an excellent range of activities for members and their
families are sometimes included too. You quoted two sentences from our
monthly federation newsletter. You could have mentioned the visit of
the Abertillery Male Voice Choir on Saturday April 11th and our competitive
drama festival the first week in April. The educational opportunities
in the March newsletter include a talk on Nuclear Power, a bird watching
day, schools on painting, sewing and basketry, a workshop at the Swan Theatre,
courses at our very own college and an International Evening. On the
sporting side in that same newsletter we offer swimming, bowling, bridge
tennis, scrabble, golf, water sports and skittles.
          I challenge Mrs. Green's Over Sixties Club who are quoted as having
a much jollier time to join WI and come with us on the trips advertised
this month. They include The Guildhall School of Music, a flower festival,
the Edinburgh Tattoo and a tour to Holland and Germany.
          Besides getting these opportunities our members get a full yearly
programme of events and meetings run by their own WIs. Our subscription
is £5.60 per year. Do you really think, as you say in that article, that
we fear competition from rival groups? I invite you to attend some of our
events and find out the truth.

          Yours sincerely,
                    Jill Hammonds. W.F.W.I. Press Officer.

1987 Letter refuting the decline of WFWI

Radio Stations were very helpful in publicising WFWI, especially in the 80's and 90's. BBC Radio, especially BBC Birmingham's Time Off programme, broadcast information on the Diamond Jubilee events, Radio Wyvern broadcast something every day about WI in the week when the Centenary of its Canadian birth was celebrated in 1997, whilst Radio Hereford and Worcester, who had regular WI slots during the 80's and 90's, brought a huge mobile aerial to Pierpoint St so that they could broadcast a programme live from the house on this auspicious 100th birthday. The vast majority of broadcasts by this station were during the day but an evening Desert Island Discs featured a selection by Mary Davis.

Jane Garvey of Radio Hereford and Worcester liked to call in Mary Davis, when County Chairman, for her early morning programme. Mary was asked to give her input on a variety of subjects including, in 1991, answering questions about the Resolutions at the forthcoming Triennial General Meeting at the NEC, Birmingham. Many other serious topics were explored such as rape in marriage and the future shape of the BBC, but it was a discussion on sexism in the WI which generated the most comments ever received by the programme and which led to a great deal of publicity.

A reported new edict from Brussels was the topic. Single sex organisations would have to open membership to both sexes. As a result, by 1993, WI would have to be renamed as

'The Country People's Friendship Group.' Maurice, introduced as a French Eurocrat, argued for the motion whilst Mary vigorously upheld the status quo. Many women contacted the programme to say how much they were against the idea. Many men made contact to ask how they could join. The bemused office staff at WI House were besieged by members' calls. Few of the callers seemed to have noticed that it was the 1st of April.

Margaret Deakin spoke on Radio Hereford and Worcester in 1993 regarding WI's role in adult learning whilst Freda Davies was approached to take part in a weekly broadcast on best buys - a look at local greengrocer's prices, during her Chairmanship. The start of the final Ashes test in 2005 apparently demanded a rendition of Jerusalem to be broadcast. Radio Hereford and Worcester came to the office where five members and a husband duly obliged. Katie Johnson, the presenter, couldn't stop laughing for the rest of the morning's broadcast.

Members of various sub-committees gave interviews to Radio Hereford and Worcester. Julia Rogers explained her love of cake making, being asked as a WI member in National Cake Week and in 2015 Sue White talked about WFWI's younger members.

In 2017, Jane Garvey was pleased to provide this comment for the book:
"I have so many happy memories of working with my WI friends in Worcestershire. Sometimes our conversations were serious, of course, but we also had a lot of laughs: and the April Fool is the best example. It really got people going! It left me with an enduring respect for this very special organisation. In fact, I went on about the WI so much that my mother joined her local branch. And she's still a member, over twenty years later."

2004 Interviewing Clarissa Dixon Wright.
Vicky Coghlan, Suzanne Owen, Trisha Waddington

2008 Mad Hatter's Tea party

Television has also featured WFWI, firstly in 1982 when Yorkshire TV shot scenes for the Worcestershire recipes in its Farmhouse Kitchen series. In 1994 BBC1 showed Worcestershire's Three Counties Marquee, though hopes of a huge audience were dashed when it was shown at 11 pm. The BBC filmed Anne Nicholas making plum jam at the House in 2000 and the new House was filmed in 2006 by BBC4 for a programme entitled 'The Hunt for Middle England' when, Christine Hickman-Smith recalls, the discussion was conducted whilst ten members, mainly from Executive, made gift boxes. Suzanne Owen was interviewed for National BBC when she spoke, as County Chairman, in support of Bill Bryson's campaign to reduce street furniture. The Let's Cook initiative generated a lot of TV and Radio interest in 2007 as did the Eco Teams.

Busy schedule for federation

THE short list of resolutions for the Women's Institute meeting in London in June, has now been published.

Included among a wide variety are proposals on subjects as widely diverse as the cutting of coastguard services, live animal experimentation for non-medical research and the acceleration of combined heat and power schemes.

Care and thought have been given to the problems of both young and old as is shown by resolutions dealing with child abuse and with subsidised travel for schoolchildren at one end of the age scale and a plea for special psycho-geriatric care at the other.

A hoary old favourite on straw stubble burning makes yet another appearance and there are predictable resolutions on education and health.

A controversial resolution on the worrying question of whether or not doctors should inform parents if they are prescribing contraceptive pills for their under-age daughters is bound to invoke a great deal of discussion should it ever reach the Albert Hall.

Only one WI domestic issue is included in the short list and it is a financial one dealing with WI investments.

Unfortunately, none of Worcestershire's proposals were accepted for the list this year.

Members of the executive and organisation sub-committee have already met to discuss the resolutions and to vote on them in order of preference. Their final selection will be taken by the county chairman, Mrs Jeanne Round, to the next meeting of the national council where agin the list will be debated and another ballot taken.

The finale choice of three or four resolutions will be made by the national executive, with the council's recommendations in mind.

The assistant county treasurer, Mrs Shirley Noble, will accompany Mrs Round to the council as Mrs MaryGlaze, county treasurer, has recently undergone an operation and will be convalescing in a warmer climate. We send our best wishes to jmrs Glaze for a swoft return to health and fitness.

Our good wishes for a quick recovery, too, to Mrs Margaret Mills, the county secretary who has a broken wrist after a fall at home. Mrs Mills has bravely carried on with as much of her work as possible and she is greatly helped by the assistant secretary, Mrs Brenda Spragg. Nevertheless, is is a tremendous drawback, the more so since Mrs Mills, who lives at Kidderminster, is unable to drive her car.

Driving at any time is a hazardous business and it becomes more so in the case of a high-sided vehicle in gale force winds. It was with some relief, therefore, that the safe arrival of the exhibition bus in Worcester was greeted on what was, surely one of the windiest days of the year.

Such was the force of the wind that it was necessary to draw up an accompanying coach alongside the double-decker to shield it from too much buffeting.

It is hardly surprising that, in such terrible weather conditions and badly situated as it was in view of traffic problems for pedestrians, the bus did not prove as great an attraction in Worcester as had been hoped for by the organisers, who had done so splendidly in other parts of the county.

Nevertheless, is engendered a certain amount of interest and there were also plenty of loyal WI members who turned up anxious to view "their" bus. Anyone who ventured in was assured of a warm welcome inside the bus, however cold outside.

It was loyal memoers' hard work which gave Pershore and neighbouring WIs their greatest triumph in the country when they scooped the prize

offered by International Stores of £100 for every mile of till rill collected.

The splendid total of £1,000 was raided due, says Mrs Beth Milson, president of Pershore, to the wonderful co-operation between members and Mr Ken Felton, manager of the International in Pershore and his staff.

Mrs Milson is hopeful that one of her pet charities, a scheme for swimming facilities for deprived handicapped children who are cared for locally, will be among the charities which will benefit from the bumper total cheque of £20,000 which was raised countrywide from the till roll scheme.

Heartiest congratulations to Pershore and the other local WIs on a wonderful achievement.

by Diana Farmiloe

• Jill Williams and Sue Arnold make a nice cup of soup for Gwen Allen in the WI bus at the cathedral.

1984 Promotion Bus at Worcester

In the early 80's there was a Promotions Officer elected by the Executive but she was concerned with the sale of County items and NFWI publications. There was also a County Promotions sub-committee in the late eighties - the renamed Calendar committee. Neither are to be confused with the attempts made to promote WFWI to gain members and increase its profile. The methods used to promote WFWI have been varied.

From 1980 to 2000 sixteen promotional activities are recorded and were administered in several different ways. From 1980 to 1986 there was a Promotions ad hoc committee which undertook promotional drives attempting to stem falling membership and 1984 was a very active year in this respect as there was a Countrywide recruiting drive devised by National, including a promotional bus. Before the January arrival of the bus, WFWI advertised the event by placing 300 posters on Midland Red buses. The three sites for the National bus were agreed with the local authorities and soup was served to the visitors who turned up. However, this event was less successful in Worcestershire than elsewhere for, although reasonable numbers came at Redditch and Kidderminster, the Worcester day was a failure. Visitors were kept away by the weather and those manning the bus had to endure inside temperatures hovering at freezing point. At least they had plenty of soup.

Worcestershire's own promotion fortnight followed in June. This featured a caravan, filled with promotional material which, piloted mainly by the menfolk of committee members, visited a different area of the County each day. Unfortunately, in Pershore, it somehow became detached from its towing car and there its progress ceased. Despite the unfortunate occurrences, the twin projects bore fruit with two new WIs being formed and 184 new members recruited.

1984 WFWI's Promotion Caravan

Appointing a promotions officer in 1991, an Executive member charged with the promotion of the WI in the County, was a major change. Diana Cartmel devised some original schemes, especially the store discount scheme with thirty-two participating outlets. This idea was adopted by NFWI and a discount book is still issued to members yearly. Display boards were purchased and WIs were encouraged to borrow them to help their own promotional activities when the 'Bring Someone New in 92' promotional slogan was launched. New promotional leaflets were placed in libraries, tourist offices, Further Education colleges and with WI markets. The use of shops and libraries for promotional displays had long been used but now they were set up in Webbs Garden Centre, Hartlebury Castle, in Worcester's Reindeer Court, Beatties department store and main shopping area, at the Malvern Spring Garden Show, at pre-retirement courses and in retirement homes. A 1994 questionnaire asked WIs to give their opinions on the recent Promotion, Press and Publicity initiatives, but no record of the outcome was found.

Promotional stalls were set up at local events such as the 1993 Worcester St John's Medieval Fair at which the new lightweight display boards were used. In 1996 there was a display at the Three Choirs Festival and in 1998 a display model village costing £500 was made which attracted much attention especially when it was used at the NFWI exhibition. When borrowed it had to be accompanied by a committee member.

Most of the initiatives described above were undertaken because of a Marketing seminar presented to the Executive in 1992 by Mike Deakin, a marketing lecturer and member's

1998 Janet Clemas, Suzanne Owen display the model village

husband. He stressed the importance of promotion and media exposure, emphasising that 'Image is everything'. However, it was recognised that whilst wanting to modernise, WFWI did not wish to 'throw out the baby with the bathwater'. Later he spoke on promotion to the NFWI Executive Committee. Membership stabilised in the early 90's but, despite ongoing efforts, it began to fall again and so in 1998 a new initiative was started with the advent of the Promotion and Display Group. By 2000 this was considered not to be successful and the matter was re-thought.

The Marketing and Development Committee

The result of this reappraisal was the setting up of an ad hoc committee, Marketing and Development or MaD, in 2000 chaired by Liz Davies. Helen Carey, then National Chairman, visited in 2001 to find out what this new initiative was doing. Many of its promotional activities were similar to those of the 90's but there was a greater emphasis on providing promotional material for WIs, especially a new member's pack which explained many of the 'mysteries' of WFWI. New, even lighter, display boards were made available to WIs along with attractive promotional handouts. One of these was a promotional video which could be borrowed along with a portable TV to show the activities of WFWI, pictures for which were collected mainly from the sub-committees. Bookmarks, folders, flyers and balloons were also available. All of these were used too at Promotional Days. Day courses were offered by Advisers to help WIs to 'sell' themselves through better writing of press reports whilst sample invites for a letter of invitation to join were prepared so that WIs could do a recruitment drop in their local area. MaD, still a working group, joined the handbook sub-committee list in 2006 and 28 members have served on it, six as chairmen and eighteen solely on this committee. It has put on 35 activities, making a total of 51 promotional events in all. It took advantage of an NFWI funded £2,000 grant available for promotion leading up to the National Centenary year in 2015 which made possible the 2013 purchase of pull-up promotional banners and advertising on ten local bus routes and at Worcester's Sixways Rugby Stadium.

MaD also looked at how WFWI presented itself internally, so the County News was revamped, eventually being produced in colour and the information leaflets were overhauled and reduced in number. In 2013 a new guide was launched called 'All you need to know about running your WI' and this was introduced by the Advisers committee.

The committee targeted communities around the county and were aided by local WIs and Groups. This time 'pop up' stalls were used in shopping malls in the main towns but village fetes, festivals and other similar events were also visited. To make such events easier, 82 cardboard easels for displays were bought in 2016. Between 2008 and 2011 Worcester City's Strawberry Fair proved another good place to promote the Federation, whilst Advisers were looking at setting up workplace WIs, the first being at

2013 Christine Hickman-Smith, Mary Lou Lockyer promoting WFWI at Webbs Garden Centre

County Hall. This direct approach, and especially the huge efforts made by the Advisers, has resulted in a stable membership total since 2005, despite the fall in the number of WIs.

MaD was mothballed in 2013 but was reactivated as a working group in 2015 when it began to concentrate on on-line skills support for WIs along with presence at some outside events such as a repeat of the 2013 Webbs Garden Centre promotion. Its formation as the Marketing and Development sub-committee was announced at the 2016 ACM. It had seven members in 2017 and now concentrates mainly on the promotion of WI through social media and is reportedly well ahead of most other Federations in this respect. Sessions on the use of Blogs, Twitter, Facebook, websites and email have been rolled out, all methods of communication either in use or planned by WFWI, and one other session has given advice on publicising WI. Mention must be made though of the incalculable impact of The Calendar Girls and the slow handclapping of Tony Blair at the National Triennial General Meeting in 2000 which raised the profile of WI nationally by showing some of the aspects of WI which had been ignored by both the wider public and the media.

2013 Bus Promotion: Suzanne Owen, Mary Lou Lockyer, Christine Hickman-Smith, Patience Broad

2013 Banner at Sixways featuring Hot Peppers WI L-R Gemma Dewson; Advisers - Anne Smith, Mary Lou Lockyer, Christine Hickman-Smith, Patience Broad. Sheena Murray at rear

2005 Chris Marriott at Crowngate promotion

2013 Promoting and collecting for the Breast Unit in the Crowngate Centre Worcester

Other Aspects of the Board's Role

Service on Outside Organisations

Throughout these thirty- eight years many County organisations have been keen to have a WFWI member sitting on their committee. WFWI was equally keen to oblige. Having a presence on committees which dealt with such concerns as health, the environment, education, agriculture, consumer groups and women's welfare was a policy aim of the Federation for, through them, it could influence County affairs in the areas which formed part of the WI remit. In the early 1980's there were fourteen such appointments, nine of which were filled by Executive members reporting directly. These nine representatives were sitting on the Committees of the Community Health Council, CPRE - the Council for the Protection of Rural England, NFU - the National Farmers' Union, Old People's Welfare, the Handicapped Association, the Standing Conference of Women's Organisations and three Further Education Colleges - Malvern Hills, Kidderminster and Pershore. Four more representatives reported to the Current Affairs sub-committee: - the Women's Committee for Solid Fuel, Cathedral Flowers, Probation Service for Volunteers and the Victim Support Group whilst one for the YFC - Young Farmers' Clubs - reported to the Home Economics and Craft sub-committee. In 1982 specific instructions were devised for the representative as to her duties and reporting strategy. By 1988 it was noted that the reports were taking up too much time at Executive meetings and moves were taken to curtail their number. Only eight bodies are mentioned in 1989. These were CPRE, NFU, YFC, the Worcester and Redditch Community Health Councils, the Police Consultative Committee, Worcester Victim Support and Worcester in Bloom. The list has remained modest ever since and the role of Executive members has been reduced. By 2010 the list featured CPRE, NFU, YFC, Police Liaison, Worcester University and the County Volunteers Emergency Committee.

1991
Mary Davis at CPRE Best Kept Village award
Wyre Piddle

Tree planting marks award

A new Golden Acacia tree is now standing in Smith's Meadow, Wyre Piddle, to mark its success in the Hereford and Worcester best kept village competition.

Organised by the Council for the Protection of Rural England and the Worcestershire Federation of Women's Institutes, the competition took place in the summer when Wyre was judged the best kept medium-sized village with a population of 500 to 700.

Town clerk Pauline Monks said: "Everybody's very pleased that we won it. The judges praised the overall look of the village, commented on the village hall and the general tidiness."

◄ Lord Sandys (Council for the Protection of Rural England — right) plants the commemorative tree with parish council chairman Gary Robinson and chairman of the Worcestershire WI, Mary Davis.

It can be seen that, over the years, organisations have come and gone from the list and indeed some like the Post Office and Telecommunications panel are not included above. However, links with the farming community have always been strong. After all it was the Board of Agriculture which sponsored the early WI. It remains, at heart, a rural movement so the Federation still supports the Three Counties Agricultural Show and maintains its links with NFU and YFC.

Membership of CPRE has also been a constant. WFWI volunteers help judge its annual competition which alternates between Best Kept Churchyard and Best Kept Village. This has been done by many members, including the County Chairman who usually judges the final. Despite the lengthy process - visits were made to 58 entries in 2002 - it is reported as very enjoyable, especially the award ceremony.

There were other involvements too. For twenty years Executive supported a special WI at Barnsley Hall Hospital; this closed in 1991. From 1980 to at least 1987 a yearly supper was provided for the Handicapped Association and in the mid-eighties a representative sat on the new National Computing Centre body in Worcester.

Lobbying was also done on any subject concerning WI. Letters were sent to both County and Government bodies when WI was looking for action, usually on a Mandated Resolution but also on other issues.

To keep the Federation in the vanguard of WI affairs, constant attention has been paid to updating the knowledge of the Board and to its interaction with other Federations as well as with NFWI.

Training

The Federation has, with the one or two exceptions noted elsewhere, paid for all of the training offered to its volunteers and that for Board members is no exception.

There is mention in 1981 of Executive going to Denman for training but it is not until 1994 that it is mentioned again. Worcestershire approached NFWI but it seems that no provision for training was available. NFWI suggested that Worcestershire were 'guinea pigs' and should offer a course with a maximum of seventy attending including those drawn from other Federations. A training handbook was produced for this course. Executive also undertook a two day media training course in 1996 which included the filming of the participants' efforts. This was conducted by Rosemary McCulloch, a niece-in-law of Uncle Mac the children's' radio personality. By 1998 there was ongoing training provided by National and several courses were run in the 2000's, usually at WI House, by an NFWI Board member. Sometimes the course content was disappointing, at others valuable information was gleaned such as on Health and Safety requirements and on the need for Board members to sign a bankruptcy declaration. Each new County Chairman had an induction at Denman and these sessions often added to the knowledge of how to run the Federation and update its practices.

By 2016 there was also a rolling programme of refreshing for those who were Ambassadors.

Liaison with other County Federations

In 1980 there was a system in place whereby representatives from Worcestershire met with their counterparts in neighbouring counties. Although a six county meeting is mentioned fleetingly, those between Worcestershire, Herefordshire and Gloucestershire were a feature until 1985 when Gloucestershire announced that it no longer wished to continue. Sometimes there were joint ventures such as that in 1981 which attracted 630 members to a Law and Order Day at Malvern.

Thereafter links with other counties have depended mainly on the visits to their AGM's by Board members and more importantly, the meetings of Chairman and Treasurer with their counterparts from every other Federation at the National Council Meeting. This replaced the Consultative Council Meeting in 1982, a similar grouping event which was the forum for discussing that year's Resolutions.

The Federation and NFWI

Much of what NFWI does impacts on both WFWI and the membership at large, as has been seen through the major changes dealt with above. Each month the Federation receives copies of NFWI News and this is discussed at the Board meeting, relevant information being passed on through the CNL. Dual membership was formalised by National in the new constitution of 1991. A very comprehensive NFWI questionnaire asking for the membership's views on all things WI in 2000 led to anti National feeling surfacing in the County when some innovations resulting from the survey were implemented. Similarly, there was some dismay in 2002 at having to pay £1 to use NFWI logo.

Several Worcestershire members have been appointed to NFWI posts since 1980. Olive Odell was already serving on the National Executive and was its Vice Chairman when she retired from it in 1983. Julia Roberts joined the National Board in 2011 and is the present National Treasurer. Others who have served on National Committees and on other National initiatives include Olive Odell – ACWW Committee and the Teaching Panel, Gwen Bullas - Music and Drama, Anne Garmon - Combined Arts, Mary Davis - Forward Planning Group, Dorothy Leavey and Anne Smith - Combined Arts, Sue Stone – Education Committee, Patience Broad - Advisers Training Committee, becoming its lead adviser in 2017, Beth Milsom - Travelling Tutor, Liz Osborn - Sports and Leisure, and Sylvia Beardshaw - National Eco Teams initiative for Climate Change. Ann Quiney became the Midlands Co-ordinator for Celebrating Our Communities and Monica Carden the Regional Sports Coordinator. Others, whose service resulted from a sub-committee involvement, are recorded in the relevant section.

National arranges many events for the total membership, the most important being the National Council Meetings. At the National AGM in 1984 Jeanne Round spoke against the proposed change to the investment powers of NFWI as Worcestershire felt it would have an adverse impact on Federations. In 1994 Rosemary Roberts, seconded by Betty Johnson, spoke for the resolution on Legal Aid at the Triennial AGM held at the NEC, Birmingham.

They were pleased that it was passed with a good majority. As described earlier, Chris Marriott thanked the National Chairman Faye Mansell at the AGM in Cardiff in June 2006. The Federation also submitted a resolution to National in 1996 and two more in 2013. In 2015, for the NFWI Centenary, the first live relays of the National Annual Meeting were shown in the theatres in Redditch and Malvern.

There are many NFWI events designed to encourage members' talents. The Huxley Cup for flower arranging is awarded each year and the Federation nominates an entrant. This was staged at the Royal Show until 2002 but has been in several locations since and the Federation has had several successes in it, Brenda Beaman and Joyce Valentine coming third in 1998 and 2017 respectively. The Lady Denman Cup for writing is also entered yearly, Alison Quartermain's poem coming third in 1999. In the same year Dorothy Norman reported on her experiences in Finland having won the Grace Haddow travel bursary. In 1982 the triennial essay competition drew thirty-eight Worcestershire entries whilst the Heritage competition of 1981 saw Overbury and Wolverly do very well. In 1990, 120 members entered the Driver of the Year Competition.

Worcestershire came second in a National Competition at the 1985 Royal Show, third in 1990 with a display based on Worcestershire Wildlife, and third again in 1994 with a display based on Elgar which included a depiction of Worcester Cathedral in découpage. In 1998 Hampton WI won their way to the National Quiz Final at Denman as did Beoley in 2013, and in 2005 Menith Wood won the NFWI Community Challenge prize. National launched a competition in 2014 to find the best fruit cake recipe. The winner was to be used for the 100th anniversary cake which, suitably decorated, was cut by The Queen at the Albert Hall. Sheila O'Shaughnessy entered the competition, won the regional final in Derby and the cake was one of the final six judged at Denman. In 2015 Wells and Wyche were proud to receive their prize for winning the WFWI Centenary programme competition from Janice Langley, NFWI Chair, at Worcestershire's ACM.

2014 Sheila O'Shaughnessy

1994 National TGM - Worcestershire delegates

2011 National AGM Liverpool

Members of Worcestershire Federation of W.I's who took part in the Co-operative entry for the Royal Show Challenge Cup 1990, organized by the County Home Economics Committee, show Mr Harry Green, Chairman of the Worcestershire Nature Conservation Trust Ltd the exhibit photographed in . W.I House, Worcester.

Pictured left to right. Ms. D. Cope, Little Withy. W.I - Ms. A. Mills, Broadwaters W.I - Ms. M. Dalton, Wribbenhall W.I - Ms. A. Thompson, Abberley W.I - Ms. D. Jones, Blakedown. W.I, Mr. Harry Green - Ms. D. Webster, Hadzor & Oddingley. W.I - Ms. L. Grant, Stone. W.I, Ms. A. Heughly. Blakedown. W.I and Ms. J. Rogers, Pedmore. W.I.

July 1990.   W.I HOUSE, WORCESTER

1990 Third at the Royal Show

2015 Wells and Wyche WFWI
Programme Competition Winners

1984 Diana Cope on the right

Worcestershire has always supported National's big exhibitions. Fourteen coaches took members to see the National Exhibition at Olympia in 1983 where twelve WFWI items were amongst those on display. Members had also produced 1,000 items for sale. Two Worcestershire members participated in the simulated computer course which National put on as part of the show and Angela Thompson demonstrated soft furnishing during the exhibition.

For several years money from the sale of National's raffle tickets has made a welcome contribution to Federation funds.

Many other NFWI initiatives are dealt with throughout this book but 2012 saw the fitness orientated 'Big Walk Little Splash' and the 'Triathlon Challenge'.

NFWI Trading Arm has existed throughout the period but is now called WI Enterprises. Rosemary Roberts was the representative for some years and remembers "WI Books began in the 70's with very limited titles but it developed over the years. However, in the 80's it got itself into a pickle, but a new Board put it on the right tracks, with any surplus income transferred to the National WI funds." Books now are only a small part of WI Enterprises Ltd.

The Federation sold NFWI publications up until the early 90's, taking a cut of the profit from the sales. 'Village Voices', a book produced by NFWI to mark its 75th Anniversary sold £500 worth of copies at the 1990 Half Yearly Council Meeting.

There had been problems growing. The Federation was obliged to buy the stock and it felt subjected to unfair competition when in 1982 NFWI sold direct to bookshops at a reduced rate. As late as 2000 Julia Rogers, the then representative, was writing to NFWI again about the unfairness of their proceedings. In 1989 getting supplies of stationery from WI Books was a problem. It seems that from 1992 a member of Executive and later a member of the Fund-raising committee took charge of ordering and selling the items.

Official Gifts for National Occasions

From time to time official gifts and cards have been sent by the Federation. Most have gone to Royalty. All of these were the work of members, sometimes via a competition. The minutes note a number of gifts. In 1980 Jubilee dishes were given to the Queen on her Maundy Thursday visit to Worcester Cathedral

1981 Card for the Royal Wedding

2000 Joanne Powell with the Queen Mother's 100th birthday card

and to the Queen Mother to mark her 80th birthday. Charles and Diana received a card on their marriage in 1981 and in 2000 a special card was painted by Joanne Powell to celebrate the Queen Mother's 100th Birthday. Layettes of non-allergic wool were made for Prince William and Princess Beatrice, William also receiving a hand-made teaching book, a pair of hand engraved goblets, a family circle of love and some silk flowers. Some of the names of those who produced the items above go unrecorded in the minutes, but a card made by Kathleen Smith was sent to congratulate the Queen in her Golden Jubilee year and also a handkerchief with a tatting border made by Bessie Attenborough.

Archives

The Federation has a very large archive. It contains all of the minutes of all County Committees and many other relevant documents produced by the County illustrative of its work.

In 2003 it is recorded that an attempt should be made to catalogue the items but this did not progress and in 2005, when Pierpoint St was sold, a decision was taken to send the bulk of the early documents, especially the record books, to the County Council's Record Office. The rest were retained at Hallow. The County Record Office is now in The Hive in central Worcester. The WFWI material there is largely un-catalogued although an application for funding this is proceeding at the time of writing.

Mary Davis was appointed as County Archivist in 2006 after her work alongside Brenda Spragg in sorting out which documents should be sent to the Record Office. She retired from this role in 2015 when Sylvia Beardshaw was appointed with Val Durnall as assistant. The large number of scrap books compiled since 1918 remain at Hallow. Other picture records are kept on the office computer and members are encouraged to donate photographs of events to keep this up to date, and also to donate other memorabilia.

Social Events

Only two are mentioned in the minutes, a social evening at the House in 1985 and a skittles evening two years later. However, there were many more which were not recorded officially as there are pictures of social gatherings taking place at the homes of County Chairmen, at WI House or at other venues. Freda Davies mentions a visit to Buckingham Palace for all Federation committee members in 1993, the first year it opened to the public.

Celebrating Anniversaries

There have always been special events put on to celebrate the anniversaries not only of WFWI but also for NFWI, National and International milestones. All of them required months of planning, often a steep learning curve, and hard work in the execution, but also gave the opportunity to acquire new skills. Usually an ad hoc committee was formed for each. The national WI 75th birthday in 1990 was the first big celebration after the Federation's 60th and was marked by 'Cavalcade 90'. This was, in the main, undertaken by the Groups.

1993 75th Birthday Dinner

For WFWI's own 75th anniversary in 1993 several events were planned. These included a celebratory weekend at Betty Hudson's Merevale Farm which was dogged by inclement weather, the making of the County Tablecloth, a competition to design a garden which would be the centrepiece of the WI marquee at the Three Counties Show, a County Cookbook whose 2000 copies all sold, a County Draw which raised £1,275, a commemorative book which proved very expensive to bind, and a service in the Cathedral accompanied by gifts of embroidery and a silver verge. The dinner party for all WI Presidents held at Stourport on Severn was a huge success, especially the food, prepared by the Home Economics committee in accordance with Hallow WI's winning competition entry. A note in the arrangements for the evening shows how much attention to detail went into this type of event. It read "Buy two 40 pound turkeys now and freeze them as they are not so good at the party time in April, as it is the fighting season."

1993 Preparations at Merevale Farm Weekend

Left – 1993 CNL

1993 New County Tablecloth

1997 saw a trip to Canada to mark the centenary of the birth of WI there at Stoney Creek and 54 members journeyed to Anglesey to celebrate this with Britain's first WI, Llanfair PG, on their 82nd birthday.

The following year, the Federation's 80th birthday was marked by a party for Presidents and Group Co-ordinators, by a Home and Country Day at Bush Farm, though this was not well attended despite the beautiful weather, and by Diana Chester making the three pears wall hanging for the Denman bedroom.

The Millennium saw a Gala Dinner held at the Three Counties Showground and a record of special WI activities was made.

An exhibition at Avoncroft Museum featuring all the best of WFWI was held for the 90th

1998 Preparing for the Home and Country day at Bush Farm

birthday in 2008 along with a dinner at the Three Counties Showground whilst Groups, WIs and individuals were encouraged to walk ninety miles, a prize being offered for the best log produced, though no record of the winner was found. A new logo was produced and the current County Badge below is based on this, being introduced in 2011/12.

To celebrate WFWI's 95th birthday in 2013 a raffle for the Worcester Royal Hospital's Breast Care Unit was held and raised over £5,000.

The national WI's 100th Birthday celebrations saw the NFWI Baton progress through the County in September 2014, courtesy of the Groups, as part of its countrywide journey whilst in the Centenary year, 2015, the wildflower seeds distributed in 2014 came into flower, the Exhibition of Craft at Harrogate was attended by a group from County on a weekend break and the special Buckingham Palace Garden Party was a highlight for those who attended. Each Worcestershire WI could send a member. Three coaches, carrying 170 members departed from different parts of the County. On the walk to the Palace these ladies were treated as a London 'sight' by many tourists who took photo after photo of the splendidly attired procession.

1997 At Stourport - Celebrating 100 years since the founding of WI in Canada

1998 Two Views of the
80th Birthday Party

2008 Events recorded
on the front of January 2009 CNL

2015 Celebrating WI's 100th Birthday with a
Garden Party at Buckingham Palace

The Federation and Worcestershire Members

There would be no point in any of the above if the membership did not respond to what the Federation offered and because of this the Federation has always put its members' interests first. After all that is what it was set up to do.

It has offered them a very wide variety of activities, has tried to accommodate their wishes and also attend to their complaints. Some things remained insoluble, such as the distance some members have to travel to venues, but others could be resolved. When a questionnaire revealed that members of the Executive seemed remote and did not mix, action was taken and in 1990 members were invited to officers' homes. Falling numbers were a problem and this impacted on all members, so in 1991 there was a membership discussion which resulted in the slogan 'Bring Someone New in '92'. New members' flyers were sent out to WIs in 1993 as the recruitment drive continued by offering money prizes to WIs for increasing their membership. A few members had always been invited to lunch at the ACM and now two new members were asked in addition. In 1996 new members days were held at WI House, invitations being made to those who had joined in the last three years. Unfortunately there were some complaints over the allocation of places and one was cancelled because of snow. Certificates were presented to WIs reaching milestone birthdays and 1998 saw letters sent to suspended WIs for the first time. Chairmen had always accepted invitations to visit WIs unless a clash occurred. In 2001 members suggested summer activities at the House and although this was implemented it proved unsuccessful. By 2009 the various measures adopted saw numbers holding up well compared with other Federations and 2010 saw an increase in numbers. This total has held at about 4,000 despite the closure of WIs as most members join elsewhere.

WIs' annual council meeting

'Bring someone new in '92'

'Bring someone new in '92' was the message for Women's Intitute members last week when they gathered at Malvern Festival Theatre for the annual council meeting of the Worcestershire Federation of WIs.

The chairman, Mrs Mary Davies, told the meeting: "There are lots of women whom we should tell about our organisation – we might know that it's the best thing since sliced bread but they don't – yet."

She said the Worcestershire WIs had managed to keep their membership figures high, with about 6,000 women in 170 groups, but she still set down a challenge for the future for local groups to increase membership.

She told the delegates that at a "brainstorming meeting" last summer the executive committee had come up with some ideas for attracting new members.

She said: "We must present ourselves in a modern, relaxed and 'user-friendly' way."

And she told the assembly, one new member had said 'I've lived in the same street for 22 years, but since I joined the WI a year ago I made more friends than in the previous 21'.

Mrs Davies, stressing that WIs are more than just social groups, said: "We are concerned with conservation and health as well as supporting the campaign to keep Malvern Hills College open."

During the morning session the delegates also heard a talk from the editor of the Malvern Gazette and Ledbury Reporter, Liz Griffin, who gave members some hints on making the best of their press reports.

After lunch guest speaker Dame Jennifer Jenkins, past chairman of the National Trust, talked about the NT and its work.

She followed her speech with a slide show of projects undertaken by the NT since its formation, nearly 100 years ago.

The article gives Mary Davis the wrong surname (Davies)

86

Communicating with Members

The WIs are given the information about all the decisions taken by the Board in many different ways but the five detailed below are the most important and have been present since 1980. Communication from NFWI to the general membership comes via the Federation and so this is included here too.

The Annual Report

Until a much shorter four-page version was introduced in the late 1980's, the Annual Report sent to each WI was a booklet of some sixteen pages. It outlined the activities and membership of the Executive and sub-committees. Produced by professional printers in a revamped form from 1990, it had its coverage period changed to fit the financial year in 1993 when the start month changed from December to January. In 1994 each of the 6000 members received a copy but this has not been repeated. Reduced further by 2006, it was then combined with the financial report and the contents were streamlined, giving much less detail about WFWI activities. This has been reversed to some degree subsequently.

Council Meetings

Holding an Annual Council Meeting is one of the major things the Federation must do. It is here that all of the yearly business of the Federation is formally approved by delegates from the WIs. The first was held before the Federation was formally constituted as part of NFWI and the young WIs came to hear and be heard. Except for the discussions on Resolutions, by 1980 WIs came mainly to hear reports on all aspects of the Federation and to listen to speakers.

Much time and thought was, and still is, put into the arrangements and speaker choices, for it seems that without a good speaker numbers attending fall. It is costly to put on and the aim is to break even financially. They are usually very happy, celebratory occasions and successive chairmen have said how much they loved the atmosphere, Chris Marriott saying "So what was the fun part of being County Chairman? Our annual council meeting held at the Malvern Theatre was always an entertaining event." Christine Hickman-Smith echoes this "There were many highlights for me during my chairman's years, engaging with and listening to Inspirational speakers, Kate Bliss, Adam Henson, Blind Dave Heeley, Christine Walkden, The

1984 ACM at Kidderminster

87

Queens Chef, Mary Rhodes and Sheila Dibnah at our Spring and Annual meetings are some of them and very memorable."

The ACM, held at the end of February until the mid 1980's when it was moved to the end of March, saw no further change until 2011 when it swopped months with the half yearly council meeting. It has since been held in October with the half yearly in the spring. There are only a few venues in the County capable of holding the expected numbers, Kidderminster Town Hall and Kings School, Worcester which are rather small, Malvern and Redditch Theatres which suffer from parking problems and the Three Counties Showground suite. The Malvern venues offer a somewhat more central location within the county, so they have been used most.

2016 The Severn Hall, Malvern Showground - Jerusalem gets the Annual Meeting underway

The day is organised thus. All Federation and sub-committee members arrive early, the latter to set up their promotional stalls and, with County items also on sale, the display area is well visited by members. The Board, hoping that all previous groundwork has come to fruition, check the lunchtime catering, the reserved seats for the guests, which in 1992 included Japanese observers, and each Board member waits to welcome the person to be hosted. These include the speakers, past Federation officers, officers from other Federations and the WI members invited to the lunch. The County Secretary and Chairman run through the agenda making sure all is in place and ensuring that the flowers, usually done by a WI, are presented beautifully on the central table. This has been covered since 1993 by the County Tablecloth and prior to that date by tablecloths from individual WIs. From 1997, a first aider has been on hand to deal with any medical issues.

2015 Awaiting the start of the ACM at Malvern Showground

88

2016 The ACM in session

Most years there has been an attendance of between 800 to 1,000 members, some on the coaches provided between 1984 and 1999 by WFWI. Seats are taken, the County Chairman gives her welcome, Jerusalem is sung and then comes the business. Details of the year's activities are given by the Chairman in her address and the financial position is reported by the Treasurer. Next come the sub-committee and other reports, these since 2002 under a time constraint after members indicated in a questionnaire that they would like less time devoted to this. The WI delegates vote on the various proposals, then speakers, which for most of the 2000's included one from Taylors Tea, complete the morning session. Until 1994 a performance of some kind, known as social time, rounded off the morning's activities but owing to the difficulties of finding suitable, willing talent this has, since then, been on a sporadic basis.

Most members bring a packed lunch, eaten outside if fine, although pre-ordered food has been available in some years.

2006 ACM - Lunch break outside Malvern Theatre

In the afternoon session presentations and awards are made. They are usually to members successful in attaining the required standard for test certificates, qualifying as Judges or Advisers or winning competitions and also to WIs for passing various milestones.

The main speaker then entertains the assembly. These have featured many and varied personalities but they all seem to like addressing WIs as can be seen from Ann Widdecombe's 2016 recollections, which she happily provided for this book after a chance meeting on holiday.

"I always like addressing WIs and in March 2006 I spoke to the Worcestershire WIs Annual Council Meeting which took place at Malvern Theatre.

There had been a lot of speculation as to whether I was retiring and indeed I had made it informally clear on several occasions that I did not intend to serve beyond the end of that Parliament (2010). However, I delayed a formal announcement because I was wary of a snap Election. Had there been no time to choose a successor, I would have faced up to another Parliament. As it was, I had always intended to make the announcement on my 60th birthday which fell in October 2007 but that coincided with a great deal of speculation that there would be a snap Election because Gordon Brown had taken over from Tony Blair.

Nevertheless, in the interim, I was answering questions fairly straightforwardly about my intentions. However, the Worcestershire WI was the first occasion on which I had answered such a question from a public platform and there was an immediate flurry of press interest and Worcestershire WI became the focus for many questions from eager journalists."

It is gratifying that this chimes with Chris Marriott's recollection. "Particularly entertaining was when we had Ann Widdecombe as the guest afternoon speaker. As can be imagined she was excellent and told us of her plan to retire and not stand at the 2010 election. This was the first public announcement of her forthcoming retirement."

Clarissa Dixon Wright's presence caused another flurry of press interest and a headache for the Executive who had to deal with members of the Anti-Hunt lobby outside the Malvern venue. Lucinda Lambton's exploits, including ripping the shirt off a coach driver on her way to Worcestershire's 1993 ACM also, unsurprisingly, made its way into the papers.

2006 Chris Marriott
Ann Widdecombe

There were contingency plans put in place in 1997 when Kate Adie was the speaker at the first meeting to be held at the Three Counties Showground, but happily she was not, as feared, whisked off by the BBC to report from Albania. Imagine then the problems when, in 2017, Prue Leith cancelled the week before the ACM.

MALVERN: Bombshell from Conservative MP at Women's Institute meeting

March 2006

Widdecombe tells the WI she's retiring from politics

EXCLUSIVE
BY REBECCA FISHER
01905 742260
rf@thisisworcester.co.uk

HUNDREDS of Worcestershire WI members were in the audience to hear colourful MP Ann Widdecombe announce her retirement from British politics.

The Conservative favourite was addressing 800 members at their annual council meeting in Malvern Theatres yesterday.

Unbeknown to them Miss Widdecombe was about to drop the political bombshell that she would be retiring at the end of this Parliamentary session.

News of her retirement came as a surprise to Mid-Worcestershire MP Peter Luff, a fellow Conservative who worked as her Private Parliamentary Secretary during John Major's Government in 1996-97.

Mr Luff said there had been hints, but no announcement.

"Ann's the kind of person people get passionate about and, whether you love her or hate her – and I have done both in my time, the Parliament will be a more poorer place without her."

A spokesman for the Conservative Party later confirmed it was the first time Miss Widdecombe had discussed her retirement plans in public.

Miss Widdecombe - MP for Maidstone and the Weald – told the audience she planned to move to Dartmoor and buy some dogs to walk, continue to write her novels and hopefully do some television work.

For someone so used to being in the public eye, she said it was the bleakness of the moors that attracted her.

"I can't wait to be near no people," she added.

Earlier Miss Widdecombe had revealed she wanted leadership of the

Liz Davies, left, and Ann Canham, right, from Worcestershire Women's Institute, with Conservative MP Ann Widdecombe at their annual council meeting at Malvern Theatres yesterday. Picture by Sam Furlong. 13591003

"Whether you love her or hate her, Parliament will be a more poorer place without her"

Conservative party in 2001, but failed to receive the backing of Westminster despite having the support of the country.

Among the packed audience was chairman of the Worcestershire Federation of WIs Chris Marriott who agreed that politics would be duller without Miss Widdecombe.

"She is quite a character," she said. "But I think the members understood her time had come to retire. It was an absolutely wonderful speech."

Miss Widdecombe also announced her support for The Bromyard Three gollies. Herself the proud owner of some gollies, she discussed her hatred of all things politically correct.

But when asked if she thought women would do a better job at running the country, she had no qualms about upsetting her female listeners.

"No, I don't think women would do a better job," she said. "I don't think it matters if you're a man, woman, young or old – all that matters is that whoever is in charge has got there on their own merit."

As well as touching on serious matters – such as the state of the country's prison service – Miss Widdecombe also took a lighthearted look at life in Westminster and about her time on programmes such as Celebrity Fit Club and Ann Widdecombe To The Rescue.

"If I can beam myself into people's lounges as a human being they might think they've got to know me," she said.

"Then, when I'm talking politics people might get to the second paragraph instead of the second word!"

One does not expect a racing tip at an ACM but that was what the audience got from speaker Muriel Allen, the first woman governor of a men's prison. She gave one for the 1999 Cheltenham Gold Cup and the horse won.

Allowing them the pleasure of meeting the large number of members present, all the County Chairmen seem to have enjoyed their ACMs although many admit to being nervous before the start. Pat Harris was so overwhelmed by the thought of her first council meeting that she had been unable to write a sufficiently good address before leaving home. Inspiration came as she drove to the venue. The unlikely source was the back of a lorry!

There have of course been minor hiccoughs. In 1980 lunch tickets had to be issued for members and visitors as the year

IMPULSIVE: Lady Lucinda, who was offended by a V-sign

Lucinda locks horns

M'lady tears shirt off a rude driver

before fifty-eight and not fifty guests had turned up. At one of Jeanne Round's ACMs the introduction of the morning speaker did not, unfortunately, go exactly to plan, the member of Executive saying, "Let me introduce our speaker who in the summer propagates his plants and garden and in the winter propagates his family."

2015 Trudi Tayloe with the mailing   2016 Fiona Layton centre with office items at the ACM

One major problem came in 2001, the year of Foot and Mouth, when the large meeting was cancelled and replaced by a much smaller affair in a town environment at the Christopher Whitehead School, Worcester. By that year concern about attendance was growing as many WIs either apologised for not sending a delegate or did not respond to the ACM invitation at all; twenty-eight being recorded as failing to do so in 2008. The Home Economics and Craft Rally was added to the ACM in 2010 when the event returned to the Three Counties Showground. It was here that the National Centenary baton was handed over to the West Midlands Federation in 2014 at an ACM held six weeks early to accommodate the baton's smooth progress around the Country.

The Half Yearly Council, later Spring Meeting

Interim reports have been given at this meeting to keep the membership up to date with the Federation's affairs. The venues for this have been far more varied. Many, by design, have been in the south of the county, with Evesham Arts Centre and Pershore Sports Centre and High School being used. Although a lower key affair, this follows a broadly similar pattern to the ACM. However it still demands the same organisation, attention and time from the Board and Office staff as the larger event.

2006 Half Yearly at South Bromsgrove High School

In the spotlight

1988 Half Yearly Council meeting

In 1994 the speaker failed to appear. From possible disaster came a success, for Freda Davies presided over an open forum, taking questions from the floor, a format which prompted thank you letters from members for a most enjoyable time. Oddly enough, in 2006, adversity again prompted congratulatory letters when Chris Marriott chaired the meeting in Pershore at a venue with no heating and no catering facilities.

By 1998 the half yearly council meeting was attracting fewer members and, in 2001, 52% said they did not want it at all. Attempts were made to improve this situation. Evening meetings were introduced and, using smaller venues, the event was held twice in different parts of the County for a time from 2008. However when the event swapped months with the ACM in 2011 it was renamed the Spring Meeting.

Much is demanded of the office staff on the long days of both these types of meeting. The Administrator is at the venue very early to make sure all is in place. She must make sure that the day runs smoothly and take the minutes, whilst the Assistant presides over post and other stationery for WI collection.

At the end of the day the office staff make sure that all the papers and equipment are loaded into the vehicle which brought them and returned safely to WI House.

The County News and mailings

'The Worcestershire WI County News', the word County being dropped in 2008, is still usually called 'The County News Letter' or CNL. It has been the most direct way of communicating to Worcestershire members what is happening in the County. One copy has always been given to each WI so that they could pass on the information to their members at their monthly meeting, but members have always been encouraged to have their own copies, purchased either personally or by their WI. The cost in 1980 was 90p for the eleven editions. It has always carried information on news and events from the Federation Committee, Advisers and the sub-committees and before the advent of WI Life important information from NFWI. Paid advertising, by both line and flyer inserts, has also been a constant and this has been generating income throughout the period. Contributors, usually the chairman in the case of the committees and the County Chairman, submit copy about six weeks before distribution. It is then put together by the Administrator and published by a local firm. After proofreading it is printed and returned to the office for packing into envelopes along with the other monthly mailing for WIs. The responsibility for packing has changed over the years. Until about 2000 it was part of the Assistant Secretary's duties. After that date it has mostly been done by Executive/Board volunteers. Occasional mistakes were made with the number of copies enclosed but, despite being an arduous task, it was generally completed smoothly.

By 1989 there was insufficient space for all the information and so, still covering four sides, its size was increased to A4. This change led to a loss and so the price per annum was increased to £1.20. Pat Harris was appointed as editor with a brief to include more information from WIs, especially unusual news. By 1996 the font size was increased and an editor was again felt necessary in 2001. It was noted in the next year that fewer members were taking copies and that they did not like the inserts. By the end of 2004 the Marketing and Development ad hoc committee gave recommendations for an overhaul.

The suggestion of in house publishing was rejected as it would need a large number of volunteers, so the price structure for adverts was reviewed and a new printer sought. Fewer commercial inserts were to be approved despite the loss of revenue and the number of flyers limited. All of this was introduced in early 2006. Further improvements were made in 2008 when the County News was increased to eight sides per issue, full colour was introduced and members were encouraged to

2007 CNL - Last of the old format

2008 CNL - First of the new format

provide photographs for the front cover and for the WI contributions. The number of issues was reduced to ten in 2010 by pairing the months from July to December. In 2012 the pairings were changed to July/August, October/November and December/January as this better served the WIs but were changed again in 2016 by altering two pairings to June/July and August/September. In 2013 patterns and recipes became a regular feature alongside the existing news from WIs and adverts. The yearly price per member in 2017 was £2.45. In 2016 a group looked at the existing format and a questionnaire on CNL was undertaken. Members requested full pages for the WFWI diary and for the Round the County feature. NFWI agreed that the County News could be transmitted digitally (at a cost of £30 pa per WI or 5p per member) and in 2017 WFWI sent out another questionnaire asking membership views on a digital CNL at £1 per head.

Communications from the Office

There is much communication by phone and letter between the office and the WIs especially for the urgent communication of information, for bookings and for queries. This continues but today as much as possible is done by electronic means which saves both time and money.

By 1995 the use of the email and internet was spreading outside academia allowing paperless contact between organisations and individuals. The first reference in WFWI minutes is in 1997 when it is noted that having internet provision was useless if it was not linked to NFWI. Computer equipment was upgraded in 1999, one of several required over the coming years. A year later the cost of email was investigated. The purchase of three modems in 2002 to connect to the internet opened the way for the Federation to utilise the World Wide Web by creating a website, as National had already done. This needed someone who knew how to do it and was eventually set up a year later by a contact of Heather Jefferies.

In 2006 all Federation committee members began receiving minutes by email and each WI was requested to name a volunteer so that they too could receive communications in this form although it was appreciated that there were some WIs which could not offer this. Meanwhile the website was not working well. In 2006 Pam Lowe offered to take a course in web design, as professional companies were too expensive, but on Pam's retirement from Executive in 2008, Jill Taylor became the web master and utilised an advert free site costing £30, £72 in 2017, which she still maintains. She was also the Federation's Digital Champion, an NFWI initiative, from its inception in 2013 until 2017 when Digital Teams supplanted Digital Champions, MaD taking on the team role. Members are always reminded that there is much more information on the net to supplement that in the CNL.

By 2011 WI was using social media. A twitter account was linked to the website in that year which also saw all Federations incorporated into that of NFWI. The WI Moodle was introduced in 2013 and a call was made for Moodle Magicians to help others navigate this internal network which is only available to members. By 2017 this was overloaded and 'MyWI' was introduced by NFWI for new members. In 2015 WFWI was recorded as using Facebook, noting also that the Board was to oversee its social media sites to safeguard its reputation. It also trialled email fliers. A WFWI blog is to be introduced in 2018

By the Millennium NFWI had realised that it did not know who its individual members were and therefore could not, unlike most charities and organisations which relied on subscriptions from members, contact its members directly. By 2002 NFWI signalled that they were moving towards the creation of a membership database, a part of the cost cutting, modernisation and rationalisation of the movement and WFWI members were asked to provide an email address if they had one. Members of Executive attended seminars on this database which is now named The Membership Communication System - MCS. The original system, as supplied by the company who designed it, allowed outsiders to access it. NFWI suspended the self-regulation facility making the site much more secure. Once implementation began, training in its use was given to the County Secretary.

The MCS was launched in 2004 and was being explained at annual meetings by WIAs. One member per WI was to be trained in its use and then become responsible for filling in the details of all the members of that WI. This database would then be sent to both the Federation and National. It was not entirely well received. Letters from several WIs were sent declining MCS. Some WIs would not or could not give a name as representative and some individual members disliked the idea of their details being on a database.

Suzanne Owen remembers it thus. "2004 saw the introduction of the MCS (Membership Communication System) which was set up to improve communication between National, Federations and the WIs. I seem to remember a great deal of angst and consternation and many training sessions to get this set up in the WIs. Indeed a great deal of effort and hard work by Executive and WI Advisers, including help given to WIs who were not computer literate, eventually led in 2007 to a report that MCS was working well."

The 'bible' for contacts and speakers within the county, it has served as an indispensable tool for all those who receive it. A free copy is issued to WI presidents and secretaries, Group Co-ordinators and County committee members. Put together by the Administrator from details sent in by WIs and committees, it can be out of date when it returns from the printers. It almost always is when received by the recipients so quickly does the information change.

In 1980 it was called the 'County Handbook: Panel of Speakers and Demonstrators.' In 1986 'Demonstrators' was dropped after a revamp whilst in 2010 'Handbook' was replaced by 'Yearbook.' In 2011 the present title 'Worcestershire Federation of WIs Yearbook' was adopted, 'Speakers' being removed completely and being given their own publication from 2013.

Until 2005 it was printed and published in Derby by Aces Publicity, thereafter Lance Print of Kettering took over.

The book has retained its A5 size throughout and some supplementary correction sheets were sent out periodically to try to keep the information current but

1980-2007 front cover   *2008-2010 front cover*   *2011 onwards front cover*

the 2008 experiment of a replaceable loose leaf style was not repeated. As the updated pages had to come from the printer this format was abandoned on cost and inconvenience grounds.

Decorated with the Worcestershire Black Pear symbol, its cover was matt until 1997 when it was replaced by a glossy finish and a coloured picture has adorned the cover since 2011. Special years were celebrated by special covers. In 2013 it began to span two years.

In 1980 the Diamond Jubilee edition contained information, in the following order, Office and House, lists of VCOs, Group Secretaries, Marketing Society details, the Panel of Speakers including Welfare Organisations, the list of WI Presidents and Secretaries plus twenty-eight pages of adverts which offset printing costs. Adverts continued to support the production costs with coloured versions appearing in 2001 and they filled nineteen pages in 2017/18. The changing needs and emphasis in WFWI is reflected in the handbook layout. The Executive Committee was included in 1983, Presidents and Secretaries were moved forward in 1985 and in 1993 a list of sub-committee members was added. The hand drawn map of the location of WIs introduced in 1996 was replaced in 2004 by a computer version which could be more easily amended. Holding Trustees names appeared in 2009. In 2017 NFWI advised that all old handbooks should be destroyed and not recycled so that the data was safeguarded.

Speakers

Provision of and easy access to good speakers has been paramount in WFWI thinking as their delivery forms an important part of the educational brief. Much time and effort has gone into making sure they reach an acceptable standard.

In 1980 the system for recommending speakers for inclusion in the handbook lay with the sub-committees. Each committee interviewed those connected with their speciality and then recommended their inclusion in the book to Executive. Interviews took place when the committee met and in 1980 it was reported that some potential speakers could not make these daytime meetings.

In 1987 Executive took charge of interviews and decided that they would take place on one evening with members attending and voting on the candidates' suitability. In early 1992 the evenings were stopped but by popular request reinstated later in the year and about 40 of these meetings have been arranged by the Board. By 2002 four Speakers evenings were needed and were always well attended. A £10 fee for inclusion in the handbook was introduced in 2003. This rose to £30 in 2012 and speakers were also charged £10 to appear at the selection meeting. If more than one WI reports that a speaker has failed to please then the person is informed and the Board removes the entry.

NFWI Magazine

Since 1919 a monthly magazine has been the means of communication from National to its members. Initially called 'For Home and Country', which was the motto adopted by the first National Executive, it had become 'Home and Country' by 1980. It was not included in the subscription and members paid an extra subscription to have the 12 copies per year. Eileen Chapman was appointed to the magazine's Speaker's Panel in 1994.

Through the magazine, WIs and Federations were encouraged to share their ideas, opinions and accounts of their events with the Country wide movement. It was the job of the Executive member appointed as Home and Country representative to collect these within the County and send them to the editorial staff in London. She also was tasked with trying to raise the number of subscribers in the County. Alongside WI items the magazine also carried recipes, craft projects, stories and many of the features typically included in other contemporary women's journals.

1980-2007   2007 onwards

Each WI appointed a magazine secretary and she received the magazines by post and was responsible for their distribution to her members. The system seems to have been fairly straightforward, the minutes only noting a problem for National in 1981 in that Printel, their printer, had found it much more difficult than expected to put names and quantities required onto their computer. By 1988 though, it seems that there were fewer contributions being forwarded by Worcestershire members because the Representative made a plea for articles. This was perhaps regretted when in the next year a letter was published from Little Comberton WI stating that "The WI had an elderly image and the Worcestershire Federation held all their classes in the daytime," but this was followed by some more cheerful news in 1992 when Worcestershire had the greatest number of Federation contributions.

In 1993 the magazine went on general sale in an effort to boost circulation. From the mid-nineties delivery to WIs was plagued by delays and delivery problems and numbers subscribing fell. Despite the continued attempts to boost sales in the new century made by WIAs and the Magazine representative, the efforts were hindered by continued poor delivery, third party marketing to local WI representatives and whispers that many members did not want a magazine anyway.

NFWI introduced direct mailing in 2005 but having asked subscribers for their mailing details they then lost part of the list. Worcester members did not receive copies for January to March 2005 and a letter of complaint was sent to National head office.

Against this background NFWI announced that the magazine was to be part of the increased subscription from 2007 and would be mailed to all, 50% of those members who replied having voted for this in a recent questionnaire.

Worcestershire Federation Executive had a very difficult period at this time. Chris Marriot remembers "2007 brought another new change. NFWI had decided to increase the WI subscription which would include a magazine called WI Life. This would replace the old Home and Country magazine which some members paid for. This would be delivered to every member. Feelings on this move were very divided with some members being quite hostile to the change."

Letters were received regretting the decision; seven WIs considered their removal from the movement, so strong was their feeling about this action and two WI annual meetings were reported as "unpleasant." The reactions reflect similar concerns to those voiced on the introduction of the MCS. WI Life, the renamed and revamped magazine, was launched in 2007 and the eight issues a year continue to be received through the post by each member.

Advisers

This committee, formerly known as the Organisation Committee, is not a Federation sub-committee. Its membership consists entirely of those who have been trained and appointed by NFWI as WI Advisers - WIAs or as they were known until 2001 Voluntary County Organisers - VCOs. From 1982 to 1995 the Voluntary County Markets Organisers - VCMOs, also attended the committee meetings, though they came under the umbrella of Home Economics and Craft. The ten monthly meetings were reduced to nine in 1987 but two social meetings, one in summer and one near Christmas, have also been held for some time.

A feature of the movement from the start, Advisers play a very large part in the running of both County and WI affairs and so their training is funded by the County. In 1985 a letter was sent to National deploring the long wait for this training. Likely candidates are invited to observe for three months and are co-opted onto the committee for that period. If the

Served as Adviser	
Grace Adkins	Beryl Hines
Lillian Angell	Doreen Jeeves
Anne Ballard	Pat Jewkes*
Margaret Bazley	Betty Johnson
Sue Bearcroft	Janice Jones*
Betty Bell*	Jean Kennedy
Wendy Booth	Margaret Kent
Anita Boston	Margaret Lane
Pauline Briggs	June Lennox
Patience Broad*	Mary Lou Lockyer
Diana Cartmel*	Chris Marriott*
Sue Chilton	Bunty Masters
Janet Clemas	Ann Meredith
Freda Davies	Margaret Mills
Mary Davis	Greta Mitchell
Rosemary Edwards	Olive Odell
Pat Elliott	Iris Montgomery
Joan Ellis	Pat Ogle
Pauline Etheridge	Liz Osborn
Jules Evans	Suzanne Owen*
Ann Evanson	Betty Padmore
Pat Farell	Sylvia Perkins
Diana Farmiloe	Rosemary Roberts*
Sandra Farquhar	Julia Rogers
Morag Ford	Jeanne Round
Valerie Freeman	Anne Smith*
Mary Friel	Lisa Snook
Mary Glaze	Helen Starks
June Green	Nanette Turner
Jackie Gregory	Patricia Waddington
Dorothy Hamer	Sue White*
Jill Hammonds	Marjorie Whiting
Pat Harris*	Pam Williams
Antoinette Harris	
Christine Hickman-	* = Chairman
Smith*	

work appeals and the candidate is deemed suitable by the committee, her name is submitted to the Board and, if accepted, training begins. It is a very rigorous course, which involves observation of trained WIAs in the field, and, since the mid-nineties, written assessments which gives it the equivalence of an 'A' level. It always includes one or more residential courses of up to a week's duration, usually conducted at Denman, but at least until 1992 there were also four one day courses held at Guildford and Keynsham. Once trained their service was usually long as only 68 have served, 14 on this committee only and 12 as chair. Worcestershire has more WIAs than most Federations.

Sue White described her training in the September 2011 CNL. "The past year has been a most enjoyable and personally fulfilling period as well as a steep learning curve. I felt lucky that, all along, Worcestershire's Adviser team were so very supportive and full of encouragement. There were three sojourns at Denman with other trainees, where I was ably tutored and guided through four modules covering finance, history, marketing and communication. Our tutors managed to harness our enthusiasm and mixture of talents to become ambassadors for the WI movement. Despite the hard work it was an enjoyable and often hilarious time. One of the highlights was a trip to NFWI headquarters which gave an appreciation of the breadth and depth of the organisation as well as the WI's spheres of influence and initiatives." Five years later and writing as chairman of Advisers she was inviting others to follow the same path saying "Worcestershire is one of the WI's flagship Federations because of our forward thinking and planning. We also recognise the potential for women around the county to be inspiring and inspired and work hard to provide as many opportunities for this potential to be realised. I can tell you that it is very rewarding to be part of a dynamic and enthusiastic team of committed people."

Rosemary Roberts remembers her pre-Worcestershire views of VCOs. "As a new mum I joined the local WI. Annual Meetings were held in March and it was 'de rigueur' that we wore hats and gloves at the meeting as we had a visiting VCO attending. They were treated like royalty. Some years later I was asked if I would consider being a VCO. I would be invited to attend a meeting at the County Headquarters and if they liked me they would consider inviting me to train with them. I didn't accept. On moving into Worcestershire I was interested to observe the same organisation with the same aims and objectives but a different approach to them and WIs who were friendly towards each other. I accepted training in this County!"

Qualified WIAs must attend refresher courses and other training so that their understanding of WI matters is always up to date. All of this makes quite a call on County finances. In 1986 the bill to the County for training was £900 with a further £650 spent on

2000 Advisers Social with Betty Johnson[17]

refreshing and other schools and there was a call for the committee to cut down on its costs. Several methods were looked at such as charging a fee for attendance at a WI meeting, visiting WIs in a smaller radius to reduce mileage claims and combining some activities. Paring back has continued ever since.

In 2017 there were twelve WIAs listed in the handbook plus three in training. This compares with sixteen in 1980. Numbers have varied, a low of nine plus two in training being recorded in 2007. Yes, the number of WIs had fallen in the interim period from 177 to 125 but the workload undertaken and the dedication given continues to be exceptional. In 1992 the minutes show that the twelve VCOs were insufficient to provide the assistance needed but recruitment was increasingly difficult. 1987 was the first recorded example of a potential candidate declining co-option because of work and by 2002 the record shows that many of those approached to be WIAs said they were too busy to contemplate taking on the role.

As well as learning about WI in training, Patience Broad being appointed by NFWI as a WIA training adviser in 2010, they have had to assimilate knowledge on new innovations. They have had to master dealing with much new technology including power point usage, social media, how to use the Moodle and WI internet sites, the MCS (Membership Communication System) and financial affairs data including charity law, VAT and Gift Aid so that they could help WIs struggling with new ways of doing things. Proficiency in the new technology did not always come easy. The minutes in 2003 reported that the WFWI website was telling the world that "All our WIs are very difficult." NFWI was contacted quickly to amend the statement to the intended "very different." Each year WIAs received fresh information at the meeting with the County Chairman and Treasurer who reported on the decisions made at the National Council. This in turn could be relayed to WIs. One of these decisions, relayed in 2015, caused some anxiety as all members of WI committees

---

[17] Standing L-R   Doreen Jeeves, Joan Ellis, Greta Mitchell, Anne Smith, Suzanne Owen, Mary Lou Lockyer, Ann Canham, Freda Davies, Jackie Gregory, Chris Marriott, Sylvia Perkins, Julia Rogers, Janet Clemas, Bunty Masters. Seated L-R   Janice Jones, Marjorie Whiting, Betty Johnson, Iris Montgomery.   Not in picture - Rosemary Edwards, Sandra Farquhar

had to be informed that they were Trustees of that WI but it was well received by the membership. A five year plan was agreed in 2016.

About 1998 - Advisers' social at Anne Ballard's home[18]

The primary role of a WIA is to support the Federation's WIs. Any problem or question about the running of a WI received by County is referred to a WIA. A free visit, with a three-scale charge thereafter, for attendance at a meeting was replaced by a two scale charge in 1986. This was replaced by the present three scale charge about 2010. Until 1988, WIs could ask for a particular VCO but then a VCO was assigned to a Group. However, requests for individuals are accommodated if possible. In the early 80's with 175 WIs, over 270 visits were made each year, the number dropping to 135 by 1996 when there were 159 WIs. Most visits were connected to the Annual and Resolutions meetings but some were to sort out difficulties. In 2016, 62 visits to WI annual meetings were recorded. This was when most WIs combined this meeting with the Resolutions meeting thus reducing the demand

---

[18] Pictured - Anne Ballard, Joan Ellis, Liz Osborn, Julia Rogers, Janet Clemas, Freda Davies, Jackie Gregory, Chris Marriott, Sylvia Perkins, Marjorie Whiting, Janice Jones, Bunty Masters, Mary Wehner, Suzanne Owen, Ann Canham. Not in picture - Rosemary Edwards, Anne Smith

for WIA visits. WIAs also gave advice by phone or letter. Despite all this support, badges were issued in 1990 as it was felt that members did not know who their VCOs were. A new badge was adopted in 2001. In 1984 they also began taking sales items to any WI meeting they attended and this lasted for some years.

Most WIAs have anecdotes about WI visits and many are about the difficulty of finding the venue especially on a dark or inclement night before the advent of satellite navigation. A particular aversion for Greta Mitchell was the night walk through a graveyard to a certain meeting hall, so eventually her husband came along to enjoy this evening too.

Rosemary Roberts writes that "The reluctance to join the committee is nothing new. At one Annual Meeting I failed to get a President. It was almost 11.00 pm and no amount of persuading and cajoling, almost to the point of nagging, produced one. I asked the Secretary to write to every paid up member and inform them that at the next meeting we would be discussing and possibly suspending the Institute. Once that discussion had taken place and the vote in favour of suspension was passed, all bills would be paid, potential speakers cancelled and the rest of the money would go to WI House. There it would be held for three years and if no re-formation of the WI occurred in that time County would keep the money. By 11.15 pm I had a President! It was 12.20 am when I got home and my husband said you are not to go any further than Worcester to a WI! You will not know how many WIs 'moved into Worcester' after that night."

She also remembers that "At one meeting we had a speaker who droned on for ages and despite the usual polite remarks could not be stopped. I nudged his leg. Unfortunately, a loose thread caught in my engagement ring. I do not who was the most embarrassed, him or me, because as I pulled my hand away so the seam of his trousers came undone."

Thank you speeches are another source of anecdote. Perhaps the most unfortunate was that recounted with much amusement by Jeanne Round who was thanked with these words "We are so sorry you got lost on such a foggy night and so very sorry that you didn't stay lost." Stunned silence followed. The blushing speaker hurriedly corrected herself to "glad" in the last part of the thanks.

2017 Advisers and Trainees[19]

Initiatives were introduced to help WIs. In 1980 stronger WIs were urged to adopt a smaller WI to help make them more viable and a special WI at Barnsley Hall Mental Hospital was supported until its closure in 1991. A new members' leaflet was compiled in 1990 and new members' evenings were held occasionally. From 1992 a theme was devised for the WIs' annual meetings. In 2008 a twinning system was introduced for the 90th birthday year. Several questionnaires such as those in 1999 and

[19] L to R Back: Sue Chilton, Lillian Angell, Anne Smith, Helen Starks, Karen Worboys , Sally Grainger, Susan Reeve Front: Margaret Bazley, Pat Jewkes, Christine Hickman-Smith, Suzanne Owen, Sue White, Lisa Snook

2004 asked WIs what they would like to see implemented and Programme Competitions have been held with Lickey coming second in the National competition of 2010.

The Advisers have to deal with falling numbers and the closure of WIs. Each month they report on the WIs they have visited or advised. If a WI is struggling, WIAs give more support and will take over as President or Treasurer for a time to keep it going if filling these positions is the problem. However, if in the end a WI has to suspend, a WIA must conduct the wind up meeting. She must arrange for all its records and assets to be transferred to the Federation where they are held for three years with the exception of the financial accounts which are held for seven years. During this three year period the possibility of reopening is explored. If this does not occur, NFWI issues a closure notice. Any assets are used to fund the founding of new WIs and the records go to the County Archive.

BARNSLEY HALL Women's Institute was formed as an Institute in a Worcestershire Mental Hospital eight years ago. The emphasis of our WI meetings is on 'normality' and rehabilitation into the community, so each meeting is the pattern of WI which is easily recognizable by patients when they return home.

Even the patients who are confined to bed are not forgotten because at Christmas time committee members visit the wards and sing carols requested by the patients.

Patients who wish, and are able to travel, are taken by mini bus to the County Carol Service which is held annually in the County, and this occasion is looked forward to with great excitement largely because of their involvement with other WI members outside the hospital.

A typical WI monthly meeting when the programme is arranged with an emphasis on 'music' (which is in the capable hands of Mrs Gwen Bullas, County Music Chairman and a member of Barnsley Hall committee), commences with the singing of 'Jerusalem'. This is a highlight so we sometimes sing it twice. We then have a song with a simple refrain, the words of which are visually displayed. The leader and committee members sing the song through and most of the members are soon able to join in, and although they may not produce a very tuneful

sound, they sing lustily and with great fervour.

Percussion instruments made from discarded squeezie bottles filled with rice, dried peas or sand, pebbles, bunches of keys, cowbells and drums are given out, and all members are encouraged to take one and these are used in most of the songs producing a noise and rhythm which has to be heard to be believed.

Other simple songs and rounds follow, and sometimes two groups compete to see who can sing the loudest. Sometimes humorous short poems are read by members of the committee and Mrs Bullas always enquires, before the meeting closes, if any member would like to perform an item of her own choice. One member named Lily who has been a patient for many years, always sings a special song which is her 'party piece' and what a joy it is to see the relaxed expression on her face at that time.

Very often male patients join us and are made welcome and also members of staff.

Everybody laughs, sings and enjoys themselves in the relaxed atmosphere which makes these musical meetings so rewarding for all concerned.

Above: Gwen Bullas' 'music' meeting
Photo: Bromsgrove Messenger

1979 Singing at Barnsley Hall Special WI

However the committee also researches areas of the county suitable for opening new WIs. Sometimes they are re-foundations, others are entirely new and in total 57 have been founded over the whole period. Particularly encouraging since 2000 has been an upsurge of interest from younger women which has led to the founding of several new WIs often with less traditional names and methods of working.

Interest in these new WIs has sometimes been so strong that, as happened in Bewdley in 2014 and Barnt Green in 2016, up to 75 ladies have attended the introductory meeting. Since 1992 there has been some provision in the committee's budget for financing speakers and meeting places in the early days of a new WI. The new millennium has seen an increase in this most helpful funding and in the 21st century £100 per new WI has been available, this being increased to £150 in 2015. For Rosemary Roberts "The lowlight has to be the suspension of a WI. When they have run their course and it is impossible to get a committee then close them with dignity. It is unfair on the existing members to make them feel guilty that they can no longer continue. Highlights are obviously starting a new WI with excitement, enthusiasm and appreciating the new skills many women now bring to WI."

A total of 401 activities of many different kinds have been carried out and, although fourteen of these have been of a promotional nature, most of the events put on by this committee offer training. These are aimed especially at the officers of WIs, and are usually delivered in house. There have been 33 for Presidents and 26 for Secretaries, these called Really Useful Days from 2014. 71 have been for Treasurers and these have included 11 for

Gift Aid. 27 Programme Planning days have been held and 18 events have been for Committee Members who are helped further by a written training programme produced in 2016 and sent out to the WIs. Three new members' days have been held. Initially providing workshops for IT, these have been handed over to MaD since its re-formation as a sub-committee in 2016. Numbers attending have varied. There was surprise in 1986 when the provision of food at a training evening brought in far more people than usual and some catering has often been offered since. Some events are very well supported as in 1995 when over 350 attended a 'Now you are on a committee' day. The venue for training schools has usually been WI House but other places around the County have also been used to reduce members' travel time and so encourage participation.

2016 Awards for Public Speaking Skills

Forty-five Public Speaking schools have boosted the confidence of Federation members in this skill. Many members mention that this aspect gives them concern when asked to stand for office or to give a vote of thanks. In the early years, verse speaking was part of this programme and in 1993 a competition was held. There were thirty-two entries at four venues, the winner being Blackwell & Burcott. There have been several gatherings for new members both day and evening, eighty-two enjoying one coffee morning at WI House.

Each year every WI sends to County a financial report and WIAs are responsible for scrutinising these and for checking the declared numbers in a WI against the fees sent in. They have also facilitated training for new IFE's - Independent Financial Examiners.

Throughout the period, this committee has been responsible for organising the Resolutions process in the County which is part of the campaigning aspect of WI, so it has often been helped in this by the Public Affairs Committee.

The journey of a resolution is long. The National Board receives suggestions for resolutions each year. It reduces the number and those chosen are discussed in each Federation. A vote is then taken. Those receiving the greatest support are placed on a short list and are then debated at WI level, a representative casting the ensuing vote at the National AGM.

Until 1982 the County Chairman and others attended a yearly Consultative Council where the proposed resolutions were also discussed, after which they reported back to the Organisation Committee. From 1983 an Executive member was appointed as Resolutions Officer to oversee the process and this lasted until 1990 when a VCO was appointed instead. From 1977 to 1989 the yearly list of National Resolutions was discussed at a County Mini Consultative Meeting but thereafter at the Resolutions meeting. There WIs could learn from experts what the impact of approving the motion would be. VCOs were also on hand to help when each WI debated and voted on the resolutions at their own meeting. In 1993 the notes from National were very late and the suggestion was made that NFWI should send them directly to the WIs. In 1993 too, WIs were asked to conduct

2008 Worcestershire's Resolution explained in Worcestershire Life

their own Resolutions meetings if possible as there were too few VCOs to go round. The same year saw the appointment of a Resolutions Officer, a position which continued to be active into the new century. It was noted in the minutes in 1995 that members were not interested in either the Resolutions or the Annual meetings, possibly because the briefings were so poor. To reduce costs, from 1994 Resolutions Meetings were held at Group Meetings and later replaced by a Resolutions Presentation Day. Decisions were taken in this way until 2010 when, through the new magazine, a one member one vote system came into operation. In 2012 the traditional May resolutions meeting also became the annual meeting for some WIs, again to save money. In 2015 the Federation Resolutions Meeting was combined with an International Day and in 2017 it took the form of a workshop.

Arrangements for the yearly National AGM, now known as the National Annual Meeting, also took up much Advisers time. They have dealt with the 38 of these to date. This entailed hosting a delegates' get together each year prior to the event, sometimes booking overnight accommodation and organising coaches for the delegates, whose travel expenses were paid for from the pooling of fares system which is administered by National. Other attendees were also able to join in the coach and accommodation arrangements if there was room but they footed their own bill. WIAs also act as volunteer stewards at the National Annual Meetings or NAMs.

During the 90's, to save money, the AGM was replaced by a Triennial General Meeting and two Intermediate General Meetings. The first TGM was held at the NEC, Birmingham and for this Cambridgeshire members were hosted by Worcestershire. National reverted to a yearly NAM after 2000.

In 1980 each WI could send a delegate to vote on the resolutions at the NAM. In 1983 it was noted in Executive minutes that again 99% of WIs were represented at the Albert Hall. The costs of each voting member were covered by National and the Federation but by 1992 these had become a drain on finances and so to reduce these costs, a Linking List was devised. WIs were placed in groups of four and the voting and reporting back for all four was done by one delegate on a rotational basis.

As well as volunteering to steward at the NAM, WIAs stewarded the Federation's 38 Council Meetings and 38 Half Yearly/Spring Meetings. They also steward at other major events such as the 37 Carol Services and at other large entertainments. A total of 161 stewarding events have been recorded.

Promotion, so necessary to attract new members, has always been an integral part of a WIA's job and the September promotional fortnight has been a yearly feature. As well as organising these, the committee has put on thirteen other promotional events. They have also joined with the Board, the Promotions Representative, or promotion committees. Marketing and Development was incorporated into Advisers between 2013 and 2015 when some IT instruction was offered. An archive workshop was undertaken in 2016.

Sometimes working conditions at promotional events were not ideal as in 1984 when the minutes reported both the icy cold of National's promotion bus and the untimely demise of the Federation's touring caravan. By contrast, June 1984 saw an excellent promotional event in beautiful weather at the Guildhall in Worcester. This featured every aspect of WI and attracted a large number of visitors. 1992 saw involvement in the County's Bring Someone New initiative. 1999 was the year of the Stop the Drop campaign with a £75 grant from National for the formation of a new WI. 2008 saw a drive for each WI to increase its membership by at least one which proved pretty successful as 2010 showed a net increase of 400 members. WIAs joined in the Board's initiatives in 2012 to promote WI with the Centenary grant money.

Questionnaires were sent out occasionally requesting the membership's opinions. That of 1993 was minuted as showing that some members thought some VCO's patronising and poorly informed whilst that of 2005 revealed that few members knew much about the Federation or National, depressing reading for those working so hard on WFWI's behalf. They have worked constantly to improve the perception of those who fill this demanding and most important role. Indeed, a Hereford Federation adviser who attended a 2017 meeting commented that she found the content very interesting and was surprised to see how active WFWI advisers are.

Groups

The Advisers' final responsibility is for the Groups. This tier is not an official one in the WI Movement and not all Counties have it. Groups were set up in Worcestershire in 1920. They aim to foster regional fellowship and the chance to hear speakers whose charges may be out of reach for smaller WIs. The WIs are thus grouped on a geographical basis. A WIA has been appointed to each group since 1991 and for a short time from 2000 an Executive member was also appointed. In 1980 there were twenty-three Groups, by 2017 they numbered fourteen. Each has a Group Secretary, renamed Group Co-ordinator from 1994, who organises its programme and general running and 151 ladies have served in this position, 91 in this role only. Two meetings a year are held by Advisers for the Co-ordinators making 76 in all over the period. Each WI in the Group takes it in turn to host the yearly spring and autumn meetings whilst the presidents and secretaries of the Group WIs also meet yearly with their Co-ordinator. An information pack was produced to guide Co-ordinators in 2006 and in that year the Groups' archives were sorted out ready for the House move.

£200 was the official amount of money a Group was to hold, its financial statements are scrutinised by the Advisers Committee and its fund-raising is subject to WI charity status, it being said in 1999 that "Groups are not allowed to fundraise for outside

Served as Group Co-ordinator

Rosemary Adams	Nita Crutch	Mary Harrison	Pam Rayner
Margaret Aldridge	Joyce Davey	Judith Hart	Grace Richardson
Daphne Allen	Elizabeth Davies	Christine Henderson	Jeanette Riddex
Peggy Amos	Freda Davies	Veronica Hill	Masie Roberts
Patsy Anderson	Mary Davies	Sylvia Hudson	Rosemary Roberts
Lillian Angell	R Davies	Jo Humphreys	Ruth Roberts
P Baker	Valerie Davies	Carol Hutchings	D Robins
Jane Baker	Kathleen Davis	Janice Jackson	Carol Rose
Anne Ballard	Helen Day	Hazel Jepson	Jeanne Round
Valerie Barlow	Margaret Deakin	Margaret Johnson	Rosemary Sadler
Janette Baston	Elizabeth Dove	Catherine Kealy	Anne Saunders
D Barton	Margaret Dufty	Margaret Kemp	Barbara Savage
Margaret Bazley	Ann Dunsby	Denny King	Gillian Smith
Eileen Beale	Mo Emmans	Kate King	Monica Smith
Sue Bearcroft	Junay England	Pam Lamming	Margaret Taylor
Sue Bell	Beryl Evans	Betty Larcombe	Maureen Thomas
Susan Bennett	Joy Evans	B Lees	Jean Thorpe
Diana Boorn	Jules Evans	Christine Linley	Jan Titley
Wendy Booth	Ann Evanson	Gill Lowe	Josie Townshend
Pat Botfield	Mrs Fabricius	Marian Loxley	Sylvia Tudor Hughes
Sue Bowes	Janet Farmer	Betty Luxton	Evelyn Upright
J Brentnall	Meg Farmer	Lorna Matthews	Patricia Waddington
Jill Brotheridge	Enid Fellows	Jean Mills	Jean Walker
Jenny Bruton	Paddy Fellows	Mary Miller	June Warner
Beryl Bubb	Margaret Foden	Claire Moore	Alison Warren
Margaret Burbey	Miss Forster	Veronica Mullholland	Irene Webb
Mrs Burns	Mary Fynn	Judy Neale	S White
Shirley Cadman	Sheila Garner	Shirley Noble	Audrey Whitehouse
Sue Canfield	Pat Gibbs	Dorothy Norman	Mrs Wilding
Monica Carden	Mary Glaze	Sue Oakley	Joyce Williams
Lisa Chambers	Olga Glaze	Joyce O'Donnell	Shirley Willis
Eileen Chapman	Sheila Gordon	Molly Oldfield	Gwyn Wilmore
Pat Chitty	Anne Green	Muriel Owen	Bea Woodfield
Mary Coffin	Jackie Green	P Pain	Audrey Woodward
M Coles	H Guest	Patricia Parrott	D Wright
Helen Coomby-Jones	Carol Hardy	Sylvia Perkins	Carole Yates
Jenny Cox	Antoinette Harris	Marjorie Plummer	Audrey Young
Irene Coxon-Smith	Pauline Harris	Anne Quiney	

organisations for, although they are outside the WI constitution, they are still within WI ethics." This led to some confusion and upset about holding a raffle but was settled as allowable if all agreed.

Although there have been changes made to the number of Groups and to the number of WIs which belong to each Group, the names Forest, Hagley, Kidderminster, Pershore, Severn, Weatheroak and Worcester Groups have survived. The changes have been necessary as WIs open and close throughout the county which can result in an imbalance of numbers. Also, the availability of members willing to serve as Group coordinators and the number of WIAs available to oversee the system have influenced the need for change.

By 1981 Malvern Hills Group had been disbanded. Bredon Hill Group followed suit in 1986/7 and some group names were changed. Leys dropped The, and Avon became Avonvale. A year later Teme Valley and Tenbury amalgamated, becoming known as Teme & Tenbury. After much discussion, 1994/5 saw a more sweeping internal reorganisation take place in the remaining twenty Groups which aimed at a more balanced distribution of WIs. There were also some name changes, especially where a Group had the same name as a WI. So Astwood Bank became Redditch, Bromsgrove added and District, Droitwich became Corbett, Malvern reverted to Malvern Hills and Martley became Elgar. In 2001 there were many vacancies for Group Co-ordinator and this situation was partially responsible for the second 2004/5 reorganisation and amalgamation. Some WIs were unhappy about the reshuffle, preferring to stay in their original grouping but this eventually settled down. The sixteen Groups which remained included the amalgamated Bromsgrove & Hillside, Evesham Vale which incorporated Avonvale and Evesham and LRS, the Lenchton, Redditch, Saltway trio.

A third reorganisation was affected in 2016 reducing the number of Groups to fourteen when both Leys and Woodbury were removed. There were no name changes but, to keep the numbers roughly even, a fairly large reshuffle of WIs was undertaken in eight of the remaining Groups. This was to be trialled for a year as some WIs did not want to move. It is mooted that Group members should be overhauled biennially.

Some Groups have an internal meeting for Presidents and Secretaries.

Besides arranging many and varied events for the WIs in the Group, the Co-ordinators have been asked to facilitate the organisation of several events for the County, some of them very large.

In 1985 the Group Secretaries organised the marquee centrepiece for the Three Counties Show, a big undertaking but not as large as the staging of 'Cavalcade 90' which celebrated NFWI's 75th Anniversary. Overseen by an ad hoc committee set up in 1988 and drawn mainly from Performing Arts, the script was written by Rosemary Grave and Joan Maybury. It depicted the changes in women's lives as seen by two female children, one upper class, one working class, growing up and living through ninety years of the twentieth century. Directed overall by Sheila Hodges, there were twenty scenes. Each Group had its own scene which was financed and rehearsed independently. There was only one entire rehearsal. The final production consisted of narration, constant movement by the miming actors, pictures projected on a screen above the stage and choirs providing the musical accompaniment. There were two performances in one day in the Severn Hall at the Three Counties Showground involving over three hundred members. A real WI community project with sixty-five WIs represented, for as well as the actors and singers many others helped by sewing costumes, finding props and supporting behind the scenes. Despite the Groups not being keen on having to finance their bit and the reported feeling that there was insufficient liaison between the committee and Groups during the gestation period, the production was a wonderfully successful and happy occasion. A sheaf of glowing thank you letters were received and it even made a small but unintended profit.

1990 Narrating at Cavalcade 90

L-R Rosemary Grave, Mary Wehner, Maureen Bowkett, Mary Davis.

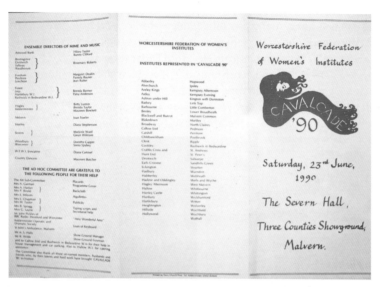

Malvern Group members rehearse their sketch for the depression years of 1930-1932 in Cavalcade 90 at the Three Counties Showground

Sport 1905-1914 was the subject of the Severn Group's sketch

Women at work and play in war and peace

The history and role of women in the 20th century was depicted in style at the Three Counties Showground on Saturday by 250 members of the Worcestershire Federation of Women's Institute in Cavalcade 90, a celebration of the 75th anniversary of the federation.

Members from Malvern took part in the production, directed by Sheila Hodge of Kidderminster and with a script written by Mrs Joan Maybury of Hartlebury and Mrs Rosemary Grave of Droitwich.

Tracing women's lives and interests from the death of Queen Victoria in 1901 through The First World War, the birth of the WI, the Depression, the Second World War, the age

of electricity and the present day, there were glimpses of the Flappers, the Talkies, a murder mystery, rock and roll and women world leaders, acted by members to words spoken by a group of narrators.

The Malvern WI Group's contribution were items on "The Depression" and "The Sixties" directed by Joan Fowler, and the Severn group presented Sport from 1905-1914, directed by Marjorie Ward and Gwyn Wilmore. The Wells and Wyche WI also played their part with others groups in the 1939-45 war years.

Cavalcade 90 was two years in the making and grew from a suggestion in 1987 by the drama subcommittee in 1987, said one of the narrators and pageant committee member Mary Davis of Wells and Wyche WI.

The next large undertaking took place in 2014 when National's Centenary Baton passed through Worcestershire. Each of the sixteen Groups devised an imaginative way of transporting the baton through its area. Members of the Groups were encouraged to support the events and so they saw the baton travel by many diverse ways: by canoe and rowing boat, by steam train on the Severn Valley Railway, by vintage cars, a bus, by bicycles and motorbike, on foot - walking or running, by pleasure boat and, very adventurously, by abseiling down Abberley Hall Clock Tower. Elgar's statues were visited and even yarn bombed, many parts of our lovely county were shown off, musicians played, Town Cryer's rang, Jerusalem was sung, many beautifully decorated celebration cakes were made and much food consumed. A very large number of members took part in this most successful event. Received on 10th September from Hereford Federation, the baton travelled through the Groups. Malvern Hills and Severn that day; Evesham Vale, Pershore and LRS - 11th; Worcester and Elgar - 12th; Woodbury, Teme &Tenbury, Forest - 13th; Kidderminster, Leys and Corbett - 14th; Hagley, Bromsgrove & Hillside and Weatheroak - 15th. The handover to West Midlands Federation took place at their ACM on 16th September.

Collecting the baton from Hereford Federation. Marion Cumella, Marjorie Whiting, Christine Hickman-Smith

Malvern Hills rider Julia Goodfellow-Smith

Yarn bombing a baton holding Elgar in Malvern

Severn Group river cruise

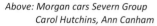

*Above: Morgan cars Severn Group
    Carol Hutchins, Ann Canham*

*Right: Evesham, LRS and Pershore Groups welcome
    the baton in Pershore*

Above: Exhibition in the Guildhall

Left: Worcester and Elgar Group procession

Below: The baton moving through Woodbury Group

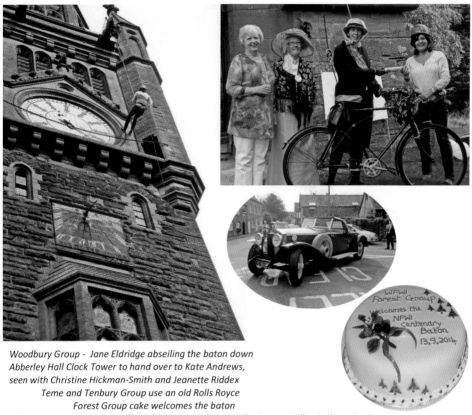

Woodbury Group - Jane Eldridge abseiling the baton down
Abberley Hall Clock Tower to hand over to Kate Andrews,
seen with Christine Hickman-Smith and Jeanette Riddex
Teme and Tenbury Group use an old Rolls Royce
Forest Group cake welcomes the baton
Gill Lowe receives the baton for Kidderminster Group at the Severn Valley Railway Station

Pat Jewkes hands the baton to the Leys Group who paddle to Wolverley

Corbett Group – Jasminka O'Hora and Karen Hewlett, in blue, ran to Chateau Impney. Cheryl Walton in red and Salt Fest re-enactors

Hagley Group singing Jerusalem outside Dunsley Hall Hotel

Bromsgrove and Hillside Group at Avoncroft. Each WI in the Group presented a resolution for the date of the building assigned to them

Weatheroak Group at Avoncroft to collect baton

Fish & Chip supper at Lickey Visitor Centre

End of journey - beacon lit on Lickey Hill with Bromsgrove Town Cryer

Handover to Jackie Gregory of West Midlands Federation at 2014 ACM

In 1985 the WRVS sought to provide emergency services via the Group system. In 1989 a co-operative competition was organised at Hurrans Garden Centre in Hagley. In 1991 classes were offered in the Group areas and in 1992 Groups held Speakers Evenings but both were very short lived as were the informal new members' evenings. Organised walks for each Group to achieve 90 miles for WI's 90th Birthday were undertaken in 2005. Individual Groups also undertake specific events. In 1985 Redditch Group made a wall hanging for the Redditch Council Offices, Bromsgrove Group held a promotional campaign and yarn bombing in 2013 whilst Hagley Group have a Pancake Race and a group ramble in most years. Many Groups organised day visits to Denman, four such being undertaken in 2000.

Bromsgrove Group promotion 2013
Top Left: Yarn bombing   Top Right: Bromsgrove library
- Jules Evans, Rosemary Mountford
Left: Worcester Group handicrafts exhibition 1980
Below: Redditch Group Wall Hanging 1985

Hagley group
Pancake Race
1982

Sub-Committees

It is the sub-committees to which members bring their expertise and pass it on to other members. However, membership of a sub-committee has also opened doors to the individuals who have served on them. These ladies have usually broadened the expertise they bring but their tenure also gives them the opportunity to acquire new skills, knowledge and organisational abilities. The members, like those on the Board, undertake a wide range of tasks to support their sub-committee activities.

The five sub-committees active at WFWI's Centenary, given in order of longevity, are Public Affairs, Performing Arts, Creative Activities, Leisure and Pleasure and Marketing and Development. In 1980 there were eight sub-committees: - Current Affairs, Music, Drama, Home Economics and Crafts, Art, Finance, Calendar and House Management. As can be seen, the present committees bear different names. This is a result of a name change for Current Affairs, amalgamation for four, the abolition of two and the subsequent introduction of three others, two of which are now combined. So really the current crop are doing the same job as their 1980 counterparts which was, primarily, responsibility for delivering the educational aspects of WFWI whilst furthering women's interests but, with the addition of a committee dedicated to leisure pursuits and a second to promoting the WI in Worcestershire. The detail for this last and newest sub-committee has been covered earlier in the book as it is part of the long tradition of promotion in the County whilst the Finance and House sub-committees are dealt with in the relevant sections.

352 Worcestershire members have served on County sub-committees since 1980. Of these 286 served on one committee, fifty-one on two, eleven on three and four on four committees. This gives a total of 437 serving positions over the thirty-eight years. Seventy-one sub-committee members have served as chairmen, drawn from the 352 members, although three chaired two sub-committees. Individual figures are given in the relevant section. As a comparison, many other Federations still have a Board member as the chairman of each sub-committee and have smaller numbers on them.

Each sub-committee is run to a predetermined remit. At present they all have the same standing orders though until about 2012 they differed. Each continues to have its own terms of reference and both are reviewed every two years. The number of meetings per year for each committee has varied, some having as many as ten, others as few as three. Individual committees have seen both an increase and a decrease in the number of yearly meetings but in 2017 all committees had six meetings a year except Marketing and Development which had three. The number of appointed members and co-optees allowed for each committee has also varied over the years. The largest committee has comprised ten appointed members plus up to four co-opted, the smallest only four with up to two co-options. It has not always been easy to attract sufficient ladies to serve and there have been several pleas for members, the first being in 1986 and the latest in 2016.

Board members may attend any committee meeting and almost all official meetings take place at WI House with the Administrator taking minutes. In 1999, sub-committee chairmen were asked not to be in the office before 10 am to allow the office staff some uninterrupted work time.

Everything each committee suggests must be approved by the BoT, but their ideas have often been inventive and always very varied. By 1984 the chairmen were meeting in January to agree the year's programme so that clashes did not occur. A budget is submitted yearly, this becoming more rigorous in 2002 and imperative in 2011, whilst three and five year plans have become the norm for forward planning, the first being mentioned in 2004. A wish was expressed for regular meetings with the Executive in 2002. Over the years, in the same ways as for the Board, there has been streamlining of meetings. Many of the decisions affecting sub-committees have already been detailed earlier.

It has also been seen how each sub-committee participates at big Federation events such as ACMs and the Three Counties Show, usually by designing and manning stalls depicting their work.

Members of all Committees enjoy a social get -together

2008 Social Gathering for all Sub-Committees

The programme of events put on by each sub-committee involves working with the office staff who provide the necessary secretarial back up. The staff mainly, but not exclusively, communicate with the members involved, as well as dealing with the organisation of the booking procedure. Whatever event is put on, at least two committee members, and often the whole number, are present and working to make it a success. Most of the committees have included catering in their events. The production of the food usually fell to the members as well as the serving and washing up.

Displays, hosting guests, locating speakers, organising a venue, the setting up and clearing of the venue, also fell to their lot, although in more recent years outside catering has been employed where the members feel unable to do this. By 2007 committee members had to pay for any event they took part in or benefitted from. 2007 also saw two other changes. The first was an attempt to address the problem of members turning up at events with no tickets which was unfair to those who had booked and paid. It also carried possible problems with WFWI's insurance. The second saw the use of space in WI House for an event become subject to a hire charge, £25 per day and £15 per half day.

25% of an event's cost was added to cover office staff time in 1988 and postage charges for events were also introduced in the 90's.

Sometimes the programme of events was disrupted. Foot and Mouth in 2001, flooding in 2007, bad weather in 2010 and various other weather phenomena have played a part as has retrenching by members when financial crises hit the country. In 2011 the sub-committees were revamped and asked to fund-raise by putting on fewer but larger events, still retaining the educational content but also providing fun.

Each committee writes a monthly entry for the County News, giving three months' notice for events. They also produce flyers to advertise the events. In the mid 2000's so many were being included in the mailing that a cap was put on their number, this being further tightened in 2011 but later relaxed again. First formalised in 2001, each sub-committee

2014 Marjorie Whiting, Liz Gardner perfect the food for the Hartlebury Soiree

can nominate ex members as friends of it and they help out when necessary. Most have social events for their committee to enjoy and occasionally all the committee members attend a joint social function such as the one in 2005 at the invitation of County Chairman Chris Marriot.

The committees encouraged the use of the Travelling Tutor scheme, initiated in 1998 and which was subbed by NFWI. Each committee also funded a course at Denman each year. Called the B Course, it allowed a committee member to learn a particular skill which she in turn could pass on in the Federation. This course seems to have been discontinued in the early 90's. Until the end of the 1980's each committee vetted and nominated speakers for inclusion in the handbook in the section given to their activities. Committee members have always been willing to go out, when invited, to give talks and demonstrations to WIs and Groups.

The Mary Pedley Award was an annual competition devised, in turn, by each sub-committee. Mary Pedley, the longest serving County Chairman 1937-54, left a legacy which funded the prize. Over the years members were set many varied challenges, each appropriate to the aims of the presiding sub-committee, so flower arranging, craft projects, menu design, literature and composing such as setting a poem to music were the type of competition held. In 1991 Barbourn WI's design for a disabled trail was so good that it was adopted for distribution by the local tourist offices. However, the previous year had seen "More written complaints about the competition" and in 1992 the competition was replaced by a yearly Denman bursary including travelling expenses.

The production of the Mary Pedley Wall Hanging in 1983 by the Home Economics and Craft committee is perhaps the greatest achievement of the competition. In 1982 each WI was given a piece of fabric on which to depict its home area. 140 embroidered panels were submitted and Stone WI's entry was judged the winner. The pieces were then sewn together into a large wall hanging measuring fifteen feet by eight feet (4.6 metres by 2.4 metres). It was displayed for many years in the conference room at Pierpoint Street and was taken out to WIs and Groups, always with an accompanying Executive member. In 2006 it was shown at the NEC exhibition of textiles after which it went on an eight month tour of WI textile treasures. Now, having been cleaned and restored, it hangs in the Worcestershire bedroom at Denman.

1983 The Mary Pedley Competition Wall Hanging

Public Affairs

88 ladies have served on this committee, 12 as chairmen and with 62 serving solely on this sub-committee. It had ten members in 2017 and is the only County committee to stand alone from 1980 to the present and one which can trace its origin back to the foundation of WFWI. First formed soon after the initiation of the Federation and known as the Education sub-committee, it was, by 1980, called the Current Affairs sub-committee. Its name was changed to Public and International Affairs in 1983, back to its 1980 name in 1991 and became Public Affairs in 2003. Despite the name changes it always, as the committee said in 1989, "Pursues the interests of members in National and International affairs and reaches the parts other WI committees do not reach."

However, this is the area of WFWI and indeed of NFWI which both members and the public in general are least aware of and least understand.

In 1980 its stated aims were to provide:
-Meetings to cover environmental, agricultural and public affairs.
-Follow up work on mandates - these are resolutions which have been adopted.
-Arrange the yearly Lucy Hingley lecture.
-Provide a representative for the Associated Council for Women of the World – ACWW.
-Pursue international interests.
-Arrange Field Study days.
-Provide members to sit on outside bodies of the judiciary, consumer affairs, environmental and agricultural groups, and health councils in Worcestershire.
-Co-ordinate the WFWI panel of speakers and vet those concerned with public affairs.
-Recommend books to read.
-Provide the expenses for the Denman cup Competition.

The 1980's minutes and County News show that apprising members of NFWI decisions and recommending books to read took up most of the committee's time. The amount of reading they undertook was prodigious and very time consuming. It placed a heavy burden on the members, so much so that they asked for ten rather than eight meetings a year to deal with the workload.

This workload did not last. By 1991 the committee was asking Executive to examine the future of Public Affairs and to determine its purpose, for most of its activities were in decline. Paperwork and discussion papers from National had dwindled significantly. The reading of books for recommendation in the CNL had been discontinued. With regard to the other aims, responsibility for the Denman Cup and the vetting of all the speakers on the panel had passed to Executive, the amount of service on outside bodies was much reduced and only a very little time had ever been allotted by the Federation to following up mandates. In addition, a questionnaire in 1984 had revealed that only eleven WIs had overseas links and that few were interested in International Affairs. The committee had, however, put on many successful and well attended events. Most of these took place in the evening thus catering for those who found it difficult to attend daytime events. Indeed in 1988, after two resignations because of work commitments, it had become the only committee to meet in the evening. After reverting to morning meetings in the 21st century, a varied meeting time and place was introduced in 2015, with some of the six being held in members' homes. It had eleven members in 2017.

Sheila Andrews, a past chairman, notes that one might be forgiven for thinking that the remit for this committee sounds boring. After reading the previous paragraphs one might well agree. However, she goes on to say that this is far from the truth.

The transformation resulted from the 1991 deliberations and saw the pursuit of more attractive and varied interests. It was decided that the committee should meet seven times a year, it would continue work on the first seven of the aims stated above and would concentrate on summer walks and the International Evening as events.

As a result of the overhaul this committee has offered 249 different events plus seven which have been cancelled and, if the approximately 180 events of the Science Programme were counted in, 429 since 1980.

The events fall into nine categories some of which have overlapping events.

The Field Study Days. These seem to stem from a new venture devised for the Diamond Jubilee when three very successful outings to the Wyre Forest took place instead of the envisaged one, as interest was much greater than

1980 Field Study Day arranged for the Jubilee

expected. Twenty areas around the County have been visited, often with a specialist informing those present. Geology, botany in different habitats, fungus, berries and butterfly forays, birdsong walks, conservation projects and farm tours, had all found a place by 1991. After this date the number reduced although there was a Wyre Forest discovery in 1998 and geology outings were popular in the 2000's.

Larger field study projects have been offered to WIs to undertake individually. National's Pathway to 21st Century Millennium Project, organised for Worcestershire by Anne Quiney, came under the Public Affairs umbrella and many WIs took part in its Parish Map initiative. A display of these maps and other material was mounted at Perdiswell Leisure Centre in 1999. In 2000 most WIs took part in a County Tree survey whist, in 2004, there was a Hedgerow survey, both being initiated by the Science Club.

Walks. The agreed concentration on summer walks has seen a very well supported programme over the years, forty-four walks being offered by Public Affairs. There have been two main types of walk, those visiting towns and those with an environmental theme. The latter rose to greater prominence as the number of field study days dwindled.

2015 Droitwich Town Walk

Starting in 1987, the town walks make up the bulk of these events and were a firm yearly fixture until 2011. Almost always taking place in the evening, the first around Worcester City had to be repeated as so many wished to attend and this happened many times when, in succeeding years, almost every town in the County was visited. Informative guides escorted the members and all enjoyed the supper which followed, often provided by a local WI. After a four-year break, popular request saw this event resume in 2015 with a visit to Droitwich, followed in succeeding years by Bewdley and Upton-upon-Severn.

The environmental walks, often to forested, heath or hilly areas, reflect both the growing concern for the planet and the wish to know more about the County's diverse landscapes.

1998 Planet Pledge part of Agenda 21
Either side of Mayor: L - Betty Rooney,
R - Anne Quiney

Environment. These walks formed a part of the environmental remit of the committee and continued the environmental awareness already apparent in 1980 when a day conference, the first of eleven events, was held entitled 'Leisure and Tourism in the Countryside, Curse or Blessing?' This was followed two years later by another on the impact of modern farming on the environment. The 1950's WI inspired 'Keep Britain Tidy Campaign' spawned a series of meetings in 1983 called 'Beautiful Britain' and since then there have been at least two concerted attempts at a county-wide litter pick. NFWI's Agenda 21 began in 1996 and, via Executive, a resolution in support of its aims was sent to National. Further pledges to help the environment were sought in 1999, Green Days were held in 2000 and

2007 Leaders of Federation's Eco Teams and report in Home and Country

2007, and in 2007 also, eight Eco Teams were formed in the Federation after the success of the Federation team involved in the National pilot group. Following this, NFWI's Carbon Challenge campaign to reduce individual carbon footprints was encouraged by the committee and by 2012 there were regular meetings with Worcestershire County Council on various environmental subjects, visits to local district environmental depots were undertaken and an environmental heritage day was held. In 2013 members joined with Worcester City Council to promote 'Love Food, Hate Waste'.

Health. The Lucy Hingley lecture on health has been given every year, 38 in all. Worcester Royal Infirmary undertook to give a free lecture in recognition of WFWI's donation of a bed and equipment in 1944 in memory of Lucy Hingley, County Chairman from 1920-31. In 2002 it was found that the plaque from the donated bed had been lost in the move to

1944 Dedication of the Lucy Hingley Memorial Bed at Worcester Royal Infirmary[20]

2013 Lucy Hingley Lecture at Worcester University

---

[20] Front- Ladies - Matron, Miss Hingley's Housekeeper, Lady Davies, Mrs Holland Martin, Mrs Pedley
2nd row – Hon. Mrs Blois, Miss Tomkinson, Mrs Winnington.
3rd row - Miss Hill, Miss Bayshaw, Miss Gibbons, Mrs Odd, Mrs Coldicott . Back - not known

the new hospital site. Executive decided in 1984 that, after forty years, the hospital had well and truly discharged its obligation to the Federation and need no longer provide a speaker and venue for the lecture. Since then, at a variety of venues, professionally trained speakers have enlightened members on all kinds of subjects from transplants and keyhole surgery to ophthalmology, dementia and bladder control. Some of the lecturers used highly coloured pictures and in the case of a lecture on urology these proved "too graphic for several members who left the room looking queasy."

The lectures are always well attended, in 2017 a larger lecture theatre had to be found to accommodate numbers for the macular degeneration talk, so it is curious that, over the years, some proposed health days and discussions have had to be cancelled through lack of support. Other health initiatives were much more successful. In 1985 a drug watch forum was held, in 1988 flyers encouraging smear testing were sent via the CNL, whilst in 2006 a simple osteoporosis test was offered so successfully that it was repeated several times. By 1993 over 1,000 members had completed the basic lifesaving course offered through the Royal Life Saving Society and this association continued until 1999. Linda Bagley who had been WFWI representative on the County Health Authority, was elected to it in 1986, becoming its chairman in 1989. She also served on the Year of the Homeless panel. A committee member served on the County Carers Scheme for four years in the mid 90's when rural stress and chemicals in the body were also subjects of day schools. At the 2005 ACM the committee petitioned for an MRI scanner. In 2007 first aid courses are mentioned and that year there was a healthy eating morning which, together with the 2010 detox your home day, followed on from concerns about chemicals in the body. In 2011 the Worcestershire Royal Hospital wished to raise money for a new breast cancer unit. Embraced by BoT, Public Affairs was an enthusiastic supporter, issuing information on breast care, making it the subject of the Lucy Hingley lecture and organising a charity bucket collection (see photo page 76) as well as the collection of bras. The bras could be of any age and condition and were to be given to a charity after they had been joined together in an attempt to make the world's longest bra chain. However, the organisation rested with an outside body and regretfully the event did not achieve its goal.

2011 ACM Members wave a collection of bras

Involvement with Resolutions. Each year NFWI asks Federations and individual WIs for topics which can be accepted as Resolutions. This topic is dealt with in the Advisers' section. Those passed at the National AGM become known as mandates and a large part of Public Affairs time has been devoted to their implementation. The copious amount of reading mentioned earlier was often on mandated matters. Climate Change is the mandate which has received the most action from members in recent years. NFWI's Climate Chaos initiative was supported and in 2015 some members attended the London Climate Rally. This was followed up by a request for Climate Ambassadors in 2016 and with the Green Heart Day on Valentine's Day 2017 to publicise Climate Concern. To aid this, patterns for green hearts were given in the County News and many were displayed at the Spring meeting.

The Federation too has its own mandates, especially in the early years. The minute books show that from 1980-91 there were Federation resolutions tabled at County meetings, either by the Board or by individual WIs. These were voted on and the nine that were approved were mandated for action, usually by the Public Affairs Committee. They were also sent to National for consideration for the national list. The subjects which received the go ahead were:- the wearing of hats when horse riding, varying the National Standing Orders, two on subscriptions, banning the sale of videos to minors (this put forward in 1983 by Public Affairs), the running of the Stoke Mandeville Games (this was passed after a difficult debate but the majority was insufficient to forward it to National so an insert in Home and Country was decided on), election to National Board, banning the consumption of alcohol in Worcester Streets (Worcester City Council refused to back this) and packaging. Time constraints at general meetings seemed to be the death knell for in-house resolutions. There are 177 pre-1980 resolutions tabled and logged at the back of the ACM minutes book but from then on, with both less time for and certainly less interest in this aspect of Federation life, the number logged declined although several are mentioned such as the 2007 resolution on Parity of Funding in Care Homes which was passed and sent on to National.

However, by 1991 with interest in resolutions declining and the committee reporting there was a low attendance when it had helped at the Resolutions Meeting along with Advisers, the suggestion was made that the meetings should be at Group level to save expense. Collaboration with Advisers continued but it was noted in 2003 that there never seemed to be enough time to deal with mandates and so in 2004 they tried to arrange a workshop on those agreed in the past. 2010 saw an effort to boost awareness when a day combining resolutions and current campaigns was tried. This approach has continued to the present with the 2015 event being combined with Worldwide Women's Afternoon and interest in Resolutions seems to be growing, especially in the newer WIs. The committee appears to have been involved in about 26 Resolutions days.

Outside bodies etc. Naturally, the part of the committee's remit which led to the reports to the committee from members on outside bodies, the action taken on NFWI initiatives and the provision of meetings for agricultural and public (current) affairs issues led to an eclectic mix of events being held. It must be noted here that education was not one of the spheres mentioned for outside bodies in 1980 and yet committee members have sat on many such panels and, in line with 1985 NFWI advice, appointed a Voluntary Education Adviser. Discussion groups ran for a while from 1981, the future of the family was considered in 1982, and in 1984 a discussion day on the European Parliament was held. Twenty years later, one on 'Europe and Us' did not attract sufficient numbers to go ahead. A rural bus questionnaire was sent to WIs in 1985 as part of the Transport 2000 initiative and received a good response. The replies were analysed by the County Transport Department. The 1988 Worcestershire Wildlife Week at the Guildhall was supported, whilst 1989 saw interest in Worcester's archaeological dig and a Federation resolution passed which called for curbs on drinking in Worcester's streets. The same year computer classes were arranged at Kidderminster and Pershore colleges, though not all were satisfied with the quality. Those held in 2003 were better received. 1990 saw seminars on women's tax. The same year, the committee's own research on packaging found that most of it seemed necessary. This led to a display of packaging being mounted at Hartlebury Museum in 1993.

An enclosure about pension provision was inserted in CNL in 1994. The early 2000's saw Fair Trade Fortnight introduced. This continues and fairly traded products are used whenever possible at WFWI events and meetings. The embracing of several campaigns including protecting the postal service, looking into the production of genetically modified foods and the Water for All initiative have been done enthusiastically. The 90@90 project examined the National Movement in its 90th year. Saving the honey bee became a priority in 2009, along with an association with the Asha Centre in Worcester - several members trained to be mentors to the vulnerable women helped by this Centre. 2010 saw a conference on the radicalisation of vulnerable minorities and much support was given to the 'Women reaching Women' initiative, with 100 members attending a large exposition at the Guildhall in 2009. Bugs and food hygiene were on the agenda for a day school in 2013.

International affairs. The International Evening, held yearly until its last mention in 2013,

2013 International Evening
L-R Sheena Murray, Georgia Jacobs,
Sheila Andrews, Linda Edmondson

focused on one country. Generally a talk, often by a native, was given about the country, although music, pictures and dance have also featured and the venues were enlivened by displays and the wearing of national costumes. A typical meal was researched and a menu devised by the committee who, until recently, also cooked and served it and then did the washing up, usually for over 100 participants. Not every country could be covered in the period but the 34 evenings have almost spanned the alphabet as both Botswana and Zimbabwe have been featured.

In 1982 the committee was wishing to spend more time on international affairs but the notes above show there was limited interest. Publicity was needed. An international newsletter was begun in 1985 and there is mention in 1990 of a meeting of international representatives from the WIs.

Each year 'pennies for friendship' are collected, though the committee noted in 1986 that, "the coins need to be larger." It must have worked because in 1996 Worcestershire, with £3,831, raised the fourth greatest amount sent to NFWI and again in 2014 Worcestershire gave £4,368 the fifth highest amount. These donations go to ACWW - Associated Council for Women of the World.

In the minutes there is little mention until 1990 of ACWW, which was formed in 1929, beyond the occasional reference to the 'pennies' collection except for Alfrick's 1982 win in its Triennial greeting card competition and an international needlework competition in which Mrs Kellett of Hartlebury reached the London finals. In 1990 the pennies collection was moved from spring to the autumn to avoid cheque overload in the office and the same year past County Chairman Olive Odell gave a talk on WI Internationally. She had been associated with the ACWW National committee since 1981 and she became its secretary after completing her work as Vice Chairman of National Executive in 1983. This talk was followed by a fund-raising coffee morning and, from then on, giving aid overseas, though not always through ACWW, featured much more prominently. In 2007 the Executive approved an upgrade in its membership of ACWW.

2013 Supporting International Women's Day

That is not to say that aid had not been sent abroad before for, in 1983 goods and clothing were collected and dispatched to Poland, in 1986 a fund-raiser took place to buy both medical and sewing materials, including sewing machines, for Uganda and in 1991 a collection of Gulf Goodies was made for troops serving in the Iraq War. By 1992, 600 Jhuggi jumpers, knitted by members from all over the county, had been sent to India after an appeal for garments to keep children warm. Monetary collections were made to support the recruitment and funding of nurses and midwives in the Maldives who could then address the very high infant mortality rate there.

The problems in the Balkans saw aid packages sent to Slovenia in 1993, sewing materials for Romania in 1994, these partly bought from the proceeds of a quilt raffle, and mittens for Bosnia in 1998. Also supported in this year was the South African shirts into dresses scheme, whilst in 1996 there was a call for used spectacles and over 500 pairs were collected for Age Concern to donate for use in Africa. 2005 saw donations collected for the SE Asia Tsunami victims. In 2016 knickers were collected and sent, together with locally made washable sanitary towels and sewing cotton, to the Congo and Malawi.

1991 Jhuggi Jumpers Appeal

1994 The Romania Appeal

Not all aid sought was for use abroad and British causes included the 1987 clothes donations to battered wives through Worcestershire Women's Aid. Acorns Children's Hospice, Worcester was helped by the collection of old ink cartridges and old mobile phones for recycling whilst in 2003 jewellery was collected for the National Heart Research Fund. In 2016 St Paul's hostel and Droitwich food bank were supported by members' donations of food, bedding and toiletries.

The most sustained effort for ACWW took place between 1998 and 2007. Aid was sent to The Gambia through the work of Jackie Gregory, the ACWW representative and her Gambian contact. Donations were requested at Council meetings and members provided not only 7,645 more Jhuggi jumpers but 130 shoe boxes of assorted toiletries and household goods in 2001 and, who can forget this appeal, 1,643 pairs of knickers. Monetary aid was funded by the sale of marmalade. This was made by Jackie and decanted into the thousands of jars she collected from members at meetings. In 2002 WIs were assured that holding a raffle or other fund-raiser for ACWW was not breaching the charity rules.

Between 2010 and 2015 support was given to specific ACWW campaigns, with jewellery weighing fifty-three pounds being collected as part of the fund-raising. The two year Indian Villupuram project, the Ghanaian traditional birth attendant's scheme, the water and

Learning Computer Skills in India

sanitation installations in Bangladesh - for which Worcestershire raised £2,600, and the training of 20 eighteen-year-old Indian girls in computer skills, again showed the ongoing concern and generosity of members. Santa's Socks raised £900 for ACWW in 2016, the year the ACWW world conference was held in Birmingham. Worcestershire members were generous in the craft items they donated for sale, the Performing Arts committee provided entertainment and Marjorie Whiting was very honoured to be asked to read a Shakespearean speech at the event.

Doreen Jeeves as ACWW representative had much success in raising the profile of ACWW. In late 2016 Val Durnall took over and a target of raising £3,000 over two years for the New Hope Gardening project in Zimbabwe was agreed. ACWW Promotional items such as donation boxes, bookmarks and label templates were also made available and, in 2016-17, six talks were given to WIs.

Permanent links overseas were also forged between Federation members and the Uetze

2016 Gifts made by Worcestershire members for sale at the ACWW conference

branch of Germany's Landfrauen. These originated in the pen friendship of Betty Steel

WFWI Exchange with Germany 1990 – 2015

Betty Steel of Droitwich WI and Inge Römmert of the Landfrauen of Uetze (near Hanover) met through the ACWW pen scheme. There were 14 exchange visits in all. In Germany, there were visits among other places to Berlin, Dresden, Lübeck and Rothenberg and in Britain to Exeter, York and Llandudno, and, of course, Worcestershire.

Having fun together

First visit to Worcestershire 1990
Barn Dance at Hanley Castle

Learning together

Denman College August 1994   Haus am Steinberg in Colsar February 1994

Exploring together

Conwy Castle July 1990   Schloss Muskau July 2015

and Inge Rommert. Every visit since its inauguration in 1990 has been organised by Lynda Bagley and alternated between visits to Germany and hosting the German ladies in Britain. Each time a comprehensive programme of events, visits and entertainment was devised for the ladies who stayed in their hosts' homes. The increasing age of the participants has, however, led to the demise of the exchange, the last taking place in 2015.

Language classes were put on from 1988. These were designed to give enough knowledge for the increasingly popular European holidays with French, German and Italian tuition being given until 1990.

Other activities. Public Affairs did not have outings as a specific aim in its objectives but outings to all kinds of places allowed members to experience first-hand many of the committee's stated aims. The first recorded outing occurred in 1995 when a trip to Waddesdon Manor was offered. The large number who wished to go encouraged further outings and these often had a scientific or environmental theme. The 17 places visited include the Thames Barrier, the Fox Talbot photographic museum, the National Space Centre - twice, Jodrell bank and the Knighton-Powis observatory, Bletchley Park - twice, St Fagan's open air museum, the Houses of Parliament, Sarehole Bog, the Cotswold Farm Park, London, the Big Pit, the National Arboretum which attracted 3 coach loads, Worcestershire Wildlife Trust's Smite Farm and the Good Food Show.

The more locally based Faith Visits began in 2005 with outings to Beoley parish church and Worcester Cathedral. Running until 2011, they were so well supported that several were repeated, some up to three times. Every faith represented in the Midlands was offered, a wonderful chance to learn about the different religions practised in the Country and very warm welcomes were found everywhere. Sheila Andrews remembers "The lunch at the Sikh Temple, eaten sitting on the floor along with several hundred others was both delicious and memorable whilst the Buddhist Temple was very tranquil. The priest at the Greek Orthodox Church had limited English but was a great communicator and made everyone laugh whilst the food offered by the ladies, especially the cakes, was 'to die for'. On one visit to the Hindu Temple members were asked to help themselves to some of the fruit offerings. Several chose coconuts which were then stored on the coach racks and bombarded the passengers when the driver braked suddenly. Just imagine the insurance claim if anyone had been hurt. The ladies at the Shia mosque seemed very uneasy about the visit as they had so little to offer in the way of refreshment. All was explained when one slipped her card to Sheila who was the organiser saying - If you come again, please let me know, we didn't know about your visit."

Science Club is another successful aspect of Public Affairs. This was proposed in 1995 in view of a grant on offer and this aim was strengthened after a joint course on genetics held with Hereford and Gloucester members at Denman.

In 1997 a £1,500 grant was received from COPUS, the Committee for the Public Understanding of Science. The first meeting dealt with science in the garden and forty-four members attended. Science boxes for use by WIs were made up and by 1999 the club was holding twelve meetings a year, half being outside visits. The secretary was Janet Clemas. It was noted in 2000 that Worcestershire was the only Federation with regular science meetings. The variety of topics was wide as the 2009 programme shows and in 2011 WI House became too small for the indoor meetings so a new home was found at Holt. Since 2012 it has been known as WFWI Science and four one day schools per year were held. These were discontinued in 2014 but began again in 2016 with one school per year. Science Club and WFWI Science together held around 193 events.

SCIENCE CLUB PROGRAMME 2009

Meetings are held on the first Monday of the month at 1.30pm unless otherwise stated.

Date	Subject		Venue	Cost
5th January	Members' Afternoon Spaghetti bridges		WI House	£2.50
2nd February	Earth Heritage Trust Liz Alston		WI House	£2.50
2nd March	Forensics. Mr Tristram Elmhirst		WI House	£2.50
2nd April 2.30pm	Visit to the Assay Office		Jewellery Quarter, Birmingham	£6.00
11th May 1.00pm	Visit to Tardebigge Cider (including buffet lunch)		Tutnall, Bromsgrove	£6.00
1st June	Recycling. Debra Parker of MHDC		WI House	£2.50
13th July	Meadow walk followed by supper		Eades Meadow, Fosters Green Farm, Hanbury	Via office
3rd August 2.00pm	Visit to Uncllys Farm		Bewdley	£1.50
7th September	Guest speaker		WI House	£2.50
5th October 2.00pm	Visit to Harris Brush		Stoke Prior, Bromsgrove	£1.00
2nd November	Origins of Cultivated Plants Murray Mylechreest		WI House	£2.50
7th December	Members' Afternoon		WI House	£2.50

We are not a closed club. You are welcome to come to any meeting that takes your fancy. However, would those wishing to go on one of our visits please ring Janet on 01905 371488, as our trips may need to know numbers and you will need directions to the venue. Join us and find out just how enjoyable science can be.

2009 Science Programme

2002 The Science of Cooking

2007 Visiting a Nuclear Bunker

A Visit to an Industrial Plant

2013 WFWI science day at Alvechurch

Performing Arts

This committee was formed in 1988 as Music and Drama when those two individual committees were combined. Both are very old committees being linked together at the beginning of WFWI and only separating after the Second World War. Collaboration continued between the separate committees, for many events and productions contained both music and drama. The combined committee was renamed Performing Arts in 2000.

65 ladies have served on this committee since 1980, fourteen as chairmen, with 35 serving on no other sub-committee. Since 1980, 275 events have been offered, 161 being musical and 114 drama, including 11 joint ventures. Eleven further events were cancelled. If the 55 'Singing for Joy' meetings were counted as one event then the offerings for each would have been more equal. Both music and drama had many cups, some valuable, to present to competition winners. Most of these were sold in 2008 to finance the purchase of new computers as by then there were few events of this kind being held.

The committee has met six times a year since 2011 and had nine members in 2017.

As the events offered are usually either music or drama each facet has been treated separately.

Music

The main activities in 1980 centred on rehearsing the seventy strong Federation Jubilee Choir drawn from fourteen WI choirs and perfecting the performances for 'Jubilee Jems'. However, there was time to arrange four church organists' schools and a music workshop too.

In the 80's, choirs were a very important feature in the committee's planning. Many WIs had their own choirs, and both competitive and none-competitive events and festivals were held regularly at Federation and National level. Through these choirs and competitions many members improved their performances and went on to take part in

1980 The Federation Jubilee Choir

both regional and national events. In the eighties, two Worcestershire members, Gwen Bullas and later Dorothy Leavey, sat on the NFWI Combined Arts committee, Gwen serving as Vice Chairman and the NFWI representative on the standing conference for amateur music. In 1981, twenty-eight members formed part of a National choir performing 'Early One Morning' in Preston. This piece, commissioned by NFWI, was written and conducted by Antony Hopkins. Joy Evans, who had a solo part, sat next to him at the meal afterwards and remarked that she was surprised how popular it was. Immediately realising her faux-pas, she was very glad when he replied composedly, that he wasn't.

1980 Singers and Dancers from Jubilee Jems[21]

Rehearsals for this national concert took place at Pierpoint Street as did some National ad hoc music committee meetings. Visits elsewhere for competitions often meant an overnight stay and members in the host region offered accommodation. Most were very hospitable but one member remembers being dropped at a house late one night and, without a word being spoken, being ushered up to a small bedroom. The following morning, she replied, yes, when someone enquired if she had been given breakfast. "You were lucky. That doesn't often happen in that house."

A rare payment, of £25, was earned in 1981 by a county choir for performing on BBC TV's 'Pebble Mill at One' programme, but usually choirs sang for love, singers taking part

---

[21] Singers - Grace Adkins, Gwen Bullas, Rosemary Sadler. Iris Bonehill not pictured. Dancers - Pat Baines, Rosie Baines, Barbara Gould, Sheila Howes, Pam Pedersen, Pat Powell, Gill Silcox, Irene Warder.

in all the Federation Pantomimes and at many other WFWI events. Work commitments and changing interests, along with the lack of pianists, led by 1987 to the closure of many WI choirs, despite the relaxation of rules which allowed one third non-members. Those which continued had some success in the 1989 Nat West choir competition with Pedmore and Wychbury choir and Wolverley choir reaching the regional final. Wolverley was in the final held in St John's Smith Square, London where they had a lot of support from Worcestershire members. A conductor's stand was purchased to mark this achievement. Wolverley also won the Staffordshire cup in 1994 and entered a NFWI competition in 1998.

Choir really on song

Wolverley Women's Institute choir will be battling it out in London on June 6 for the title of W.I. National/West Choir of 1990.

The race for the title started in the Autumn of 1989 at the Hereford and Worcester Federation rounds when Wolverley, together with Pedmore and Wychbury, won the right to represent

Worcestershire in the Regional round at Barry, South Glamorgan on March 17.

Wolverley won the day in the face of stiff competition from nine Welsh choirs and several others from the Midlands area to go forward to the national finals at St. John's, Smith Square, London. They will compete

against choirs from Derbyshire, Gloucestershire, Surrey, Durham, Essex and Leicestershire, Rutland. Wolverley W.I. choir was formed 42 years ago and gives its services to many charitable events throughout the area under its conductor Mrs Jean Small. The accompanist is Mrs Jean Ovens.

1989 Wolverley Choir in National Final

Trophy triple is repeated

PROUDLY showing a trophy treble they won recently are the sweet-voiced women from the combined Pedmore and Wychbury WI choir.

The 18-strong choir picked up a hat-trick of cups at the WI Worcester Federation Music Festival for the second successive time.

Two years ago they won three trophies and they repeated their success at Worcester's Guildhall in the event, held every two years.

The choir, formed 17 years ago, came top of the class in the madrigal and alternating soprano and alto voice sections. They won

the cup awarded to the choir with most points overall.

They were led by Mrs Gwen Bullas, of St Peter's Road. Pedmore and musical accompaniment was provided by Mrs Mary Marshall, a Stourbridge music teacher who has been with the choir since they were formed.

Picture are — back (left to right): Joyce Leach, Elmina Harris, Joyce Westwood, Jill Dyas, Joan Hare, Mary Fowler, Pam Turner, Peggy Gittins; front: Elsie Bingham, Gwen Chater, Audrey Bennett, May Mayers, Gwen Bullas, Joy Evans, Madeline Beasley, Ann Tandy.

1985 Pedmore and Wychbury Choir

Guildhall hosts county music festival

PETER AINSLEY

●The Worcestershire Federation of Women's Institutes Music Festival was held at the Guildhall, Worcester on Saturday. Left: Blakedown ladies waiting for their turn and right, tie Stourton members, who sang "Dance To Your Daddy."

Despite the decline of individual choirs, a WFWI choir has been assembled each year for a Christmas entertainment, requiring several rehearsals beforehand. The committee usually put on a Carol Concert, generally to capacity audiences, although it has had different formats and names such as 'Christmas Crackers' and 'Christmas is Coming'. Merren Anthony conducted this event from 1989 to 2012 when Tim Morris took over. Various venues have been used, the first being Sansome Walk Methodist chapel. There was always an organ accompaniment and in 1990 the comment was made that organist Maureen Bowkett could write a book on the organs she had played for WI. Many singers enjoyed this yearly get together and the choir increased in size. The largest mentioned had 207 members and so a larger venue was sought. Pershore Abbey was the favourite between 1986 and 1989 although Worcester Cathedral was used in 1987. This latter venue required a fund-raising event to defray the rising costs, but on return to the Pershore venue a few operational difficulties arose when in 1989, only the week before the date, the committee was told that a wedding with a christening would precede the concert.

A four o'clock wedding meant that timing was tight for the six o'clock start. The bride, following tradition, was late. VCOs and committee members found themselves acting as witnesses at the christening and then as ushers after the wedding. The account of this function in the Annual Report stated, "The occasion was certainly memorable if only for the speed of evacuating the church of 450 wedding guests and filling it with 450 WI members on the coldest day that December." The utter confusion which could have prevailed was avoided and the Abbey was made ready with only a five minute delay.

1988 Federation Choir; Carol Concert at Pershore Abbey

1980 Joan Philips conducts Carol Rehearsal at Sansome Walk Chapel

Late 1980's Carol Concert at Kidderminster Joy Evans - soloist, Maureen Bowkett - organist

Winter conditions caused at least one cancellation at the next venue, Kidderminster Town Hall, though fortunately rearrangement was possible in January. Here the traditional catering by the committee, mainly mince pies, continued more easily. Smaller audiences led to Hallow Church being the venue in 2015 and the event is now enjoyed biennially.

WI anniversaries such as significant birthdays often included a Cathedral service for which a large choir was needed. Small local groups rehearsed for many months and the choir only came together on the day, sometimes having a rehearsal on site, but the results have always been pleasing.

A WI choir made a CD in 2005 and in 2011 'Singing for Pleasure' was introduced, continuing for over four years. Members joined in the monthly get together as and when they wished and the experience was enjoyed until 2016. Meanwhile, NFWI announced the 'Singing for Joy' national choir competition to celebrate WI's hundredth birthday and WFWI joined in though their two competition pieces did not make the final.

2013 Singing for Joy. Merren Anthony conducting, Shirley Fieldhouse accompanying

There were three competitive music festivals organised biennially from 1981 to 1985, but the one planned for 1987 was cancelled at the amalgamation of the committees.

2014 Musical Soiree at Hartlebury Castle

Choirs have played a very significant part in the musical programme of Performing Arts but by no means the only one and as the number of choirs declined so other types of event grew in popularity, many being excellent fund-raisers, and thirty-four of this type of event have been organised. The summer musical soiree with supper at Hartlebury Castle, first held in 1996, continues to play to capacity audiences. It features different artists and musical genres each year and so many applied in 1999 that a second performance was sought but could not be arranged. Male Voice choirs and brass bands proved popular for a time as did visits to the Eisteddfod at

1994 Joseph from Scratch: Judy Neale

Llangollen. Elgar's Birthplace was visited in 2001 and Musical Lunches commenced in 2006. There was a very successful Old Time Music Hall at the Guildhall in 1984 though that in 1993 at the Swan Theatre had to be cancelled despite the huge amount of work that had gone into it.

Alongside these large events several day courses and sometimes a competition were organised each year. In 1984 the Mary Pedley competition, setting a given verse to music, attracted forty-nine entries and there was a successful carol writing competition in 1996. Thirty-three musical workshops and several impromptu singing days, as well as four talks on aspects of music have been organised. The variety in these events was wide. Instrument days, hand bell ringing and fun days of many kinds including workshops for music hall turns and 'Sing Messiah'. Musicals were 'done from scratch' in a day. The cast of 'Joseph' looked particularly fetching in their cloaks and turbans - it is amazing what a few tea towels and scarves can achieve. For 'Noah and His Floating Zoo' not only were the songs and movements practised but animal masks were made and then worn for the performance.

Songs from the Shows and the access to travelling tutors complete the kind of thing on offer for the musically minded member.

Scores and other material could be borrowed from the music library until this was disposed of on leaving Pierpoint Street.

Drama

The ambitious, high standard and successful five-night drama festival held at the Redditch Palace Theatre was the Drama Committee's main event for the 60th Jubilee year. Twelve WIs performed their piece, three per evening, with those judged the best performing again at the Saturday night Gala. 1980 also saw the conclusion of the NFWI drama competition called Scene Eighty which had started in 1978. There had been ten regional finals for the one act play entries. Worcestershire's entry was produced by Peggy Cox and two courses were required to help preparations as "the

DRAMA FESTIVAL

Evenings Tuesday, 29th April-Saturday, 3rd May 1980

at

THE PALACE THEATRE, REDDITCH

ONE ACT PLAYS, REVUE, DRAMA, COMEDY ETC.
ADJUDICATOR: MISS PATSY YARDLEY

Programme:
TUESDAY: 1. Ipsley;   2. Mrs. Drinkwater (Rowney Green)   3. Wolverley
Mrs. Farmiloe (Hadzor & Oddingley)
"Duologues"
WEDNESDAY: 1. Chaddesley Corbett; 2. Pebworth; 3. Kington with Dormston.
THURSDAY: 1. Blakedown; 2. Cradley; 3. Hopwood.
FRIDAY: 1. Stoke Prior; 2. Wychbury; 3. Alvechurch.
SATURDAY: GALA NIGHT.
Adjudicator: Miss Patsy Yardley, Birmingham School of Speech and Dramatic Art.
Tickets: £1.00 Tuesday - Friday.   £1.25 Gala night, Saturday.

WI drama groups did not understand what was needed." Extracts were used during social time at the Diamond Jubilee Celebration Conference in 1980. Although Worcestershire did not have a place in the final which was held at Stratford in 1981, many members joined the audience.

By 1980 the cost of buying scripts and the like had become too expensive for many individual WIs and the committee was pleased to build up a library of one act plays and scripts. It had also bought a professional lighting system. These items were stored in WI House and items could be borrowed by WIs for their own productions, selection being made from the catalogue detailing what was on offer. Inevitably the plays became depleted in number when copies failed to be returned whilst the lights gave many a headache as they were often not returned in the original condition. It became increasingly difficult and expensive to mend the lights. They were withdrawn in 1988 and disposed of in 2000. The library was dispersed when the Pierpoint Street house was sold.

1980 Drama Programme

A very large drama wardrobe had also been built up from which items could also be borrowed and of course could be used for Federation performances. Some of the costumes were old and some very valuable and many of the latter were, over the years, found secure homes in museum collections. The costumes often needed attention but the biggest single input of time was given in 1984 to 1985 when two members spent a hundred hours over fifteen months overhauling the garments. In 1990 the drama wardrobe was considered a fire risk and its contents were reviewed. By this time the number of items hired out had reduced greatly. Talks about the wardrobe were offered and from 1991 an 'Antiques Clothes Show' was devised to entertain WIs and Groups who booked it for their meeting. In some years this totalled 8 to 10 visits for the committee member in charge of the collection.

When Hallow was purchased in 2005 this collection was also dispersed as there was insufficient storage at the new County Headquarters.

The most rewarding activity for the committee though was the organisation of events where members could perform and show off their talents and fourteen of these large-scale activities have been undertaken.

The Drama Festivals, often of a week's duration, required judging and the, mainly non-WI, judges sometimes needed accommodation. It seems that they were not always the easiest of guests. One drama judge locked herself in her hostess's toilet and the bolt had to be unscrewed before she could get out. Initially she wanted someone to climb in through the first floor window but the only candidate for the job, the thirteen year old son of the household, quite sensibly refused. On another occasion a judge got lost on the motorway and had to be rescued. She also asked her hostess to iron her dress, quite clearly expecting this as part of the service.

These festivals which were organised by both National and the Federation became less frequent as time went on. They were held in 1982, 1987, 1995 - by then including choirs, and in 1998 and 2006. Festivals required a great deal of both organisation and time input for those involved, so the disappointment was great in 2000 when National cancelled its Drama Festival. All was not lost though as Worcestershire's entry was performed at the half-yearly council meeting and also on Radio Hereford and Worcester. The same station did a live broadcast from WI House during the lead up to the pantomime in 1997. Lunch was laid on and the outside broadcast van with its huge aerial mast was allowed to park in Pierpoint Street.

Denman too held drama competitions. 'Times Remembered' organised by Anne Nicholas came third there in 1995 and 'A Woman's Place', about the beginnings of WI and written by Ann Moore for the 2001 NFWI competition at Shaftesbury, was performed there in 2009.

The 2001 cast of 'A Woman's Place' was well acclaimed at the Shaftesbury competition but whilst there for the weekend, the unthinkable happened for, despite there being an ample gin supply, the tonic ran out. Marjorie

2001 Drama Festival play – A Woman's Place [22]

Whiting, being the youngest, was sent out for more supplies as the hotel staff were too busy with a wedding to help, but she drew a blank and tap water had to suffice. In 2015 excerpts from 'Cavalcade 90' were performed in the Hive as part of Worcester's Being Human Festival, where items from WIs' archives were also displayed. This marked the continued and increasing interest shown by Worcester University in the WI's role in the County. At the 2016 ACWW Triennial meeting in Birmingham members of this committee staged jam sessions and Marjorie Whiting read 'This Sceptered Isle,' John of Gaunt's speech from Shakespeare's Richard the Second.

The costumes for 'Cavalcade 90' were designed and made by Di Cope, who also created many of the pantomime outfits. The pantomimes have been a success over the years, both financially and in providing great entertainment and fun. All of the productions had good receptions, with many congratulations both verbal and written.

These are quotes from the sheaf of letters, housed in the WFWI archive and received after the 1986 performances of 'Snow White and the Seven Dwarfs', the script of which was written by Joan Maybury and Rosemary Grave.

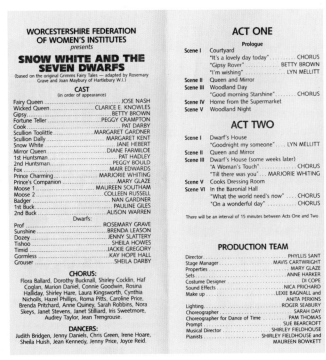

WORCESTERSHIRE FEDERATION OF WOMEN'S INSTITUTES
presents

SNOW WHITE AND THE SEVEN DWARFS
(based on the original Grimms Fairy Tales — adapted by Rosemary Grave and Joan Maybury of Hartlebury W.I.)

CAST
(in order of appearance)

Fairy Queen	JOSE NASH
Wicked Queen	CLARICE E. KNOWLES
Gipsy	BETTY BROWN
Fortune Teller	PEGGY CRAMPTON
Cook	PAT DARBY
Scullion Toolittle	MARGARET GARDNER
Scullion Dally	MARGARET KENT
Snow White	JANE HEBERT
Mirror Queen	DIANE FARMILOE
1st Huntsman	PAT HADLEY
2nd Huntsman	PEGGY BOULD
Fox	MAIR EDWARDS
Prince Charming	MARJORIE WHITING
Prince's Companion	MARY GLAZE
Moose 1	MAUREEN SOUTHAM
Moose 2	COLLEEN RUSSELL
Badger	NAN GARDNER
1st Buck	PAULINE GILES
2nd Buck	ALISON WARREN

Dwarfs:

Prof	ROSEMARY GRAVE
Sunshine	BRENDA LEASON
Dozey	JENNY SLATTERY
Tishoo	SHEILA HOWES
Timid	JACKIE GREGORY
Gormless	KAY HOPE HALL
Grouser	SHEILA DARBY

CHORUS:
Flora Ballard, Dorothy Bucknall, Shirley Cocklin, Haf Coglan, Marion Daniel, Connie Goodwin, Rosina Halliday, Shirley Hare, Laura Kingsworth, Cynthia Nicholls, Hazel Phillips, Roma Pitts, Caroline Price, Brenda Pritchard, Anne Quiney, Sarah Robbins, Nora Skeys, Janet Stevens, Janet Stilliard, Iris Sweetmore, Audrey Taylor, Jean Trengrouse.

DANCERS:
Judith Bridgen, Jenny Daniels, Chris Green, Irene Hoare, Sheila Huish, Jean Kennedy, Jenny Price, Joyce Reid.

ACT ONE
Prologue

Scene I	Courtyard	
	"It's a lovely day today"	CHORUS
	"Gipsy Rover"	BETTY BROWN
	"I'm wishing"	LYN MELLITT
Scene II	Queen and Mirror	
Scene III	Woodland Day	
	"Good morning Starshine"	CHORUS
Scene IV	Home from the Supermarket	
Scene V	Woodland Night	

ACT TWO

Scene I	Dwarf's House	
	"Goodnight my someone"	LYN MELLITT
Scene II	Queen and Mirror	
Scene III	Dwarf's House (some weeks later)	
	"A Woman's Touch"	CHORUS
	"Till there was you"	MARJORIE WHITING
Scene V	Cooks Dressing Room	
Scene VI	In the Baronial Hall	
	"What the world need's now"	CHORUS
	"On a wonderful day"	CHORUS

There will be an interval of 15 minutes between Acts One and Two.

PRODUCTION TEAM

Director	PHYLLIS SANT
Stage Manager	MAVIS CARTWRIGHT
Properties	MARY GLAZE
Sets	ANNE HARKER
Costume Designer	DI COPE
Sound Effects	NICA PRICHARD
Make up	LEXIE BAGNALL and ANITA PERKINS
Lighting	ROGER SEABURY
Choreographer	SARAH DAY
Choreographer for Dance of Time	PAM THOMAS
Prompt	SUE BEARCROFT
Musical Director	SHIRLEY FIELDHOUSE
Pianists	SHIRLEY FIELDHOUSE and MAUREEN BOWKETT

1986 Snow White programme

---

[22] L-R   Marjorie Whiting, Sylvia Cartwright, Diana Hackett, Diana Farmiloe, Mary Wehner, Irene Hoare performing the play for the German exchange members

Three members of the audience wrote: "Costumes and sets were tremendous and Elk-on John was about the best panto animal I have ever seen." "It outshone the professional panto I saw recently." "There was a wealth of talent amongst the large cast." A cast member wrote "A concept of involvement, teamwork and friendship prevailed throughout, a magical time in the lives of those who have taken part." County Chairman Greta Mitchell said that it was the highlight of her final year and an event to remember.

It had not augured well for 'Snow White' at the beginning in 1984. The ad hoc committee chaired by Jeanne Round reported "Although there are about 170 WIs and seven thousand members in Worcestershire, only just enough turned up to cast the panto parts whilst the chorus is thin and many more are needed for back stage and front of house." Perhaps the enormous commitment in time and effort put people off initially as from October 1985 to February 1986 there would be forty-six rehearsals, including one technical and two in full dress, plus the four performances. However, things improved. Walt Disney Productions had given permission and the committee began to source sponsorship, find a lighting company, organise the hire of village halls for rehearsals and negotiate special group rates on the train to Malvern from Stourbridge for the performances. Anne Harker was in charge of the set, music was under Shirley Fieldhouse's baton whist the director was Phyllis Sant, who continued in the role despite having had to leave the drama committee as she had begun full time work. Di Cope not only designed the 150 costumes but also made them aided by the one other member who volunteered to help.

1986 Snow White cast on stage

Big break for panto moose

That old theatrical expression "break a leg" has a special significance for two brave ladies in the county WI's pantomime "Snow White and the Seven Dwarfs."

For they will be expected to cavort all over the stage and clamber down to the auditorium of Malvern's Festival Theatre disguised as a pantomime moose.

And they have only just begun to rehearse together for their special double act as Elk-on Jon, the moose.

Organisers of the pantomime issued a desperate plea for volunteers for the part after the original Elk-on Jon dropped out.

"I was originally the prompter for the pantomime," said back half, Mrs Maureen Southam.

"But I was volunteered for this part. I don't mind as no-one will be able to see me!"

Luckily the front half, Mrs Colleen Russell, is already a friend of Mrs Southam's.

"They have to be very agile," said Mrs Jeanne Round, one of the pantomime organisers.

"They have to go from the stage into the auditorium which means negotiating boxes and so on.

"But they are insured against accidents."

1986 Elk on Jon, the Snow White Panto animal

Disaster struck with a month to go when in January the front half of Elk-on Jon was lost. An appeal in the County News pleaded for someone willing to step into the front half of this pantomime animal and luckily someone did. A two page spread in the Worcestershire and Warwickshire Life gave excellent publicity, along with flyers and write-ups in other local newspapers and this helped provide capacity audiences at each of the four performances with 3,200 being entertained in all. All were delighted with the £3,500 profit made though not so much with the video, available for hire by WIs, which was of poor quality.

'Jack of Hearts' was performed ten years later and casting and rehearsals began in 1997 for 'Simple Simon', performed in 1999 and written by Andrew Wehner. Both of these received many congratulatory comments, but the next pantomime, 'Hansel and Gretel', which auditioned in 2007 failed to cast the leads and so was cancelled. This did not, however, see the end of panto, for in 2013 there was a panto workshop called 'Cinderella and Sleeping Beauty'.

A large production named 'Fifty Golden Years' was a great success in celebrating the Golden Jubilee of Queen Elizabeth II in 2002. Performed at the Swan Theatre it was narrated by Bill Maynard, a friend of Anne Moore. There

1997 Rehearsals for Jack of Hearts

were three performances and a Worcester Evening News critic wrote, "A huge success, nostalgia reigned supreme and it was lively throughout." It was entirely produced and written in house, involved over sixty members and raised £3,000. In all the committee has staged ten large festivals, shows and competitions.

Also in the same year, 2002, Wolverly choir took part in a Denman Festival and Performing Arts won third place at the Denman Fanfare with an entry based on the first performance in Worcester Cathedral of Elgar's 'Froissart'.

1997 Jack of Hearts cast take a bow

2008 saw the start of a series of Murder Mystery Evenings. These were generally performed in village halls, have included dinner, and have been very well supported. A small cast performs a script written by Andrew Wehner or Pat Gale and its members then visit each table to discuss the likely outcome. The five put on to date for Federation members include one at the Croome Court WI Day but additional outings to Groups and WIs have increased this number.

Like the Music side of Performing Arts, Drama has offered courses and day schools, fifty-five in all, on most aspects of performance and the following list illustrates the choice that has been offered. Drama schools including a Wilde day at the Swan Theatre, characterisation days, stage management, verse speaking, group speaking, poetry days, stage lighting, writing days, tap dancing and mixed drama fun days. A 'Strictly WI Ballroom Blitz' day was followed by 'Strictly Samba' and 'WI's Got Talent' days. Visits to theatres have been arranged at Stratford, Malvern and Buxton, the last for a Gilbert and Sullivan festival. Barn dances were popular in the mid 90's whilst the seven literary and two musical lunches embracing a wide variety of subjects have proved very popular in the 21st century as did the poetry reading with tea in 2017.

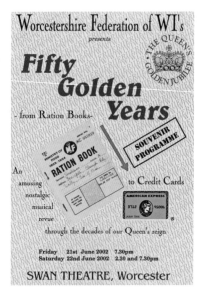

A Nativity play competition in 1991 had twelve entries and was won by Offenham WI. Open days at the House have been popular and WI Drama representatives were tried out in 1992.

Katie Johnson of Hereford and Worcester broadcast a series of talks by the committee on theatrical themes in 2007.

Creative Activities

Served on Creative Activities Committee

Rosemary Adams	Diana Cope	Nora Henderson	Mrs Revers
Karen Albert	Elizabeth Cornish	Christine Hickman-	Jane Richardson
Joan Allen	Louise Craske	Smith	Judy Robinson
Helen Allen	Christine Cross*	Anne Hingley*	Mrs Rock
Pat Baines	Eileen Cross	Kathleen Hollands	Julia Rogers
Pauline Bamber	Margaret Crowther	Marion Inman	Jeanne Round
Mrs Banks	Judith Cussen	Pat Jones*	Sheila Rust
Eleanor Barrett	Margaret Dalton	Val Kilmartin*	Betty Scanlan
Cicely Barnes	M Daniel†	Pat Lane	Rosemary Schafer
Brenda Bemand	Sheila Darby	Sue Lloyd	Margaret Shaddock*
Sylvia Bettison	Anne Day	Pam Lowe	Cilla Skinner
Rosemary Bezzant	Janet Denny	Betty Luxton	Hazel Smith*
Betty Birch*	Eileen Dixon	Christine Manderson	Jo Stevens
Sheila Bishop*	Elizabeth Dow	Jill Martin	Hazel Stewart
Betty Boffey	Ann Dyer	Anne Martyr	Sue Stone
Dorothy Bond†	Barbara Edwards	Lorna Matthews	Judith Stubbs*
Meg Bourton*	E Edwards	Pauline Milnes	Margaret Taylor
Maureen Bowkett	Maureen Egglington	Beth Milsom*	Gillian Thomas
Anne Boyce	Mrs Entwhistle	Elizabeth Mitchell	Joan Tipping*
Joyce Broome	Jill Ewance	Elizabeth Mountford	Rita Tysoe
Jenny Bruton	Joan Fowler	Margaret Neale†	Beryl Village
Shirley Cadman	Mary Fynn	Laura Nicholls	Shirley Vizard
Eileen Chapman	Joy Gammon*	Anne Nicholas†	Mrs Wakefield
Jean Checkley	Ann Garman*	Shirley Noble	Mary Wehner
Angela Chipp	Lesley Grant	Margaret Norris	Mary Wilkes
Jacki Clarke	Cherry Greaves	Liz Osborn	Shirley Willetts
Vera Clarke	Joan Green	Elizabeth Parker-	Janet Williams
Susan Clemants	June Green	Jarvis†	Jill Williams
Mrs Clews	Catherine Guest	Christine Parsons	Gwyn Wilmore
Raley Clifton	Beryl Halsall	Jan Pearce	Heather Winspur
Vicky Coghlan*	Jill Hammonds	Joy Peers*	Valerie Wood
Mrs Cook	Anne Harker	Joanne Powell*	Dee Woolford
Helen Cooke	Barbara Harris	Reta Powell	Rosie Wynne*
Alison Cooke*	Stephanie Hartley	Edna Pugh	Anna Yelland
Cynthia Cooksey*	Mrs Hatfield	Roma Punt *	
	Christine Henderson	Monica Rees	* = Chairman

† = also VCMOs

Other VCMOs not on the Committee were - B Capewell, Sheila Clarke, Margaret Upton

In 2008 Home Economics and Craft joined with Art to form Creative Activities. The combining of the two was first discussed in 1987 but not activated. It had difficulties initially as some members continued to have separate meetings and one member felt that the committee had moved away from Home Economics and so she could no longer contribute. 139 ladies have served on these committees, twenty-one as chairman and 103 on these sub-committees only. Together they have put on 1,268 events: 664, including 228 craft loan visits, on the Home Economics and Craft side, and 604 on the Art side which includes 380 painting days. 25 events have been cancelled. The committee has met six times a year since 2011 and in 2017 had ten members.

As with Performing Arts, the activities of the two original sub-committees are dealt with separately.

Home Economics and Craft

This sub-committee was first formed in 1976 when the Produce and Handicraft Guilds were discontinued by National. These had been set up in 1918 to teach members the relevant skills and often to allow the sale of the goods produced. Worcestershire members expressed sadness at their passing.

In 1980 there were 10 appointed members and up to four co-opted members, and in 1990 there were 7 members and two co-options. This reflects the variations in members which have been adopted over the years. In 2005 they were seeking new members. Despite this the committee has put on some 664 separate events in these 38 years and one lady who came as an observer to a 1990 meeting was quoted in the minutes as saying "How surprised she was by the wide scope of the committee's work."

Rallies and Conferences. The main objective has always been to foster members' interest and expertise in food, the home and craft. To encourage this there have been 38 Rallies organised at which members' achievements and skills could be displayed in the various food, craft and floristry competitions. Last mentioned in the CNL in 1998, nineteen Autumn Conferences also took place at which members could learn from experts on a wide range of subjects.

The Rally was a big event. Its primary object was to give members the chance to showcase their talents whilst learning from other members. Individual and co-operative classes were both offered and WIs could select members to enter each category. As with any exhibition an enormous amount of time and thought was put into the event. Each year a new schedule was devised and dispatched to the WIs and once the entries were received, the staging had to be worked out and the judges organised.

THE ENGLISH countryside makes a pretty picture — especially when the needle-wielding women of the WI get at it!

As part of an international competition being staged by the Associated Country Women of the World — to which the WI is affiliated — members of the Worcestershire Federation have been stitching up our rural heritage.

They were asked to embroider a countryside scene, to represent the county at national level, and maybe world-wide when the international judging is done in Vancouver at the ACWW's triennial conference in June of next year.

The Worcestershire appeal attracted thirty entrants from institutes throughout the Federation, most of them on display at their craft rally at the Malvern Winter Gardens, with Mrs Celia Kellett's entry in pride of place.

Mrs Kellett, from Hartlebury, won her way to London for the next round with a corpulent compilation in rich russets, browns and greens — her needlecraft clearly depicting hills, fields and a country cottage framed in the heavily laden boughs of an old apple tree.

Many of the pictures were recognised landmarks of Worcestershire, like Eckington bridge, Blackwell Church

and the Folly at Earls Croome, while others were more general displays of fruit, trees, and flowers, birds and butterflies, corn fields and tractor tracks.

There was even a reminder of winter — a snow scene tinged with silver frosting, a busy hedgerow harvest and a black and white interpretation of the Black Country, each one putting a little bit of England back on the map.

"We are extremely fortunate in this country to have such a wonderful heritage. We really must do all we can to preserve it — and not only in pictures," said Home Economics chairman, Mrs Cynthia Cooksey from Colton Hackett, a reminder to us all to care for our countryside.

Even closer to home, local members vied for a place in the Federation's "Kitchen Window" competition, a co-operative effort from institutes to include produce from the kitchen garden; an unusual preserve, a piece of needlework and general staging judged during the rally.

Mouth watering marmalades, relishes, jellies, curds, chutneys and candies, embroidered aprons, what-not holders, gadget covers, herb holders, egg and tea-pot cosies, oven gloves and scissor tidiers set among flowers, fruit and miniature vegetable baskets gave the judges a difficult time.

Eventually, they made up their minds and put Fladbury WI in first place, Feckenham in second, and Upton-on-Severn, third. Welland was highly commended.

•EDNA PUGH, Cynthia Cookson and Beth Milsom, with Mrs Kellett's winning entry in the WI craft fair at Malvern.

1982 Rally

WI annual Craft Rally

Women's Institutes from around the county attended their annual home economics and craft rally at Kidderminster Town Hall.

National Federation executive member Mrs Anne Morris and Mr Richard Craven, of Anvard Wools, Church Lench were the main speakers.

A "Here's Health" competition for the best bakery, craftwork, home-made drink and flower arrangement was won by Hartlebury WI, and the individual scarf-making contest was won by a member of Webheath.

•Left to right: Carol Graham, county secretary Beth Milsom, organiser of the Craft Fair, Greta Mitchell, county chairman, Mrs Brenda Zych, Mayoress of Kidderminster and Ann Morris, National Federation WI Executive.

•Richard Craven, speaker, with models Vicky Coglan, Suzanne Owen, Maureen North and Diana Cope at the WI Craft Rally.

1988 Rally: Interviewing Anne Hingley

1985 Rally

The programme for the day always included speakers or demonstrations as well as updates from the sub-committee. After judging was completed, those attending could view the exhibition and sometimes lunch was available. The Rally was a very popular event especially in the first half of the period under discussion. In 1983 there were so many entries that staging them all at Malvern Winter Gardens was difficult and it was agreed in committee that a rethink was needed. However, in 1990 when ninety-nine WIs participated at the same venue there was insufficient space again, the minutes recording difficulties because of overcrowding. So, by 1995 the Rally was being staged at a larger venue, Perdiswell Leisure Centre in Worcester. Over 500 attended and there were entries from more than seventy WIs. In 1998 novice classes were introduced to encourage those who had not won before but in 2001, with costs escalating and the number of entries falling, the rally was renamed the 'Spring Food and Craft Show'. Two years later it found a different venue at the Ramada Hotel, Stourport and, having become a loss making event, it was combined with the ACM in 2010. It has continued to attract entries, for in 2015 there were 293 separate entries and in 2016, 208. The organisation of these events entails an enormous amount of work each year. The organisation of the entries for this, and any other WI show, is governed by rules laid down by NFWI and every WI is encouraged to have a copy of 'On with the Show' which explains them. The shows held by WFWI required a committee member to be skilled in staging. Anne Garman and later Ann Hingley could offer this expertise and they gave advice on how to start, how to set up the exhibits especially for the co-operative class and explained the marking. Ann Hingley became a staging judge in 1994.

The Autumn Conference which featured excellent speakers also entailed detailed and extensive organisation. Having been very popular in the early eighties when numbers twice demanded two dates, it then seemed to suffer from unpredictable demand. It was cancelled in both 1985 and 1995 but, by contrast, in 1996 the venue was changed because so many applied. It disappeared from the calendar in 1998, partly because it was vying with the ACM for speakers.

2016 ACM   Above from top – Setting up; Judging: Viewing

Below - Trophies

Above   2016 ACM
Some winning entries

Classes and Courses. The committee has offered a great number and variety of classes, courses and demonstrations whose duration could be from half a day to being spread over many weeks or even months. These have been for both craft and home economics and fulfil the teaching remit of this sub-committee.

Every type of craft seems to have been explored but those connected with sewing, knitting, needlework, box, toy and jewellery have made up by far the largest proportion. Some of the 226 craft titles have been intriguing with pot et fleur, terraria making, bazaar ideas, pergamano, etui boxes, tea bag folding and trapunto arousing great curiosity.

The home economics offerings have sounded less exotic but the 1980 Evening with the White Fish Authority at Bromsgrove Swimming Baths conjures up some interesting visions.

Sugar paste cake decoration accounted for nineteen of the 102 food based events whilst preservation courses have appeared very regularly. Gardening or flower arranging featured twenty-nine times and thirteen staging classes have been run. Most of the courses were delivered by committee members though from 1984 some of those running over weeks or months were offered at local colleges such as Evesham, Pershore or Kidderminster so that members could gain recognised qualifications.

Often follow-up courses were requested in both craft and home economics but this was not always beneficial as there are several instances of cancellation through lack of support or a loss being made when members failed to turn up. In 2009 round the kitchen table classes made a debut but were found to be outside the Federation's insurance cover.

In 1987 the committee began fund-raising for a demonstration mini kitchen at WI House which would make the delivery of food based courses much easier and this was installed in the Pierpoint Street conference room by 1989. There was a dispute about the quality of the finished article with the firm entrusted with the work and, after a solicitor was consulted, the firm removed it and Hatt Kitchens installed the one which remained until the sale of the premises.

Food hygiene courses were introduced in 1992 as regulations for dealing with food involving public participation were tightened by Health and Safety legislation. For a time a group of embroiderers began to meet twice monthly at WI House, beginning in 1995.

1980 Olive Odell right, demonstrating baking

About 1990 Horticulture Certificate Course at Pershore College

Quite a number of the courses mentioned above were Certificate courses for which a NFWI qualification could be awarded. Several were put on each year allowing members to reach a designated standard in the chosen craft or home economics discipline. These certificates were awarded at ACMs. Ratified by Executive each year, a Test Certificate Organiser and an Assistant were appointed by the committee from its numbers, the first renamed Skills Co-ordinator in 2004. The Certificate Officer met with her peers in other

1987 Machine Sewing Class making Stuffed Toys

2013 Knitting Class

Sugar Craft Certificate Course
Tutor Sheila Bishop on left

2015 Crochet class

About 1990 A staging class by Anne Garman

2013 Flower Demonstration by Joyce Brewer

federations at a yearly conference in London. In 2005 the Skills Co-ordinator explained that her role includes the recording of all classes done by the Federation so that the education element can be provided to the charities commission. Yearly figures are rare in the minutes but in 1989 they show that over 2000 students had attended Federation schools and classes. She also looks for finance, sponsorship and grants to put on the courses.

In the 1980's women were being urged to return to work but WI members found that the WI certificates were not regarded as a qualification by employers. Steps were taken to rectify this by forging links with County's Further Education and Horticultural Colleges so that the certificate courses could gain recognition. The appointment by Executive of a Voluntary Education Officer – VEO, began in 1985. Beth Milsom, the first of these, was much involved with this development, as she had a great regard for the education of women.

A talented seamstress working in Further Education Colleges, she both shared and increased her knowledge with the WI. Her service on the Executive and Home Economics committees opened new horizons as she gained a much deeper knowledge of financial management and honed her organisational skills. These led

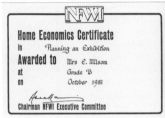

1994 Beth Milsom

to a further teaching qualification in psychology. Her thesis for this course was based on the WI as an educator of women. Sometime later she decided to use her expertise to set up her own bridal business and became runner-up in the 1994 Worcestershire Women of the Year Award, later being invited to the Women of the Year Awards in London.

Others who gained accreditations from the courses run for the WI at these colleges went on to use them as a basis for a career or part time interest in such spheres as cake making, catering, dressmaking, costume making, horticulture, floristry and toy and gift making.

Suzanne Owen and Vicky Coghlan attended a certificate cookery course at Kidderminster College in 1994 little thinking they were doing more than making up the numbers. A second course followed and after completion in 1996 their qualifications allowed them, when asked, to cater at many and varied WI events and especially at six consecutive Three Counties Shows for WFWI, the first in 1997 and then every three years until 2012. They look back on these Shows as being very hard work but so much fun.

2008 Upstairs Downstairs Christmas Demonstration[23]

---

[23] L-R Rosemary Adams, Val Wood, Ann Day, Christine Hickman-Smith, Hazel Smith

Judges. Some who reached the required standard went on to train as NFWI judges in the relevant discipline. There have been fifty-nine members serving as judges. Some are qualified in more than one discipline. In 1980 there were thirty judges listed in the handbook, fifteen in cookery and preservation, eleven in crafts and four in flower arrangements etc., three of the names being found in two areas.

Served as Judge

Bessie Attenborough	Mrs Hingston
Mrs Austin	Kathleen Hollands
Ruth Baster	Marjorie Honeybone
Sheila Bishop	May Lloyd
Betty Boffey	Vivien Lloyd
Maureen Butcher	Anne Martyr
Jean Checkley	Olive Mason
Angela Chipp	Diana Milligan
Vera Clarke	Pauline Milnes
Margaret Collins	Sheila Nash
Elizabeth Cornish	Olive Odell
Louise Craske	Freda Page
Margaret Crowther	Pat Parker
Margaret Dalton	Christine Parsons
Anne Day	Joan Peck
Janet Denny	Enid Peel
Eileen Dixon	Joy Peers
Mavis Drew	Roma Punt
Eileen Fincher	Jeanne Round
Betty Foster	Hazel Smith
P Freeth	Diana Staines
Joy Gammon	Hazel Stewart
Antoinette Gilmour	Sue Stone
Shirley Graham	Beryl Stuart
Lesley Grant	Mrs Targett
Diane Harper	Joyce Thomas
Barbara Harris	Rita Tysoe
Christine Henderson	Beryl Village
Sandra Hill	Shirley Willetts
Anne Hingley	

In 1984 when twenty-five names were listed, a distinction was made between NFWI qualified and County Recommended judges. The number serving at any one time has dwindled over the years, the low point until recently being in 1995 when there were only twelve. A real effort was made to increase numbers and from 2000 to 2006 there were twenty or more. Decline set in again and in 2017 there are only seven though one person judges in three of the five disciplines. These five are cookery, preservation, sugarcraft, crafts and flower arranging. There are also three judges awaiting full training from NFWI and are listed as County Recommended judges.

The job is very time consuming and for most of the period a judge paid for her own training which is expensive and very exacting. At first Olive Odell seems to have been involved in training but usually it has been done at Denman. There is a practical exam and a viva. Judges also receive regular refreshing. In general, judges do not judge their own Federation's competitions. They judge at other Federations' competitions, at some WFWI events, at WIs and for outside bodies. Beryl Village's experiences on TV are recounted in the article opposite. There is a set rate to charge when judging plus travel costs. They aim to encourage, educate and enlighten with their comments.

Sheila Bishop, in 2017, is the most qualified judge in the whole of NFWI and has been a judge for cookery, preservation and sugar craft in Worcestershire throughout the period. Recruited by Olive Odell when doing City and Guilds food studies, she has overheard many comments about her judging and usually they are fine. However, not all have been complimentary but the most extreme was from a member who said "Fancy saying that, she should be shot."

Judges meet twice yearly when jobs are apportioned and the judges' co-ordinator is appointed. Occasional, 'Meet the Judges' sessions are also held for members. Like

Advisers, judges attend regular refreshing courses. The number of shows judged during a year by the Federation's judges has varied but the seventy-four in 2005 is the highest recorded.

In 1999 Barbara Harris, along with Sue Stone, trained as a judge at a time when the requirement of holding a City and Guilds certificate was still mandatory. To encourage more judges to train the Executive was paying half of the £400 cost or the full amount if the person remained as a judge for two years. This was discontinued in 2011 as the Federation could no longer afford it. Barbara judged sugar craft for the certificate classes and someone from Denman always came to check her decisions. In 2015 she was judging the cookery entries at Winchcombe Country Show when she noticed Gryff Rhys Jones on the other side of the table, accompanied by a cameraman. Startled, she stopped work but the cameraman said "Please keep doing what you are doing because I want to film you and especially your WI Badge." This programme was broadcast in 2016. Barbara judges, on average, eleven shows a year and they are mostly held between July and September.

Top   WFWI Judge Sue Stone's story

Right   2007 WFWI Judge Beryl Village's TV assignments

■ SUE STONE, Member of the Board of Trustees, writes "You never know where joining the WI will take you." I can really empathise with this little phrase. Cookery has always been a hobby of mine. As a 16 year old I can well remember receiving my latest copy of 'Supercook' and preparing supper for my parents every Saturday, talking to myself throughout the entire process – out loud!!!! After attending a fair few evening recreational cookery classes, I ventured into the City

and Guilds Cooks Professional course thinking I would just do one year. Then I did two, and, well, I finished the course. So three years later I did take the final exams and thanks to an excellent tutor (Jackie Emeny) and the support of family and friends I achieved a good result. This result enabled me to take up the next challenge, to be a WI cookery judge. Under the guidance of Beryl Village and Sheila Bishop, two ladies with such a wealth of experience, I managed to qualify. This led me into training to teach my sk and from there I became heavily involved with Let's Cook. This project took me to be part of the National Education Committee and from there I have been asked to help create and judge some super competitions including the Saturated Fat competition. Hence the picture below!!! So fellow members, don't be afraid to have a go, you never know where you will end up and, remember, you can always say no!!!!!

The Great British Village Show

Being a member of the WI can get you into all the best places as National Federation Cookery and Preserves Judge, Beryl Village found out. You may have seen her recently on The Great British Village Show on the BBC. This is her story…

The journey into the world of TV began in the summer of 2005 when I was part of a group interviewed by Rick Stein and later appeared in his Christmas Show Special. In the spring of 2006 I was invited to attend an interview along with other National Federation of Womens Institute Judges for a series to be produced for the BBC. Within a couple of days I received confirmation that I had been selected with Lyn Blackburn to judge the food classes and Jackie Woolsey to judge the knitting in The Great British Village Show.

In July the first of the six semi-finals began in West Sussex. 12 yard Production team, the judges, film crew and Angelica Bell arrived at the hotel on the Saturday. Introductions were made over dinner. Sunday at 6 am the crew left for the site and at 7.15 am the Judges were collected by taxi. The exhibitors were already at Petworth setting out the exhibits and we had breakfast from the mobile kitchen until called to pre-judge the exhibits. We returned to wait for the film crew to take us through the judging in front of the cameras.

Alan Titchmarsh and James Martin arrived mid-morning, the public, at lunchtime. Soon the marquees were full, cash changed hands at the stalls and people settled in chairs or on the hay bales to enjoy the entertainment. The weather was glorious and so this set the pattern for the semi-finals as we moved in following order through Somerset, Derbyshire, Cambridgeshire, Cardiff, and West Yorkshire and onto the ultimate

venue at Highgrove for the finals.

On Sunday October 2, 2006 my sister June and I travelled to Gloucestershire. Sunday evening at dinner the wine flowed, party night combined with nervous tension at the thought of the following day but we all retired early to our respective rooms. Monday dawned, the weather once again beautiful and along with the guests we were transported to Highgrove. The semi-finalists arrived with guests in time for breakfast and people were moving around the lovely gardens of Highgrove. After the judging had finished his Royal Highness Prince Charles and his wife Camilla Duchess of Cornwall arrived. We were introduced and shook hands. After exchanging a few words they moved on to meet the exhibitors. The marquee held the strawberry jam and rich fruit classes, and one or two exhibits were tasted before they left. Lyn and I ran to the Orchard Room which housed the Sugarcraft Novelty Cakes and once again the Royal couple approached and paused to chat. The Duchess, who is a WI Member, asked about the WI's involvement to which I replied: "Who better m'am to take care of the food section?". The winners collected their awards and the day drew to a close. Screened in 2007 on BBC2. ■

To find a WI near you contact: WI House, 7 Elgar Business Centre, Hallow, Worcester WR2 6NJ. Tel: 01905 641658, email wfwi01@tiscali.co.uk or visit www.womens-institute.org.uk.

Beryl Village above centre

Craft Collection. A committee member has responsibility for the Craft collection. There were separate museum and craft collections which brought together the best work of members and other donated items. They contain individually worked pieces in many mediums along with WI banners, tablecloths and other regalia. Both were set up in 1980, being unified in 1987. The collection is available to non-WI groups as well as WIs and the officer takes them out several times a year, explaining and displaying the contents. The most visits recorded in one year, 1995, numbered eleven. The collection has been taken out about 228 times in the period. The contents of the craft collection were catalogued and photographed in 2016.

WI Markets formed another facet of this committee until 1995. In 1980 there were fourteen weekly markets held around the County, each headed by its own organiser. They in turn were overseen by a Voluntary County Markets Organiser - VCMO, chosen from their ranks, who attended the Organisation Committee and the National Markets' meetings and paid their own training costs. There have been eight VCMOs who are named on page 143. The markets were held at Bredon Hill, Blackwell & Burcott, Bromsgrove, Droitwich, Evesham, Hagley, Malvern, Pershore, Redditch, Stourport, Stourbridge, Tenbury Wells, Upton-upon-Severn and Worcester where the market had, prior to 1980, operated outside WI house. Rubery was added in 1984. WI Markets were severed from WI in 1995 because of the charity laws and by this time only ten venues were in operation as those at Blackwell & Burcott in 1983, Bromsgrove in 1992, Rubery in 1993, Stourport in 1992 and Stourbridge in 1991, had closed.

Markets were set up in 1919 to allow members to sell anything they produced to the public and thereby earn some income. Each marketing society operated as a separate company, membership was available by purchasing a 5p share and it was the only part of WI which men could join.

Tightening of Environmental Health laws was first noted by the committee in 1984 when the VCMO reported great concern amongst members after an officer in Wychavon had notified all producers that their homes were liable to inspection. Salmonella hit the number of egg producers in 1989 as most felt it was uneconomic to incur the subsequent testing cost. By then a parcel scheme had been introduced but some markets were in

1955 WI Market outside WI House in Sansome Walk

2016 Country Markets at the ACM

difficulties because of the reduced number of producers. Nevertheless the total turnover that year was £186,000.

▲ Piles of goodies on offer at the Worcester WI market.

spectrum

Market forces delight fans of the WI

Special report by MIKE PRYCE.

IT was a bitter cold morning, but quarter of an hour before opening there was already a queue outside.

It has probably been like that for the past 75 years, ever since the ladies of the Women's Institute decided to hold their first market.

Shoppers who know they're on to a good thing get in first for the goodies.

This is where the "jam" bit, out of the "jam and Jerusalem" image, comes from.

You want jam?

It's here in abundance. Blackberry, loganberry, strawberry, blackcurrant, gooseberry - in fact just about every jam you can thing of.

Thick, fruity and homemade, it might cost a touch more than the supermarket "super saver" lines, but then it's in another world.

Open a jar, bring a spoonful to the mouth and it's the taste of the countryside in summer, green fields, clear blue skies, the sun shining through farmhouse kitchen windows on to pine tables, while gingham curtains flutter in the warm breeze.

Open your eyes again and you're in St Clement's Church Hall, Worcester, on an extremely parky Friday in the middle of winter.

The consolation is that you're in a gourmet's Heaven.

Because these ladies know how to cook.

The biscuits melt in your mouth, the pastry is as light as air and you would kill for the cakes.

There are cherry cakes, almond and cherry, coconut and orange, jam and cream sandwich, chocolate marble and chocolate chip — with real chocolate!

Not to mention scones the size of your hand palm, shortbread like it should be, pasties that owe nothing to mass production, golden sausage rolls, country apple tarts with sugar on top and rock cakes, all brown sugar and currants and very yummy.

The list seems everlasting.

Lined up on trestle tables, it all looks like some gigantic cricket tea.

All you need is the marquee...

Special service is flourishing

YOU can get a special Christmas or birthday surprise courtesy of the WI.

Just as flowers can be arranged on the Inter Flora network, so can goodies from the local WI market be wrapped and delivered as a gift.

"Just tell us what you want sent where or how much you want to spend and we'll organise it," said Worcester WI market organiser Mrs Heather Clark.

"We contact the WI market for the area and they wrap up the gift and deliver it."

Using the service, a lady from Callow End sent a home made Dundee cake and mince pies to a friend in Sussex as a Christmas present for just £6.35.

"I gather it was very well received," Mrs Clark added. "It's a real surprise to get something home made like that. It makes a very unusual gift."

WORCESTERSHIRE WI MARKETS

► Bredon Hill (Eckington): Friday 9.00-11.00. White Gate's Garage, New Road, Eckington.
► Droitwich: Friday 9.30- 11.00. Old Library.
► Evesham: Friday 8.30- 11.00. Wallace House, Community Centre, Oat Street.
► Hagley & District: Friday 9.45-11.00. Community Centre, Worcester Road.
► Malvern: Friday 8.45- 11.00. Lyttelton Rooms, Church Street.
► Pershore & District: Saturday 9.00-11.00. Avon Leisure Centre.
► Redditch & District: Friday 8.30-12.30. St Stephens Church Hall, Church Green.
► Tenbury Wells: Tuesday 9.00-12.00. Scout Hut, Main Car Park.
► Upton-on-Severn: Saturday 9.00-11.00. Church Rooms, Old Street.
► Worcester: Friday 9.30- 11.30. St Clements Hall, St Clements Close, St John's.
The next Worcester WI market is on Friday, February 18.

▲ Barbara Edwards unloads goods from her car boot for sale at the market.

February 1994 Article in Worcester Evening News

In 1994 Markets celebrated its 75th anniversary with a special market held at the Guildhall, Worcester but the next year all the Marketing Societies had to leave the WI. They became a limited company called WI Country Markets Ltd. Eventually in 2004 it was renamed Country Markets because it had no association with WI and the name led to confusion. Worcestershire's Marketing Societies also lost the right to a free room at WI house but continued to hold meetings there and used it as their regional office address. A legal agreement was drawn up later between WFWI and Markets to confirm this arrangement but they held their last meeting at the House in 2013 and now only retained the address. They continued to sell their goods at all of WFWI's functions after the severance but as time went on the association waned and Markets now appear only at ACMs. The number of centres has also continued to fall, the remaining five at Droitwich, Hagley, Malvern, Pershore and Tenbury Wells being listed in the 2017/18 yearbook.

Involvement in County Exhibitions. There have been several large special County exhibitions put on over these years, each being organised by an ad hoc committee, mainly drawn from both this and the Art committees. During the Diamond Jubilee year there was a large display of items at Evesham. In 1981 the very large 'Pride and Joy' exhibition, whose ad hoc was chaired by Margaret Crowther, took place at North West Worcestershire College and ran from Wednesday to Saturday. There was also a preview evening about which the ad hoc had mixed feelings; it was a good public relations exercise but they could have used the time for arranging and staging. Having already received and processed the items in the previous week and then organised the judging, the committee was at full stretch for a fortnight. Mrs Anne Harris, the National Chairman, came to the preview and was delighted with both the high standard and the involvement of NFU and YFC. Jeannine McMullan of Woman's Hour opened the event which attracted over 1,000 people. There would probably have been more if there had not been poor weather on the Saturday, the national financial situation had been more favourable and the venue more central to the County. The exhibition did prompt a complaint about food waste which led to a resolution on the subject being debated but not upheld at the next ACM, but it also prompted many congratulatory letters.

1987 Treasures and Pleasures Schedule

1987 saw the three day 'Treasures and Pleasures' competitive exhibition held at Perdiswell Leisure Centre and again this committee was heavily involved in both the arrangements and the delivery of the event. Some classes were offered to prepare for this 1987 show including terrarium making, pot au fleur and staging. The collective class had to use the material, yarn and seeds sent out by WFWI. 93 WIs took part but some thought standards too high.

However, Rosemary Roberts had this comment on the collective class. "The Grow, Cook and Sew was a successful 'shop window' on Worcestershire WIs and all that we do. It covered virtually every discipline from literally planting the seed to cooking the produce." She added "In the sewing sections I particularly remember the wonderful samplers which were made. The one which stood out for me was one of the British Isles with every county stitched in a different stitch and done as a black and white work."

The Board expressed concern over the escalating costs during the gestation period but the event was a great success. Lunches were offered and despite being non-profit making there was a £460 surplus.

The National 'Millennium Craft Spectacular' held at Tatton Park displayed the highest standard of WI work in the Country and Worcestershire was proud to have several items selected including the work of Brenda Banner, Ann Brookes, Jean Brown, Monica Clarke, Sylvia Harris and Susan Shaw. These followed in the path of Ann Garman whose work was exhibited at the 1990 NFWI exhibition.

Flowers in Patterned Pots by Ann Garman (Worcestershire).

1990 Displayed in the NFWI Exhibition

2000 Susan Shaw's embroidery: Scenes of Chaddesley Corbett for the NFWI Millennium Craft Spectacular

2008 and 2011 saw further large undertakings by County. The first was held at Avoncroft Museum, Bromsgrove to celebrate WFWI's 90th Birthday and although all the sub-committees played a part, craft was important and of course the whole display had to be staged, Anne Hingley undertaking this work. The Croome Court WI Day of 2011 was again a combined sub-committee event with tea, scones and fresh fruit being served in the marquee by this sub-committee.

In the eighties especially, sales of work took place. The 'Welcome In' craft sale of 1982, undertaken in Worcester Guild Hall, was the first of these. Members were encouraged to dress dolls for sale and there were many other items too which Group Secretaries were asked to house for the November event. Successful financially, it was an excellent showcase for WI craft and produce. The 1986 Easter Extravaganza was a joint enterprise with the Promotions committee. Easter goods of all kinds were on offer and so were ploughman's lunches.

WFWI 90th Anniversary Exhibition at Avoncroft Museum 2008

2008 - 90th Birthday Exhibition at Avoncroft

The following description of such an event was found in the archive. "You can probably imagine the time taken in arranging all the various exhibits - scarves, hats and jewellery - to best advantage. However, we appeared to have an over-enthusiastic customer who could not wait for the sale to commence: she would persist in taking first one hat and then another and each time turning to the mirror to view the result on her head. Having told her there was no selling before the official opening, it was exasperating to see her trying on yet another hat. The request was repeated with this rider, in any case the hat you have just put on does not suit you. Really, she replied, I would have you know that this is the hat I came in."

Almost every year there were other commitments. There were regular requests for the committee to cater at other Federation events. The Carol Concert's mince pies, other music events, town walks, sports days, tennis tournaments, the Caravan Rally, Federation celebrations, the Fishing Weekend, a tasting day for British Food Week at WI house and for visitors from other Federations are among those minuted. In 1989 a tea for Asian ladies was organised as part of the English League's efforts to have closer links with these growing communities in the county.

The committee, through an ad hoc chaired by Anne Hingley, initiated the first joint enterprise with Worcester & District Health Authority and Worcester City Council in 1992. It was held at the Guildhall and called 'Looking Good: Feeling Great'. This was the first time that health promotion had been offered jointly with the local

SEPTEMBER 1992
WORCESTERSHIRE W.I.
COUNTY NEWS
County Chairman: Mrs. MARY DAVIS   County Treasurer: Mrs. FREDA DAVIES
County Secretary: Mrs. Brenda Spragg   W.I.House 11 Pierpoint Street Worcester WR1 ITA
Tel: Worcester 22575

W.I. House is open to members:
9.00 – 4.30 Mondays — Wednesdays
9.00 – 5.00 Fridays
PLEASE NOTE THE COUNTY OFFICE AND
W.I.HOUSE ARE CLOSED ON THURSDAYS

County Office Hours:
Mondays   9.00 – 4.30
Tuesdays & Wednesdays 9.00 – 1.00 & 2.00 – 4.30
Fridays   9.00 – 1.00 & 2.00 – 5.00

WORCESTERSHIRE FEDERATION
in conjunction with
Worcester & District Health Authority & **Worcester City Council**
present a
HEALTH PROMOTION DAY FOR WOMEN
"Looking Good — Feeling Great"

AT THE

THURSDAY OCTOBER 15th

OPEN FROM 10am - 4pm
Admission Free

INFORMATION STANDS
ADVISORY SERVICE
MAKE-UP DEMO'S
COLOUR-CONSULTANT
ENVIRONMENTAL DISPLAY

GUILDHALL IN THE HEART OF WORCESTER

KEEPING FIT DISPLAYS
BY WI MEMBERS
FOOD DEMONSTRATION (WI HOME ECONOMICS)
COMPETITIONS — PRIZES
PLENTY TO SEE & DO

IN THE INTERESTS OF YOU, YOUR FAMILY AND THE COMMUNITY'S HEALTH — SEND FOR A LUCKY FREE PROGRAMME — APPLY TO COUNTY OFFICE WITH SAE
PRIZE DRAW WILL TAKE PLACE FROM THOSE SHOWN ON THE DAY — YOUR CHANCE TO WIN A DAY FOR TWO AT 'RAGDALE HALL', MELTON MOWBRAY, LEICESTERSHIRE

156

providers. Many meetings were held with local authority staff and a wide range of health, beauty and fitness products were exhibited along with goods for sale and demonstrations. Bromsgrove WI gave Keep Fit displays and the sub-committee demonstrated healthy snacks and other foods.

Anne Hingley

Through undertaking such enterprises for the WI and her interest in health issues, Anne was asked to an interview in 1992 for the position of chairman of the NHS Wolverley Disability Trust. The two other candidates were professionals but she was successful. She considers that her CV, compiled largely from the voluntary work done with WI, played an important part, whilst the leadership and management skills learned from other members whilst sitting on both Executive and Home Economics committees were invaluable. Along with all this involvement, Anne undertook WI certificate courses and gained a sufficiently high standard to go on to train and qualify as a Staging Judge. She considers that the unconsciously assimilated acquisition of all her skills, whilst having the satisfaction and fun of organising WI events, has allowed many doors to open for her. What were those doors?

In 1995 she became chairman of the South Birmingham Mental Health Trust, leaving in 1998. In 2004 she ventured into local politics, first as a ward councillor and later as a County Councillor. She became Mayor of Kidderminster in 2011 and in 2017 was elected Chairman of Worcestershire County Council. She says "I owe far more to the WI than it owes me," and this echoes the many similar comments of other members.

The sub-committee participated in Worcester County Council's Apple Day in 1993 which was considered a poor event. However, in 2009, an SOS from the Lord Lieutenant led to the provision of cakes for and the serving of tea at the Land Army Veterans' party at the Guildhall. Worcester magistrates, between 2006 and 2008, held mock trials for school children in the new Court Building and WFWI provided the catering for the magistrates' lunches on these occasions.

Catering was usually on offer at the committee's own demonstrations and talks, especially in later decades. This was particularly successful at the yearly Christmas event.

2009 Let's Cook course run by Ashton Underhill WI

The challenges posed by some venues were usually overcome by WI initiative, as at the 2003 event when there was no hot water available for the necessary chores.

Other cookery based activities included the time in 1982 when Yorkshire TV asked for Worcestershire recipes for their TV programme entitled 'Farmhouse Kitchen'. The dishes to be sampled were cooked by the sub-committee. In 1992 WFWI produced its own recipe book,

'Favourite Tastes from Worcestershire' and for this four committee members had the task of tasting all 170 recipes. In the same year Worcestershire was chosen to pilot an NFWI project for meal cookery. In 1997 there was a cooks' quiz, in 2000 Anne Nicholas demonstrated plum jam making on BBC2 and WFWI took part in Worcester County Council's Ready Steady Cook competition. Let's Cook started its first course at Kidderminster College in 2007 and up to 2010, nine courses of these lessons were offered to encourage basic home cooking and nutrition. Funding came from various councils for this County wide initiative.

On the craft side, there were many competitions to enter and the committee was responsible for all the arrangements. Some of these occurred annually like the NFWI Huxley Cup. This is awarded for flower arranging and a Worcestershire member is nominated for the honour of doing the County's entry. This was staged at the Royal Agricultural Show at Stoneleigh until it closed in 2002 and since then the venues have been in a variety of places. There was also the yearly Royal Show Challenge Cup awarded for a cooperative entry which aimed to test the ability and craftsmanship of WI members. Worcestershire has gained a second place and two third places since 1980. Other competitions were contested and Shirley Barlow was second in the 1994 Guernsey Flower Competition.

The minutes show that two NFWI design awards have been won, that in 1980 by Janet Wooldridge for a model of Fagin and a 1984 carpet design by Jennifer Page. Photographed in 2010, Liz Cornish's quilt came second in the Makower Challenge, thus replicating Muriel Farrer's achievement in 2000. Suzanne Owen remembers that in 2006 "The National Needlework Archive asked for help from the Federation and WIs to photograph and record the needlework and textiles owned by the WI. The Archive is used for research and raising the profile and esteem of needlework in the community. I wonder how many hundreds of banners and tablecloths are recorded!"

Within the County, Rally competitions led to the production in 1998 of story sacks which were later given to schools and in 2006 tactile books for the Clear Vision project were given to children with impaired vision. In 1986 there was an embroidery competition held for

1980 Janet Wooldridge's Fagin   *1995 County Sampler Winner*   *2010 Liz Cornish's quilt*

the Wildfowl Trust and in 1988 an ad hoc committee was formed to deliver an entry for the William and Mary Tercentenary competition.

In 1991 a competition was launched for a county tablecloth design. It was won by Di Cope and stitched by a group of six members led by Margaret Dalton and Kath Hollands. It was unveiled at the 75th Birthday ACM and is pictured on the back cover of the book. Lesley Grant of Stone WI won the County Sampler competition in 1995. A similar competition for a wall hanging for the Denman bedroom was won by Diana Chester in 1997, for the 80th birthday year. A County Banner is mentioned as being made in 1996. The Mary Pedley competition wall hanging from 1982 inspired the committee in 2000 to ask each WI to produce a second 'block' to depict their community. These were made into three wall hangings which are displayed in the committee room at WI House. Additional blocks for the wall hanging are being made for WFWI's 100th birthday by WIs formed since 2000.

1988 Display for the William and Mary Tercentenary

Outside organisations asked WFWI for help, most notably Huntingdon Hall, Worcester who in 1985 asked if 400 seat covers could be embroidered. The cushions had a red background with cream and green motifs. Home Economics and Craft committee took on the responsibility for this project led by Beth Milsom. By 1988 they were all duly made by WI members who had inundated the committee with offers, but in the end it was felt that the WI received scant recognition for the part they had played.

The County Museum at Hartlebury requested that an exhibition of WI work be displayed in September 1992. Staged by this committee and called 'Not all Jam and Jerusalem', it encompassed all aspects of WI activity.

In 1993 display boards were purchased for promotional purposes and were first used when WI was promoted in Worcester cathedral.

Women's Institute gives pupils the sack

◄ Women's Institute chairwoman Joy Pers presents a story bag to Cranham Drive language centre pupil Robert Jone

Picture: Martin Humby. 59980/33

RALLY MAY 1998

PUPILS at two county schools got an early Christmas present when they were presented with special story sacks by Worcestershire Women's Institute.

The sacks were made by WI members as part of a competition at the WI's Home Economics and Crafts Rally at Perdiswell Leisure Centre, Worcester, earlier this year.

Each of the 15 sacks donated — six of them made by WI member Beryl Village — contains a variety of toys designed to stimulate learning, including board games, puppets and soft toys.

At least one lucky youngster also received a Postman Pat steering wheel to accompany reading.

WI chairman Joy Pers this week presented the sacks to delighted youngsters with special needs at Cranham Drive Primary's 'I Can' Early Language Centre, Warndon.

Also benefiting are pupils at Burlish Nursery School in Stourport-on-Severn, which will shortly be opening a new language centre of its own.

2000 - 144 WIs each created a block for the wall hanging

BERROW'S WORCESTER JOURNAL, JULY 1, 1988

4

A long hard sew

Women's Institute members all over the county are working flat out making seat covers for the Countess of Huntingdon Hall in Worcester.

About 50 seat covers have been completed since the project started in 1986. The first covers were finished for the Three Choirs Festival in August last year.

All in all about 400 seats have to be covered and ex-chairman of Home Economics and Craft now county vice-chairman, Mrs Beth Milsom said although they've still got a long way to go, this summer should see the centre section of the Hall completed. She estimates the whole task should take another two years.

Approximately 200 women and some men are busy sewing from about 60 WI centres. Mrs Milsom said people have been really enthusiastic about the job

with covers being taken to Canada and America to be finished on holidays, some forming groups just to do them and some women even learning canvas work especially to help.

She said: "We're very pleased to be doing something for the city of Worcester — this is the first major heritage project to be done by the WI."

Each cover takes about 100 hours to complete. They are based on a very simple design like a Victorian tile, in three colours, cream, light green and brick red. Workers each use different stitches so each cover looks slightly different.

Mrs Milsom said the project was not limited to WI members or even women, so anyone who would like to help for the satisfaction of knowing their work will be part of Worcester's heritage for years to come should phone her on Pershore 553092 for canvas and wool.

Above: 1988 Presenting the cushions for Huntingdon Hall, Beth Milsom on right

Left: Report about the project

When WFWI were asked to participate in the first Malvern Autumn Show in 1995 this committee had a large input into the exhibit and stand. Both Radio Wyvern and Radio Hereford and Worcester often asked members on to their programmes. Mostly the programmes were recorded but occasionally were nerve rackingly live.

The committee also undertook craft commissions from other sub-committees. In 1982 bridge cloths were made from old curtains, sashes have been made for various events, whilst tabards were made by some members in 1994 for use when serving food. In 2001 Action Packs which WIs could borrow were produced and promoted. Donated sewing machines though proved a headache as they were deemed unsafe. WI Home Economics and Craft Secretaries days were held. By 2002 it was felt that a PA system would be a great asset and so the committee held fund-raisers for this. In 2011 a visualizer was purchased to help improve the audience's view of demonstrations. The WI marquee at the Three Counties was always well supported with both static material and demonstrations.

A Friends of Home Economics and Craft was set up in 1992 and reconfirmed in 2000 and the friends are invited to social occasions.

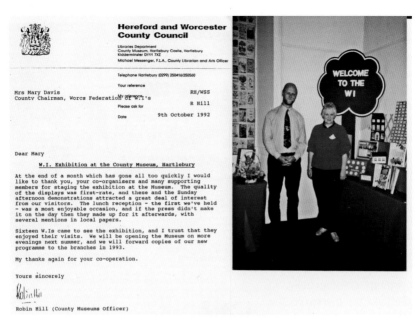

Hereford and Worcester County Council

Libraries Department
County Museum, Hartlebury Castle, Hartlebury
Kidderminster DY11 7XZ
Michael Messenger, F.L.A., County Librarian and Arts Officer

Telephone Hartlebury (0299) 250416/250560

Your reference

Mrs Mary Davis   RH/WSS
County Chairman, Worcs Federation of W.I.'s

Please ask for   R Hill

Date   9th October 1992

Dear Mary

W.I. Exhibition at the County Museum, Hartlebury

At the end of a month which has gone all too quickly I would
like to thank you, your co-organisers and many supporting
members for staging the exhibition at the Museum. The quality
of the displays was first-rate, and these and the Sunday
afternoon demonstrations attracted a great deal of interest
from our visitors. The lunch reception - the first we've held
- was a most enjoyable occasion, and if the press didn't make
it on the day then they made up for it afterwards, with
several mentions in local papers.

Sixteen W.Is came to see the exhibition, and I trust that they
enjoyed their visits. We will be opening the Museum on more
evenings next summer, and we will forward copies of our new
programme to the branches in 1993.

My thanks again for your co-operation.

Yours sincerely

Robin Hill (County Museums Officer)

1992 Display at Hartlebury Castle - Not all Jam and Jerusalem
Robin Hill-curator, Anne Hingley

Art

This committee, like all the others, could put a member forward for the County Sponsored B Course at Denman. This opportunity, discontinued in 1990, allowed the member to learn something new and then use the knowledge to put something back into the community. Di Cope feels that this opportunity was almost life changing as it opened so many doors. She had left school at sixteen despite wishing to stay on and suddenly, here was this exciting, wonderful course which gave her confidence in both her abilities and in herself. She has built a career around her art and handicraft talents but has also made huge contributions to events held by the Art, Home Economics and Craft and Performing Arts committees. A wonderful example of what the WI can do for a person and of course what they in turn can do for others in the County.

There has been a WFWI Art sub-committee since 1963. This grew out of the Art Club which began in 1961. It lost its individual identity in 2008 when it was joined with Home Economics and Craft to form Creative Activities. The minutes show that it was not an entirely happy union at first and it must be said that the number of art based events put on by the combined committee has been reduced by roughly two thirds, excluding the summer painting days.

These summer painting days, with evenings added in 1992 for those who worked, have averaged ten per year over the period. This means that the committee has had to find 380 venues, a mammoth task as permission must be sought from both private and public owners for the group to pitch their easels. Since 1998 they have also arranged an end of season celebratory meal. The days are often held at members' properties for many of these provide interesting corners to paint. The continued attendance illustrates the dedication of the many participants in pursuing and developing their artistic talents.`

224 courses and classes have been offered by the committee, those covering some aspect of painting or drawing form almost half the total. All levels of ability have been accommodated from complete beginner, like Cynthia Jones featured, to those who sell their paintings commercially. In 1984, demand for places on the courses was so strong that the committee recommend to the Board that "Due to excessive oversubscription for classes an overall policy should be adopted for the allocation of places and this policy communicated to members. This might alleviate the disappointment of members who feel that it is not worthwhile trying to attend classes."

Demand for certain events continued, well illustrated in 2013 when the 'I wish I could draw' course was so popular with beginners that it had to be repeated in 2014. The 1990 competition to provide a picture for the Denman bedroom appealed to the more accomplished as did the chance to exhibit. From 1984 to 1986 a postal art course was offered so that demand could be accommodated. Every painting medium has been offered with

Discovering talent at the WI

CYNTHIA Jones discovered a new magic recently. She went along to the WI's Portrait School for the day — and found she could do it.

She was over the moon with excitement. "I've never tried anything like this before," she said. "It's been marvellous — I'm so pleased with the result. I shall be doing a lot more now."

She is one of many women who are finding that WI activities can change their lives.

The Worcester Federation has a lively Art Group, some of whom are experienced and well-qualified, and some of whom are like Cynthia — complete novices discovering a new and exciting form of expression, and their own hidden talents.

Cynthia Jones completes her first attempt at a portrait.

1982 Art course inspiration for Cynthia Jones

1998 A summer painting day

1997 Art Lunch at the end of the summer painting days

oils, watercolour, pastels and acrylics mentioned and so too has every subject from landscape to human figure drawing, from pets to botanical illustration, miniatures and still life.

Calligraphy which was particularly popular in the first two decades, collage, batik, card and paper days, sculpture with various materials, dabble days and photography make up the rest of the art forms on offer. Those held towards the end of the year often had a Christmas theme. Photography has been of greater interest since the advent of the digital camera, six courses being offered since 2008.

2010 Digital Camera Class

Exhibitions. Until 1995 an exhibition of members' artwork was put on biennially, then every four years until 2008. Since then two have been mounted, making eighteen in all. Major County exhibitions were usually staged in the intervening years. Worcester Cathedral and Worcester's Central Library and Art Gallery have been hosts to the larger events but most often WI House or several regional libraries and halls have been the venues.

The amount of work needed to put on exhibitions was quite daunting. The categories were chosen and the schedule sent to WIs. The entries were usually received at WI House over a few days. They were then transported to the venue where the display was arranged for public viewing as well as for judging, normally by non-WI judges. There were 315 entries for the 1983 regional exhibition and a large number for the County exhibition at the City Art Gallery a year later.

Artwork was also displayed and sometimes offered for sale in other places. From 1981 pictures could be displayed on the picture rails in the conference room at WI House and other artefacts such as ceramics could be placed in the display cabinets. Pictures were provided for the Denman bedroom, alternating yearly with Warwickshire, whilst in 1998 ten items were chosen for NFWI's 75th Anniversary Craft Display in Nottingham. A public sale was held at WI House in 1990 when the paintings were hung on the railings in Sansome Walk. Members' pictures were chosen for the calendar in celebration years and a competition was usually held to provide a design for County tea towels, Christmas cards or a card to mark a special national event such as in 1997 when Norma Timms won the design competition to mark 100 years since the start of WI in Canada.

Artwork was also displayed when Worcestershire hosted the Three Counties Refreshment marquee, where the committee often put on painting demonstrations or encouraged children's participation. In 1993 the children could enter a competition to depict the WI. One drew an octopus; considering what a diverse organisation we have this seems to have been a very insightful child.

In 1984 the committee painted several huge panels to beautify the Worcestershire catering area at the Royal Show. The next year Worcestershire art was featured in Home and Country magazine, in 1990 forty banners were made for 'Cavalcade 90' and in 2003 Cinderella's coach was made for the Carol Concert.

Outside speakers and committee members gave twenty-four talks, lectures and demonstrations. The talks ranged over subjects such as individual painters, painting techniques and art history but the committee

1997 Norma Timms card for 100 years of WI

ceased putting on demonstrations in 1991 when they felt that they were no longer able to carry all the necessary equipment up the flights of stairs in WI House.

In 1980, and again in 1992, financial difficulties are mentioned in the Art minutes. Fund-raising events were introduced, twenty-four in all, most being outings usually visiting museums or art galleries around Britain. A shoppers' lunch was offered in 1980, a ploughman's lunch two years later and several coffee mornings were held at WI House where art was on display. The committee also held two weekend holiday breaks.

In 2008 one of its members, Joanne Powell, became an Associate of the Society of Women Artists – one of only 140 worldwide.

2016 Members' artwork at the ACM

Leisure and Pleasure

This committee was formed in 2011 when the Sport and Leisure sub-committee amalgamated with the Fund-raising sub-committee. In 2010 the Sport and Leisure sub-committee could not find a chairman and so amalgamation with Fund-raising was suggested. It did not find favour at first but eventually the merger took place in 2011 and the joint committee has functioned since as Leisure and Pleasure. Operating in the 1980's, the previous County Promotions sub-committee members are included in the following figures. There have been 88 members serving, sixteen as chairmen, although Greta Mitchell chaired the two separate committees, and 48 serving on this sub-committee only. A total of 558 events have been staged with a further 31 cancelled. Each of the original sub-committees will be dealt with separately.

Sport and Leisure

The Executive Committee provided some sporting activity for members between 1980 and 1983 for there is mention in the minutes of golf and tennis competitions, a swimming gala and a sports day at Perdiswell Leisure Centre which could accommodate 1,500. The introduction of bridge days at WI House in 1982 heralded the provision of leisure pursuits too and in 1983 Sport and Leisure was inaugurated as a new sub-committee to offer those activities which were increasingly being looked for by members alongside the traditional WI interests. The initial narrow range had expanded by 2017 with forty-six different sports and pastimes tried by WI members over the thirty-five years to date. 342 events have been offered in total. Jill Hammonds and Peggy Mytton had served for

Served on Leisure and Pleasure Committee

Joan Ainsworth	Mrs Knight
Sheena Aitken	Clarice Knowles
Jane Baker	Mary Lou Lockyer
Anne Ballard	Iris Montgomery
Eleanor Barrett	Mollie Long
Margaret Bazley*	Pam Lowe*
Sylvia Bettison	Barbara Maskell
Joy Blakeway	Bunty Masters
Beryl Bubb	Diana Milligan
Angela Burden	Margaret Mills
Megan Bury	Beth Milsom
Marion Cadbury	Greta Mitchell*
Ann Canham*	Fiona Mitchell
Monica Carden*	Pam Morton
Diana Cartmel*	Janet Murphy*
Janet Coe	Peggy Mytton*
Pat Crook*	Shirley Noble
Freda Davies	Margaret Norris*
Elizabeth Davies	Liz Osborn*
Margaret Deakin	Barbara Pallister
Sheila Dent	Kathleen Pardoe
Liz Dove	Elizabeth Parker-Jarvis
Margaret Dufty	
Ann Edwards	Sylvia Perkins
Beryl Evans	Nita Pritchard
June Garvey	Roma Punt*
Lesley Grant	Jane Richardson
Anne Green	Grace Richardson
June Green	Rosemary Roberts
H Guest	Julia Rogers*
Heidi Hague	Evelyn Rose*
Jill Hammonds*	Jeanne Round
Pat Harris	Elizabeth Rowley
Janet Harris	Rosemary Sadler
Marion Hawkes	Shirley Smith
Christine Henderson	Anne Smith
Dallas Henderson	Mary Thorpe
Christine Hickman-Smith	Sylvia Tudor Hughes*
	Patricia Waddington
Sandra Hill	Mavis Ward
Pauline Hopwood	Mary Wehner
Eileen Howard	Marjorie Whiting
Betty Hudson	Christine Williams
Sue Jennings	Lynn Winters
Betty Johnson	
Janice Jones	* = Chairman

21 and 15 years respectively when they retired in 2004 and one committee member, Liz Osborn, served on the National Sports and Leisure committee.

1986 Sports' Taster Day at Perdiswell

None of the activities has had a continuous presence during the sub-committee's life. The bridge drive comes closest, appearing yearly from 1984 until 2017. 33 of the 34 days were run by Diana Cartmel, Freda Davies taking over in 2017. Diana tutored all of the 21 sets of bridge lessons offered by the Federation, the last being in 2009. The lessons were very popular and by 1995 over 1,000 members had taken the opportunity to learn the game. Diana knew something about bridge when her own WI asked her to take a class but was certainly not a teacher. Expressing her reluctance on getting home that evening, her husband's bridge partners encouraged her to do it, promising to supply the notes, hands etcetera. It went well, another door opened and she developed her teaching talents. The rest is Sport and Leisure history.

2014-15 Skittles competition

Diana Cartmel, in blue, at a bridge drive

A skittles tournament was re-instated in 1987. The response was overwhelming and the challenge has been taken up each year since with a record ninety-five teams taking part in 1995. The event is organised by placing each six-member WI team into a group on a roughly local basis. The winner of each group plays either in the semi-finals or just the final depending on the number of teams participating, the winner holding the trophy for a year.

In 1997 the rules had to be clarified and yet again in 1999. Despite these problems and the dwindling number of skittle alleys available for hire, this competition is still going strong after thirty-one years. Competitions are eagerly and energetically contested by all teams but can also be a source of fellowship between WIs.

Smite or Cornish skittles, a variation of the game, was trialled in 2011 and a set was bought for hire by WIs.

The competitive spirit of the movement is also displayed at the quiz evenings. Seventeen contests have been arranged since its 1990 inception as Sport and Leisure's competition for the Mary Pedley award. Offered on a biennial basis at first but becoming an annual event in 2007, it has attracted as many as 112 teams, each consisting of four players. Such large numbers have required as many as three venues around the County. Two winning teams, Hampton in 1998 and Beoley in 2013 went on to play in the NFWI finals.

There has been success at National level too in table tennis, with Peggy Mytton and Diane Bidwell winning for three successive years

2015 Smite set on show at the Three Counties. Marion Cumella

1990 Table Tennis Peggy Mytton, Diane Bidwell

between 1994 and 1996 and coming second in 1997. The first of the eight table tennis tournaments was mentioned in 1989. The other tennis, lawn tennis, offered by the County, also had national finalists in Clarice Knowles and Jean Kennedy, who took part at Queen's Club in 1987. There were twenty-nine tennis events in the County, fourteen tournaments,

1980 Tennis Lesson by Mrs Purchon

1987 Clarice Knowles, Jean Kennedy

Bowling maidens over

Bowling 'em over — WI members took part in a bowls tournament at Droitwich's Vine Park recently, and found it exciting and, occasionally frustrating.

BERROWS JOURNAL

19. 6. 85

eleven courses of lessons and four social days. Another racquet sport, badminton, had four courses devoted to it.

Green bowling was first offered in 1984 and there have been seventeen bowling events and one tournament. Indoor mat bowling was added in 1990. Four more sets of lessons and a tournament followed and a County team reached the National finals in 1993.

Golf was an early passion for Federation members. Aspiring golfers were offered twelve sets of lessons. There was a competition in 1980 and this one, like all the other seventeen, was organised by a non-committee member. The weather was not always kind. In 1994 the twenty-nine competitors played in appalling weather. A joint golf and croquet day was offered in 1996 whilst the skills of croquet could be learned in the eight sets of lessons or taster days offered. That of 2004 was oversubscribed with forty-six lucky members taking part. The latest taster day was held in 2012.

Swimming too was an early sport on a County basis when in 1981 a gala took place. There was much swimming organised at local and group level but the sub-committee has offered nine swimming events including several very successful sponsored swims. One yielded £1,000 which was

1980 Golf Lesson

168

divided equally between the Federation and WIs, whilst that of 1986 raised money for Denman. Other water based sports have been few and unlucky. Fly fishing went ahead twice but an aquarobics course planned for 1993 was cancelled through lack of interest, a water sports day in Sandwell Valley was cancelled by the venue, the Foot and Mouth outbreak put paid to a sailing course in 2001 and the brine baths visit of 2009 failed when the venue stopped trading.

1999 Betty Johnson go-carting

There have been seven Sports Days and two health and fitness days which have often allowed minority sports to be tried. One such was go-carting in 1999 with the press featuring the County Chairman in her car. It was hoped that the Archers radio programme would advertise the health and fitness day arranged jointly with Home Economics and Craft in 1992, whilst a Sports Council grant aided the sports day in 1986.

One Rummikub and nine Scrabble competitions have allowed members to exercise their brain power whilst accuracy of eye was fostered by six darts and pool evenings, and two archery and two snooker coaching events. Success at the snooker table made one participant comment "Oh what a thrill to pot a black!"

Some activities have been offered as a one off. Sixty-three people enjoyed hot air ballooning in 1996 despite one balloon coming down with a bump in a cow field in Powyke, somewhat short of the desired destination. Netball, gliding, abseiling, line dancing and a gym visit also fall into the single event category, whilst talks, rounders and clay pigeon shooting have been tried twice. Thirty members, many from newly formed WIs, enjoyed the second shooting day held in 2015 and a karting and crossbow day was offered in 2017. There have been four car maintenance and driving courses and in 1990, 120 Worcestershire members entered the NFWI car driver of the year competition. Four horse riding events, of either a day or weekend duration were enjoyed, the latter at Llangorse in Wales. One of

2015 Clay Pigeon Shooting

13th JUNE 1996
BALLOONING FROM WORCESTER RACECOURSE TO MADRESFIELD.

1996 Hot Air Ballooning

the three orienteering competitions attracted sixty participants, whilst of the five cycle rides one, the ten mile ride in 1985, took the form of a treasure hunt.

To all this must be added five activity weekends away and ten outings to a wide variety of venues such as the Horse of the Year Show, Porton Down, local farms, canal trips, skid pan driving and pamper days.

Numerically, walking events have been the most prolific activity. Thirty-six varied walks have been arranged. One was a town ghost walk but the rest were in Worcestershire's beautiful countryside, the one through the Wyre Forest alone attracting eighty-six participants. There have been ambles followed by tea, more energetic walkers' walks, rambles on hills such as Bredon, Kinver and Clent where fifty took part, walking weekends on Exmoor and in the Elan Valley, a walk along the Severn Valley preceded by a train ride, and walks to view flora and fauna, these including orchids, fungi and butterflies, and to hear the birds' morning chorus in spring.

Added to this there were four larger walking events. In 1995 many members accompanied Freda Davies on her walk around the county when she passed through their part of Worcestershire – see page 59. The Millennium 'Ride and Stride', part of National's 'Fitness for Life' initiative, allowed twenty-eight WIs to contribute 22,000 miles and some very beautifully illustrated logs of their walking and cycling routes. This inspired many WIs

2015 WFWI day ramble around Abberley

2014 Visit to Wimbledon

2008 Celebrating walking on the Worcestershire Way

2017 One of three successful dragon boat days at Pershore

to hold at least one monthly ramble which was useful again when supporting the 2015 'Moon Mission'. Here the aim was to accumulate the miles to the Moon through the combined hiking activities of participants and was organised by the University of Worcester. WFWI's 90th Birthday was marked by walking 31 miles of the Worcestershire Way. Done in five stages during May to September with transport to and from the route, parts were attempted by many and twenty-five members completed the whole length. The weather was not always kind. It varied, as it must have done for all the outside events. These walkers experienced everything from torrential rain to hot sunshine but held a celebration at the finish which featured a wonderfully iced cake.

In 1986 a system of WI sports representatives was started although this seemed to fade away fairly quickly

Most of the events offered by Leisure and Pleasure have been ascribed to their original committee but a few new ideas have surfaced such as dragon boat racing, zumba and tai chi days. In 2011 a Federation sports representative was appointed in response to a NFWI initiative whilst in 2014 taster days were offered through Sue Bentley, a club and volunteer officer funded by the Government and Sport England. Joint sub-committee events were being encouraged by the Board, and Leisure and Pleasure provided a diamond talk at the 2012 Jubilee Garden Party, a treasure hunt at Arley Arboretum organised with Public Affairs, a 'Behind the Scenes at Wimbledon' visit, so popular that it was run twice and the arrangements for the London Eye and river boat trips as part of the Federation outing to London in 2013.

Fund-Raising

In 1987 the Executive was worried about the financial state of the Federation, especially as to how to keep course fees at a reasonable level during a time of rapidly rising costs. The solution was the initiation in 1988 of a Fund-raising ad hoc committee which would provide money for the general use of the Federation.

However, it would be erroneous to think that there were no dedicated fund-raising efforts before 1987. A County Promotions sub-committee had been active since at least 1954 selling items to the membership and to the public at outside events. This was renamed as the Calendar sub-committee in 1980, renamed again as Sales Promotions and reverted to County Promotions in 1983 to reflect the increasing range of goods for sale. Evelyn Rose was its chairman from 1980 to 1986, followed by Roma Punt until it was disbanded in 1988. Fifteen members served on this sub-committee and are included in the total for Leisure and Pleasure.

The 1988 ad hoc committee was such a success that in 1992 Fund-raising became a permanent sub-committee. It was chaired from inception to 2002 by Greta Mitchell who remained on the committee until 2013. It has had a total of five chairmen and one of them, Julia Rogers, served on the committee for 17 years. From 1988 onwards it has put on 218, mostly large, events.

It took on the lucrative sales side of the former County Promotions committee, continuing both to produce a yearly calendar and to sell goods. The goods are referred to as County Items and continue to be offered to both members and the general public.

Over the years the County Items have included stationery and cards, small gifts, diaries, tea towels, bags, scarves and, occasionally, clothing with a WI County Logo. Members were encouraged to produce designs for the special Christmas cards and tea towels sold by the Federation, often in a competition organised in conjunction with the Art sub-committee.

2012 Selling County Items at the Three Counties
Janet Allbutt, Janet Murphy

The rest of the merchandise has been chosen by the member of the committee nominated to look after this aspect of fund-raising and which, over the period, has contributed many thousands of pounds to Federation Funds. It is a demanding job. These goods must be sourced, approved and marked up for sale and each year there is a stock-take. The stock in 1984

2015 Three Counties. Selling haberdashery-a new venture

comprised 2,700 sheets of wrapping paper, 1,000 sweet making books, 550 tea towels, leisurewear comprising six trousers and two navy sweatshirts, 42 jotters, 21 boxes of postcards and one pack of stationery. County Items are generally available at WI House but are also taken to most County events, especially council meetings

The person in charge of the County Items transports them, sets up and sells at whatever venue is visited. Selling opportunities have arisen by request at WI and Group meetings and at Market venues. They are also sold at local fetes and County shows, especially the Three Counties, where they bring in income from the public and at the same time help to promote WI. This person became known in 1992 as the Publications Officer as the role also included selling NFWI merchandise too, especially their publications. The name was changed to Sales Officer in 2002 for by then the amount of NFWI merchandise sold directly by WFWI had diminished.

The position of Sales Officer was advertised in CNL in 2011, and 2015 saw a rethink on County Items. New items were sourced and in 2016 blue boxes containing them were made up for WIs to take out and sell at their own meetings or events.

In 1980, £1,240 profit was made from about 12,000 calendar sales and a County calendar continues to be produced yearly although with a much-reduced number, down to 2,000 in 2015, fewer in 2016, when to add to the decline some of the batch had to be returned as they were printed badly. Perhaps fewer paper calendars are now used because more use is made of digital organisers. In most years members' photographs on an aspect of Worcestershire have been featured, but in celebration years members' paintings have often been used. In 1986 there were 151 photographs submitted and it was very hard to choose only twelve. The size and layout has varied but the illustration has almost always been a detachable post card.

| 1980 | 1986 | 1997 | 2017 |

To these sales' staples the ad hoc committee in its first year added some interesting new ideas These were the 200 Club with its own account inspired by the successful 1986 grand draw, a male voice choir concert, a grand sale, a flower arranging evening, a fashion show, catering at the Heart of the County show at Grafton Flyford and a Christmas shopping outing to Bath.

The years have proved that the original events offered by the ad hoc committee were ones members most liked to support. There have been thirty Christmas shopping trips since 1988, with Bath and Cardiff seeming to be favourite destinations as they have been visited three times each. These usually attract members in the hundreds but the largest number of coaches recorded was sixteen to Cardiff in 1995, a total of over seven hundred people. A Saturday was offered in 2008 but this did not prove popular as numbers were well down. Most trips went smoothly, but in 1989 fifteen coaches fought their way through fog to Oxford, in 2010 one coach did not reach Nottingham because of an accident and another year a husband was left behind in London. The minutes report that apparently his wife didn't seem at all bothered by the loss. Throughout these tours only two persons are recorded as having missed the return journey, although eight were left behind at Blakedown on one London outing, this happening because someone had changed the pick-up point with the coach firm but not agreed it with the organiser. Town centres have been the main destinations but Chatsworth, for its Christmas decorations in the house and market in the grounds, proved very popular in 2013 with over five hundred participants. A craft fair at Blenheim Palace in 2015 was greatly enjoyed and three coaches took members to Waddesden Manor in 2017.

A summer outing was introduced in 1990 and there have been twenty-five of these to date, mainly to scenic towns. Three weekend visits have been enjoyed such as that to Kew and Wisley Gardens, whilst the day trips to Trooping of the Colour, river cruises and stately homes have been much enjoyed. One day trip in 1996 to the Derbyshire well dressings produced an interesting moment for County Chairman Mary Wehner. She boarded each coach as they prepared to leave Buxton and gave a small speech, hoping that the members had enjoyed the day. On the last coach she was surprised to be thanked in a broad Yorkshire accent. The realisation dawned that she was on the wrong vehicle. She had not been addressing Worcestershire ladies at all but some tourists from further north. In 2017 a visit to Salisbury Museum was offered to see the knitted spoons done by WI members countrywide but was cancelled through lack of support.

There have been eight events featuring entertainment by choirs and jazz groups and seven events with a flower arranging or gardening theme, the largest being the 1988 flower festival at Hartlebury. Six fashion shows, including one in 1994 which welcomed members of the Scottish Women's Rural Institutes and the 'Looking Good: Feeling Great' days, have influenced members' wardrobes. Maybe some of these clothes were worn at the twenty or so lunches or suppers featuring a celebrity speaker. Topics at these lunches have ranged from antiques to the River Severn, A Woman to the North Pole and a Victorian Christmas, whilst well known speakers such as Jennie Bond have been engaged for celebration years such as the Queen's Golden Jubilee. Hats were encouraged at the six summer tea parties of the 'noughties', especially at the Mad Hatter's tea party for WFWI's ninetieth birthday.

The sale of bulbs began in 1991 and has continued off and on ever since, whilst the fund-raising quiz, one hundred questions on topics such as colours or motorcars, starting in 1994, had a loyal following through its ten variations. Special evening store openings for members at Beatties and Lakeland in Worcester were much appreciated as were the very large craft fairs organised during the 1990's at Worcester's Guildhall with fifty stalls and catering to tempt the visitors.

2012 Fashion Show at Hartlebury Castle

The committee members themselves provided the catering for most of the functions which involved food, including Harvest lunches in 1994. These lunches proved particularly hard work.

In 2000 the Board approved a Friends of Fund-raising team to help out when required. In 2003, in line with Health and Safety rules, committee members who were responsible for food at events obtained food hygiene certificates but for the last few years, food has often been brought in as the committee had begun to find the catering was too much for them.

The monthly draw, with cash prizes, continued for twenty-one seasons. At first named the 200 Club, this was changed to the Supporter's Club in 1994. In 2011 it became Worcestershire Winners but then NFWI informed WFWI that charity law only allowed individual participation. Thus, many of the WIs had to drop out rendering it unfeasible and it was discontinued.

Special celebration events have been organised. The first summer outing was Fund-

2008 Committee members in the kitchen at Little Witley[24]

raising's contribution to NFWI's seventy-fifth anniversary whilst their Worcestershire cookbook marked WFWI's seventy-fifth year (see pages 61 and 157/158). Recipes were donated by members and the book was launched, with a demonstration of some of the recipes, at two venues. 140 came to Hanley Swan and such was the demand that Chaddesley Corbett had to host two sessions as 347 booked there. At both Chaddesley demonstrations police traffic wardens were needed to control the event.

The train outing was brought back for the same 1993 celebrations and the visit to Cambridge was heavily over-subscribed with 811 wanting the 341 places on offer. It went ahead with the addition of two motor coaches carrying those from the south of the county. Although successful, its organisation was fraught with problems and this really was where the train outing finally went into the siding for good.

In 2006 the move to Hallow meant that at least one committee member had to give up as she had no transport, and, at this time the holidays were brought under the wing of Fund-raising, staying until 2010.

In 2011 when major fund-raising events were again brought under the Board's direction the name was no longer describing the work of the committee and so Fund-Raising merged with Sport and Leisure to become The Leisure and Pleasure sub-committee.

---

[24] L-R Julia Rogers, Pat Crook, Liz Osborne, Janice Jones, Greta Mitchell, Molly Long, Margaret Dufty

Centenary Preparations

So, the wheel has come full circle for this book. Almost at the start, the Diamond Jubilee Celebration events were covered: Part One now ends with the plans for the celebration of 100 Years of the Worcestershire Federation. These are well advanced and the membership can look forward to a very varied year of entertainment.

2017 The Centenary Ad hoc Committee[25]

An ad hoc committee was set up in 2015 to formulate and co-ordinate the activities and the BoT asked Christine Hickman-Smith to be its chairman. Those who make up the rest of the committee are the County Treasurer Sue Chilton, cakemaker Sheila O'Shaughnessy, Centenary Book author Sylvia Beardshaw, Suzanne Owen, together with representatives drawn from Advisers and the five sub-committees. The same representatives for some of the latter come to all the meetings, whilst others send different members to the two or three meetings per year. Minutes are taken by a committee member and issued by the Administrator after being approved by the BoT.

The first item off the ground was this book. It was introduced at the 2013 ACM and the Federation WIs were each asked to write a page for its second section. Its launch is planned for the 2018 Spring meeting.

From 2015 the following plans were gradually put in place.

Rose Bank Vineyard in Fernhill Heath agreed to dedicate its 2016 vintage of Phoenix white wine grapes to bottles labelled to celebrate the Centenary. WI members were invited to pick the grapes and this was done in October 2016. Bottled at Halfpenny Green, it went on sale at the 2017 ACM.

For 2018, a Centenary Lunch, a Grand Draw the proceeds of which will go to the County's Hospices, a garden display at the Worcester Breast Unit, flowers in Worcester Cathedral, a coach trip and a walk on the Evesham Blossom Trail, and a buffet lunch and a piece of celebration cake for all attendees at the 2018 ACM, are being arranged.

A resolution on mental health, submitted by Louise Jones of Callow End WI and taken forward by the Advisers, has made the national shortlist. Advisers will also organise carpet bedding in Kidderminster. Hot Peppers WI also plan carpet bedding in Upton on Severn. Public Affairs will assist with the Resolution and make a banner featuring 100 years of campaigning. Performing Arts plan a Musical Evening at Avoncroft Museum which will feature many varied artists and the lighting of the grounds. They are also planning a Carol

---

[25] L-R Back - Janet Murphy, Sue Chilton*, Sheila O'Shaughnessy*, Patience Broad, Pat Jones, Sylvia Beardshaw*
Front - Marion Cumella, Marjorie Whiting, Christine Hickman-Smith*-chairman, Suzanne Owen*
*= permanent members; sub-committees send various representatives

Service in the Cathedral with a members' centenary choir. Creative Activities have asked all WIs formed since 2000 to complete a panel to be added to the 2000 wall-hanging and much of this is completed. They will decorate a Christmas tree at the Cathedral with glittering baubles made by members. Marketing and Development launched a logo competition in 2016, which was won by Gemma Dewson, and are producing a diary of events in the form of a bookmark for distribution to the WIs. Leisure and Pleasure decided on events with a water theme and these will be delivered through the Groups. It will arrange dragon boat races too and a Christmas card competition. It is also ordering or commissioning centenary items for sale - a calendar, a tea towel (draft shown below) and a hessian bag both featuring the winning logo, a mug, and notelets depicting the 2000 wall hanging.

*2016 Grape picking at Fernhill Heath
for the Centenary Wine*

With many of the plans now in place, it is the Board of Trustees which will be overseeing the Centenary Celebrations.

**The Board of Trustees of
The Worcestershire Federation
for 2017/18**

Sue Stone - Chairman
Sue Chilton - Treasurer
Margaret Bazely
Marion Hawkes – Asst Treasurer
Anne Smith – Vice Chairman
Rosie Thom
Sue White – Vice Chairman
Marjorie Whiting
Rosie Wynne

*Top row:
Rosie Thom, Sue White, Margaret Bazely, Marion Hawkes, Rosie Wynne
Front row: Anne Smith, Sue Chilton, Sue Stone, Marjorie Whiting*

Part Two

The WIs of the Worcestershire Federation

The map[26] shows the 125 WIs of the Worcestershire Federation which are listed in the 2017/18 Yearbook. It will be seen that there are four WIs based just outside the northern county boundary but who choose to be in the Worcestershire Federation - Kinver Village, Pedmore, Stourton and Wychbury.

---

[26] The original version of this map was a large A1 size format, made in 2003 by Sylvia Beardshaw for the Marketing and Development Committee for use at promotional events. A digitized version was kindly prepared in 2004 by a friend of the author and 'WI Husband', Ron Fenney of Leicestershire. The WFWI version is now updated annually by the printers of the Yearbook. It replaces a hand drawn map which had appeared in the Handbook since 1996.

No celebration by WFWI would be complete without the individual WIs writing about their activities since the Diamond Jubilee: the author's thinking in 2013 when asked to write this book. Having seen examples of this type of work, both in WFWI archives and at Denman, such a second section would add greatly to the volume, thus covering every aspect of the WI in Worcestershire 1980 to 2018.

Each WI was asked to produce one page about their activities and to nominate a member to oversee its production. Some WIs produced their page very quickly, the largest proportion, with some encouragement from me, by the December 2016 deadline. Others remained outstanding but, with even more chivvying, by mid-September 2017, all were gathered in. Editing was done where necessary and, as with the rest of the book, my husband has been good enough to format the pages. Each WI has been sent its page for approval.

At first, many were daunted by the thought of trying to pack nearly forty years of their WI's activities into 500 words or 450 plus a photo or two. The guidelines also stated that they could show themselves however they wished, in picture only, concentrating on one facet or any other way they devised. Taking up the challenge they have provided a rich tapestry of life in the Federation's WIs and I thank all the contributors for their work, their help and the joyous way in which the overwhelming majority approached their page.

In 1980 there were 177 WIs listed in the handbook. As the Centenary approaches, 125 are listed in the 2017/18 yearbook. The table below shows how the number of WIs has decreased over the decades since the Diamond Jubilee. It also shows the falling membership, though this has stabilised in the 21st century.

	Number of WIs	Total membership[27]
1980	177	7300
1990	167	5920
2000	157	4945
2010	134	About 4000
2017	125	4139

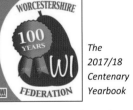

The 2017/18 Centenary Yearbook

As in other Federations, the map is not static, for new WIs open and existing ones close. The decade by decade number of WIs in the table therefore belies the fact that there have been a total of 235 individual Worcestershire WIs during the period. Of these 235, 108 have closed and thus many WIs which existed between 1980 and 2018 are not represented in the following WI pages. A few closed WIs did accept the invitation to submit a page and some have closed since submitting their page. All of the closed WIs are named at the end of this introduction.

Of the 177 who enjoyed the Diamond Jubilee, 91 remain open. Of the lost 86, nine are recorded as having enlarged with current WIs and two joined bordering counties to ease travelling. The remaining 75 were closed. The names of four were subsequently used by a new foundation – Arley & District, Barnt Green, Webheath and Welland.

---

[27] All totals except for 2017 are taken from the Annual Financial Reports

58 WIs have been added to the County since 1980. Kinver Village joined from a neighbouring county and five are re-formations, the four noted above plus Wychbold which had just closed by 1980. Of these 58, twenty-four have closed and thirty-four remain active.

It is interesting to look at the formation dates of our WIs. The data summarised in the table below has been provided by WIs, WFWI's MCS and NFWI. NFWI were unable to supply opening dates for 21 WIs which were active in 1980 but have since closed. Nine of our present WIs were formed before the Federation came into being in November 2018, although there had been a Conference since 1917. The nine, in order of longevity, Pershore – 1916; Bromsgrove, Hadzor and Oddingley, Mamble-cum-Bayton and Hanbury – 1917, have all celebrated their own centenaries, whilst those formed in 1918 will celebrate along with the Federation in 2018 and they are Salwarpe, Malvern, Wolverley and Droitwich Spa.

Year opened	Active in 1980 or opened since 1980	Of which not active by 2017	Still Active in 2017
Pre 1920	15	4	11
1920s	47	23	24
1930s	27	9	18
1940s	19	8	11
1950s	15	6	9
1960s	28	13	15
1970s	5	2	3
Not available but pre 1980	21	21	-
1980s	14	9	5
1990s	18	11	7
2000s	6	2	4
2010-2017	20	2	18
Totals	235	110	125

Our 125 WIs have a very wide range of member numbers, the smallest having only 8, the largest 83. The numbers in the table below are based on data from WIs and from the County office.

Number of members in a WI	Number of WIs
Under 20	21
20 to 29	27
30 to 39	36
40 to 49	21
50 to 59	10
60 to 69	5
70 or more	5

A list of the 125 current WIs, shown by year opened, is at the end of the book.

The 131 WIs who provided an entry for the book were asked where they meet and if they had changed venue since 1980. 81 replied that they meet in a Village Hall or Community Centre, 35 meet in a Church or Chapel Hall, 5 use Schools, 4 use Memorial or Remembrance Halls, 2 meet in Scout Huts, 2 at Bromsgrove Stroke Centre, 1 at a Senior Citizens Centre and Queenhill and District owns its own hall. Thirty-one are noted as moving premises with one, Pershore, selling its own hall to Pershore council but being given free access to its present venue. Two meet in one village hall in summer and in another in winter.

Meeting times and days vary. 109 record evening meetings, 16 meet in the afternoon, 5 in the morning and one meets in the afternoon in winter and the evening in summer. Wednesday is the most popular day for meetings with 51 WIs choosing it, 30 choose

Thursday, 25 Tuesday, 24 Monday but only one meets on Friday. Whichever day is preferred the second one in the month is most popular with 71 WIs meeting then. 33 meet in the first week, 24 meet in the third week and only 3 in the fourth.

2016 Display at ACM celebrating Pershore's 100th Birthday - the first in Worcestershire

1978 Queenhill and District members care for their hall

Most of the WIs existing between 1980 and the Centenary take their names from their location although some names like Oak Apple, St Peter's, Swanpool and Trotshill Totties all in Worcester, Chad's and Somerleyton in Kidderminster, Hot Peppers in Upton-upon-Severn, Honeybees at Honeybourne, St Gabriel's in Hanley Swan and the two Bookends, Early and Late Editions, do not necessarily proclaim their location without a bit of thought. The Bookends were named for their meeting place at Alvechurch library. Late Edition was subsequently renamed to become Ark Angels. This is the name of the Ark meeting room at St Laurence's, Alvechurch. Pump House in North Worcester is also named after its meeting place. There were three names inspired by workplaces. Abberley Clockwatchers takes its name from the clock-tower in the grounds of the school where they meet. Two others, County Hall Swans and Malvern Mods also had workplace names but have closed. The less obvious names geographically usually occur when further WIs are formed in a location. This is the case with Brockencote in Chaddesley Corbett, Wychbury of Pedmore, Whitton and SPArkles in Droitwich Spa, and Finstall Cross is named after a pub in Finstall. Kingfisher in Redditch, now suspended, is named after the naval ship which Redditch town has long supported.

Apart from name changes on enlargement, four other WIs besides Ark Angels have been noted as having a name change. Barnards Green became Malvern Green, Cropthorne added Charlton, Hillside, which took the name of the Hillside Telephone Exchange became Hillside@Alvechurch, and West Malvern Wenches became West Malvern. Also, Hagley became Hagley Afternoon although it seems that by 1980 it was generally known by the latter name.

By 2017, the minutes show that many WIs had their own email address and websites. 20 had a generic email address, 24 had a website, 16 were on Facebook.

1998

The many activities of the WIs are shown in the following pages but additionally the achievements of the WIs include Fairfield winning the press report competition in 1997, Mamble-cum-Bayton campaigning to save facilities at Kidderminster Hospital and in 2017 Hot Peppers reaching the final round of Tonight at The London Palladium, a TV show with Bradley Walsh, although they were unable to take part.

Quotes from Ripple WI on their page highlight the joys of membership and the benefits it brings, as do quotes and comments on many other pages. Most prospective members go along in the company of an established member and WIs cannot charge anyone for entry but can ask for a donation. Perhaps the most bizarre introduction to WI came from cutting the front lawn. Nothing unusual about that you might think until it is realised that the passing WI members were stopped in their tracks when they saw that a pair of scissors being used for the task. Intrigued, they asked why it was being done this way. Well, the shears are locked in the shed and I promised to do it, was the reply. Recognising good WI material, they invited her to their next meeting. How right they were, Jeanne Round became County Chairman in 1981 and is still a staunch WI'er in her 90's.

With 235 WIs in total during the period covered by this book and 125 still active, this is what happened to the 'lost' 110: -

Two left the Federation to join neighbouring counties:
  Bredon (founded 1923) to Gloucestershire 1980
  Cradley (founded 1938) to Herefordshire 1980

The nine recorded as having ceased on enlargement with a current WI are:
  Astwood Bank (founded 1933) enlarged 1997 with Cookhill, *named Cookhill*
  Cofton Hackett (founded 1948) enlarged 2005 with Finstall, *renamed Finstall & Cofton Hackett*
  Crabbs Cross & Hunt End (founded 1965) enlarged 2007 with Ipsley, *renamed Ipsley with Crabbs Cross, later renamed Ipsley*
  Earls Croome (founded 1938) enlarged 2015 with Ripple, *renamed Ripple & Earls Croome*
  Hagley Evening (founded 1965) enlarged 2015 with Hagley Afternoon, *renamed Hagley*
  Hill & Moor (founded 1939) enlarged 2005 with Fladbury, *renamed Fladbury & Moor*
  Kempsey Afternoon (founded 1966) enlarged 1998 with Kempsey Evening, *renamed Kempsey*
  Rushwick & Upper Wick (founded 1938) enlarged 2005 with Cotheridge & Broadheath, *renamed Broadheath with Rushwick*
  Suckley (founded 1950) enlarged 2004 with Alfrick, *named Alfrick*

Where an enlargement takes place the WI which ceases is treated as closing immediately – there is no period of suspension – and all its records and assets are transferred to the enlarged WI.

The remaining 99 which closed are listed on the next page with their original formation year, where known, and the year of suspension. The official closure does not occur until three years after suspension. Some of these 99 may have ceased on enlargement but no such information has been found. Arley & District is shown twice as the WI which started in 2001 took the same name as the one which closed in 1992. Those on the list shown as closed in 2015 onwards are still suspended as at the end of 2017.

WIs which Closed between 1980 and 2017, or are suspended
(with year of formation where available, and year of suspension)

Arley & District 1945-1992
Arley & District 2000-2016
Avoncroft 1991-1995
Barbourne 1986-2003
Barnsley Hall 1971-1991
Barnt Green 1916-2001
Belbroughton 1922-2013
Berrow & District 1944-2005
Birlingham 1922-2007
Bookends First Edition 2010-2012
Bournheath 1958-1994
Bretforton Pre 1980-1990
Broadwaters 1990-1992
Broadway 1919-2004
Broomhall 1997-2013
Burford 1923-1994
Charford Estate 1966-2002
Church Lench Pre 1980-1983
Churchill Pre 1980-1986
Claines 1920-2002
Cleeve Prior 1945-2014
Comer 1991-2014
Cookley 1929-2016
County Hall Swans 2007-2011
Defford 1963-2014
Drakes Broughton & District 1959-1995
Eastham Pre 1980-1983
Elmley Castle 1922-1998
Evesham 1992-1997
Great Witley 1922-2014
Grimley 1921-1995
Habberley 1966-2017
Harvington 1924-2013
Headless Cross 1929-1993
Heightington 1944-2016
Heronswood 1986-2008
Hindlip Pre 1980-1985
Honeybourne 1926-2003
Interfield & Half Key Pre 1980-1982
Kingfisher 1985-2015
Knighton On Teme 1925-2006
Lickhill 1995-2012
Little Comberton Pre 1980-1995
Lindridge 1919-1994
Lower Wick 1997-2000
Lyppard Grange 1995-2005
Madresfield 1917-1994
Malvern Common 1928-2007
Malvern (Barnards to 2009) Green 1992-2016
Malvern Link 1946-2005

Malvern Mods 2014-2016
Malvern Wells Pre 1980-1987
Marlfield 1984-1987
Norton & Lenchwick 1929-2009
Offenham 1925-2003
Ombersley & Doverdale 1920-2010
Overbury Pre 1980-1984
Pickersleigh 1966-2014
Pinvin Pre 1980-1988
Pound Green & Button Oak 1953-2010
Rochford & District 1964-1996
Romsley & Hunnington 1939-2008
Ronkswood 1991-1992
Rous Lench Pre 1980-1985
Rowney Green Pre 1980-1989
St Andrews 1968-2005
Sandhills Green 1966-2004
The Shelseys 1960-2004
Sherrards Green Pre 1980-1984
Sherwood Pre 1980-1988
Shrawley 1920-2002
Sinton Green Pre 1980-1990
Stakenbridge Pre 1980-1981
Stanford & District Pre 1980-1989
Stock & Bradley 1988-1991
Stoke Bliss & Kyre 1931-1983
Stoke Prior 1931-2015
Stoke Works Pre 1980-1983
Stone 1921-2011
Stoulton & Wadborough Pre 1980-1992
Strensham 1977-1993
Tardebigge 1921-1993
Tibberton 1946-2004
Trimpley & District 1950-2003
Upton On Severn 1960-1998
Upton Snodsbury 1984-1989
Victoria 1991-1995
Warndon 1969-2006
Webheath 1959-2005
Welland 1925-2003
West Malvern 1936-1998
White Ladies Aston 1982-1984
Whittington & District 1939-2014
Wichenford 1944-2004
Wilden Pre 1980-1990
Winyates Green 1983-1995
Worcester Centre Pre 1980-1990
Wribbenhall 1928-2013
Wychbold 1988-2014

Some of the dates are based on their entries in Handbooks and so may be out by the odd year

Abberley

In 1980, Abberley WI had been established for nearly sixty years, but the exact date of formation, due to a missing minute book was lost in the mists of time.

It was in fact founded in 1921 and in 1923 contributed £50 to The Hut, most probably a prefabricated World War 1 army hut. This first Abberley Village Hall was the home for our WI and the Cricket Club until St George's Hall, a new brick hall opened in 1937.

In 1987, the 50th anniversary of St George's Hall was marked by celebrations including a cricket match between the WI and the Cricket Club. The 70th anniversary was celebrated in 1991, two years later St George's Hall was sold for development and another new hall was built very close to the site of The Hut, opening in 1995. The WI planted the gardens around the hall and, in 1997 members celebrated the centenary of the creation of the WI movement in Canada.

During 2011 older members reminded their committee that we should be celebrating our 90th year! We applied to the Heritage Lottery Fund and were successful in obtaining a "Your Heritage" award which really enhanced our 90th anniversary celebrations.

We started by planning the 2012 programme of monthly meetings themed around issues that had significant impact on women's lives. The grant funded heritage professionals to train us how to research our history and get our own archives in order. Our first official event was an exhibition of memorabilia and displays about Abberley since 1952 for the village Queen's Diamond Jubilee celebrations on a shockingly wet weekend in May. We held an official 90th birthday party on the day that the Queen had visited Worcester and officially opened The Hive. Guests included all current members, seven past Abberley WI presidents and the County Chairman. WI members researched, gave talks and wrote blogs on what they had discovered, our in-house IT expert trained us to scan and edit historic photographs and we had training on oral history recording. Finally, we used the scanned photographs and our research to create a book "Abberley Lives" covering the twentieth century history of the village. The final act was to deposit the sorted and listed archives at the new record office at The Hive, so that future members don't have the same problem working out how old we are.

Abberley WI members at their 2016 annual meeting posing in their charity shop challenge outfits – bought for a combined total of £350.

The Inspiring Women rebranding, our 90th birthday celebrations and the WI centenary have all resulted in a much higher profile for our WI which, in the UK WI centenary year, now boasts a thriving membership of over 40 members.

Abberley Clockwatchers

Abberley Clockwatchers WI was founded by a group of mothers from Abberley Hall School, in October 2009.

We are a small but vibrant group of around 20 members, some with a connection to the school, others from the local area. We host our meetings within the school and as a rule we meet every second Wednesday of the month at 9.15 am. New members are always welcome.

Our programme is a mix of activities, speakers and trips. For instance, over the years we have had an archery lesson with a Paralympian, a Zumba class and tried Belly Dancing! We've enjoyed wine tasting and fabulous lectures on reading paintings, the history of pearls and the Mandalay School for the Deaf. We've had trips to Daylesford for a floristry lesson and enjoyed the wonderfully decorative Laskett Gardens in Herefordshire.

We celebrated the WI Centenary within the Woodbury Group, with one of our members abseiling down the Abberley Clocktower with the centenary baton! Members of Clockwatchers and Abberley WIs watched from below with a celebratory glass of champagne and waited for the baton to reach the bottom and be handed on to the president of Abberley Village WI. Members also attended a special Centenary Dinner within the group.

Alfrick

Alfrick village is a civil parish in the Malvern Hills district of Worcestershire, seven miles west of Worcester.

The Alfrick WI was founded in December 1946 so in 2017 we will be in our 71st year. We are currently 24 members and we meet in the village hall in the evenings, on the 2nd Wednesday of the month.

About 16 years ago we combined with Suckley WI and until recent reorganisation have been part of 10 WIs known as the "Elgar" group. We have now joined the "Malvern Hills" group.

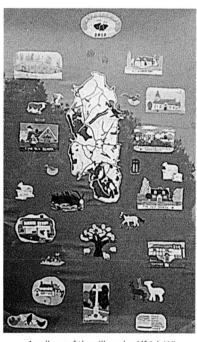

A collage of the village by Alfrick WI

We have always been a busy WI. In 2010 for the opening of a re-vamped village hall, we created an embroidered collage of the village which now hangs framed in the foyer there. In March each year we organise the schedule for the WI open class section of the well-known Alfrick Show which is always on the first Saturday in September. We take part in the County skittles competition and were lucky enough to be winners in 2012 and 2014, and runners up in 2016.

Over the years we have held birthday parties to celebrate our founding, and had many Summer Garden parties in June in members' lovely gardens, to which we have always invited Elgar group members. They have joined us too at many Christmases for lovely food and entertainment from stage struck Alfrick members performing silly pantomimes, rhymes and jokes to great applause. The Elgar group instigated their own Carol services, where Alfrick has had its turn to use our church to take part.

We have organised several group meetings in Alfrick and given a helping hand in the WI marquee when Worcestershire has its turn at the Three Counties Show.

Apart from writing reports about our WI for our local parish magazine, many members are involved in the community, representing us on the village hall committee, working for the church and working as volunteers in our village 'community shop'.

So, with regular meetings and several prospective new members, Alfrick WI hopes to continue for many years to come.

Alvechurch

In the centre of Alvechurch Community
We have 60 Members

We meet in our Village Hall

Planting daffodils for the Millennium

Maintaining Alvechurch Memorial Village Green

St George's Day celebrations for the village 1999 – 2016

St George's Day

ALVECHURCH W.I.
invites you to our
Diamond Jubilee Tea Party
at the Village Hall
On Monday June 11th at 6.30 pm
Dress code - Elegance, Diamonds, Pearls,
Red, White and Blue, Crown, Tiara

Celebrating the Queen's Diamond Jubilee in 2012 with a special tea party

Annual Alvechurch Picnic in the Park

Areley Kings

Areley Kings WI was formed on 2nd November 1926 with 50 members and met in the Parish Rooms, a tin roof building with very few amenities. By 1980 the membership was 74. We celebrated our Diamond Jubilee in 1986 with a dinner and each member received a souvenir programme and contributed to a nostalgic journey through 60 glorious years since 1926. A new village hall was opened on 6th March 2004 and our WI held its first meeting there on 19th April.

Membership has always been good. In fact, at one point, we were considering splitting into two, one in the daytime and one in the evening!

The basic topics at meetings haven't changed over the years – Denman's apparent continuous demise, complaints over rising subs and whether we should limit refreshments to biscuits only.

Produce and Craft were the mainstays in the 1980's. It was debated in 1981 whether a member could demonstrate how to bone a chicken! I don't think that it was taken up. We soon modernised and progressed to talks on reflexology, yoga, acupuncture and even a talk by a Mastermind Champion.

Our membership has always been active at county level and we produced our own VCO (as it was then called) in Julia Rogers, a Federation Chairman Mary Wehner and an Arts Chairman Margaret Shaddock.

Reading the minutes of past years, I was struck by the way no-one was referred to by their Christian name – always Mrs Jones, Mrs Smith etc. It was only in the early part of this century that we were given an identity and our names used.

In the centenary year 2015 we streamed the broadcast of the AGM from the Albert Hall to our village hall and invited all the WIs in the Forest Group to attend and celebrate with us over lunch. It was a fantastic success.

In 2016 our WI was 90 years old. We are still going strong with 50 members – funnily enough the same number as we started with all those years ago in 1926!

A sociable group where you can try something new

Who: Ark Angels WI is a young, dynamic group. Meetings take place at the Ark in Alvechurch. The group has 30 members who are predominantly mums with children at the local school.

Achievement: Revitalising the WI and making the values matter to the next generation.

How: Taking into account the pressures faced by working mums and applying the WI principles to that demographic.

Do: In traditional meetings they made Jam. At Ark Angels WI we made samosa.

Ashton under Hill

Formed in 1941, with a continuous membership of around 45, Ashton WI has had a lively history. Major highlights since 1980 have included hosting BBC's *Gardeners' Question Time*, and *Any Questions*. Members have enjoyed many organised visits varying from Highgrove or the Birmingham Jewellery quarter, to Tyntesfield, Painswick and Slimbridge. Alongside joining in with WFWI and Evesham Vale group trips, there have been adventures in Scotland and cycling in Cornwall plus participation in German exchange holidays.

Several shows have been staged by and for members including *Calendar Girls*, *Rhyming Cinderella* and a sketch based on the *Antiques Road Show*.

Our active visiting speaker programme saw personalities such as Percy Thrower, Nigel Rees on *Family Sayings*, Kay Alexander on *Life at the BBC*, Trish Steward of *Calendar Girls* fame, and Sir Ross Simms, writer of *Heartbeat*. Other topics have included *Nuclear Electricity*, a *History of Fashion*, *How to look after Pearls*, and a talk on *Evesham Street Pastors*. Craft and activity classes have included painting, smocking, crochet, creative embroidery, sugar work, calligraphy, belly dancing, cookery, IT skills and golf croquet.

Over the years Ashton WI members have produced a wall hanging depicting village life, a patchwork quilt, a Millennium Map of the village, and have published two highly successful cookery books, in 1981 and 2014. Members have also helped raise funds for the Parish Minibus, a new village notice board and the planting of commemorative trees and bulbs. Our skills have been on display when flower arranging for Worcester Cathedral and the many successful entries in WI craft events. An exhibition of memorabilia and photographs to mark Ashton WI's 75th and the Queen's 90th birthday was staged as part of the village's yearly Open Gardens weekend, at which the WI always serves tea and cake for visitors. Once every two years we also run a stall such as the Tombola at the Village Fete.

Fun and friendship is our WI motto so social activities are numerous and include Murder Mystery evenings, concerts, quizzes, skittles, theatre trips and visits to gardens and historical homes. In Ashton we try to encourage membership by having a varied and interesting mixture of learning and entertainment. One of the most popular activities is a monthly walk, usually finishing with lunch at a pub. Attendance has never been better and Ashton WI is a successful and forward-looking group, always searching for different and enjoyable events and speakers for our members.

Astley

Astley's formation meeting was in November 1925 with its first formal meeting in January 1926. Having started off in a wooden hut, our current membership of 28 now enjoy the facilities at our lovely new Village Hall, built in the 1990s.

Over the years we have proudly supported the local community by supporting Astley Church's fundraising, undertaking local litter picks, providing wonderful cakes for village events and organising a First Aid training session for local people in the Village Hall. For ourselves, we currently enjoy skittles and a monthly lunch club and craft club.

Having entered into County competitions, we have enjoyed success with a number of first and second places (and some highly commended) in the floral displays and we are particularly proud of Astley's first place in the Choral Festival in 1985 from which evolved *The Shrinkin' Violets*, our singing, drama and 'have a go at anything' group. Not only have they entertained Astley members and guests but also WIs further afield and performing at the Diamond Jubilee County Celebration as the closing act. *The Shrinkin' Violets* enjoyed great success at the 2006 Drama Festival performing a recitation, a humorous sketch based on an improvisation and our original 'Astley Rap' written to highlight some of our events and interests.

As the longest running WI in Forest Group, we were honoured to be asked to hand over the baton as part of the Centenary Celebrations. The day began with a tea party in the Wyre Forest, followed by a cavalcade of classic cars to the hand-over at the Severn Valley Railway for its next leg of the journey by steam train. A day to remember!

As the Twentieth Century ended and the Twenty-first began, to commemorate this milestone, the Astley WI Millennium wall-hanging was completed. A collaborative project, members produced hand-stitched pictures of local landmarks and sites of importance which were then sewn onto the backing. It was a labour of love and it has pride of place in the Village Hall. Another source of pride for us is when Astley's Marjorie Whiting was elected County Chairman in 2014.

One of the highlights of the early 2000s was our classes on the 'ComputaCoach', a fully equipped bus where attendees learnt to use the computer. Apart from being great fun, it brought us into the Twenty-first Century ready to face the technological age but we didn't leave behind our core values of Fun, Friendship and Community.

Badsey

Badsey WI was formed in March 1927 and has always been an active and thriving Institute. Since 1980 perhaps the most significant change has been the advent of Information Technology. We have accepted this change here at Badsey but not without some difficulty. We enjoy the web sites; Moodle and the MCS data register, downloads and the help for treasurers. Extremely helpful is using e-mail to get in touch with other Institutes and Federations more quickly and efficiently, though not always!

Badsey WI in the last 40 years or so has grown and is even more active and, dare I say, vibrant. The main aim of Fun, Friendship and Education has always been at the forefront of our WI. We have had our highs and lows but by working together have overcome any difficulties as they have arisen.

FUN is the order of the day which we have in plenty. Holidays at home and abroad, outings, theatre visits, lunches, walks, skittles and many, many more. **FRIENDSHIP** is abundant and new members and visitors are always sure of a very warm welcome. We support each other in so many ways, visiting when ill or incapacitated, providing transport for those who need it and supporting events individual members may have arranged to raise money for a Charity, be it be from doing a sky dive, as one younger member did, to attending teas, quizzes etc. **EDUCATION** plays a big part in our WI. We give a generous Denman Bursary and, as well as having interesting speakers, we have our own in-house tutors who hold regular art, card making and embroidery classes.

One of the most memorable events for our WI was the Millennium year when, with a lot of hard work and grant applications (never easy to obtain), we were able to plant over 5000 thousand crocuses in our Churchyard and hundreds of daffodils along the outside walls of the Church, and landscape the Garden of Remembrance, where a plaque is placed in acknowledgement of our work. For the 100 years of WI celebrations, we had a beautiful bench made which, suitably inscribed, was presented to the village.

Bra Cancer Challenge   *Our Millennium Gift to the Village*   *Carol's Charity Sky Dive*

Now with 52 members, we meet in the Remembrance Hall and look forward in our 90th year to keeping up the core values of our WI whilst maintaining the traditions that have been built up over years. We progress and change but keep the aims of the WI which was founded to educate, help and empower Women.

Barnt Green

Barnt Green reformed in 2017. Originally formed in 1916 by Lady Margesson, Barnt Green was the first WI in Worcestershire. 2016 would have been its centenary year, so its reforming is timely. After more than a ten year break we are back with a bang, with 70 ladies becoming members in the first few months.

We have already enjoyed some fascinating talks, embraced needle felting and Bhangra!

In Barnt Green there's a new WI.
Please come and give us a try.
There's drinking and dancing, fun and laughter,
All the things that you are after.
So don't think twice and don't be shy
Hip hip hooray, for the WI!

By the "Bah Humbug" team

Barnt Green WI meets at 7.30pm on the third Thursday of the month at the Barnt Green Baptist Church.

Bentley Pauncefoot

We might not have been mentioned in "Madam President: Fellow Members", the 60th Anniversary book, but there is no doubt that by then, having been formed in June 1963, Bentley Pauncefoot members were most definitely active and signed up to the ethos of the WI.

Like the world at large, Bentley Pauncefoot WI has not stood still over the past forty years, but has continued to evolve, building on its firm foundations. Minute books, scrap books, photographs and the reminiscences of members record our progress. The famous annual Pancake Race, held on the lane outside the Village Hall, still taking place in the 1990s, and the outings and sports days held for members' children may no longer happen, but many other activities have continued or have begun since then.

Particular events: the annual May Lunch, Produce Show and Christmas Party with home-grown entertainment, have always been permanent features in our calendar, though the entertainment at the latter - the (riotous) Pantomime - is a little less exuberant these days. Regular activities such as our monthly Book Club, a weekly Tai Chi class, visits to gardens, historic buildings, the theatre, cinema and walks arranged by members are enjoyed. Our 'making' renaissance - entering Federation competitions and the innovation of running successful Rag Markets - is rewarding. We reach out to the wider community, by raising money annually for a local charity and by filling boxes for Samaritan's Purse. Thanks to our Speaker Finders, monthly meetings are enhanced by interesting and often challenging talks; fun is in social time! In October 2016, one of our members, an engineer, spoke about, and demonstrated, the influence of modern technology on our lives – truly 21st Century! Our Committee works tirelessly for us.

A day to remember in 2013 has to be 6th June. On this day, in Bentley Village Hall - the same date and venue as our very first meeting – we celebrated our 50th Anniversary. What an amazing event! To say the hall 'buzzed' with the sound of eighty voices is an

understatement, as members, both current and former, and friends gathered. The superb lunch, floral decorations, home-grown entertainment and, naturally, the cutting and eating of the celebratory cake were enjoyed by all. We toasted, with gratitude, our founder members, who left us such a superb legacy. A copy of our Anniversary booklet, to which we all contributed, was presented to everyone, as a memento; fifty years of memories, in words and photographs. Although each contribution was unique, they were united, because certain words – 'friendly', 'happy memories', 'interesting', 'fun and laughter' – occurred again and again. Later that year, a packed hall of members and villagers witnessed the unveiling of a celebratory plaque and viewed our archive of books and photographs.

We currently have 56 members. New members are welcomed, new ideas flow, but one thing, we hope, will never change – the beautiful view towards The Malverns from our home, Bentley Village Hall.

Beoley

Beoley WI's first meeting was at Beoley Village Hall, where we meet to this day. The founder and first President was Lady Norton. There are now 53 members, and we are in the Weatheroak Group with six other local WIs, taking it in turns to host Group meetings twice a year.

Beoley holds monthly meetings, although June's is usually an outing organised by members and August's is a walk and dinner out. At our meetings, besides singing Jerusalem and hearing about all the trips and events we may go on, we have had a huge variety of guest speakers, followed by tea and home-made cake, a raffle and the judging of our monthly competition.

We have a Birthday Tea in March, a Harvest Supper in October, an American Supper at our AGM in November, and supper or party food in December with entertainment which is usually musical. Members also enjoy theatre trips, often to The Palace in Redditch. Our Quiz team has won the Worcestershire Cup in successive years.

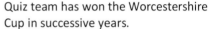

Our Craft Group meets once a month to create and chat. Beoley has held various craft workshops, including silk painting and stained glass. We hold an annual Christmas Craft Fair and also an annual Jumble Sale. We have an enthusiastic and talented Performing Arts Group, which graces various events. One member represented Worcestershire in a national golfing competition.

We have planted two enhancing trees: a flowering cherry at the Village Hall and, on a green in Beoley, a Millennium Black Pear Tree, this being both Worcestershire Federation's symbol and an ancient symbol for the county.

As 2019 draws near, we look forward to a future of continuing and enjoyable meetings and events in the good company of our members with all their many and various experiences, talents and skills.

Bewdley

At time of writing, Bewdley WI is just 2 years old, founded in October 2014. We meet on the first Monday of the month, 7.30 pm, St George's Hall, Bewdley and have 43 members. We are mere toddlers in the long and fruitful family of WFWI. All of our Forest Group partners have a much longer history, although sadly the WI in our sister settlement, Wribbenhall, just across the River Severn, closed a few years ago.

Bewdley is a small town, a lively, active community with many long established cultural, educational and charitable organisations. Bewdley has an annual Festival, the Severn Valley Railway, a great museum with modern craft workshops, street fairs, a carnival and many opportunities for the involvement and engagement of all generations. How could a new WI possibly compete and provide interest and entertainment for our busy population of cultivated, intelligent, creative and busy women? It is, of course, work in progress, but maybe we can summarise our endeavours so far around three principles:

Firstly, variety: our meetings have included talks on local history, ecology and wildlife, a sombre reflection on the Battle of the Somme and the hilarious memoirs of a cartoonist. We have enjoyed demonstrations by a chocolatier, a baker, florists and gardeners and have been on our feet with yoga and rather loud in a percussion workshop. We have a BWI Book Club, which, in collaboration with the local Library has promoted eclectic reading and our Art and Craft group produced a memorable Centenary WI Duckhouse (complete with guardian Cuthbert the rabbit) for the 2015 Bewdley Festival, and a stunning mural to disguise hoardings protecting a building project in the town (Banksy beware!).

Secondly, we have been able to introduce our membership to participation in the Worcestershire Federation and the National WI. Members have attended Annual Council meetings, training sessions, archiving instruction and practical art and craft workshops. We have lively debates over Annual Resolutions, and, prompted by the Food Waste Campaign, now have a relationship with a local Food Bank.

Finally, and perhaps most importantly, we have learned so much from each other. In 'social' meetings, members have shared their passions and their skills – cement mixing in Italy, poetry composition, geology ..... Members participate enthusiastically, suggest new departures creatively, welcome visitors warmly and bake most deliciously. They are everything we are, and we thank them!

website: www.bewdleywi.org.uk

Blackwell and Burcot

By 1980, which was our WI's 50th Anniversary, times had changed since our formation in 1930 as Blackwell WI. We had added Burcot to our Institute; meeting at Burcot Villge Hall, our numbers have grown to 65.

From those early days, our meetings now are much livelier occasions. We have speakers on such diverse subjects as The Battle of Worcester to Yoga and Tai Chi, we have trips to the theatre, to interesting places, some historical, some for shopping! We help our local villages at their fetes and have raised money to donate a stage and skittle alley to Burcot village hall, have planted trees in both villages with a grant from Taylor's Tea and we have had computer classes - a necessity as our members are all retired, being an afternoon WI now.

We started an allotment in 2009, have litter-picked both villages, dressed up in tin hats and gas masks to join in with Bromsgrove Council to mark the beginning of World War One and dressed up again to join with our group at Avoncroft Museum of Buildings to pass on the Centenary Baton. We were allocated the Chapel so dressed as Victorians, played the harmonium and sang "All things bright and beautiful"!

We have raised money for ACWW at meetings and by doing Sponsored Bluebell Walks on the Lickey Hills with members from other groups. We have connections in Africa, knitting blankets and babies vests for their old and young.

In 2012 all members had a whole page to show their lives in two books to celebrate the year of the Queen's Diamond Jubilee, a lovely treasure for our archives. These were displayed at the weekend celebrations with the Village Hall when we used half of the Hall to display the work of our WI and the other half for the Hall activities. We had Appalachian Dancers, children's racing and the WI put on a superb tea. We still use a tablecloth embroidered in 1970 at all our meetings and in 2014 our craft ladies made and embroidered a banner which shows the link between Blackwell and Burcot - the famous railway Lickey Incline. We have helped serve teas in the Three Counties Show WI tent and joined in many Federation and Group activities. Many of our members have enjoyed courses at Denman College and have passed their knowledge on to other members.

In 2015, WI's Centenary year, we are celebrating with a party at our local retirement home with a skiffle group! We also took part in the Bromsgrove Festival by having a stall in the High St advertising our WI and selling our craft work and cakes. Two of our members had a wonderful time attending the WI Garden Party at Buckingham Palace and the AGM at the Albert Hall.

Blakedown

Blakedown WI, started in 1920, has always been a forward looking, well supported and much enjoyed WI with a monthly meeting of intelligent and progressive women who enjoy a diverse range of opportunities and each other's company. A monthly luncheon club, walking group, two book clubs, drama group and craft club as well as outings to local gardens, the seaside, Christmas markets, interesting speakers and brain testing social time make us second to none. The Annual Christmas meeting and pantomime are firm favourites for our members and visitors. Our WI means everything to us.

In 1982, our WI took over the land adjoining our railway station planting it with shrubs funded by various events. This was our effort to keep Britain tidy promoting a national campaign by British Rail. Blakedown WI was honoured in London's Guildhall for its efforts.

 In 2000, the WI embroidered a large Millennium tapestry of the village as it then was, to hang in our Parish Room. Local school children took a great interest in this depiction of their village. A time capsule, containing a contribution from every WI member, was buried in a secret place on the village Millennium Green, an area planted with trees and spring bulbs for villagers to enjoy.

In 2016, after an absence of some years, the WI revived the annual Produce Show. A huge success, it drew together the villages of Blakedown and Churchill with an amazing range of exhibits, craft and culinary skills with classes for everyone to show their talents. Children produced rubbish monsters and miniature gardens, men baked cakes and artists and photographers stunned us with their talent.

We have 55 members and meet in the Blakedown Parish Room.

Bockleton

Location

The very rural hamlet of Bockleton is situated in the west of Worcestershire between the market towns of Tenbury Wells, Leominster and Bromyard near the Herefordshire border. We have members living in both of these counties.

History

The Institute was started in November 1966 and we held a celebration lunch in Tenbury Wells in November 2016 to celebrate our Fifty Year Anniversary. We still meet in the Parish Hall where the first meeting was held and have the same third Wednesday of the month as our meeting day.

Organisation

During the last few years our member numbers fell but to overcome the difficulty of finding a volunteer to organise the yearly programme of speakers we adopted the following strategy. Each member took one month and was responsible for organising a speaker or activity for that month and so we have a wide and interesting range of meetings involving local speakers, hands on craft activities, visits and a garden picnic. This has worked so well that we still use this method every year and because our numbers have increased our officers do not take a month but other members do take their turn.

Activities

During the early years of the Institute we had an active Drama Group presenting plays in the Parish Hall and wider afield. We have a tradition of entering competitions at local Ploughing Matches, Bromyard Gala and Tenbury Show which involve many members of our Institute in arts, crafts and cookery. For many years we have entered the County Skittles Competition and were winners in the 2009/10 season despite being such a small and remote Institute. We once reached the final of the County Quiz which was held in the Guildhall in Worcester. We also enjoy visits to local places of interest and join coach outings organised by County and coach companies, some involving hotel stays. Recently we have been to The Shard in London, Blackpool Illuminations, Royal Ascot on Ladies day, Chatsworth and Blenheim. Members also involve themselves in an annual early spring Litter Pick along their own patch of verge along the lanes.

Finances

To help pay for speakers, activities and hire of the hall for our monthly meetings, we hold a successful Jumble Sale each year in March at the Parish Hall with customers queuing outside waiting for the doors to open. This event is necessary for our finances as membership contributions alone would not be sufficient.

Biennial Show

Every two years we hold our own Craft and Produce Show in the Parish Hall. The judges are always so pleased and surprised at the quality and quantity of entries and what a marvellous display we have for our small Institute. We have handsome trophies for the winning members.

The Future

Our Institute, though small with 16 members, is thriving and we look forward to many more years of knowledge, friendship and fun.

Broadheath with Rushwick

Broadheath's first WI was established in 1923 and lasted just a few years before closing. Our current WI grew out of Cotheridge Women's Institute, affiliated in 1922 and becoming Broadheath and Cotheridge in 1951 as the number of members from Broadheath increased and meetings moved to Broadheath Memorial Hall.

Cotheridge and Broadheath offered a lifeline to the members of Rushwick and Upper Wick in 2004 and in January 2005 the combined Institutes became Broadheath with Rushwick WI. Current members come from both villages and beyond.

Since the millennium we have changed our meeting times from afternoons to mornings and our membership now spans five decades. An active recruitment campaign and an upbeat approach has borne fruit and new members. At present we have 19 members and hope to continue to grow further.

From amongst our membership we draw on amazing skills to provide us with talks and demonstrations of a high standard. We encourage visitors and members of the community to join us in many of our activities. Recently we held a successful village event with a wonderful evening of homemade 'Soup and Puds'. This really increased our funds, always a challenge as a small WI, and plans are being made for another community event next year, besides stalls at various fetes selling handicraft items, cakes and other produce.

We make sure there is a good mix in our annual programme and of course trips out are a winner. As a small WI it is helpful to be able to call on members to give talks or demonstrations and sometimes they are just the best. In the past couple of years, talented members have demonstrated exquisite Japanese silk and Hardanger embroidery, ceramics, beading, beautiful gift wrapping and  quilting. We have learned how to prepare the perfect race-day picnic and members have transformed our hall and catered for our own Christmas lunches too.

In April 2017 we hosted the Elgar Group meeting, welcoming around seventy ladies with an excellent supper and speaker. Yolanda Campbell had everyone spell bound with her stunning floral displays. The evening was a great success, proving that small WIs can achieve big things.

2017 has been an exciting year with some good speakers, the Group meeting, lots of visitors, a trip to the Lavender Farm at Broadway and trying new activities such as dragon boating. We are spreading our wings, reflecting the interests of new members, and embracing the future in a positive way. We very much look forward to celebrating our own centenary in 2023.

We meet on 2nd Wednesday of the month at Broadheath Memorial Hall at 10.30 am.

Broadwas-on-Teme

Upon checking our Records, Broadwas was a very popular and strong WI in 1980 with 33 members; we are very familiar with so many names from the Register as they are still Members today. Noticeably, the computer age was a thing of the future and our Record books are all hand written, beautifully hand written and legible with Members addressed by their title of `Mrs` or `Miss`. Today we all address each other by our Christian names, sometimes struggling to remember a surname!

First prize was awarded to ... Broadwas WI

Broadwas has many photographic memories from the 1990's as someone had the forethought to purchase a photograph album, and we found a lovely photograph from Broadwas Village VE Day Celebrations when our WI entered the decorated float section, the theme being `My Village`. The emphasis of the float was the WI in wartime, with `Make do and Mend`, preserving and coping with rationing, all familiar to the WI from its beginning.

Our then very active and busy President, Pat Smith, sent a letter to the Prime Minister Tony Blair petitioning that Pensions should continue to be paid into a local Post Office account as not everyone had the means or ability to travel into town to collect their Pension. The usual standard letter from the Department of Trade and Industry was received and nowadays most people have their Pensions sent electronically. We have to move with the times!

Pat had more success with her petition to our local MP at the House of Commons supporting free Bus Passes as we still enjoy free travel within the County today.

Broadwas continues to support both Village events and WI resolutions and petitions. We have our Annual summer outing in August, often connecting with a Speaker who has been to us. We have seen the newly-restored Perseus and Andromeda fountain at Witley Court, taken a guided tour around The Chateau Impney at Droitwich and, after a four year wait, went to the home of HRH Prince Charles at Highgrove.

Unfortunately, one of our Members slipped in the Royal mud and broke her arm! She was regally treated by the Medical staff but another Member and husband took her to hospital. A letter was later received from Highrove asking after her health and inviting the two Members, and husband, for a return visit; they sensibly went in the summer on a dry day.

Along with Broadwas Croquet Club, some WI Members being very good players, a tree was planted at the Village Hall to commemorate the WFWI 90th Birthday.

Now, in 2016, Broadwas has a membership of just 19, meeting at the Village Hall. Small as we are, we are still a strong, active group, supporting many WI events. We hosted the Elgar Group Carol Service in 2015 under the direction of our President, Jay Popplewell, we have also hosted Group Meetings and even have an enthusiastic Skittles Team.

Sadly, some past members of Broadwas WI are no longer with us but, through our Record Books and Photograph Albums their names and faces are a constant reminder, never to be forgotten and to inspire us into the future.

Brockencote

"You will support me, dear, won't you." With these words the Brockencote WI came into being. Our first President, Kath Grange, asked her friends to support her in starting an afternoon WI. Our inaugural meeting was on the 19th February 1992 where the name was chosen from: Chaddesley Corbett Afternoon, Chaddesley Corbett Four Square and Brockencote, with the first meeting of Brockencote WI being that of Wednesday 18th March 1992.

The first year's report gives a true account of our doings and intent. With the ideas and energy of Kath Grange and the skilled midwifery of Diana Cartmel, Brockencote WI was born. Jobs were freely allocated and several of us left that afternoon wondering what on earth we had let ourselves in for. After a year of meeting, talking, listening and laughing together, friendship has taken over and we all look forward to the third Wednesday of the month.

We have planted trees, had many guest speakers over the years, and talks and demonstrations by members with an enthusiasm, particular skill or interest in a variety of subjects. Outings include Hidcote, Lichfield, Shugborough, Bourton on the Water, Gloucester, Evesham, Snowshill Manor, Hardwicke Hall, Coventry and Ryton Gardens, Ludlow, Stockton Bury and Dorothy Clive Gardens. We look back with pleasure at our meetings in our members' gardens, tea of course included.

In our 25 years, with our salmon lunches and coffee mornings, we have supported various charities - Air Ambulance, Acorns Trust, Stroke Association, Guide Dogs for the Blind, Swan rescue, etc. We have knitted jhuggie jumpers and at present Teddies for Tragedies. We have photographs of members wearing Easter Bonnets in 1998, performing in costume on the stage in 2000 and many others of us just enjoying the company of WI friends at various venues. It is never too late

Past and present Presidents and Secretaries

to take up a new craft as the award of our 'Brockencote Plate' attests, from art to winemaking, collage to cookery, embroidery to patchwork and beyond (including jam making).

In 2015 our two joint presidents attended the 100th celebration of the WI held at the Royal Albert Hall in London and have wonderful memories of such a special occasion. We celebrated our 20th Birthday with a special tea at Stone Manor in 2012 and this year our 25th Birthday at Whitlenge gardens, on a beautiful sunny day. As our first president drew on her circle of friends initially, we do not have a core base but our 30 members are drawn from a wide area - Worcester to Kidderminster, Stourport to Bewdley, Hagley to Hartlebury and beyond. Without the hard work of our committee, helpers and members, we would not be characterised by welcoming everyone to Chaddesley Corbett Village Hall each month with friendliness and informality.

Bromsgrove

In March 2017 Bromsgrove WI celebrated its centenary, so it is officially 100 years old and still going strong!

Bromsgrove WI is the second oldest in the Worcestershire Federation. Its membership has fluctuated over the years and at present has a small but active membership of 12.

Its very first meeting took place in the ladies waiting room at Bromsgrove railway station and has had many 'homes' over the years. For the greatest number of years in one place, from September 1962 until December 2015, the WI met at the Bromsgrove Masonic Hall.

A move became necessary because of the town centre redevelopment and so from January 2016 the WI has met at the modernised and recently-opened Life After Stroke Centre in Bromsgrove.

The WI's activities, in addition to the monthly meetings, have varied over the years. In the 1980's there were enthusiastic keep fit classes and until 1990 the WI ran a stall at the annual Elizabethan Market for which it won a prize for the best dressed stall in 1988. Since then members have met to play bowls, skittles and whist, enjoyed walks with the Bromsgrove Group and at present enjoy meeting for craft and poetry.

The WI has always supported local projects and charities by making clothes and knitting for the premature baby unit; it provided a new television for Bromsgrove hospital in1991 and, from 1983 to the present time, members provide small Easter Eggs placed in knitted chicks for the pupils at Chadsgrove School who all have life challenging difficulties.

Bromsgrove WI members have supported the NFWI campaigns, ACWW, Federation events and Group activities. Each month we participate in an activity or hear from a wide range of inspiring speakers, and we enjoy our social time having tea and a chat. The friendships formed within the WI are very important to all the members.

Bromsgrove Belles

Bromsgrove Belles is a very young WI, which was formed in June 2015, by its President Carla Priddon and a group of friends. Carla had enjoyed belonging to a WI when she lived in London; on her return to Bromsgrove she decided to form a similar WI.

Bromsgrove Belles is not only a young WI, but has a young membership and modern outlook. Members range in age from early thirties to eighty plus years. There are 30 members at present, with more than twenty attending every meeting. Visitors are welcomed to meetings, several of whom have joined over the last year.

The group now meets at the Life After Stroke Centre, on the second Monday of the month at 7.30 pm. Initial meetings were at Bromsgrove Golf Club, followed by a spell at St John's church hall, where access was found to be difficult. Members have found the new venue pleasant and inviting.

Regular activities outside formal meeting times are a book club and supper club which meet monthly on alternate 2nd Tuesday evenings at 7.30. Venues have varied from members' homes to local pubs and other eating establishments. Members also enjoyed a day out at Denman College, many returning with enthusiasm for the food provided and the many opportunities to learn new skills or to improve on existing ones available at the college.

There has been an eclectic mix of speakers and activities over the last year. Easter saw members making Easter bunnies, from knitted squares. In the Autumn, a session on origami was run by two members, and at another meeting members had fun taking part in Qi Gong, a gentle martial art. There have been talks from guides at local historic houses and gardens. One member was a 'games maker' in the London 2012 Olympics; she gave a very interesting and pictorial account of her experience. Other talks have included 'Impostor Syndrome' and a visit from the Cinnamon Trust. The last meeting of 2016, a Christmas special, included hand bell ringing, with some members taking part.

In the coming year Bromsgrove Belles are looking forward to welcoming speakers imparting their knowledge of scarf tying, personal colour, genealogy and first aid among other interests.

We are very pleased to work with the Basement Project as our designated charity. The Basement Project is based in Bromsgrove to help young people with housing and other difficulties, up to the age of 25 years.

Bromsgrove Belles is looking forward to its second year as a Women's Institute, welcoming new visitors, who we hope will become new members, and the continuing support of old and existing members.

Broome

Broome WI in the 1980's was a flourishing group with about thirty members. They met on the first Tuesday of the month in the afternoon. Very active with craft groups, book group and walking group; members participating in the competitions held at the Annual meeting. Each year they entertained disabled members to a Garden Party. Over the next 12 years as members grew older, numbers dropped. In 1990 Broome celebrated their 50th Birthday. WI member Mrs Green presented ink drawings of the village.

In 1991 a group of younger ladies became members and were persuaded to form a committee with one or two of the older members, providing the meeting could be changed to an evening, as they had jobs during the day. This was agreed and the evening meeting took place on Tuesday 4th February 1992. Looking through the records it was interesting to see that the subscription was £9 in 1992. The time of the meeting was changed again in 1995 to the third Wednesday of the month and Broome has continued to meet at this time.

We celebrated our 60th Birthday in 2000 and presented two Hawthorn Trees to Broome Church. Broome grew in numbers and we enjoyed a Christmas visit to Denman in 2005 and have photographic evidence of members singing The Twelve Days of Christmas with great expression. In 2009 we enjoyed a visit to The National Arboretum to see the WI seat and were humbled at the realisation of the sacrifice made for us to be able to live as we do now.

We hold a Garden Party in the summer at the home of one of our members to raise funds for the year. In 2015 it was our 75th Birthday, so we donated a Bench that sits outside Broome Village Hall where we meet each month. Now in 2017 we have thirty five members and enjoy many activities together, and have some very interesting speakers every month. We are proud to be part of Worcestershire Federation.

Callow End

Callow End WI itself is approaching its Centenary. Its first inaugural meeting was on Thursday May 19th 1921. When the Village Hall opened in 1926 this became the WI's home and continues to be. In 1981 its Diamond Jubilee was marked with a Church Service, the gift of a china thimble and a meal together.

Throughout the 1980's Callow End WI produced and performed an annual Pantomime. Such productions were Snow White and the Four Dwarfs, Pollyanna and the Bear, Cinderella, Aladdin, The Sleeping Princess, The Three Bears and Hansel and Gretel. Three shows were always performed and had wonderful reviews in the local press. Scripts were written by a well-remembered member, Connie McEvoy, and also to mark Callow End's 80th Birthday she wrote a poem which sums up the spirit of Callow End WI.

> "When Callow End began its WI
> With several kindly ladies who did try
> To make their monthly meeting night
> Cheerful, interesting and bright,
> Tho' Canada first evolved this scheme-
> In Callow End, here – you have seen
> That as the years have rolled along
> Your WI is still going strong."

Participation in Federation events has been important especially skittles with several wins over the years. A panel for the Federation Millennium Banner was embroidered and ten Sweet Chestnut Trees were planted on the Old Hills.

Outings over the years have been important. They visited Exeter and Sandy Bay, Stratford upon Avon to walk in Shakespeare's footsteps with Bernard Pumphrey and also visited the gardens at Highgrove, the home of Prince Charles. Individual members have also taken part in NFWI events; on 31st July 1995 one of our present members, Jean Luty, represented us at a Buckingham Palace Garden Party. Another member, Muriel Jones, received Maundy money in 1980.

Callow End WI always tries to include every member in activities, so in 2004 it was decided that a new tablecloth was needed. Each member was asked to embroider her own square. These were made into the tablecloth we use today with new members added as they join.

Just as today, good speakers were important. Members have been from Bahrain to the Canadian Rockies; from Faberge eggs to Royal Worcester Porcelain. There is however always room for the serious side; one evening's talk saw "The Law today as it relates to Women" but then next month saw a magic show.

New members are always welcome and encouraged to come along and there is always a friendly competitive edge but when, in February 1985, a talk from local pharmacist Mr Ogle on Homeopathy saw a competition during the tea interval to find as many words as possible from "Homoeopathy," this was taken to the limit when on Mrs Carter's first visit she won the First Prize. Callow End WI continues to be well supported with 27 members and still upholds the sentiment of those ladies who started the WI all those years ago. Hopefully the WI will continue in Callow End for many years to come.

Callow Hill

Callow Hill WI was founded in 1947 and met in the Methodist church schoolroom. After some years numbers had increased beyond the capacity of the room and the group moved to Gorst Hill Parish Rooms in 1976. According to the reminiscences of a founder member (now deceased) numbers increased to such an extent that it was decided to form two smaller groups – Callow Hill WI and Far Forest WI - although this has not been confirmed. In 1990 Callow Hill WI moved back into the Methodist chapel where we still meet today in a well-equipped and cosy environment on the edge of the Wyre Forest.

In the period since 1980 Callow Hill WI has been involved in a number of local events. Over the years, members have entered the Far Forest Show to compete for the WI Shield awarded to the WI with the most points. Callow Hill won the shield on many occasions with items of craft, flower arranging, cookery and photography. Callow Hill WI has always supported both Forest Group and County events.

Until recently the group ran a monthly competition. In the past these were arranged by individual members on a rota basis and included such things as "Guess the dish", "Guess the smell" and "Guess which country the cow comes from"!

The group also had its own annual produce show when members competed for a cup. Entries for flower arranging, cookery, craft and photography were all judged by fellow members who put pennies with their favourite item. Proceeds were sent to Pennies for Friendship.

In the past members produced an annual pantomime.

We have had celebrations for our 40th, 50th and 60th anniversaries with special meetings and meals, and we are currently discussing arrangements for our 70th anniversary celebrations in 2017.

In 2014 our numbers dropped and we were faced with the possibility of closure as the viability of the group was in question. This was a sad time as everyone valued the close friendship of the group. It was decided to try moving the meeting time from an evening to an afternoon meeting. This has proved to be very successful with several members returning so we now have 19 members.

We have a varied programme with outside speakers covering a wide range of subjects. Talented members of the group also lead workshops in flower arranging and various crafts. These practical sessions are always enjoyable. We also have social afternoons with games and quizzes etc.

As well as the monthly meetings, we have an informal get-together on the 4th Wednesday of each month when we meet for coffee and/or lunch at a variety of local venues. They have included local cafes, National Trust properties and garden centres.

There is usually an outing organised in August. Visits have been made to Waddesdon Manor, Blenheim, Chatsworth House and Highgrove Gardens. We have also been to Abby Cwm Hir, Wightwick Manor and Hanbury Hall around Christmas time.

Callow Hill WI is a welcoming group whose members all value the support and friendship of its members.

Catshill

Since 1968 the fledgling Catshill WI has progressed. Every month members have enjoyed meetings with talks as diverse as old bottle collecting to jewellery with thousands of pounds worth of gems on display and tasty cookery demonstrations, especially the tasting afterwards!

'Hands on' meetings have been well supported and have included pottery, china painting, floral art, calligraphy, enamelling, rag doll making and patchwork. Creating a summer hanging basket led to a lovely display that particular summer.

We have supported local events and charities. We purchased chairs and a table for our Village Hall (which is where we meet) when it was refurbished and recently enabled the installation of an electronic screen with a Community Grant from the County Council. Our Charity Jar, which is donated annually, has helped local causes that have appreciated our help.

Over the years our craft skills have provided goods for sale at the Catshill Carnival which was succeeded by the Village Fund Day, then the Village Hall Craft Fayre and in 2015 we took a stall at the Bromsgrove Carnival Street Fayre.

2008 – Members of Catshill WI arrive by bus in Birmingham City Centre on their way to visit the National Trust's Back to Back Houses

Also during this time, we have enjoyed well over 50 visits around the Midlands and beyond, as well as participating in the audience at the BBC.

We have always been pleased to host Group Meetings, and the highlights have included cookery and flower arranging demonstrations, an Antiques Roadshow and a Magic Show.

This is our 49th year and, with a current membership of 18, we look forward to celebrating our Golden Anniversary and a very bright future.

Chaddesley Corbett

In 2018 Chaddesley Corbett WI will celebrate its 98th Birthday being one of the earlier WIs formed in Worcestershire. Its membership has always been good with a peak in 2015 of 87 which necessitated the introduction of a waiting list to keep within the Insurance requirements for the Village Hall.

Friendship and fun have always been the heart of the WI with members enjoying monthly walks known as Nora's Rambles, craft evenings, lunches, a book club, skittles and outings. Supporting our community has been a top priority over the years. We have assisted in all the Village fundraising appeals, such as Wake 88 and the Centenary Roadshow, but special mention must be made of our successful application for a £5,000 Lottery Grant to source and purchase chairs and tables for the refurbished Village Hall in 2000, pictured below on our return from the temporary meeting place at Bluntington Methodist Church Hall. Both the grant and our donation to the refurbished church bells at our village church, St Cassian's, were for the Millennium.

The Annual Village Fete always saw the WI providing afternoon teas and, in 2016, a pudding evening was held to raise funds for the Village defibrillator. Over the years we have supported various courses, often led by one of our members. They have ranged from many crafts such as soft toy making, basket weaving, upholstery and pottery through art classes, to  historical projects. Some of these courses have resulted in sales of work in the village. We have also provided refreshments and help for some village school events and projects. We have planted trees to mark significant occasions and looked after the village flower trough. Our tablecloth is covered in embroidered name squares of members past and present.

Members of our WI have been active at Federation and National levels. Since 1980 there have been three members serving on the WFWI Board of Trustees, one becoming the third County Chairman from our membership. Two members became WI Advisers, fifteen have served on County sub-committees, others took such roles as Denman Tutors, a Denman Guide, demonstrators, Eco team leader, County Archivist and Federation Digital Champion who also created and manages the Federation Website.

In addition, at our meetings we have enjoyed an excellent range of speakers on historical topics, many of which have been followed up with a visit to a place of interest. We have taken part in demonstrations on cookery and gardening, and had other informative talks on everything from pearls to event catering, hats for occasions and costumes of Peru. We have a hugely talented group who have every year entered the WFWI competitions and, on a number of occasions, have been extremely successful.

Chad's

Chad's WI began in October 2012. We meet in St Chad's Church Hall and have an average of 30 members. Our committee always provides a varied itinerary of monthly talks and activities, as well as special outings and an annual open meeting. Visitors are always welcomed and enjoy delicious, homemade refreshments.

Our monthly Craft Club allows members to learn and practice new skills. These have included crocheting, knitting, making gift boxes and bags, screen printing and glass painting. Our members enjoy sharing their talents and new ideas for craft work.

In 2014, we dressed up in all our finery to receive the Centenary Baton at the Severn Valley Steam Railway in Kidderminster. Our own celebration was aboard a barge for a jazz evening on the Stourbridge Canal, a very enjoyable evening for all of us.

We end each meeting with a "Cynthia's Smile" moment (in memory of a very dear founder member) – a joke to send us home with a smile on our lips and joy in our hearts.

Childswickham

Childswickham WI was founded in 1928 and meets in the local Memorial Hall. Membership has fluctuated over the years but, since celebrating our 80th birthday, has almost doubled. A lively programme of speakers, activities and outings has been key to attracting many new members. Bursaries have been used for craft activities, such as pottery, Christmas decorations, flower arranging and jewellery making. On the 400th anniversary of Shakespeare's death in 2016, we visited the RSC for an educational behind the scenes tour "From Page to Stage", focussing on costumes and rehearsal. Membership now stands at over 40.

One member created a wonderful new cover for the President's table to replace the original, more fragile, cloth. This (pictured above) incorporates colourful appliqué work showing local produce, asparagus, plums and apples, with the WFWI and NFWI logos on the sides.

Over the years we have planted daffodils to enhance the village and have instigated and supported other village activities, such as fetes, open gardens, garden parties and clean-ups. We also raised money for a bench to commemorate the Queen's Golden Jubilee.

Recently, prompted by a new member, we have become concerned about the provision of hearing loops in all public places and have been working on a relevant Resolution.

Clent

Carrots keep close company with Clent WI. During the annual September show, held with Clent Gardening Club, carrots appear solidly, spruced up and sturdy, sitting on plates close to fellow competitors; those garden blooms and frilly flowers, jams, chutneys, cakes and crafts. There are photographs to prove that they were there, though Clent WI carrots mostly remain just out of shot. Unseen they may be but we can hear them. Note: These carrots have not been genetically modified but, as they are dangled, communicative sounds have been clearly evidenced by sharp ears.

Listener responses are variable.

Category 1 - 'YES! Let's get started!' Category 2 - 'No, not me. I couldn't.... Could I?' 'You can do anything.' Carrots whisper.

'I don't know anybody. I'm new and I'm too busy with my family and my job and....'

'Why not take time out? New friends? Oh, and PD James is set to reveal her darkest plots in Worcester on Friday. Can we offer you a lift?' (Overheard some 20 years ago.)

Listening to carrots may lead to surprising things. Getting into television! Imagine: Shefali the weather girl is heading home, John Craven is at his desk, leaving the studio empty, open to you and friends: Are you up for presenting the news? For smiling sweetly as dismal weather fronts approach? For recording the Afternoon Play? Can you cope with the noises in the Archer's kitchen? You don't know?

Well, we could do with more models for the Fashion Show. You'll be good. All shapes needed. No matter you haven't done it before. We're looking for a Christmas Fairy to flit about a bit, no need to do the decorations. Maybe you could do a Strictly, gliding 'Stately As A Galleon' from the front door, or just write a little limerick or bake a pie, make a salad or a trifle or join the Crafty Crowd in making paper bags and cutting up string, or come out wandering with us, checking out good food and drink.

WHAT? You will... You would love that! Can we offer you a lift?'

Founded 1929, we meet in Clent Parish Hall and have a 2016 Membership of 46.

Clifton upon Teme

Clifton upon Teme WI was formed by Elizabeth Daniels in 1964 when, returning to live in the village she recognised the need for an organisation to bring together local women and the many newcomers moving in. Every woman on the electoral roll was contacted and with the help of WFWI and a dedicated committee, Clifton WI was born and is still alive and well 52 years later.

Looking back through our scrapbooks we find two benches. The first, presented to Clifton to commemorate the NFWI Golden Jubilee in 1965 still stands on the village green. Also, pictured above, is a tree seat which was given in celebration of our own WI's 50th birthday in 2014.

Over the last 40 years, our WI has been involved in a variety of local activities including Clifton's "1,000 Year Pageant" held in the grounds of Woodmanton Manor in 1977 and celebrating local historical events and people.

Inspired by the Diamond Jubilee of WFWI in 1980, scenes from village life were recorded for posterity by our WI members on a specially embroidered wall hanging presented to the Village Hall where it still hangs today.

A new Millennium scrapbook was begun in 2000 and is still being added to but these days many photographs and articles are sent by email or appear on our website and so are more difficult to conserve. Members enjoy having their correspondence and minutes to read digitally but we maintain as much information as we can for future members to look back on.

Clifton is part of the Elgar Group enjoying regular meetings together. Smaller membership numbers these days limits our attendance at some events but we always try to support the Spring and Autumn council meetings where Federation news and excellent speakers make it such an enjoyable day.

An integral part of the village, our WI continues to offer catering services for local social events and funerals, and teas for visiting groups. This keeps our profile high and helps with our funds. Last year we inaugurated a "Great Clifton Bake Off" competition which was very well received. Another is planned in the autumn.

Clifton remains an attractive and pleasant village in which to live, once being dubbed "The village with a heart that has been beating for 1000 years". Set to grow if planners have their way, long may it continue so.

We meet every second Tuesday, Clifton Village Hall at 7.30 pm. 18 members plus 1 dual.

Cookhill

Membership has remained fairly stable, some ladies having been members for over 40 years. There was an influx when Astwood Bank WI closed in 1997. This brought many members, financial assets and a set of handbells which were refurbished after a grant from the Parish Council and much fund raising in January 2001. These were played by a group of enthusiasts for all members' enjoyment, other WIs and funerals. Numbers were further increased when Crabbs Cross and Hunt End closed and many members came to join Cookhill, making a valuable, enthusiastic active contribution. We now have 40 members.

The ladies have raised funds over the years for Air Ambulance, Primrose Hospice, Birmingham Children's Hospital, Worcester Acorns Hospice, ACWW, Salvation Army and Alexandra League of Friends for whom we knitted Easter chicks by the hundreds for sale in the Hospital Coffee Shop.

Members had fun and raised money holding many activities some of which are Black Country, Cockney, Bavarian, Horse Race, Medieval and Barn Dance Evenings. Garden Meetings were held to celebrate the Queen's various Jubilees and meals out for WI birthdays and anniversaries. Outings were enjoyed to a Well Dressing, Althorp, Oxford, National Arboretum as well as many local places of interest. We are a very gregarious lot, supporting group and council meetings en mass. Members frequently attend Denman and County arranged courses for subjects such as crotchet, lace making, silver jewellery and life style.

Fun activities enjoyed by the ladies are still skittle evenings, joining the County skittles league and winning the Group Kurling Tournament. Throughout the years, we have supported the Village Hall with fund raising, especially during the refurbishment. Petitions were sent to councillors and our MP trying to get the speed limit through the village reduced. Members held a VE Anniversary Party providing villagers over 70 with a celebratory free meal.

For the Millennium, it was decided to plant a Black Pear tree in the village hall car park; this was arranged with a party and ceremony. Unfortunately, it was later knocked down. We thought we would try again and on September 16th we celebrated the centenary with a coffee morning and planted a special WI Centenary Rose in the village hall Memorial Garden.

Our last main activity was to hold a garden party at a member's home to celebrate the Queen's Birthday. The garden was festively decorated, out came the tea and cake - down came the torrential rain, ending up with a squash in the conservatory.

Let's hope Cookhill WI continues as a happy, healthy and successful WI to the next Millennium.

Cookley

Cookley WI, formed in March 1929, met and held events in the ideal venue, the Village Hall, until it closed in 2002. We had problems finding alternative accommodation. Numerous places were tried, including two pubs and the Church, before we settled on the village school. Not ideal, but we are grateful for somewhere to meet. In all that time we did not lose one WI member, they were all very loyal and still are. Unable to attract new members, our numbers have dropped from 60 plus to about 24 and we are struggling to stay open, but keep on hoping.

Older members tell of many happy and hilarious evenings in the past. In particular, parties in the Village Hall with husbands invited and hosting the village over 60's with a free meal and well received in house entertainment.

The annual Flower and Produce Show, like other events, finished with the Village Hall closure. Open to all villagers, there were many categories like largest onion, marrow and straightest runner bean, whilst the craft section attracted many entries and was enjoyed immensely. The first prize was 30p and a little certificate; great days. We also lost the Spring Fayre, held on the Saturday before Mothering Sunday for which we made lots of small items and flower arrangements for the children to purchase.

In 2006 the Lottery Awards for All, made us a grant of £3,000 to attract new members from the village. We organised a day at Denman College to learn crafts, visits to Worcester Porcelain Factory and Museum, Botanical Gardens and Stately homes, lectures on Royal residences and antiques and held six craft sessions. Over 40 ladies from the village joined us for the outings and 6 ladies became new members of our WI.

Many handicraft classes have been held, the most challenging was to cover an armchair, but all went down well and members are always keen to learn something new.

We celebrated our 70th Birthday by having a 1920/30 theme where everyone came as a "flapper" with headbands and appropriate outfits. At one of our Group Meetings we were honoured to have NFWI Chairman Barbara Gill attend, a delightful lady who sadly died at an early age.

Cookley WI is especially proud of two members. Mrs Jeanne Round, one of our very loyal members, has been Cookley President three times, Group Secretary, on the WFWI Executive Committee becoming, in 1981, County Chairman and on the NFWI Royal Show Committee and says how much support she received from Cookley members and how much she enjoyed her three very happy years as County Chairman. Mrs Gwen Palmer is another lady to be admired. This year (2015) she reached her 102nd birthday, anyone looking at Gwen would think she was at least 20 years younger and (surely this must be a record) she joined WI in 1941 and is still a very active and loyal member.

Unfortunately, since writing this piece, Cookley WI was suspended in December 2015.

Cropthorne with Charlton

Cropthorne with Charlton WI, founded May 1947, meets on the second Tuesday of the month at Cropthorne and Charlton Village Hall. In the 1980's "with Charlton" didn't appear on documents; members came from both villages AND during the winter months the venue was The Old Schoolroom in Charlton, though someone did go down two hours in advance to turn on the electric heaters hanging on chains from the rafters!

There has always been an eclectic mix of speakers, outings and activities: history, geography, the arts, cookery and a huge range of alternative medicines over the 40 years. Inspiring and educational speakers, some reminding us of our youth with games, songs and corsets, some making us laugh, some bringing us close to tears. Memorably, Terry Bullingham, the Falklands veteran, and Don who, aged 11, lived in Japan and became a prisoner in WW2, his sample of daily food was an eye opener, 300 calories.

We have had a variety of musical events and can be persuaded to sing along. Food and chocolate seem to appear regularly over the years at meetings. Serious national and international issues are also well represented.

Visits have always been popular to farms, chocolate factories, stately homes, the races, and theatres. A 1983 committee meeting notes "a pantomime would be more suitable than Sweet Charity"! The post-Christmas meal is always memorable especially in 2011 when vehicles struggled through the snow and ladies arrived in wellington boots, with a change of shoes of course.

Sport has been represented by skittles, golf and a Federation tennis champion, who remained a member into her 90th year. Some lighter aspects include line dancing, solo ballroom and belly dancing with ladies joining in, hip scarves a wiggling.

At the 50th Birthday meeting the full name was re-instated, a certificate was presented and a tree planted. Unfortunately, the certificate, photos and scrapbooks were victims of the floods in 2007. The Millennium was celebrated with the provision of an engraved carafe and tumbler and, as with the president's lectern, a WI husband carried out the craft work.

During the village hall refurbishment, The Den at Holland House was home in 2010/2011. Now the hall is again the regular venue, spacious and warm for meetings, group and federation events, and most notably the Centenary celebrations of 2015 with members, families and friends from across the county. Each village was presented with 100 spring bulbs, daffodils on The Green in Charlton, crocus and daffodils in Cropthorne.

Members have always been willing to step up and contribute their services for village events, cakes still in demand. For many years the produce and craft show attracted folk from around the area as members showcased their talents.

Membership numbers have see-sawed, almost to closure during 1985 and 1995. There are now over 40 members from Charlton, Cropthorne and other villages. This reflects well on the varied and interesting programmes produced by the "youngsters".

Have things changed? Of course, but WI remains informative, interesting, friendly and fun.

Crowle

Crowle village lies approximately five miles east of Worcester. We have about 500 houses and a population of 1200. The properties are a range of various designs from thatched, black and white to modern. Whereas the village was once centered on agriculture, few people are now connected to farming.

The WI in Crowle started in the old village hall next to Hunts Farm (riding school) in April 1941. It had no electricity so meetings were held in the daytime, and no running water so this was carried from Sadler's Farm across the road.

Members were young mums and old residents that rarely left the village. In the early 1970's the WI provided a break for pensioners and for mums child rearing.

In 2000 a new village hall was built with modern facilities.

Today most WI members are retired but still actively involved in events and we are trying to attract younger members.

We have lost our village shop, dentist, butcher, baker, greengrocer, doctor's surgery and petrol station but kept the school, Post Office, pub, plant nursery and a limited bus service. A fishman from Grimsby, a milkman and paper delivery are all that call now. The demise of the local trades happened after the large supermarkets opened nearby. The remaining church is poorly attended. Some organisations in the village continue to thrive including cubs, scouts, pre-school and Crowle Players.

WI membership is approximately 40 and stable. One of our members, Betty Johnson who lived at Sale Green (a nearby parish), was our President, and then in 1999 became County Chairman. We were very proud of her.

Our meeting is the first Wednesday of the month at 7.30 in the Parish Hall. We pay £1 towards tea and coffee and raffle. Business first, keeping it brief as our own Newsletter gives the schedule of WI forthcoming and local events, then a speaker. Refreshments, chat and time for members to browse leaflets and news of other upcoming events end the evening. Members tend to leave at 10 pm.

Crowle has a 10K race around the local villages which attracts 600 runners from all over the country. The WI serves the usual tea and cake, the pre-school provides children's entertainment and the church a barbecue. The proceeds are then shared and we generally enjoy an August trip. We have visited Cardiff, Buckingham Palace, Blenheim, Chatsworth and Highgrove.

At the top of Froxmere Road is a small patch of ground which the WI adopted for many years - planting daffodils plus a bench commemorating the Queen's Silver Jubilee in 1977. Due to the ageing of WI members it was passed to the local parish to tend. In 2015 the WI planted wild flower seeds ready to celebrate 100 years of Worcestershire WI in 2018. We look forward to our legacy. It is still referred to as The WI Garden although it is now maintained by Crowle Parish Council which also erects Christmas lights on the trees on the patch.

Cutnall Green

It is comforting to think that WI ladies have continued to meet and support each other in our village for the past 85 years. In previous years it has drawn from surrounding cottages and farms, then from the new houses being built and with more ladies driving and our reputation of being a friendly group, they have come from further afield. We have 34 members and meet in our Memorial Hall.

Every Autumn we would start preparations for the Derby and Joan Christmas Party. We would prepare a two-course meal for 100 guests in a tiny, basic kitchen. Local farmers would donate turkeys and beef. A small bottle of whisky each helped our guests to better appreciate our home-grown entertainment of pantomime, sketches and dance routines, accompanied on a piano which, due to the ever-present damp, had notes missing. In time this ended, professional performers took our place, but members continued to produce a large buffet for social events of 90 plus people.

WI Centenary Party, September 2015

Our new Memorial Hall was built and we had supported the fund raising. We continued our meetings enjoying a wide variety of speakers, often complementing them with our own ideas. One was a trial with members playing lawyers, judge, witnesses and the accused, with the remainder being the jury.

One year we were very lucky to be accepted for a lottery grant which enabled 19 members to enjoy three days at our wonderful Denman College, enjoying courses in cookery, craft and therapy skills.

Having visited many stately homes including Buckingham Palace our highlight was our visit to Highgrove. Of course, the Prince wasn't in residence but we were made very welcome and enjoyed the wonderful gardens, each one discovered by entering individual doorways created by using gifts presented to him from all corners of the globe. His influence was everywhere.

Another memorable visit was to a family-owned mansion house in Wales. Each room was decorated for Christmas. We commenced our tour through the beautiful rooms when the lights went out. The guide produced a pencil torch and we stumbled after her in the dark as she made her way through each room highlighting the decorations as she went. Unable to obtain a reviving drink following the tour (no electricity) we clambered aboard our coach, set off home, only to come to a halt after a few miles on a very dark lane to be informed that we had run out of fuel!

Dodford

Dodford WI was formed on 26th October 1956, when 52 ladies enrolled. The venue at that time was the old Dodford Memorial Hall. Dodford is a Chartist settlement and this aspect has played an important part, especially in recent years.

In the 1970's concern arose at the condition of the old Memorial Hall and fundraising commenced to build a new Village Hall, with many villagers coming together to achieve this, including the WI. The new hall was built alongside the old hall to enable continuity of use. In 1977 the new hall was officially opened and the old hall demolished to make way for carparking. So, in the 1980's, the WI held its meetings in the brand new, centrally heated hall.

In 1996, to celebrate our WI's 40th Birthday, a 'Red Hawthorn' bush was planted at the village hall to commemorate this, and also a booklet was produced by Diana Poole entitled '40 Years of Dodford WI'. In 2006, when it was time to celebrate our 50th Birthday, an additional booklet was produced by Sheila Bretherton and a group photograph taken. Joan Davis, our longest serving founder member, cut the birthday cake. And in 2016 we happily celebrated our 60th birthday.

1999 saw the celebration of 150 years of the Chartism settlement with a procession from Dodford School to the Dodford Inn, and of course the WI assisted.

In 2003, at our 500th meeting, the hall committee stated that £30,000 was required to carry out repairs to the new village hall, especially the roof. So more fundraising began, and, as you might expect, this figure rose but eventually, with the aid of grants, the hall improvements materialized, and is now much used.

Fundraising always plays an important part in the life of any village, and over the years the Dodford WI has been there to help, from WI Pantry at the local Fete to Enjoyable Fashion Shows which were held in 2007, 2008 and 2009 when WI ladies paraded the 'catwalk'.

In 2008, Dodford was twinned with Belbroughton and Hartlebury for the County's 90th Birthday. One of the events was a Kurling evening, great fun.

As part of the WI Centenary celebrations, in 2014 the WI Baton arrived at Avoncroft and six members of Dodford WI took part representing local Nailmakers, with sumptuous refreshments in Guesten Hall.

Dodford WI now has 18 members and looks forward to the next celebration in 2018 and reading the WFWI Centenary Book 1980-2018.

Drakes Cross

Drakes Cross was the third WI to open in Wythall. The oldest is Wythall WI founded in 1934 and this was followed in 1969 by Hollywood when Wythall WI could take no more members. Both meet in the evening. About twenty years later some ladies were looking to attend an afternoon WI and so, in 1992, Drakes Cross was formed.

Wythall Baptist Church Hall, behind Wythall Village Hall, was chosen as the venue for meetings and we remained there until it closed in 2016. We now meet in Kingswood Meeting House.

We have eight members. All are pensioners and the eldest is over ninety. Three of the eight are founder members of this WI. One member joined the WI sixty-eight years ago when she was fourteen.

The smallness of the membership is making it difficult to pay for our meeting venue as this new one is more expensive than the old. Despite this, we continue to enjoy our monthly get together and we always support our Weatheroak Group Meetings.

The number of car drivers has dwindled to one so we can't get about as much as we used to. We do not attend Federation events because of this, and because they generally involve a fairly long journey from our location on the north-east edge of Worcestershire.

We are too arthritic to do craft now but we did in the past and are very proud of the beautiful WI banner we made.

We still enjoy a speaker at most meetings and especially remember an afternoon with Marietta, the ACWW contact in The Gambia, when we were enthralled by her talk and enjoyed sharing the afternoon tea with her afterwards. Sadly, the photographs from this occasion are no longer available to us.

Although we are not very active, we still have three events on our yearly calendar.

We raise much needed money for speakers by holding a Hot Cross Bun morning on Maundy Thursday as we have been doing every year since we were founded.

Our July meeting has been held at a member's home for many years now and our December meeting always takes the form of a Christmas Dinner held at a local pub.

How long we can keep going on is a question we are facing.

Droitwich Spa

Droitwich Spa Afternoon WI is the oldest WI in Droitwich, celebrating 100 years in existence in 2018. It is a small, friendly group with 14 members, meeting every first Wednesday afternoon of the month at 2 pm at Rotary House, Droitwich. Our meetings are varied with speakers covering a wide range of topics from creative ideas such as jewellery and lace making, as well as flower arranging, through local history topics such as the history of Kays, Worcester to presentations about far flung projects in Nicaragua, to training as a paramedic and working in radio.

During the summer we have held meetings in the outdoors, often at the President's or a member's home. These are very informal gatherings and are always subject to the British weather!

A variety of venues have been chosen for outings such as a wander around Spetchley Gardens in Worcester, a day trip to Denman College, a trip to Buckingham palace and a holiday for a number of members in the Lake District. These outings which supplement our usual meetings allow members to mix and interact in different environments.

We support local charities as much as possible such as supporting the Breast Cancer unit and creating "Twiddle Muffs" for our local hospital. We also support international ventures such as knitting bears for a school in Burundi and having a Tree for Life planted in Anantapur, SE India through Taylors of Harrogate in 2002.

Our members come from all walks of life but over the years have contributed to this WI, to the WFWI and to the National Federation through their time and enthusiasm. One member even bequeathed a gift for an annual bursary to be awarded to a WFWI member to attend Denman College for a training course of their choosing.

Droitwich Spa Afternoon WI is proud to be part of the WFWI and the National Federation. We are proud of our (nearly) 100 years of history and hope we will be able to continue for another 100 years.

Delivering our donations to Worcestershire Breastcare Cancer Unit, December 2013

Our fund-raising stall in town, November 2016

Eckington

Village life is an integral part of Eckington WI and we have always kept our profile high in the village. Whether it be having our own float in the 1980s village carnival and parade, providing cookery lessons at the school, or manpower to the local Music Festival Eckstock, we are active contributors to village life. Recently we undertook a new venture by organising a village garage sale. Our first was in 2014 and given its success, is repeated annually.

We do like to get out and about, join in celebrations, even try the occasional competition. One of our main achievements was winning the Silver Cup in 1981 for our entry in the 'Off to Playschool' Co-operative competition. In 1990, Eckington were the only WI to perform alone in the WFWI Cavalcade, presenting a Murder Mystery. Fast forward to 2008 when we celebrated our 70th Birthday with a party held in September for current and past members.

2015, we all celebrated the WI Centenary Year. We had members attend the Palace Garden Party and the ACM at the Albert Hall and we held our own Garden Party in August with all members dressed in their finery enjoying a fine afternoon tea! A new experience was the Tea and Tents Festival 2015; four of our members attended and were inspired by the range of ages, activities and enthusiasm that we aim to bring to our own WI.

Although perhaps a more mature WI, we have accepted change, adapted and are always looking for new ways of recruiting and retaining, taking advantage of social media with our Facebook Page and website. On researching the Eckington WI Record Book though, it is clear there is one thing that has not changed over the past 40 years. In the Committee Annual Report 1999, it stated "we may not be the biggest institute in the county, we may not be the institute with the most number of young people in the county but we must be one of the most happy, friendliest groups". So yes, we are still small (34 members in 2016, meeting at the Village Hall) and still a happy group. With our 80th birthday to arrange in 2018, we hope to celebrate it with friends new, current and past.

Evesham Vale

Over the past nine years Evesham Relay for Life has raised £655,840 – a phenomenal amount for a small country town. For the past four years, members of Evesham Vale WI have assisted Evesham Relay by helping to provide refreshments for the teams and individuals taking part during their final weekend.

What is Relay for Life?

Relay for Life is an inspirational year-round event bringing communities together to show that united we are stronger than cancer. Teams of friends, family and colleagues rally together, raising as much as possible through the year for Cancer Research UK.

The Relay

Relay is the celebration of everyone's fundraising efforts. Teams come together for one weekend each year, set up camp and with the celebrations in full swing, members of each team take turns to walk around the track for the duration of the Relay. All Relays are overnight, marking the fact that cancer never sleeps. As the evening draws in, everyone gathers to light Candles of Hope and pay tribute to those whose lives have been affected by cancer. Bags are lit up by a glowing candle with poignant messages of remembrance and celebration and line the track to create a moving and unforgettable moment. At the end of the Relay, everyone joins together for a final lap to celebrate their fundraising achievements and look back on an unforgettable Relay for Life.

Our members were impressed by the people taking part in the fund raising who were so enthusiastic and dedicated. It was a very humbling and enlightening experience to witness so many people co-operating in such a worthwhile cause, all or most having lived with or experienced cancer.

The following are thoughts from our members:

➢ We would not normally say that a couple of hours spent pouring cups of tea and coffee is the most inspiring way of spending your time! However, it can be, if you are on the WI team helping out at your local Relay for Life event, in aid of Cancer Research..... one thing they have in common; they want to help beat this awful disease. Many are survivors or carers. It was a privilege to serve them, the WI in the community, all pulling together in a great cause.

➢ The time flew by – so humbling to see everyone so upbeat about a serious illness.

➢ Babies, toddlers, the teenager that you just knew had an amazingly courageous story to tell – senior citizens and everyone in-between. Humbling and inspiring – such a privilege to be able to help in a very small way.

➢ Every face that passed by our refreshment stall told a story. People big, small, young, old. Bravery, hope and a sense of humour had helped them survive and live on.

What an inspiration – to see so many smiling faces. A fantastic event with amazing people. What a fabulous team they are!

Our WI has 32 members and we meet at Bengeworth Church House.

Fairfield

Founded in 1932 Fairfield WI celebrates its 85th birthday in 2017. During that time membership has remained fairly constant, between 30 and 40, with an age-range of 30 to 80 plus years.

Our rural setting is reflected in the proportion of members we have from farming families blended with a wide variety of other professions e.g. health workers, teachers and civil servants, as well as those running their own businesses. Throughout the years our meetings have been held in the Village Hall which is sited alongside the church at the centre of the village. During this time although the building has been modernised, it has remained on exactly the same site. Our meeting at the heart of the village is very much the ethos of the Institute.

Whilst we continue to promote and take part in an ever widening variety of experiences, for the past 22 years our major event has become our Annual Produce Show. We believe this is an example which clearly demonstrates the extent to which WI is involved in our village community and is committed to bringing people together.

On show day, many and varied classes are open to both WI and non-WI exhibitors. Through this we endeavour to facilitate the mutual sharing of skills, whether it's in growing flowers, fruit or vegetables, making preserves or baking, flower-arranging and photography or making craft items. Following the excitement of judging and prize giving amidst a great hubbub, all parties participate in an eagerly awaited Produce Auction.

We are convinced that this event serves to connect people of all ages in a world that seems to be increasingly electronically connected and less invested in growing and creating things for others. At Fairfield WI we recognise the importance of community, true friendship and welcoming new opportunities for learning.

Far Forest

We work for Home and Country
As on through life we go.
With "Fellowship" our motto
We Knit and Cook and Sew.
Our interests are varied
From Walks to Bottled Fruit.
We work and play together
We're the Women's Institute.

We start each monthly meeting
With a joke to make us laugh.
We give out Birthday Posies
Business time we've cut in half!
Our Speakers all inspire us
On subjects by the score,
We eat delicious suppers –
No-one could ask for more.

Each month we have a Craft Night
When we meet to learn new skills.
We also love to natter
As the air with laughter fills.
Rag Rugs and making Boxes
Some things that we have tried
And Breast Care Unit pillows
We've handed on with pride.

With Jumble Sales and Outings
Our life is never dull
We're there for our community
And live life to the full.
With Skittles, writing Recipe Books,
Treading the Boards in village shows,
Our Catering is famous
Demand just grows and grows.

We go to Denman College
For courses of all kinds.
Each year we give a Bursary
To improve our members' minds.
We've studied things like Dowsing;
Made windows in Stained Glass,
Whatever course is chosen
It always is First Class.

One day each year in August
We support the local Show.
Make 400 packs of Sandwiches -
It really is "all go"!
With a thousand cups of Tea to serve
And Cakes and cans of Pop –
When we've worked for eleven hours
We all are "fit to drop"!!

"Jerusalem's" our anthem,
We aim to do our best.
With offering help to others
We never seem to rest.
But working well together
We're always "on a high".
We value special friendship
We're Far Forest WI.

This poem can be sung to the tune of the British Grenadiers!

We recently moved to the Far Forest Pavilions, Callow Hill, having previously met at The Far Forest Centre. Current membership is 20.

Feckenham

Our group of 20 members meet at the Village Hall, Feckenham.

One recent event which has stood out for our group as a real achievement was the Feckenham Open Gardens and Church Flower Festival. This event takes place every three years, and has grown in popularity since its inception many years ago. 2015 was busier than ever and during the entire weekend of the Festival we were truly pushed to our limits. Feckenham WI's task is to provide light lunches, teas and cakes at the village hall for the visitors. We rose to the occasion and, although exhausted by the end of it, we all felt extremely satisfied with a job well done! Added to this, some of our members are also part of the church flower arranging group and had worked hard during the Friday creating beautiful arrangements for the event, and of course they also had their gardens open!

Fortunately, the weather treated us kindly which might well be why there was an abundance of visitors. Our members met at the hall early in the morning with a supply of homemade cakes and an eagerness to make the weekend a success. What we didn't expect were the coaches with hordes of people to add to our ever-growing workload. Sandwich making was the first job which worked rather like a production line with Doris Burley, our eldest member at 90 years old, sitting and making sandwiches all day. As people visited the hall, we soon got through our supplies which were supposed to last for the two days. New supplies had to be purchased for Sunday's opening. To give you an idea of how busy we were, here are a few supplies and quantities we got through during the weekend: 28 loaves of bread, 40 litres of milk, 120 tea bags, 10 packets of coffee, 3000 serviettes and 13 dozen plain scones.

The list could go on as we made sure we provided a large selection of sandwiches and cakes – all of which was eaten! We also had a few girls serving and a number of washing up helpers in the kitchen.

The whole festival was a huge success, with the money from the open gardens going to the church fabric fund. The money taken by the WI ensures we are in credit for the next three years and also enabled us to donate £1,000 to the church. After expenses, we raised a total of £3,669.

It was supremely satisfying for all of us to learn the final figures and fully comprehend how successful the weekend really was. We received many lovely comments praising our wonderful food and efficient system! We truly worked as a team and without this I doubt it would have experienced the same success.

Another highlight for our group which must be mentioned, was the planting of a Yew tree in the church yard in 2009 to celebrate 90 years of the WI in Feckenham. Our Centenary celebrations will be in 2019.

Fernhill Heath

The early years of Fernhill Heath WI are a bit of a mystery. What is known dates back to 1970 when a lady called Pat Clarke joined the WI in the village and became President. She held this role for 2 years, but unfortunately the WI closed in 1972 as there was no volunteer for President.

Fernhill Heath Mk2

In late 1997, Sylvia Perkins and Suzanne Owen delivered leaflets through the doors in Fernhill Heath, inviting anyone interested in setting up a WI to attend a meeting in the Memorial Hall. Eileen Kilminster was one of the ladies who decided to attend and whilst on her way to the meeting, she began to catch up with another lady who turned to her and enquired "are you going to the WI meeting? Shall we go together?" That was how Eileen met Barbara Hartshorne. This meeting was very well attended and with much enthusiasm for a WI, so Sylvia and Suzanne arranged a further meeting. It was made clear that three ladies would be needed to take on the Officer roles. If no one volunteered the WI could not proceed and these volunteers would be needed at the next meeting.

The second meeting was not so well attended, maybe 40 to 50 ladies covering about four rows of seating in the hall. No-one volunteered for the roles, so Sylvia and Suzanne started to go along the rows asking each person in turn. The question was "Would you like to be President, Secretary or Treasurer?" There were no volunteers until they reached Eileen in the middle of the third row. She said yes to the Treasurer's role and then persuaded Barbara, who was seated next to her, to take the role of President! A lady called Isobel Reynolds agreed to become Secretary for the first 12 months. Fernhill Heath WI had officially come into being; there were 9 official members at the start, rising to 14 by the end of the year.

We now have 26 members as of April 2016. Meetings used to be held at the Cedars, but in 2012 we moved to the Baptist Church Hall. The WI is well run by a committee of nine ladies who meet once a month. We are a very active group with Craft, Book and Walking sub-groups. We also take part in the County Skittles and Quiz Competitions. Alongside these activities we run theatre, ten pin bowling and other interesting outings.

Fernhill Heath WI also takes part in the annual 'Fun on the Brum' event. This summer fayre for all the village has grown in popularity and strength over the last couple of years and is now seen as a real highlight in the village – raising money for charities and a great day out for all the family. The photo taken from the Fernhill Heath WI Refreshment Stall in 2016 shows how busy it is!

Finstall and Cofton Hackett

In the centenary year of the WI, boxes of our records dating back to the first meeting in 1937 were discovered stored in the loft of our meeting place, the Village Hall. These showed how much both Finstall and our WI have changed over the years to the present day.

In 1937 Finstall was a small, close knit village community. Many villagers came from families who had lived here for generations and many worked on the local farms or were from the large houses in the area. It was these "ladies of the manor" who started Finstall WI. The records from the early years show how closely they kept to the aims and objectives of the WI.

From the 50's to the 80's the membership grew to over seventy, many coming from beyond Finstall and we were very active with a Craft Group and Drama Group performing plays. They entered cakes, jams, chutney etc. in competitions and often won prizes - they even had a Home Economics Secretary! They organised outings, theatre visits and lobbied the government on issues of the day such as free school milk. Finstall too was expanding with hundreds of houses built on any available farmland near the village. In spite of this, with increased mobility, the two local shops closed. The post office was kept open briefly following a WI-led petition but eventually closed. Finstall underwent a massive change and lost its sense of a village community. The improved road network made commuting easier and many residents work well away from the locality.

A new WI, Finstall Cross, was formed which, having evening meetings rather than our afternoon meetings, has attracted many working women so that our membership is mainly those who have retired and tend to be the less energetic elderly. Although our membership declined to the teens, it has now stabilised at the mid-twenties and we continue to have a wide and varied programme of talks and visits. We hosted a successful Spring Group Meeting in 2015 and we have a reputation for holding very good parties. We organise two coach trips a year in which many members of the local WI Group participate. Every year, we have a fund-raising Garden Party and Coffee Morning, a Christmas and Birthday Party, and a New Year Meal at a local restaurant. We have a Poetry Group, have recently started a small Craft Group and we run a bookstall at our meetings for members to exchange books.

Our meetings are held in Finstall Village Hall which has recently been completely refurbished with re-decoration and a modern heating system. In 2005 we acquired seven new members and a new name when we absorbed Cofton Hackett WI which closed due to falling membership. Sadly, only one of these members remains. Hopefully we can continue for many more years, though Finstall will continue to change as more local land is earmarked for building. We meet at 2 pm on the first Monday in the month and welcome new members who will find us friendly and caring.

Finstall Cross

Finstall Cross WI was formed in October 2009 with 14 members and increased to 61 by 2016. Finstall Village Hall is our venue and we are named after the public house opposite. Due to the size of the hall, the fire restrictions and, possibly our popularity, membership reached its capacity by 2016 and a bye law was read at the annual meeting setting the membership limit to 60. Visitors are always welcomed and could become members as and when numbers allow.

Our WI has been described by a local authoress as a feisty, vivacious group of ladies who "do things and achieve a lot". We certainly pack events into our itinerary with monthly supper club, book club, craft club and knit and natter afternoons. Weekly, we explore the local district on foot! Trips have become an almost monthly event and have included Berkeley Castle, Malvern Well Dressing, Liverpool, The London Poppies, Highgrove and many more. There are often up to three events in the same week. A few of us went to Tea and Tents, an amazing event. WIKenders is a new club introduced in 2016 for members who may want company at the weekend either to go to a pre-arranged event, or for a last minute get together.

Helping those in need has become an essential part of our WI. We have knitted beautiful trauma teddies so that our local fire service and the British Red Cross disaster van can give a child comfort when they are involved in a difficult situation. New toys and books have also been sent to the disaster van. Colourful jumpers have been knitted for children living on the border between Thailand and Burma. We have knitted squares for a local church to make into blankets to be sent to a fistula hospital in Ethiopia. Christmas presents are sent to the lonely in Bromsgrove via the Salvation Army.

Environmental concerns have led us to travel to London to lobby Parliament about climate change, litter pick the local area and plant new meadow seeds.

To celebrate the WI centenary anniversary in 2015, we set ourselves various challenges: - walk 100 miles, swim 100 miles, raise £100 for charity, lose 100 lbs, collect 100 tips to publish and donate 100 items to local organisations. These targets were mostly achieved – in fact, we walked over 1,000 miles, raised £206 and donated 307 items.

We are a very friendly and youthful (in mind if not always in body) group of ladies, who enjoy exploring new opportunities.

Fladbury & Moor

Formed 18th March 1930 - 37 Members meet at Fladbury Village Hall
SNIPPETTS FROM OUR SCRAP BOOKS

April 1997 - National Spring Clean time, so very appropriately on St Georges Day, a band of WI members, wearing emblazoned tabards and armed with gauntlets and pokers, set out to deal with Fladbury's litter.

'Up the creek without a paddle' – Fladbury & Moor branch took part in the Fladbury Paddle Club Regatta. A couple of evening practices under the instruction of some young Olympic hopefuls. On the day members set off to compete against other local teams. We wore our green shirts and life jackets and paddled the bell boats too fast to count. There was much cheering from the crowded banks of the River Avon, alas, we didn't get gold, or silver or even bronze, but we did have fun and it was the taking part that counted!!

When I thought about joining Fladbury WI, I had just moved into the place,
I hadn't a clue about who was who, or which name to put to a face,
Well it wasn't too long, or so it seemed to me, that I felt like a really old hand,
What with raffles and jumbles and shows and the like, and all manner of things being planned,
When the inevitable happened and I received the call, to think about joining committee,
I put my name forward at the AGM; to refuse to would seem such a pity,
And I thought, what's the harm? And I don't really mind, I'd willingly help all I could,
And the ladies are friendly, jolly and kind, and so it seemed to me that I should,
Well the voting took place for the president's post, and was duly elected,
But imagine my surprise, when she asked me to be, The Secretary, (not what I expected),
Well twelve months have passed by since that fateful day, and despite being new to it all,
I've had lots of fun, and done many things, and I'm glad now I answered the call.

January 2000 - The gift of a Sanctuary cushion and ten kneelers for the choir, undertaken by the WI Millennium project, was presented to and blessed by the rector at a short ceremony preceding the parish communion service. An illuminated plaque in beautiful calligraphy now hangs in the area of the choir explaining the project, for the benefit of future generations.

April 2003 - Fladbury WI Players and friends presented **Snow White** at Fladbury Village Hall and due to the enormous success of this production, and subsequent demands for more, the WI Drama group has diversified and is now known as Fladbury Players.

June 2009 - Our garden meeting: We wandered around the gorgeous garden with wine glasses in hand, murmuring 'What's that called?' 'Can I have a cutting?' 'until the evening cooled and we reluctantly moved inside. There we partook of the sort of spread only the WI can achieve. By mutual consent, calories did not count that evening – it's sort of WI magic.

November 2005 - Two separate WI's which went their separate ways at the outbreak of the Second World War in 1939 have reunited after 60 years. The new organisation will be known as Fladbury & Moor WI.

Foley Park

Foley Park WI was founded in 1984 for 'Mums at the School Gate' and meets as an afternoon group. This has proved to be a successful arrangement for old and new members who do not want to be out in the evening, but want to enjoy the friendship and activities that the WI offers. Foley Park WI has evolved into a friendly active group, with Summer rambles, Theatre visits, County activities and a Summer outing as well as other social events.

In 2014 we celebrated our 30th Anniversary with a tea party at which current and past Founding Members were present. We meet on the second Tuesday of the month at Foley Park Methodist Church, DY11 6LD from 1.45 pm and we have about 35 members at present.

A Typical Summer Outing. Off to the Cotswolds. First stop Moreton-in-the Marsh on market day and very busy. Look! A lovely pub with a very pleasant courtyard for coffee. Plenty of 'retail therapy' then time to drive on to Bourton on the Water. What an idyllic afternoon: children paddling in the shallow river, families picnicking on the river banks, a street performer entertaining, cream teas, exploring this lovely place. All too soon, time to board the coach for our journey home. What a perfect day!!

A Group Social Evening. It's our turn to host The Leys Group Social Evening. What to do? Talks on Victorian Corsets? "Painful!" Flowers in bra cups? "Odd!"... Or ask our Actors to put on a Murder Mystery Play. The night is arranged, and on the evening Members arrive in strange cricket gear. Knobbly knees are bared and eccentric village ladies are all suspects! Roles are played with gusto, and fits of the giggles. The Murderess is revealed as the Lady Cricket Captain who has been given OUT, when not, and has bashed the Umpire over the head with her bat, not her handbag!

Walking For Health! We took up the Federation's challenge to complete 100 miles of activity during The WI Centenary Year, linking in with The University of Worcester's "Moon Mission". Again in 2016 these local rambles have proved very successful giving an opportunity for us to meet on 5 or 6 occasions in spring/summer for a leisurely stroll, followed by well-earned refreshments. These socials have now become a regular part of our programme and we hope to continue finding more walks and encouraging our members to "walk for health".

Celebrating the Queen's 90th birthday

Franche

Franche WI celebrate their 50 years of existence in February 2017. We will be holding a party with past members in attendance. One lady who has been a member almost since its onset will be helped by our current oldest member to cut the anniversary cake.

Whilst we are by no means a big Institute, what we lack in numbers we certainly make up for in enjoyment, good speakers and outings. We regularly attend the live theatre, go on various trips and have lunch meetings, as well as participate in the Worcester WI skittles competition. Our recent trips have involved a visit to The Royal Opera House London and the last visit was to the BBC studio in Birmingham.

One of our most enjoyable outings was that visit to the Royal Opera House in 2015, funded by the Hamlyn Trust and NFWI to see the Nutcracker Ballet. So memorable, the atmosphere with hundreds of WIs from all over England was magical.

Sadly, under the re-organisation, the Leys Group has disbanded, but we have had many enjoyable get-togethers with the Leys Group, including the Queens Jubilee.

The Queens 90th Birthday found us donning our posh frocks for an afternoon tea.

We are now one of the smaller WIs so funding speakers can be a problem, hence the fund-raising effort. Our home made cakes and preserves went down a storm.

We have 18 members and meet at St Barnabas Community Centre, Franche.

Frankley

Frankley WI was formed on 14th May 1946. Currently the meeting venue is St. Leonard's Church Hall. In past years, meetings took place in a room variously described as the Village

School, Village Hall and Church Hall. For a few years from 2002, while the new St. Leonard's Church Hall was being built, they moved to St. Christopher's Hall, Holly Hill.

In 1980 there were 38 members of our WI. This slowly reduced to about 20, but then started rising again and now stands at 27. In 1981, committee member Mrs Clark was praised for having served for 35 years and, in 2015, committee member Mrs Charles retired after serving for 35 years. This almost covers the 70 years of our existence.

In 1989 there was a memorable meeting when founder member Mary Parker gave an account of receiving Maundy Money from the Queen in Birmingham Cathedral a few weeks earlier. The presentation case of coins was much admired.

In the 1980s and 1990s Frankley WI organised regular trips to places of interest – museums, stately homes, gardens and factories. In recent years, members have more often joined with other WIs for visits but have started to make regular theatre trips.

Over the last 40 years Frankley WI has taken part in skittles, group walks, group crafts, litter picks and fund raisers. Frankley WI still holds an annual produce show and often enters some of the classes at the WFWI creative crafts competition. Frankley WI awards two trophies each year. One is for the member with the highest overall skittles score in WI competitions. The other is the Olive Risbridger Trophy, awarded to the member who

participates most frequently and successfully in meetings, games and competitions.

In 2014 our current committee dressed as members of an Edwardian showman's family at the Centenary baton handover to West Midlands at Avoncroft museum. We had great fun acting our parts.

Members also attended the Buckingham Palace Garden Party and the NFWI AGM at the Royal Albert Hall in 2015. We are looking forward to participating in the WFWI centenary celebrations in 2018.

Great Comberton

Great Comberton is a small Women's Institute with a current membersip of 15. It has continued to meet monthly through its loyal band of members and hardy support of the presidents through these years, Peggy Foster and Eileen Pieters, and the secretaries, Eileen Pieters and Mary Rednall (yes Eileen was a glutton for punishment). They handed over only recently to Anne Reynolds and Jude Wood.

Our Women's Institute not only has monthly afternoon meetings in our village hall but has, over the years, been involved in local issues, such as supporting the refurbishment of the hall and the war memorial, and planting daffodil bulbs at the entrance to the village.

Coil pot we made as a group

After listening to the speakers, they join us for tea

Visit to Spetchley Gardens

Coffee mornings supporting worthy causes, bike rides around Bredon Hill and hosting visits from Women's Institutes, some all the way from Wales, have all been tackled.

Now regular Nosh and Natters are held in the village hall to bring together residents over coffee and cake.

Guarlford

Guarlford WI meets on the second Tuesday evening of the month in the attractive upper room of the Village Hall, which was once a malthouse, built around 1870. The village lies beneath the beautiful Malvern Hills, surrounded by farmland; there is a church (St Mary the Virgin), the award-winning Grange Farm Nursery and two public houses, but no longer a school, shop or Post Office.

The year 2016 marked an important milestone for Guarlford WI, as it was 75 years since the Institute was formed. Previously ladies had been members of the WI in the neighbouring village of Madresfield, which was set up in 1917 as "Madresfield, Newland and Guarlford Women's Institute". From 1941 the ladies of Guarlford held their own meetings in what was known as "The First Aid Point", set up in the stable of the Rectory, moving to our present home in the Village Hall after World War Two. The 2016 photograph shows member Liz Tidball cutting the 75th Anniversary cake, also celebrating her birthday that day.

Since 1941, and even 1980, a lot of things have changed: the Committee and members can now communicate through e-mail, most drive to meetings instead of walking or cycling, and we have our own pages on the village website, www.guarlford.org.uk. In essentials, however, we are still very much as we were all those years ago – about 20 members offering friendship and interesting meetings, at which we enjoy traditional topics as well as new ideas. There is a Skittles team and a Quiz contingent. We are still involved in helping the local community: for example, every year we use our crafting skills for a local charity – in the Centenary year we joined forces with some of the ladies of St Gabriel's WI, Hanley Swan, to make 100 cushions and bags for patients who had had breast cancer operations. In 2016 we were knitting blankets for premature babies.

At our 75th Birthday meeting on June 14th we were pleased to welcome our County Chairman Marjorie Whiting, our Rector Revd. Sue Irwin and members of other local WIs with lively entertainment from The Elderly Brothers and excellent food. (Guarlford WI has a good reputation locally for its delicious catering.) So one thing has not changed over the years – the members of Guarlford WI enjoy a good party!

Habberley

Habberley WI has 31 members and has met at Habberley Scout Hut since 2014. We were founded in 1966, meeting at St John's Church Hall. During the time since then we have gone through challenges and changed from an evening meeting to an afternoon one. Our meetings have been focused very much on members' wishes so that the interests of all participants of varying skills are considered. As well as learning new skills such as craft, cooking and needlecraft, we have fun at social time with quizzes, beetle drives, film shows, outings and lunches.

In 1984 to celebrate our 18th birthday, a commemorative silver medallion was struck by a member's husband, Harold Badham, which is worn by each serving president. Engraved on it is a picture of Pecket's Rock, Habberley Valley. The same year a member, Greta Mitchell, was County Chairman. We have had three serving trustees on the County Committee.

Our craft work included, in 1986, making objects from pewter; a photograph of one of these plates was published in the county calendar. 1990 saw us knitting hats and jumpers for the premature baby unit at Birmingham Hospital. More recently we have made gel flowers, an iced plaque for a Christmas cake and a hanging Christmas tree made of card. Several times we have entered the Co-operative class at the Home Economic Rally and in 2000 at Perdiswell we won our class! Success was in our bones and we managed to win this wonderful accolade on two other occasions. We held a biennial Produce Show in September where husbands and children were encouraged to enter too. 1996, 1998, 2004 and 2007 photographs from members were published in the County calendar, subjects being Daffodils at Kidderminster Hospital, Worcester Cricket Ground, Poppy Fields at Blakedown and Arley Arboretum.

Over the years we have enjoyed many outings including a visit to a Well Dressing, Chester, Buckingham Palace, Tea at the Ritz, Weston Park, Great Witley Church, Burford, Weston Super Mare and Llandudno to name but a few.

In 1998 we joined a march to save Kidderminster Hospital from being downgraded.

Together with afternoon teas we collected recipes to put together into a book and sold copies to help with fund raising.

Members are happy to respond to the needs of the Community and for many years we have been pleased to arrange a 'Litter Pick' at Habberley Valley where numerous bags of rubbish were collected.

We have a link with a WI in New Zealand and exchange calendars at Christmas.

Whilst in the Leys Group we enjoyed many entertaining and educational speakers. In 2001 together with other group members we put on a craft display at Bewdley Library. In September 2014 we met as a group to accompany the 100 years NFWI Centenary Baton being transported down the canal to Wolverley before it continued to the next area.

WI membership can be very fulfilling and this is just a small selection of what we have enjoyed through the years.

Unfortunately, since submitting this, Habberley WI was unable to continue and was suspended in January 2017.

Hadzor and Oddingley

Hadzor and Oddingley WI met in Oddingley from their formation in 1917 until 2014 when the Church Hall closed, moving to the neighbouring village of Tibberton in January 2015. Members always enjoy entering events and competitions, winning the Mary Pedley Award in 1980 with a beautifully decorated poem on  blackberrying and jam making.

In the 1990's we celebrated our 80th birthday in the garden of a member's home in Hadzor. We enjoyed orienteering in the Wyre Forest and entering the Home Economics Rallies.

Hadzor and Oddingley WI were delighted to win the Home Economics Rally in 2006 and even more thrilled to win it again in 2007, the year of our 90th Birthday. A celebration lunch was held, photographed by the local newspaper; there was also afternoon tea with a marquee in a member's garden with guests, strawberries and sunshine.

Blackberries 1980

In 2011 we won the Co-operative Cup at the Annual Council Meeting followed by the runners-up shield in the County Skittles Competition in 2013. 2017 sees the 100th Birthday of Hadzor and Oddingley WI with much celebration and possibly blackberry picking.

For over a hundred years friendship, fellowship and support has been at the heart of Hadzor and Oddingley WI. Over that time members have enjoyed many outings, coffee mornings, monthly competitions, groups for sewing and craft, walking, bridge, play reading, the occasional litter pick and maybe blackberrying. 29 members now move forward in the same vein

Hagley (Late Hagley Afternoon)

In its 50th year Hagley Evening WI found it impossible to continue and the decision was made to enlarge with Hagley Afternoon WI to become, in 2015, Hagley WI. Members are mostly in the "retired" age group so activities are now confined to more sedentary pursuits which are suitable to their mobility and financial status.

Hagley Afternoon has entered competitive events arranged by County and other organisations, with some degree of success. Also, visits have been organised to different venues to educate or entertain members. Classes have been arranged to teach various skills – among others Christmas baubles, beadwork, pressed flowers, embroidery techniques and decoupage have been tried. In the past there has been considerable success in competitive drama. Now Hagley WI are reduced to the "HAGS" (Hagley Autumnal Girls Society!) whose activities are confined to trying to entertain its own members!

Occasional afternoon music events, which appeal to a wide variety of tastes, have been enjoyed. We have had small groups dedicated to members' particular interests, such as walking, Scrabble, craft etc. Craft continues with a monthly Knit and Knatter group. Whilst not being confined to knitting, this group has supported many charitable organisations. Quilts have been made for Pro-Linus. Baby clothes for the neo-natal unit at a local hospital is ongoing; jumpers and hats have been made for needy children in Africa. The current project is to knit blankets for the Fistula Clinic in Ethiopia.

To mark the Millennium, Hagley Afternoon and Hagley Evening WIs mobilised the community to produce a Tapestry. It is composed of small representations of village organisations, produced by the members of those organisations, and also of historic sites in the parish. The various parts were put together by members of the two WIs and the tapestry, which hangs in the foyer of Hagley Community Centre, was unveiled by Lord Cobham on 16th September 2000.

An important part of Hagley WI's activities concern care for the community. The local hospice is supported – one member being involved in caring for the garden which was adopted several years ago by Hagley Group. Another project is to support the local Women's Refuge by holding a monthly collection of items urgently needed by the women and children.

Two benches have been provided at Hagley Playing Field, the first to commemorate Hagley Afternoon's 90th Birthday and later, 95 years of WI in Hagley. To finance the benches the bulk of the money was raised by a number of highly successful Fashion Shows kindly organised by Debut, a local Hagley business.

To fund charitable activities, we have held jumble, table top and bring and buy sales and hosted Coffee Mornings, Afternoon Teas, Lunches and Garden Parties. Currently, funds are being raised to support Denman College and the project to build a Community Hub in Hagley.

Hagley WI continues to thrive although the numbers have dropped considerably from a membership of 125 with a Committee of 12 in 1980 to about half that number. We enjoy monthly meetings and extra activities as they did, but times have changed and our WI has changed with them.

We continue, also as they did, to consider ourselves a caring, friendly and welcoming Hagley Womens Institute.

Hagley Evening

Hagley Evening WI was formed in 1965; younger Mums needed their husbands to childmind so they could not go out until evening. Their first meetings were held in the new Community Centre, later they moved to St Saviour's Church Hall and finally to the Free Church Hall. Throughout its nearly 50 years, membership was always around 30 to 35 and when in 2015 we joined with Hagley Afternoon WI, there were 30 enrolled members. Unfortunately, a number of ladies could not manage a Monday afternoon meeting due to long standing commitments so they did not rejoin.

Members have always supported County events especially the Council meetings, the Lucy Hingley lectures and lunches with a speaker. We have competed at the County Rally with some success, and good friendships have been made whilst preparing the exhibits. One of the highlights of our year has been an evening visit to a garden, usually an NGS garden with tea and cakes!

In the community, we have helped at the Annual Hagley Fete making and selling cakes to raise money for the Community Association. For many years we made and sold cakes for the Hagley Village Show which we ran in conjunction with the Gardening Club until 2009 , exhibiting and providing stewards on the day.

In 2009 we held a Debut Fashion Show and donated £450 to our local Hospice, Mary Stevens. We also helped create a garden there, planting shrubs and bulbs and finally we planted the Jam and Jerusalem Roses.

Each year, until the landslides of 2010, we served refreshments at Arley Station, on the Severn Valley Railway, for the arrival of the Father Christmas Special trains full of excited children heading for his Grotto; this was always the last Sunday before the 25th – hard work but great fun!

Many of us are enjoying WI as part of Hagley WI and we look forward to many more years of friendship as members of WI.

Hallow

Hallow WI has always maintained a healthy membership since its inception in 1943, with numbers averaging 70 annually. Throughout we have held our meetings in Hallow Parish Hall on the second Thursday of the month.

Memorable events since 1980 have been the appointment of Freda Davies (a member since 1965) onto the WFWI Executive Board in 1986, then becoming County Treasurer in 1990 and in 1993 being appointed County Chairman.

In 2006 a large number of Hallow members were part of the fantastic WI trip to China and in 2013 Hallow WI celebrated its 70th birthday with President Freda Davies at the helm!

The year kicked off in April with a 'lunch with speaker' - the National Flower Arranger Andrew Lloyd. In June we had a Celebratory Dinner with illusionist Bertie Pearce to entertain, a celebratory cake and our oldest member, Mrs Edna Wilde, who unveiled a new tablecloth which the Craft Group had made.

This was the culmination of a number of years spent talking about producing a new tablecloth but it seemed such a daunting task it never got started. However, the Craft Group led by Jeanette Riddex, decided that for the 70th birthday celebration it would become a reality and with the purchase of a piece of dark green material from the Rag Market in Birmingham, they set about producing a design. They looked at different ways of incorporating the lovely embroidery from the old tablecloth but that would have meant cutting it up, so it was decided that everyone would embroider flowers and fruits from all seasons either onto a piece of the green fabric (after we had cut out the main cloth) or directly onto the cloth. Everyone, from experienced needlewomen to ladies who had never embroidered at all, produced a beautiful array of flowers and fruits which were arranged in a swag, a painting of Hallow Oak Tree with our dates and gold lettering (made from a charity shop find!) finished the design. Hallow was very fortunate at that time to have a member who used her expertise with sewing machines to finish the project and she added the embroidered part of the old tablecloth to the other end of the new cloth.

That same year Hallow WI won The Shrawley Cup (an annual competition held within the Woodbury Group) in the Summer and also won the WFWI Challenge Shield and the Rose Bowl at the Annual Council Meeting in October for their entries depicting 'Celebrating 95 Years'. A very memorable year.

Hampton

As our WI entered the 1980's we had upwards of 50 members, and the subscription was £3. Our meetings had a good mix of interesting speakers, along with outings and theatre visits, and participation in group and county events.

At Christmas 1981, we went carol singing around Hampton, donating the proceeds to our local cottage hospital, where a day room was being built. This was repeated in 1985, when funds were given towards a new operating table. In 1988 there was further fund raising for the Worcester and District Scanner Appeal, and also for a local hospice.

1982 saw the 700th anniversary of St Andrew's, our parish church. Amongst other celebrations was a medieval pageant, with some of our members taking part.

In 1986, we organised a visit from Canon John Eley (the Cooking Canon), who had a successful cookery show on TV at the time. He came and demonstrated a range of dishes in a marquee on the vicarage lawn. It was a very enjoyable summer's evening.

In 1989, we celebrated our 21st birthday, with a celebration meeting, at which many former members were present, many of them travelling long distances to be there.

During these years, our meeting place had been a rather run-down wooden scout hut, with minimal facilities, which was sometimes challenging when it came to catering. The community had been fund raising for many years, and we did our part, but it was a drop in the ocean, considering the amount needed to build a new brick scout hall. Luckily a local charity and local government together provided the bulk of the money, and in 1992, the new premises were completed. It was lovely to be able to hold our meetings in a warm comfortable space, with good kitchen facilities. The meeting place of a WI is so much bound up with the traditions, memories and character of the group.

From this: *To this:*

In 1998, our quiz team won the Worcestershire heat, and went on to win the Inter-Federation semi-final against five other counties. The final was held at Denman College, but unfortunately, we did not win on that occasion!

Moving into the 21st century, things continue much the same – interesting speakers, outings and theatre visits, raising money for local charities. A highlight in 2012 saw a group of us going for afternoon tea at the Ritz. Another lovely occasion! For the Centenary Year, in 2014 we welcomed the Centenary baton on its journey through Worcestershire, and our president was amongst the 8,000 members who attended the 2015 garden party at Buckingham Palace.

In 2016, unfortunately our membership of 38 is growing older, with little sign of new young women coming along. However, as Hampton, like most other places nationally, has a great many new homes being built, we have hopes that new members will come along. To this end, our President is organising a leafleting campaign, so fingers crossed!

Hanbury

Hanbury WI is a thriving heritage group with 36 members in 2016 ranging from 32 to 94 years in age. We believe in having fun and building friendships. Living in a rural community with a well-established WI, we take pride in caring for each other. Our members meet in the evening once a month with a varied programme of speakers, demonstrations and "have a go" sessions where we try out new skills like scrapbooking, glass decorating and felting. In addition, we have an informal book club, craft-club, cookery club and of course Group Skittles team.

There have been many special occasions over the last 40 years including our WI 75th (1992) and 90th (2007) celebrations, Queens Jubilee (2002) and Royal Wedding (2011) which involved friends and family, along with annual social events in August. We show off our new skills at our annual Flower, Craft and Cookery Show which has taken place nearly every year over the last 100 years. We keep it up to date with new classes each year. The most popular classes in 2016 were colouring and photography, which everyone could enter.

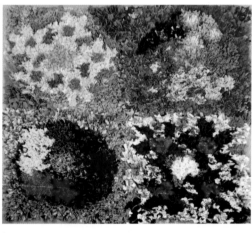

We choose a local charity each year and raise funds by having a stall at Hanbury Village Fete, jumble sales and an annual summer coffee morning. This year, to support one of our members and because we all know someone, we raised money for the newly formed Worcestershire Breast Unit Haven, breast cancer support charity, by making "Hanging Bra-skets". This was very successful and the village proudly displayed their bra-skets all summer long!

2016 has found us preparing for our Centenary year. Many special events are planned with our May meeting being held at Hanbury Hall, the roots of our WI, as Lady Vernon was our first President in 1917. All of our members have been involved with designing and making a commemorative Rag Rug depicting the seasons to represent the ongoing community spirit of our group. Much investigating of minute books, scrapbooks and photos has shown the rich history of Hanbury WI over the last 10 decades. This will be shared with our members and at the Annual Council Meeting during 2017.

Hanley Castle

Hanley Castle WI was formed in February 1921 and by 1980 had a membership of over 70. However, some of our older members were finding evening meetings irksome, and it was decided to set up a new afternoon WI. As a result, in 1993 St Gabriel's WI was founded. This naturally had an impact on our membership, some no longer came to our meetings, but a considerable number became dual members, enjoying both the afternoon and the evening meetings. We now have over 50 members and meet in Hanley Swan Village Hall in the parish of Hanley Castle.

Over the years our WI has evolved. Initially the monthly meeting almost stood alone, now we have a number of groups that get together between the monthly meetings. These include the friendship group who meet for a cup of tea and a chat, the eating out group, a readers group who gather to discuss their chosen book and walkers who enjoy two forays a month, one long and one short. Swimming, tennis and craft sessions have also been popular. A Parish Map was produced in 2001. We also organise informal visits to local attractions such as Sudeley Castle, Harvington Hall, Spetchley Gardens, etc.

Each month, in an endeavour to keep our members fully informed, we produce a Hanley Homily, containing reports of the past month's activities and details of events for the coming month.

AND, in between all of this, we participate in Worcestershire Federation events, (a number of our members have held office in WFWI and are active on sub-committees) and always enter the Skittles and Quiz competitions.

Hanley Castle WI has always been involved in the local community in Hanley Swan and Hanley Castle. For many years we created a float that took part in the August Bank Holiday Fete and Flower Show and some years ago our last effort was on the theme of the TV series "Upstairs, Downstairs". We also enter the Village Open Gardens annual scarecrow competition and won first prize one year with our scarecrow celebrating the foundation of the WI movement.

In addition, we provide the refreshments for the Village Flower Show with the money raised going towards the Show funds. We support the annual Big Lunch, join in the annual Litter Pick, provided tea and cakes for a local archaeological dig – in fact where ever we are needed, we are there!

On the fun side our talented members wrote, produced and acted in pantomimes for the enjoyment of both villages and also created smaller dramas for our members.

At our meetings, we have, through sales and raffles, raised money for local worthy causes, including Malvern Community Hospital, Worcester Breast Care Unit, Worcestershire Cancer Aid and the Midlands Air Ambulance.

Hartlebury

The 80s. In 1980 Hartlebury WI was invited to London by the London Welsh WI. They sang carols in Regents Street and were entertained to supper. Records show that Hartlebury enjoyed a party. There was a return visit for Hartlebury's Diamond Jubilee and in May the Bishop of Worcester held a Thanksgiving Service in the Chapel of Hartlebury Castle.

A WI of keen, energetic competitors who did well; activities included yoga, bridge, first aid and French and their diverse programme included water divining. Always attending craft rallies, the report mentions "The triumph of Mrs Lloyd's oven glove in the handicraft competition" but skittles needed more practice.

The 90s. 1990 was slightly less formal and "there were colour co-ordinated flowers on the president's table, which often matched their outfits". There were Polish and Italian evenings and two meetings were struck by power-cuts so they read poems by torchlight.

There were great celebrations in 1993 as they won first prize for the Co-operative and even more amazingly, reached the semi-finals of the skittles. Hartlebury would do teas for other occasions in the village but by 1995 their Spring Party was "in the modern style – we sat back and were waited on and nobody made a thing or washed a dish"

At the 75th anniversary, they dressed as bright young things of the 1920s and put on an "old style dramatic entertainment of typical WI sketches".

Perhaps things became a little too laid back at the end of the decade as the Christmas party was in April. The members learned about Brum Grub – HP Sauce, Bird's Custard and Typhoo Tea and the skittles team lost every game.

The 2000s. The 80th birthday was celebrated in style at The Pleck where some early meetings took place. Foot and Mouth disease affected many of the trips and they won one skittles match. In 2002 it was decided that weekly practices at the Talbot skittle alley might be a good idea, particularly if it included lunch. This paid off because by 2006 they reached the semi-finals again!

For the Queen's Diamond Jubilee we used new flower arranging skills for a Flower Festival. On a visit to the Morgan Car Factory, bins of aluminium offcuts were raided for attractive flower accessories.

Hartlebury WI meet at the Parish Hall and continue to attract new members - we reached 40 in 2016. We have excellent trips for culture, exercise and sociability and sometimes the real treasures are right on our doorstep. In 1921 they learned how to skin a rabbit and make gloves – we continue to craft, compete and party, with the same spirit.

Heightington

In the 1980's Heightington was about half way through its life as an Institute. Small, with a reputation for being rather elite, it paid its way by hosting High Teas in the Village Hall.

There is no village, just a few houses set individually in the countryside. Members come from up to 10 miles away and private transport is essential – many members sharing journeys. Members are loyal, happy to take office and very generous with offers of help or hospitality.

Our first meeting was at Heightington village hall on April 12th 1944 with 30 members joining. It would appear that it was difficult to get to the subsequent meetings during the war, as records show that over quite a period of time, at most, nine people attended. War time must have made things very difficult. Heightington now has a beautiful new village hall where we continue to meet on the second Monday of each month, in the mornings, as most of us are more awake then!!!

We have had all sorts of speakers, both academic and practical, on, for example, Pearl Button making, local landscape clock tower, and the Origins of London Stores, but perhaps the most enjoyable are "home-grown" demonstrations such as cookery or "my most memorable experience" (ranging from starting work as a librarian, or standing on a pile of coal to get at a key, to turning on the electricity to launch a ship!). We have also had "Favourite Readings" and extracts from favourite books.

We have been on outings with other WIs with the County. Perhaps the most memorable was a visit to the new Bull Ring in Birmingham before it was opened, (the first outside body to be invited). It was very special and we achieved fame because a photograph of the assembled ladies appeared on the front page of the Birmingham Post, taken from the back. Truly a sight to savour! We toured the whole complex, including parts we do not see now it is open. After this outing we were more conventional: Highgrove and The National Arboretum at Alrewas, which awed us as it does everyone who visits.

The interests of members range from paragliding, sewing, embroidery, knitting, flower arranging, painting, photography, drama, dog training and showing to many more. All are happy to share their talents and one member has directed two pantomimes. One was 'Cavalcade 90', a pageant celebrating 90 years of WI in Worcestershire as seen through the eyes of two girls, one rich, one poor, from 1900 to 1990's. It started with Queen Victoria's funeral and proceeded through Amy Johnson (where everyone was an aeroplane) and concluded with a Grand Finale.

In April 2014 we celebrated our 70th birthday with a "posh" tea party, of which we feel our founding war time sisters would have approved. We now look forward to celebrating the arrival of the Centenary Baton in Wyre Forest Area in September.

"Sadly, since writing the above in 2014, Heightington WI has found it impossible to carry on. The average age of our 20 members is over 81 and we have been unable to fill the positions of the "officers" required. Most members have already filled the positions several times. There are also only three people who actually live in Heightington, so it is with great regret that we close after many successes and the happiness of all those past years of fellowship."

Hillside@Alvechurch

Founded 1968 and named after the local telephone exchange

We love making and eating cakes

And craft activities like the patchwork quilt

We enjoy dressing up for our group meetings

Not only do we play skittles, sometimes we win

Here we are today at the The Ark Alvechurch with 37 members of all ages

Himbleton

1992 – An oak tree was planted in memory of Lady Sandys, our first president

2000 – to celebrate the Millennium we made a new scrapbook of village life to be kept alongside the original made in 1965

2011 – past members were invited to join us for a delightful garden party to celebrate 80 years of our WI

2002 – The Queen's Golden Jubilee was celebrated with a village picnic and duck races

Regular fund raising social evenings such as progressive suppers, pudding evenings and skittles matches

WI Extra – regular get togethers for craft activities, visits or walks, usually with pub lunch

We meet in our Village Hall and currently have 33 members

Hollywood

Hollywood WI was founded in 1969 and meets at Kingswood Meeting House. It has always had between 30 and 40 members. In 2016, eight of the founder members are still active with us.

Fun has been a watchword for us. Whether taking part in the village carnival, visits to gardens and other places of interest, eating together in lovely surroundings, visiting theatres or just getting together socially it has always been the intention to enjoy our membership.

Since 2006 about half of the members have taken part in regular Pilates exercise classes. None of us are young and athletic, some have to sit to exercise and one arrives using her Zimmer frame, but again we have fun. If laughter is good medicine then these afternoons are just the best.

Our programmes of speakers are very varied and interesting. In 2013 a talk on the Fistula hospital in Addis Ababa, and the plight of its patients spurred the whole membership to start knitting blankets and later baby clothes to be shipped to the hospital. To date more than 200 items have been made and sent to the hospital. This followed on from many years of producing children's jumpers and other items to be sent to The Gambia under the auspices of ACWW.

Some of the blankets and the knitters, including some of our founder members

Members have always been involved with Group and Federation activities. The Christmas shopping trip is a highlight for some, while others enjoy attending Council Meetings, Resolution and Campaign Days and the Lucy Hingley Lecture. Members have served as Group Coordinator, Federation Science Representative and also on the Public Affairs Committee.

A Denman bursary has given members the opportunity to attend courses at the College, whilst other members have made good use of its programmes to extend their craft and other skills.

Since our foundation we have been educated, stimulated and entertained, but most of all WE HAVE FUN!!

Holt

Holt WI celebrated its 95th Birthday in 2014 in style by having Afternoon Tea at The Elms Hotel at Abberley. We have met the first Thursday at Holt Village Hall at 7.30 pm since 1919. The Hall we meet in now is the second Village Hall in the Village. The original is situated in a garden a little walk away.

We also closed for a short time during the Second World War as fuel was in short supply to heat the Hall and as a farming community members were busy supporting the war effort. We now have thirty-two members from Holt and the surrounding area.

Over the years there have been many memorable times. We celebrated The Queen's Golden Jubilee in 2002 with a Garden Party at one of our members' homes wearing something gold. We also included our families to help celebrate. We ran the Tea Tent serving Afternoon Teas at the Jubilee Gala. Not an easy feat when there were no facilities for washing up but as true WI Ladies we used our initiative.

Many outings have been organised including a trip to Kew Gardens on the hottest day in April and to Highgrove the home of HRH Prince Charles. This was when you waited to be invited and felt like a terrorist when your identification was checked as you waited to enter. How privileged we were to be there.

The year 2000 was also a busy time. We designed tea towels and fabric shopping bags which travelled around the world. Footpath Walk Books around the village were also produced. We sold 200 copies in all. A Parish map was produced by one of our members and is now hanging in the Village Hall. With the profits from these ventures we were able to buy two wrought iron benches for the then new Millennium Green.

The progression of the Centenary Baton through the Woodbury Group was celebrated by Holt at the President's home with breakfast of Bacon Butties and Bucks Fizz. The President on the back of her son's big red motorcycle then transported the Baton to the next WI.

Millennium Green Bench   Progressing the Baton

We now look forward to our 100th Birthday in the year 2019 and yet another celebration.

Honeybees

Honeybees was formed in February 2016. The members are both long standing residents of the village of Honeybourne and many new residents to the area. It has been invaluable in helping to integrate new people to the area and many new friendships have been made.

With 26 members and meeting at the Village Hall, we now have a monthly Munch Club, and Book Club. Over the past year we have had some interesting speakers but we have also spent evenings getting to know each other, learning about each other as well as swopping skills etc. We have an active facebook page and website. This coming year we hope to do many more new things and have BIG plans!!!

Hopwood

HOPWOOD VILLAGE HALL.

It was in 1920 that Lady Smedley Crooke resident of Hopwood in Worcestershire and wife of a Birmingham MP suggested to the ladies of Hopwood that they form a Women's Institute to be held in Hopwood Village Hall. This they did and their first meeting was in the December of that year.

The Institute has met there ever since, with the one exception, the year being 2014 when the ladies moved to The Friends Meeting House, Barnt Green for one year, to enable the Village Hall to be renovated. The Institute returned in 2015 in time to celebrate the Hall's 100th birthday. Some of the paint used was won by the President in a competition featured in the NFWI Voucher Book! There are currently 30 members.

In 1985 Hopwood acquired a Dutch President. Her old WI, Hilvarian Beek in Holland, was due to celebrate their 25th anniversary, so a coach load of members joined her, sang 'Jerusalem' at their party and in the President we had our very own tour guide for a week in Holland. The 1980's also found us at the Edinburgh Tattoo and a long weekend in Scotland.

Other outings over the years have had us visiting Highgrove, The Houses of Parliament with a conducted tour led by our MP, The Morgan Car Factory and the Hopwood Service Station where we planted a Worcester pear tree to celebrate our 80th Birthday The many County Outings included The Eisteddfod and County holidays to Italy and the Rhine Valley.

Hopwood members' involvement with the County Drama section has been very enthusiastic. In the 90's County Productions, our members performed in the County Cavalcade, and in the Pantomimes. In 2002, to celebrate the Queen's Jubilee at the Swan Theatre in Worcester, members performed in 'Fifty Golden Years', two of our members writing the first act. The following year at the Rose Theatre Kidderminster, members performed in the Old Time Music Hall and one member wrote one of the acts. We also performed in 'Christmas Crackers' another County production.

In 2005 we applied for a National Lottery Grant and received £5,000. With this, nearly all of our members went on a course to Denman. and for those that were unable to go, we had a Denman tutor come to Hopwood to give a talk on the history of the area. All our Group members were invited.

A local paper asked our secretary if we would be stripping off for a calendar; she replied "No we have other interesting things to do".

We are Wine Tasting, Taxidermy Shocking,
Bollywood Dancing, Steam Train Travelling,
Gin Swigging, Power Posing, Cake Baking,
Festival Serving, Life Saving, Buzzy Bee Learning,
Tea Drinking, Scrap Book Making, Crochet Teaching,
Fund Raising, Grief Supporting, Women Empowering,
Gallery Visiting, Theatre Going, Mosaic Designing,
Naked Calendar Producing, Media Courting,
Rambunctious Glorious Giggling Women.
We are Hot Peppers WI Upton upon Severn.
Founded June 2013
50 members and rising.

Inkberrow WI was formed in 1920 with a membership of 104 from 349 households. The venue for meetings is the Village Hall in Sands Road. Membership peaked at 112 in the 70's following the first large scale village expansion.

1980 was Inkberrow's Diamond Jubilee year, a celebratory meal was held at Perry Hall Hotel Bromsgrove, with Pat Jacobs a past National Chairman as guest speaker. A commemorative tree was also planted at the Village Hall field. In 1988 The Birmingham Fellowship for the Handicapped presented the Institute with a gavel and box in recognition of twenty-five years of tea parties, entertainment and fun provided by members. The Institute remained a vibrant force with members involved at all levels. Average membership at this time was 56.

In 1997 the last surviving founder member Hannah Smith died at the age of 107. Despite efforts to attract younger members, the nineties saw a gradual slide in membership to 28. Nevertheless, County, Group and village events were supported with enthusiasm and the 75th birthday was celebrated in style.

The Millennium saw an upturn in the fortunes of Inkberrow WI. The 80th birthday took the form of a 1920's style supper party and soiree with guests and members dressed in period costume. Inkberrow's contribution to the Parish Map Project was a tea towel illustrating the village streets and buildings.

In the following few years the committee gained members who had no WI background. They brought refreshing and radical ideas to bear on meetings which became less formal. Cinema, walking, sewing and two book groups were established. At this time ACWW was particularly well supported. Outings became wider in scope and with increased membership money was available to engage a different range of speakers.

In 2005 a wonderful book documenting Inkberrow as it was then was compiled, providing a valuable archive. In 2010 the Institute's 90th birthday was celebrated with a party, the planting of bulbs and a tree in the grounds of Grey Gable Surgery.

Inkberrow continues to thrive thanks to the enthusiasm and dedication of its committees, their aim being to provide fun, friendship, high quality speakers and exciting outings for its current membership of 59.

Ipsley

Ipsley is a parish within the Redditch boundary. The Institute was formed in 1966; hence we celebrated our 50th Anniversary in July 2016.

During this time our meetings have been held in only three different venues, Lodge Farm Secondary School (now Woodfield Middle School), then briefly the Woodrow Library and now Winyates Green Community Centre. The Institute began with 60 members, presently we have 54, and many enjoy the incredible friendship and support offered by the ladies. Visitors find the atmosphere welcoming and not at all "cliquey".

Our Institute is located in the NE limits of Worcestershire. However, members have always involved themselves with and supported events and activities organised by the County Office. Of the many events in the last 40 years, two come to mind – "Cavalcade 90" and the Town Walk 1999.

Cavalcade 90 – held at the Malvern County Showground, was an entertaining pageant, involving members countywide, with commitment made to rehearsals, to costume searches and makeup. It has also provided members with some really individual memories.

The Town Walk was organised by Ipsley members, with the support and assistance of an officer of the local Borough Council (Redditch was designated a "New Town" in 1964). As a result, the redevelopment caused real problems; WFWI members seemed wary of visiting Redditch. The Walk was one way of promoting a new revitalised Redditch. Institute members organised the whole day, routes and pathways, places of interest, a visit to the new Kingfisher Shopping Centre, with a hot supper served later for everyone in the Ecumenical Centre - a wonderful experience and achievement.

In July 1991 members enjoyed the 25th Anniversary with a celebration meal at the Tardebigge Restaurant. The whole year was recorded in a huge scrapbook with photographs, speakers, outings and any special events organised during that time. An Ipsley WI banner – see above – was unveiled having been designed, made and presented to the Institute by some of the members.

Similarly, in July 2016, we celebrated our 50th Anniversary with a superb meal at Bromsgrove Golf Club. Members raised funds through "kurling" evenings with partners and friends, collected coins in "Smartie" tubes and supported organised outings – Tewkesbury Market, a sail along the River Severn, London and the National Memorial Arboretum – to celebrate our anniversary in style and record it in detail in a photographic book.

Our Institute has enriched the lives of members – long may it continue.

Kempsey

One of the biggest changes to take place for Kempsey WI over the past 40 years was the amalgamation of the afternoon WI with the evening WI, as more members were working it made it unviable to continue as two separate entities. This resulted in a bigger/more pro-active evening group who welcomed the new ideas and expertise of a mainly more elderly membership.

The format in the earlier years always had four distinct sections, a business section, (more formal in those days and always addressing the President as "Madam Chairman," hats were worn and smokers had to sit at the back), a speaker, a refreshment period and always social time to follow in which all members participated (a quiz, games of beetle/bingo, crafts etc). The end of the meeting was always officially announced and then members were "allowed" to go home.

Recently the meetings are much more informal and friendly, Christian names are used and are not so divided into sections, slightly shorter in length due to the speaker sessions not being as rigid, more adventurous and not always "Jam and Jerusalem". We have a "Ladies that Lunch" group which 20 members attend monthly, a book club, theatre trips, garden parties and a team in the WI skittles league.

A lot of new homes are being built in and around Kempsey so hopefully "the future is looking bright" for Kempsey WI.

We have 31 members, meeting at Kempsey Parish Hall. The hall is built of tin with little insulation; one Christmas members' party we all had to sit in our coats as the heating had failed but we still had a great evening. The good news is that plans have been approved to build a new modern hall and the old one is going to a heritage museum.

What My WI Means to Me   By Ivy Lee (Kempsey WI)

Many moons ago now, when I joined the WI
Our President would greet us thus (with steely glint of eye):
"Would all you worthy ladies who are desperate to smoke,
Please occupy the back seats (so the rest of us don't choke!)"

But times have changed and weightier matters fill our minds today
To which our Resolutions have so often paved the way;
For instance, take Apprenticeships- ignored once without mention,
But now moved to the forefront of national attention.

And then, of course, there's Denman - an experience indeed!
Once you become addicted, it's an ever-pressing need;
Eight visits now I've clocked up, and each time a different course,
From Photography to Betjeman and Philosophy to Morse!

Our speakers are informative, light-hearted or profound,
And some simply entertain us, but we shan't forget the sound
Of our rending of "Jerusalem" echoing through the land,
Accompanied, with gusto, by a ukulele band!

But now I'm not so nimble, I can still enjoy a quiz,
An outing or a slide show, but that isn't all there is,
For WI bonds women, old and young, and near and far,
And extends the hand of friendship, no matter who you are.

Kington with Dormston

The villages of Kington and Dormston have embraced modern technology in a gentle manner. It is irritating that in 2016 we still do not have fast speed broadband although there are many businesses which depend upon the internet.

Farming is still an important industry in the area, sadly smaller farms have been swallowed up by larger units. Mechanisation on the other hand means that famers have many less workers and a field can be ploughed, rolled and grain sown all in one action as the tractors are much bigger and can pull more equipment at a time. Strong tractor lights mean that harvesting can continue until 2 or 3 in the morning provided that there is very little or no dew. With the reduction of agricultural workers, allied trades are also more difficult to find.

Development of the villages has been limited with only small infill developments. Because of the lack of good rural transport, it is necessary for a householder to own at least one car. It is not unusual to see several cars on the drives of the houses as people seek work in and around the area stretching to London and Birmingham. A sign of the times however, the children from the villages are bussed to schools in either Worcester or Pershore. A three-tiered system of junior, middle and senior schools provides the education for the majority of our youngsters. The churches have survived due to the dedication of the villagers. Kington annually holds a flower festival and fete and Dormston has hosted various garden parties in the field opposite the church!

Despite all the changes the Women's Institute continues to thrive with most interesting speakers, outings and classes. Its membership of 21 is pretty constant. One WI member runs a quarterly craft workshop ranging from card making to silver jewellery making, and several WI members run the Over 60's club for residents of the two villages and other people who live within the proximity of the Village Hall. The WI was fortunate to make a successful bid to Awards for All, a national charity, for funding to replace the worn-out heating system in the hall.

The residents are not inward looking but quietly go about their charity works, one of which is a school in Africa and the residents hold various fund raising events to enable it to continue.

A clause in the planning permission of the Village Hall stated that there should be a women's organisation involved in the hall – hence the WI. To celebrate the 75th anniversary of the building of the Hall, the 75th birthday of the WI, and the 60th anniversary of Her Majesty's succession to the throne, an embroidered wall hanging was made depicting many of the old buildings in the two villages. This was designed and worked by members of the Institute some of whom had never done cross stitch before.

Kinver Village

Situated close to the West Midlands conurbation lies Kinver, a large village in Staffordshire surrounded by lovely countryside, Kinver Edge (a National Trust property) and the Staffordshire and Worcestershire Canal. It's a lively village with an abundance of activities, societies and clubs, of which our WI is one. We are the second WI in the village. The original one opened in 1929 and closed in 1980. The WI we have today opened its doors with a Christmas party in December 1988. We were affiliated to the Staffordshire Federation of WIs but in 1993 decided, for geographical reasons, to become part of the Worcestershire Federation.

Kinver WI has some thirty members who meet on the second Monday of each month at 7.30 pm. The meetings consist of talks on a wide variety of subjects, learning new skills, social evenings and usually includes a summer evening outing. There is a monthly competition, often linked to the subject of the talk, with points awarded towards the "Gladys Potter" (a founder member) Cup. There is also a sales table for items brought by members.

December 1988 - The First Committee

At Christmas we fund a draw for two bursaries. One is for a year's membership of the WI, the other for a weekend at Denman College. When it is felt that a talk will be of particular interest the meeting is opened to all, men as well as women. The visitors get an insight into the WI and do their best to join in singing Jerusalem.

In addition to the monthly meetings, Kinver WI members enjoy numerous other events. There is a very active craft group, coffee mornings are held, and we have visits which this year (2015) included the Beacon Centre for the Blind, a lovely garden near Droitwich and the Birmingham Mint.

With such an active village, the WI is involved with community life in many ways.

For the Best Kept Village Competition members maintain a planter at the entrance to the village and organise a Poster Competition with the three local schools.

Members have close ties with the Kinver Rock Houses which are part of Kinver Edge. A number help to run the cafe and some act as stewards. The craft group has made rag rugs for the rock houses and also aprons and mob caps for visiting school children to dress up in.

Kinver WI always has a stall at Kinver Country Fayre and this year they were also invited to take part in the parade to celebrate 100 years of the WI. They did it in style atop a brewer's dray pulled by two shire horses.

In 2016, in addition to the events listed above, Kinver WI will be hosting Frampton Cotterell WI (a long standing friendship group), and King John (alias Max Keene) will be entertaining the people of Kinver (a major fund raising event).

The membership of Kinver WI remains at thirty plus, with younger members joining, so with the help of the internet the future looks promising, hopefully for another 100 years.

Leigh & Bransford

Two of our longest serving members Sue and Elizabeth, have been members for over a hundred years between them. They have seen many changes in that time, so we asked them what memories they both have of the WI in the past forty years.

What changes have you seen in the WI since the eighties? Both agreed that the relaxed approach of the WI is now attracting a varied age range. They both remember when new members had to be proposed and seconded before they could join! Many things have altered as the minutes are no longer read and a lot of communication is now done electronically.

What is your favourite memory of the WI in the past forty years? For Sue and Elizabeth, it was the celebration party for our 60th anniversary in 1994. Sue arranged a flower pedestal for the evening which was then dismantled and rearranged for the grave of Mrs Nellie Gale, a founder member who passed away a few days prior to the celebration; her two daughters were given buttonholes to take to the funeral. It was such a happy yet sad time.

What do you think Leigh & Bransford have achieved in the past forty years? Both said that it is important to keep the WI going. There have been many difficult periods with a lack of volunteers for President and committee members, but fortunately we are now a thriving group, with fun, friendship, and supporting others when they are having a difficult time. Wider interests are now catered for and we have many active groups ranging from a book club, ladies that lunch, embroidery, playlets, ramblers, skittles and local history.

Where do you think Leigh & Bransford will be forty years from now? "Big question!" replied Elizabeth. "A crystal ball would be very useful!" remarked Sue, but both agreed the world is changing rapidly. With a good leader and an enthusiastic committee flying the flag for Leigh & Bransford WI, it should flourish.

President Elizabeth Portman in 1994 with Vi Handy the oldest member & Mary Fynn the longest serving member at that time.

Sue Jones & Elizabeth Portman with our Celebration cake for our 80th December 2014

We meet at Leigh & Bransford Village Hall, with a current membership of 36.

Lenches

Nestled high in the rural Worcestershire countryside you will find the village of Church Lench. Church Lench has been in existence for more than one thousand years and is mentioned in the Domesday Book. In the centre of the village stands the beautiful church of All Saints. Next to the Church is the Village Hall - this is where the Lenches WI meets on the third Monday of every month. The Lenches WI incorporates six neighbouring hamlets, Atch Lench, Ab Lench, Church Lench, Lenchwick, Rous Lench, and Sheriffs Lench.

The current Lenches WI was formed in February 1986 with 27 members. We still have three active members from that first meeting. Our numbers have grown over the years and currently there are 42 members. Previously there existed a Church Lench WI Avon Group - we still have a 1964 embroidered tablecloth depicting 112 members' names in our possession. In 1990 a green embroidered Lenches WI tablecloth was made which we still use at our monthly meetings.

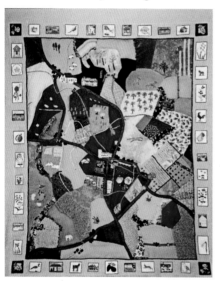

During the thirty years our WI has experienced many events, outings and craft work, the most memorable being the Millennium Project 2000 where members produced a remarkable tapestry wall hanging. The centre depicts the countryside of all the Lenches. The houses embroidered around the sides of the millennium hanging were the houses of the members who worked on the hanging, instead of signing their names. Also in the border were birds, flowers, animals and other local landmarks not included in the main picture. The tapestry took two years and some 2000 hours to complete and measures 4'6"x 5'. This is now proudly displayed in the entrance of the village hall and is here for all to see.

Over the years many occasions have been caught on camera. We have several photograph albums in our possession capturing numerous walking events, Lenches Litter Pick and a day out at Madresfield Court ending with a wonderful picnic. These albums are displayed annually at our AGM Meetings.

Members recall the wonderful opportunities Denman College Courses have given them from William Morris, cookery, singing, tracing ancestors through to a 2016 Advanced Driving Course. After taking courses at Denman, members have gone on to demonstrate at other WIs.

More importantly, the WI is an introduction to friendship not only within our local area but throughout Worcestershire and Great Britain. The Lenches WI are staunch supporters of the Worcestershire Federation events. We are all proud to be members of the WI. Long may we continue to grow and develop.

Lickey

The Institute was formed on 23rd June 1964 at 8:00 pm in the Lickey Parish Hall, now called The Trinity Centre. Fifty-seven ladies were present, but in April 1965 our one hundredth member was welcomed. She received a small gift for the honour. Also memorable - a cup of tea cost fourpence! We have continued with our monthly meetings although our numbers are down to thirty-seven. Members come and go, but we remain constant with the same aims and friendliness.

Over the years we have had many outings – the most memorable being our wonderful trip to Paris in 1989. Fifteen ladies set off on 17th February for a long weekend, coming home on 20th February. We went everywhere enjoying every minute – we caused some chaos – a very tired WI lady back in her hotel room wanted some tea. She plugged the kettle in and fused all the lights in the hotel! The crossing by ferry was very rough. Our first hotel was too – full of rugby supporters, sleeping six to a room! We quickly changed to another hotel close by. Next morning, we set off to see the sights. We had various adventures – we got lost – taking suicidal chances to cross the road and of course trying to understand and make ourselves understandable to the Parisians. We saw the Mona Lisa and the Sacre Coeur. The atmosphere in this church is unique! We had an evening boat trip on the Seine ending up with a meal at the Eiffel Tower. There wasn't a famous part of Paris we did not see. The crossing back was calm and we arrived back at the NEC, yes all 16 of us, to be greeted by our patient husbands waiting to take us home. What a memorable holiday and still talked about today.

We have also travelled to Wales and been to famous establishments e.g. Cadbury's, Wedgwood and the Lowry Exhibition. These are just a few places members have enjoyed and of course we went by coach, which we filled – it cost a lot less then.

We have always done well on the domestic front. Our Home Economics Team was super, always in the top three finishers. We are an active Institute – we take part in walking (we do live near some bluebell woods). For many years we had an outdoor Crown Bowling Group playing every Monday. We have swum in the Droitwich Brine Baths several times. We had an hilarious time with our tap dancing classes, performing in front of our own ladies. We called ourselves the 'Bluebell Belles'. We have taken part in yoga and keep fit classes and were successful in the County Skittles competition. We went to the theatre in Birmingham on a regular basis. We now have a Book Club and a Luncheon Club, each meeting once a month. Our committee dinners are excellent and our January meetings take the form of lunch at the local cricket club. Our birthday suppers are well catered for, the members producing beautiful plates of food.

We have had a choir and sung at Kidderminster at the carol concert and also in Worcester Cathedral and Pershore Abbey. We came second in the National competition for programme design in 2010. Our own embroidered cloth graces the president's table and we also have a library and a sales table. After 52 years we are still functioning, maybe with fewer members, even so we must be doing something right. It is a great tribute to the Lickey ladies and others from further away. You are always assured of a warm welcome at our meetings. Long may it last.

Lickhill

1995 – 2012

Advertised in the Kidderminster Times as 'A WI first for Town's Early Risers', Lickhill WI met for the first time on 18th October 1995 with an initial membership of 19. Originally aimed at young mothers, it attracted more mature ladies and membership grew rapidly to almost 50, becoming a vibrant and exciting new WI. We met 10 am to 12.30 pm on Wednesday mornings in the Community Hall, Lickhill Road, Stourport-on-Severn.

The programme offered a broad range of educational and social opportunities with speakers, activities and educational visits. Each year one lucky member won a Bursary and enjoyed a two-day course at Denman College.

An annual Spring lunch for members was held in February and a fund-raising Strawberry Tea, with homemade cakes, was enjoyed at the end of June. An Annual Outing took place every August and a visit to the SS Great Britain at Bristol was particularly memorable. Another event, such as a Quiz, was held in October and local WIs joined our coach to the Federation Annual Council Meeting. A walking group met regularly and community projects included knitting 'Teddies for Tragedies' and donating large print books to the local library.

As part of the Forest Group, Lickhill WI took its turn to host the meetings. A visit to the National Arboretum at Alrewas was arranged to see the National War Memorial and the WI seat. Members also supported National Federation Resolutions and initiatives and our competition entry for 'WI of the Year 2007' provided a snapshot of a year in our WI.

However, with an ageing membership, few volunteering for the committee and a poor response to a recruiting drive, it was with a real sense of regret that Lickhill WI had to be suspended at the end of 2012.

Link Top

Formed 18 March 1989 - entertainers, crafty, nimble, literary, bakers, skittles champs, good friends.

Our membership has ranged from 15 to 25. Our meeting venues :

    The Women's Institute, Bank Street May 1989 to August 1993.

    The Salvation Army Hall, Newtown Road September 1993 to January 1998.

    The Church of the Ascension Hall, Somers Park Avenue February 1998 to December 2010.

    From January 2011 Somers Park Avenue Methodist Church Hall

LITTLE WITLEY

40 YEARS ON

1980'S

In the Pride and Joy competition we won first prize.
We celebrated our 40th Birthday in the 80's.
Our WI contributed to the Domesday Book.

1990's

A member spoke at the AGM at the Albert Hall in London.
We celebrated our 50th Birthday with a Flower Festival.
Three founder members joined us for the celebrations.
We contributed a painting to the Millennium Calendar.

2000's

The Federation Tablecloth was designed by one of our members.
Approximately 90% of members have access to a computer.
The Foot and Mouth outbreak curtailed our sports activities.
We got two First prizes in the May Rally.
One of our members became County Chairman.

2010's

A member of Little Witley carried an Olympic torch in 2012.
We started four new groups: Book, Craft, Gardening & Walking.
For the Diamond Jubilee we planted a commemorative oak tree.
We currently have 39 members and meet at our Village Hall.
In 2018 we will celebrate our 70th Birthday.

Here's to the next 40 years!

The Littletons

The Littletons WI was formed in 1950 and members come from the three Littleton villages with some from the surrounding area, meeting at Middle Littleton Village Hall. Over the years, membership numbers have varied between 30 and 45; we still have two founder members (who cut the cake at the Baton Ceremony). We are a very active WI, with a Book Club, Walking Group, Lunch Club and two Crochet groups (left-handed and right-handed!!) as well as our monthly meeting. We also have craft workshops on a regular basis. In 2009 our entry won the Silver-gilt award in the WFWI competition – our first entry for a number of years. We have a skittles team who are keen but not very good. We bought T-shirts with "Littletons WI" printed on to boost the team and intimidate the opposition. It doesn't seem to work for some reason!

A "Littletons WI" Banner was made in 2014 by members making pennants, depicting their own interest. These were mounted on backing material making a banner of which we are very proud!

Over the years we have always supported village activities and in 1997 we helped provide supper and entertainment for the Village Hall's 60th Anniversary. We have raised funds to provide new curtains and tables for the Village Hall and regularly have a fund-raising cake stall at the Village Fair. Members have catered for several visiting Over 60's groups, for funerals and in 2012 the wedding reception of our Treasurer. This was a very happy event that took place at a Steam Railway Station including a ride on the train!

We organised a "Garden & Craft Show" for a number of years. We arranged a Scarecrow weekend in 1998 and 1999 and participated regularly in the annual litter picks. In 1985 some members co-operated to compile a Village Book which included interviews with local businesses and village "characters". These accounts, together with photographs, make very interesting reading, illustrating many changes over the years. We also produced a book of our natural environment and one listing all businesses and clubs in the area. In 2005 a souvenir album with photographs of every meeting, outing and event over the year, plus a short history of our WI was produced. In 2013 one member entered a competition in the WI booklet and won 20 tickets to the NEC Gardening Show. We hired a minibus in order to bring home all the plants and goodies!

To celebrate the WI Centenary, we donated an annual bursary to our local Primary School and also organised a Treasure Hunt.

We are a very busy and happy WI – always active with meetings, groups and outings – keeping to WI traditions but welcoming new ideas.

Littleworth & District

Littleworth & District WI opened in January 1978 with sixteen ladies attending. Meetings were held in the Parish Hall Committee Room, Littleworth on the third Tuesday of the month at 7.30 pm. This was a very small room which soon became inadequate and so the meetings transferred to a larger room at the Parish hall.

Record books and photograph albums show members enjoying many activities over the years especially outings to gardens and places of interest as well as village functions and celebrations. It is also clear that meetings were perhaps more formal than they are today as ladies were usually addressed as Miss or Mrs whereas now we are happy to be called by our first names.

Over the years the many members have influenced the life of the WI in the villages of Littleworth, Norton and the surrounding area but probably none more so than Miss Mary Beechill.

In recent years WI meetings have been held in a new room attached to the parish church of Norton and it is thanks to Miss Beechill that we have this lovely facility in the village.

A teacher in a girls' school by profession, Miss Beechill was passionate about education for women. As a member of the Parochial Church Council she was determined that the church should provide good Christian education for children and young people. The existing facilities in the parish church did not give much scope for this work – it was cold, there was no water supply and no toilets. Miss Beechill was a member of the Parochial Church Council and often spoke of her vision of what there could be if only sufficient funds could be found.

Miss Beechill had been a frequent visitor to Norton where her parents lived. When she retired from her teaching post in Birmingham she was able to come to live permanently with her elderly father. She continued to be a staunch supporter of the WI and all it stood for until her death in 2000.

In her will she bequeathed her bungalow to the church and the sale of this property enabled the building of a wonderful extension to the parish church. It is more than Mary could have imagined and fulfils every dream she had. It is used by several parish clubs, hosts craft mornings, afternoon teas, U3A groups, church activities and many other events. Services are held in this room throughout the winter months as it is always warm.

However, this was not Miss Beechill's only gift. As well as this wonderful legacy for the whole community she also left a large sum of money for members of our WI to attend courses at Denman College. Over the years many have been able to take advantage of this wonderful gift.

The Institute continues to meet in the Beechill Room but the meeting night has changed to the third Wednesday in the month. There are currently 21 members and we are fortunate to have one member, Mrs Rita Twining, who was there at the very first meeting.

Lower Broadheath

This WI was formed in 1971 to cater for a group of working women who wanted an evening WI. The only alternative in the village was and still is Broadheath with Rushwick, a daytime WI. We meet on the third Monday at Lower Broadheath Memorial Hall.

We have been editing and distributing the quarterly Parish magazine for about 10 years now. We are a tight knit group of nine members who particularly enjoy talks on local history. There are regular bar-b-ques and outings throughout the year. Typical of these was a walk through the lavender fields at Bridgnorth and a walk along the banks of the Severn through Worcester finishing with tea at the Diglis hotel. We compete in an annual quiz against the local Gardening Club, winning more than we have lost. We always end the year with a special shared supper at Christmas.

Malvern

Malvern WI is almost 100 years old, having been formed on 1ˢᵗ March 1918. We meet at 2.30 pm on the first Thursday of each month, except January, at Holy Trinity Church Hall. It's a very nice venue with disabled access.

WI outing in 2016 to Hampton Court in Herefordshire
Daphne Hughes, Celia Parsons and in the centre President Anne Noble

We are a very friendly group with average membership numbers between 20 to 30; new members are always welcome. We have good speakers talking on all sorts of subjects, sometimes with practical demonstrations in which we can participate.

We have a reading group which meets monthly, a lunch club which is also a monthly event, and we visit somewhere new each time within our home area. In spring and summer, we combine lunch with a trip to a place of interest, quite often a garden. We often go to a matinee at the local theatre which produces a number of pre-West End shows. Many of us also attend the cinema on a Tuesday morning. There is also a 'knit and natter' group making items for charity.

Once a year we hold a charity fund-raising event to support local charities. One year we hired a school hall to raise funds for Acorns Children's Hospice. We raised £1,000. We asked WIs in our area to join us, we sold books, cakes, bric-a-brac and had a big raffle. The local lighting shop gave us about fifty new lamp shades to sell and a man turned up with a box of freshly dug garlic. Our Adviser took on the task of selling it in the hall, and then what was left taken out into the street and sold there!

Another year we had a Home-made Soup and Desserts Lunch with a really superb speaker, we had a few stalls selling hand crafted items, another big raffle after which we served tea and cakes. We made a fantastic £800 thanks to the support of our fellow members in local clubs.

We have regular outings to a huge variety of places. One was Cheltenham Races, where we began the visit with a guided tour of the course, stables, weighing room and the jockey's room. In the afternoon we enjoyed watching the racing, it was very exciting, especially when our particular favourite was winning! We did have a bet or two and came away with a small profit.

Mamble-cum-Bayton

In 1919, John Drinkwater, 1882-1937, English Poet and Playwright, published the poem Mamble. He wrote in his first verse, "I never went to Mamble, that lies above the Teme, so I wonder who's in Mamble, and whether people seem, who breed and brew along there as lazy as the name"………. Perhaps he should have taken the road to Mamble and Bayton, where he would have found Mamble-cum-Bayton Women's Institute. Definitely not as lazy as the name, they were formed in November 1917 with initially 28 members. A local farmer disapproved of his daughters joining, calling it Women's Interference.

We are now about to celebrate our centenary in 2017. A wonderful link to our past will be our centenary meeting that will take place at Shakenhurst, Bayton, a member's home, and where Lady Margesson in 1917 explained the aims of the WI movement and where our first meeting in November that year took place. Our 24 members between them have approximately 400 years as members of our WI and 500 years overall of WI membership. Our longest serving member joined us in 1955, one joined in Wales 67 years ago, and another joined a Worcestershire WI in 1960 aged 16. Over the past four years 8 new members have joined us.

Our treasured curtains shown above have been displayed on every possible occasion over the last 40 years, as indeed they were the previous 44 years. They were designed and made in 1933 and exhibited in a Worcestershire Federation Handicraft Exhibition, where they won a Gold Star. Later they were shown at The London Exhibition. The curtains were worked on at Shakenhurst once a week, and were made to fit across the stage in Mamble Village Hall, where we still meet as we have for many decades. The village hall is 103 years old, having been opened by Mrs Stanley Baldwin accompanied by her husband in April 1914.

A photograph, the earliest we have in our records, taken outside the village hall, shows a member who was born in Mamble in 1846 enjoying a 90th birthday celebration complete with a two-tier iced cake. Our records show that the largest tier was consumed by the members. This party was held at the monthly meeting on 1st May 1936.

Mamble-cum-Bayton WI continues to thrive, enjoying all the present has on offer, looking forward to the future and naturally treasuring our long WI history.

Martley

Martley WI was formed in November 1921 with 30 members in the Chantry School Room which was built in 1913. Membership numbers have fluctuated over the years, numbering over 60 in the 1930s but settling for the most part in recent years at around 30. Meeting venues have also changed several times, starting at the Old Chantry, moving to the Memorial Hall, then Sport Martley but meeting since January 2006 in Heaton House, a warm and comfortable venue.

Over the decades Martley WI has continued to be very involved with village life, taking part in flower festivals, tree and bulb planting, a Sealed Knot event, pantomimes, open garden teas, cake and craft stalls at the Memorial Hall Christmas Fayres and the annual village Horticultural Show, to name but a few.

Regular events for the WI have also been many and varied, including weekly craft and sewing courses, fund raising mini markets on the village weighbridge, and garden meetings with fun auctions. There have been theatre visits, celebration parties, meals out,

afternoon teas and skittles evenings, as well as the monthly meetings. A recent popular addition has been the monthly coffee morning which visits assorted local garden centres and other venues and welcomes friends and family to join us.

To highlight a few particular endeavours: -

In 1980 it was decided to design and create a tablecloth to celebrate 60 years; it is still in fine condition and very much in use today.

In 2000, thanks to the initiative of one member, the idea was floated to create a Millennium map of the village. A successful application to Awards for All meant that every member of the WI received their own copy of the map; the original framed map was presented to Martley Memorial Hall in 2001.

In 2007, as part of the "Go West Teme Valley Project", several members created 75 tabards to be worn by pupils from Broadwas, Lindridge and Martley Primary Schools. The pupils acted as young time travellers and heritage knights. WI members who took part in the project were invited to attend the dedication event in Worcester Cathedral in July 2007. In December 2009, Martley WI were delighted to begin a new tradition for the Elgar Group of WIs with a Celebration of Christmas at St Peter's Church. It was attended by members from WIs in the group and was very successful.

Martley WI continues to flourish, embrace change and welcome new members as we move towards our own Centenary in 2021.

Menith Wood

In the year 2000 several ladies from Menith Wood were members at Wichenford WI and would often take friends along for the talks. It was getting so that we were almost taking over so it was decided to see if we could start a Menith Wood WI to mark this special year. We put a notice in Teme Spy the church magazine, and did a leaflet drop asking if ladies were interested. We had a favourable response so contacted WI House to see what we had to do.

A meeting was arranged for 18th September and over twenty ladies came along and met Trustees and Advisers from County. On 2nd October 2000, Menith Wood WI was inaugurated. Our first talk was on The Life of Mrs Beeton.

Several members helped to produce the Menith Wood 2000 book and the first official assignment was to help at the book signing event in December 2000.

Each year we have a Birthday Lunch. A Worcester Black pear tree was planted on our first birthday. We also planted a tree on the Queen's Jubilee. We had a party for our 10th birthday and invited local institutes and County Trustees. Unfortunately, it had to be postponed till 2011 because of bad weather!

Many members come from Eardiston and the community spirit with Eardiston has blossomed and we all join with events in neighbouring villages much more than we did before. We have all made many friends. We have recently been co-opted onto Midweek Break at Eardiston Village Hall where locals meet once a month for coffee and company. In the past we ran skittle evenings which were open to locals and were very popular. We open our talks to partners and villagers and have many WI husbands helping at events.

We have had stalls at the Lindridge show and often run soup or cream tea events to raise money for local charities. In 2011 we put on a St George's Day Barn Dance and Mummer's play and raised money to help towards the Cancer Care Suite at Kidderminster Hospital.

Most members have embroidered their name on a leaf shape on a table cloth for meetings. and a banner depicting the Village Hall has been made.

Membership has been in the twenties since we started. Several members have served at County level, Pauline Briggs was an Advisor until 2015, Linda Edmudson and Pauline are on the Public Affairs Committee. Alison Cooke was Chairman of Creative Activities and Kath Pardoe and Janet Farmer served as County Trustees. We put Menith Wood on the map.

Members have learnt to cook, flower arrange, make sugar flowers, Iris folding cards, play golf and croquet, joined choirs and taken part in drama productions and the German exchange, and been on WI arranged holidays. We were in exchange with a WI near Nelson, New Zealand for a few years when a past member, Anne Andrews lived there.

In 2011 we were featured on the village calendar as "The Calendar Girls". Several times we have hosted events and provided meals for the German exchange group and made many friends.

Mitton

Mitton WI formed in November 2013 when 21 ladies attended a meeting held at St Michael & All Angels Church, Stourport-on-Severn. The group was named after the hamlet of Lower Mitton where the canal terminus was built in the south west of the town which helped Stourport to develop and prosper; and we hoped for this prosperity. At the first meeting ladies were able to try Christmas crafts, make friends and have an inspiring evening of enjoyment which we hoped would form the basis for all future meetings.

Since that inaugural meeting, members have enjoyed a varied range of speakers, craft evenings and social soirees. One memorable evening was hosted by Fergus McGonigal, a Worcestershire Poet Laureate, who gave a humorous account of his life and read entertaining poems from his published works.

Another landmark evening saw members making a fabric flower corsage in WI colours to wear with pride. These brooches are much admired and have become synonymous with Mitton WI.

A special occasion that warranted the wearing of our corsage was the Forest Group celebrations held at the Wyre Forest Centre on Saturday 13th September 2014 when Mitton, as the most recently formed WI within the Group at that time, received the centenary baton. After delicious food, drink and good company members travelled to Bewdley and then on by train on the Severn Valley Railway to Kidderminster where the baton was then handed over to continue its journey around the Federation.

Mitton WI seeks to keep its members informed, and so in November 2014 a monthly newsletter was launched to keep everyone up to date with local and regional news and events. It is produced by a member of the Mitton Planning Group (our committee) and distributed via email.

Mitton WI members took part in contributing miles to the 'To the Moon & Back' project in 2015 organised by Worcester University which encouraged members to become active and as a result of this initiative the Mitton walking group was formed. We have also arranged competitions at the monthly meetings including cake baking, best biscuits and a table decoration to celebrate Easter which have allowed members to demonstrate their creative side.

Our President has been lucky enough to attend National Federation Annual Meetings which have included a special visit to Buckingham Palace to celebrate 100 years of the Women's Institute. This was a very special event and all the members of Mitton WI felt part of the excitement.

During 2016 Mitton WI decided to enter a class at the Far Forest Countryside Show in Worcestershire and were thrilled to be awarded the best exhibit cup for 'a tea tray for the Queen' to celebrate her 90th birthday. We hope this will be the start of many crafting achievements.

Mitton WI still meet on the third Thursday of the month at St Michael and All Angels Church, Stourport-on-Severn and in 2016 there are forty active members.

Naunton Beauchamp

The first recorded meeting took place on 29th November, 1951 and was held at The Old House, Naunton Beauchamp with two ladies taking on the post of President - Mrs Hunt and Mrs Bailey.

The Worcester News

This WI is unique as there is no village hall. From the time of its formation until June 2009 meetings were held in the homes of members, the cups, saucers and tea pot being taken to the relevant home by the tea convener.

Members come from many other villages, some of them quite a distance away. Upton Snodsbury, Libbery, Abberton, Bishampton, Pershore, Westmancote and Fernhill Heath.

WI County Events

Over the past 40 years prizes have been won for Drama – *'Isolation at Eyme'* being a great success; *'Laundry Girls'* and *'Little Benjamin'* also prize winning plays.

Awards have been received for our cookery displays and craftwork. Kathleen Smith produced the winning card to be sent to Her Majesty The Queen on the occasion of her Golden Jubilee by The Worcester Federation.

For **Catherine Guest**, the WI was her life. She was a County Executive member, The Lenches Group Secretary and Secretary of Naunton Beauchamp WI for many years. Catherine moved from the village in 1997. On her death some years later it was learned that she had left a legacy to the Worcester Federation.

Memories

- The 900th anniversary of St. Bartholomew's Church was celebrated with a Pageant. People came from far and wide, it was the largest event ever held in the village with residents fully involved.
- We discovered one of our members had been married to one of the Princes of Siam - (The King and I).
- In June 2000, Naunton Beauchamp provided the delegate to attend the NFWI AGM held at Wembley. A memorable day when The Prime Minister, Tony Blair was booed off the stage.
- 2002. Our President Helen Bower gave birth to a baby boy - James.
- The 2009 London Marathon - Sally Grainger completed this tremendous challenge.

We meet at The Village Hall in Upton Snodsbury. The membership has grown over the years and the homes are no longer able to accommodate everyone. Naunton Beauchamp now has 32 members.

North Claines WI

Home About Programme Activities Blog Contact

1985

Painting by Mrs Win
Pengelly of meeting at
Claines Institute

2016

Meeting at
Bishop Allenby Hall

Aug 2012

Garden visit

Dec 2013

NCWI panto

Mar 2014

Birthday meeting

Mar 2016

Line Dancing

Follow us on Twitter

Tweets by @northclaineswi

northclaineswi
@northclaineswi

Aren't our new members of
our WI great? All made at
August afternoon meeting.
Lots of chat, laughter and
cups of tea!

northclaineswi
@northclaineswi

Much laughter last night but
also much relevant info at
#lucyhingley memorial lecture
"Who cares about the pelvic
floor?" Good choice WFWI!

northclaineswi
@northclaineswi

Incorporated: - 24th February 1953. **First meeting: -** Tuesday 3rd March 1953, 7.00 pm at Claines Church Institute, Worcester. **2008: -** moved to Bishop Allenby Hall, St Stephen's Church, Droitwich Road, Worcester meeting at 7.15 pm on first Wednesday in the month, where we now have 42 members.

Oak Apple

Oak Apple WI opens March 1996

Oak Apple WI was formed in March 1996 with 20 members, of which 5 are still members in 2016. We have our own tablecloth adorned with leaves with each member's name embroidered on.

We originally met in a classroom at Worcester Sixth Form College for about 5 years taking our own kettle with cups and saucers each month until the water tasted tainted so we bought our own bottled water – not at all convenient. We then moved to Ronkswood Community Centre for a couple of years but got locked in by hooligans and members were worried about the safety of their cars. We moved to our current venue Whittington Village Hall in June 2003. Our numbers have remained fairly constant although we went down to only 10 in 2003, and currently in our 21st year we have 21 members.

We have had numerous themed evenings, including The 40's, Tramps Night, Scottish Dance, and on our 10th birthday we dressed as 10 year olds. At least one meeting per year we invite other local WIs to join us, usually to our popular Quiz evenings. We enjoy many outings including the Recycling Centre, farm walks, gardens and theatre trips. We have summer garden parties and rambles, including the 100 miles for the Moon Mission in 2015.

Members have knitted hats for sailors, made snowdrop crafts for St Richard's Hospice, fundraised £100 during the NFWI Centenary Year which was donated to St Richard's Hospice. We are currently fundraising for the Denman Appeal and are holding a jumble sale where everyone can come and try to find that elusive white elephant.

Pearls of Wythall

Last November the call went out... Worcestershire Federation was after members and volunteers to help form a new WI in Wythall.

Well, the call was answered... and Pearls of Wythall WI was formed! To date the group has 29 members, in just four months! We are very proud to have a younger core of ladies among us who will take the group through to the next era.

Our first tentative meeting back in January 2017 where 15 of us took part in a Tai Chi demonstration has moved forward rapidly to our best meeting to date which was Easter Wreath making in April. We have also turned our hands to chocolate making and enjoyed a fun evening learning all about which colours suit us during a Colour me Beautiful demonstration.

January 2017 (15 members)

Our enjoyment at the meetings is of course helped by half time refreshments, with delicious homemade cakes supplied by our members.

It is sure to be a busy first year for the Pearls as we have been asked to host 'The Great Wythall Bake Off' - a fun event at the local Carnival. We also intend to host a stall at one of the local School Fetes, all in addition to growing our newly formed group which meets at Scout HQ, Wythall Park, Silver Street.

So far 2017 has been kind to the Pearls, we have achieved a great deal in our first four months – long may it continue!

April 2017 (29 members)

We will strive to nurture this new friendship group, based on fun, laughter and our community.

Pebworth and District

Started in 1951. Monthly meetings on 1st Wednesday in Pebworth Village Hall.

Our members are active in every part of the community as parish and parochial church councillors, school governors, and Village Hall and Pebworth in Bloom committee members. We sing in the village choir and ring the church bells. For 25 years we have organised the village litter-pick and our teas for NGS Open Gardens and fetes are described as legendary!

Membership stands at 47 with numbers boosted recently by residents of a new housing estate, some of whom are new to WI. We retain many WI "faithfuls" - singing "Jerusalem", social times, competitions and delicious refreshments but are looking to the future by using social media and by encouraging the increasing interest in crafts. Talented members enjoy teaching their skills - art, crochet, fabric dyeing have recently been offered with the Knit and Natter group increasingly popular. Rambling and drama groups have been popular over the past 40 years (we won the County Drama Festival in 1981). A weekly Keep Fit class, started in 2010, has strong support and members enjoy success with the skittles and the quiz teams. Our noisiest and most competitive event however is the annual beetle drive.

We award a Denman College bursary, £50 annually to a local charity, and donate "pennies for friendship" to ACWW. An early morning swimathon and breakfast in 2004 raised funds for WaterAid. Fundraising events such as "bring and buys", jumble sales, car treasure hunts and barn dances, popular in the 1980s and 90s, have been replaced with talent auctions, book sales and "swishing" clothes swap events as members support recycling.

We have visited many local towns and cities for guided walks in the past 40 years and highlights further afield have been visits to Highgrove, the Houses of Parliament and Buckingham Palace. Our June meeting is held in a member's garden and July's is traditionally arranged by volunteers. We remember with special pleasure dressing up for the Mad Hatters' tea party in 1990, the carnival floats in the 1980s and the Elizabethan festival where four members took turns to ride side-saddle as Good Queen Bess! Our first book club is still going strong after 20 years. Not only have two more WI book clubs been introduced but also one for members' partners who discuss their reading at the pub while WI meetings take place!

Pedmore

Pedmore WI commenced in 1929, and we like to think it has grown and developed in line with WI ideals and beliefs. The initials WI can be seen every spring on the island which is at the centre of Pedmore, in the form of bulbs planted by our members.

Members have been responsible for many intricate items of craft, in the form of embroidery, knitting, tatting etc. and entries in craft competitions held over the years have been rewarded with many prizes. In fact, some remarkable examples of the detailed work achieved can be seen in the 'Loan Collection'. One of our members was asked to give a demonstration at the Royal College of Needlework in London. A handkerchief made by the same member was sent to Buckingham Palace and accepted by the Queen.

The Institute has over the years tried to commemorate special dates for the Country and our own area. Royal weddings and other royal dates were celebrated with parties and get togethers. The special 100th year of the WI was one such anniversary, being attended at the AGM by a delegate from Pedmore, and the garden party at Buckingham Palace by a representative from the Institute.

Pedmore has tried to be proactive as possible within the area with various petitions, whenever we thought our help might be of assistance. We have petitioned on behalf of school crossings, local hospital closures and the road signs denoting entry to Pedmore district.

We meet at Pedmore C of E School, as do Wychbury, and have a current membership of 28; we look forward to future years and a happy and prosperous WI.

Pedmore and Wychbury choir, formed from members of these two WIs and led by Pedmore's Gwen Bullas, had much success both within the Federation and elsewhere. In 1980 the choir gained three first, one second and two individual solo places in the WFWI music festival. The success was repeated two years later winning the same three silver cups for the same classes and the highest points total was also gained.

Until retirement in 2012, the choir performed many concerts and took part in various fund-raising events. These gave great enjoyment to all the audiences, and numerous charities benefitted from our singing.

Peopleton

Formed – 12th February 1930. Meet in the Village Hall on 2nd Tuesday at 7.30. Peopleton is quite a small village with currently about 600 residents.

1980-1990 – 49 members

During this decade the WI were quite forward thinking for the time with talks on Drug Abuse, Marriage Guidance, the importance of breast checks and smears and motorway driving. But as well as the serious side there was also the frivolous with Fashion Shows, Wine Tasting and a visit to Bulmers Cider in Hereford.

Visits to a vineyard, gardens and lots of local houses of interest were very much enjoyed as were the train journeys organised by WFWI.

The village fete was organised with Maypole dancing, fancy dress, sports, a band and BBQ complete with May Queen and flower girls all pulled along on a horse and cart float. At Christmas, Father Christmas arrived at his Grotto in the village hall to give out presents to the children.

A Denman Bursary was introduced and many members have benefitted from being able to attend the college for different courses, reporting back on what they have done.

In 1985 a performance of 'WInderella', was performed at Christmas to such acclaim that we had to have a second showing for the village. Unfortunately, WInderella's coach turned into a rather small 'three wheel' child's bike.

1990-2000 – 32 members

We had to meet in members' houses for four years as the village hall was closed, so goodbye to the mice and the cold and hello to a nice new, warm place to meet.

This decade we ventured into selling! We held a Car Boot Sale, but never again, someone wanted to buy the Land Rover we had come in. We also attempted a second-hand clothing sale, with much more luck.

In Tiddesley Wood we purchased a 'Rent a Nest' which was home to nine blue tits in its first year. We started playing skittles and got to the final one year. Some members joined the County Choir. We took part in 'Driver of the Year' but unfortunately didn't win, we also entered a garden design competition, held a fashion show and planted bulbs around the village hall and churchyard.

This was the decade that the members decided to sing Jerusalem only at the Annual Meeting or special occasions!

2000-2018 – average 48 members

This decade lots of things have taken place – a wall hanging was completed, with every member putting in at least one stitch, and now hangs in the entrance to the village hall.

Jam Making and Chutney classes along with flower arranging were organised for members. Christmas Angels and Trees, bags, willow weaving have all been attempted, some more successfully than others.

And, in 2002 the village was invited to another show that included four almost dressed members performing 'Hi we're the WI'.

One thing is certain about our WI, we are very welcoming, love our WI and are definitely aiming to be the same in 2018.

Pershore

The last forty years have seen Pershore WI enjoy a busy programme of events and an active membership of 40 this year.

We are now the oldest surviving WI in Worcestershire, and as such we are very proud to be celebrating our centenary in 2016. The first meeting took place in the Masonic Hall at the back of the Angel Hotel, and from 1921-1979 we had our own hall in Priest Lane. We moved to our present meeting place at Wulstan Hall in January 1979 when we sold the hall to the council due to a compulsory purchase order.

With the help of a grant from the Heritage Lottery Fund we have been able to take part in the "Pershore In WWI" project, which enabled us to research our history, while also being involved in various community events to commemorate the role of women in the First World War.

During the war years the WI was very influential in the production and distribution of food to the nation. To commemorate this, in 2016 we had a stall at the Tiddesley Wood Open Day, where we gave out seed potatoes with handouts of WWI recipes and offered free cake tasting. This enabled us to spread the word about the WI to many people.

Highlights of the year included a visit to The Eckington School of Cookery, where we were given a very interesting demonstration using recipes from the First World War. Also, a visit to Denman College was enjoyed by all our members during the Summer. Some of us researched the lives of the women who were on the first committee, and organised a walk around the houses they lived in at the time, appropriately finishing with Pimms and nibbles at our first meeting place, the Angel Hotel.

A few of us also helped research the chapter on our WI in the book "How the Pershore Plum Won The Great War", which was compiled by Prof Maggie Andrews and independent archivist Jenni Waugh as part of the work done with the help of The Heritage Lottery Fund.

As well as our association with the "Pershore In WWI" project we have also marked our centenary by knitting one hundred scarves, baby hats and blankets for charity and also filling one hundred shoe boxes for the shoebox appeal. Over the course of two sessions, we also made one hundred jars of jam.

Our celebrations will be completed when we have our Centenary Celebration at Pershore Abbey on Sunday November 20th and our Centenary lunch at The Angel on the following Monday. It has indeed been a memorable year for Pershore WI!

Poolbrook

Poolbrook WI meets in an outlying area of Malvern. The name derives from various pools and brooks running off our beautiful Malvern Hills. Our founder member was Mrs Polly Cartland (mother of novelist Barbara Cartland) who inaugurated the group in 1949. We initially met in the historic Foley Institute, moving to the more comfortable St Andrew's Hall in 2003. As the membership grew so large an extra WI was formed (sadly this is no more). Our membership is 36 in 2016.

We have been very active organising events, acting, exercising, baking, crafting, singing, puzzling and, of course, talking. We have helped in local activities including stalls at the village fete and planting roadside bulbs. Federation events have been fun with shopping trips, carol concerts, health talks and town visits, as well as providing cakes and helpers for the Three Counties Show.

Many of us have enjoyed the delights of Denman, ranging from embroidery and painting to philosophy and bread-making courses. We have visited historic Great Malvern Railway Station, Hampton Court and Weston's Cider as a group, while individuals have been presented to Camilla, Duchess of Cornwall, at the Buckingham Palace Garden party. And, of course, we have been to the Royal Albert Hall with the Queen (and thousands of other WI members!).

Our craft skills help raise funds with the best greeting cards made 'in-house'. Our skills were shown in making green hearts that were presented to local organisations to thank them for taking action on climate change – just one event of many that have featured prominently in our local paper.

Over the years a huge number of women have served on our committee developing their skills with experience and support from other members. Some have been there for a long time – others for just a year – all have helped grow our WI into the friendly, fun and active WI that we all enjoy today.

Powyke

Powyke WI opened its doors on the 15th November 1989. Initially meetings were held in the School Hall and then moved to The Orchard in Powick. We have 20 members, which includes some of our founder members.

Over the years, two trees have been planted. One marks the founding of the new WI. It has a seat around it which was reclaimed from another site in the Village and refurbished. The second was planted in the grounds of the Parish Hall to celebrate the Queen's Diamond Jubilee.

Many fundraising events for local charities have been held in the form of "Midsummer Madness", which always involved a large amount of strawberries! The WI made "angels" out of beads and safety pins for a festival at the local Church and have contributed to many Village events over the years including "litter picks". They welcomed the Olympic Torch through the Village in 2012. Over the years there have been many outings, lunches, learning new skills, sharing friendship and generally making the most of being members of the Women's Institute.

Pump House

On the 9th March 2005, a group of 19 ladies, who were interested in forming a new branch of the Women's Institute in the Barbourne area of Worcester, met with three WI Advisors to discuss the way forward. They agreed that the venue would be the former Waterworks Pump House on Gheluvelt Park and that the meetings would be held in the morning on the second Wednesday of each month. Two ladies, Sylvia Hudson and Dorothy Bucknall, volunteered to start a committee and after a little persuasion three more agreed to join them to make up a full committee. Further trial meetings took place in April and May and finally in June 2005 the Pump House WI was formally inaugurated and began regular monthly meetings. At this time the membership was up to 12 members and Sylvia Hudson had been elected as President.

Pump House Banner - 2014

At the November 2005 meeting, a WI Advisor attended and the members were told that the Pump House WI was now officially registered. All agreed that in a very short time it had become a very happy and successful group.

10th Anniversary Tree Planting 2015

By 2009 there were 30 members and currently, (2016) we have our full quota of 32, the maximum number that can meet in the room, plus a waiting list.

From our beginnings, we have developed a whole range of activities. We produced a recipe book, made visits to places of local interest, have an annual garden party and now have an active

Boat Trip (Pamela May) July 2016

book club, skittles team and theatre group. A special highlight was a coach trip to Highgrove to visit the gardens of Prince Charles. Our group "twinned" with a WI group from Lickhill near Stourport. A very impressive banner has been created by a number of members, and this is now proudly displayed at all major functions.

We are particularly fortunate with our location as currently the annual City of Worcester Show is held on Gheluvelt Park each August. We volunteered, as the local WI, to run a "home-made" cake stall, which has been very successful.

In 2015 we celebrated our 10th birthday and to mark the occasion we planted a Crab Apple tree alongside the Pump House building. This occasion also marked the 100th anniversary of the national WI movement.

Queenhill & District

Our 'home' since 1937 is a wooden hall in a corner of a field in a quiet, beautiful hamlet just outside Upton-upon-Severn. One of our main claims to fame is that this hall is ours - we own it! The location is not one people are likely to pass en-route to another town, but we do get visitors. Apart from human visitors we enjoy the company of the cows in the nearby field who like to know what we are doing, and swallows come each year to nest in the porch.

We meet on the second Thursday of each month, in the afternoon. Our membership, therefore, currently 25, is made up of those who are retired from work. A successful Promotion Day was held in 1985 with BBC trainee technicians in attendance and, more recently, information about WI work was displayed in the local library. However, it is usually by word of mouth, recommendation and invitation that our membership numbers are maintained.

As part of the local community, we raised money for local provision of alternative training for young people (2015); held Children's Days providing activities for school children during the summer holidays; made 'animals' for the model village at the County Fun Day at Merevale Farm (1993); and in 1987, members appropriately dressed up for Oak Apple Day celebrations in Upton.

Another reason for dressing up came at the 60th Anniversary dinner when members were asked to wear "Thirties' Dress, please, with all relevant glitter. Diamonds and tiaras may be worn". We enter Trivia and Skittles teams, probably with more enthusiasm and enjoyment than competitive talent.

A thriving and talented art group, that includes men and women from the wider community, meets every Tuesday. Although we have no tutor, we learn from each other and thoroughly enjoy the company and enthusiastic encouragement we receive.

Just as any home needs maintenance and care, so does ours. Donations from the Art group and from the monthly trading stall are important for this. Since the 1980s, a new kitchen and cooker, new toilets and hand basins have been installed, and the plumbing improved. More recently the hall has been decorated, new curtains hung and new chairs have replaced the old plastic ones. In 2009, the appearance of the hall changed when the wooden platform at the end of the room was removed, providing more space for our activities.

Outside the hall, two footpaths converge, and for walkers our two benches, one to celebrate the Queen's Jubilee and the other the Millennium, are a welcome sight. On a sunny day, we like to sit there and look over towards the Malvern Hills. We count ourselves very lucky to be members of Queenhill WI.

Ripple & Earls Croome

Ripple WI was formed in 1921. Two years ago members of Croome WI voted to close their group because of dwindling numbers and join Ripple to become Ripple & Earls Croome WI. We currently meet in Ripple Parish Hall and have 33 members.

A member taught us how to tie a spray of flowers

The best way to tell you what our WI is like is through the words of our members.

Sue - *One amazing thing was talking to some Ripple WI members, whose grandmothers and mothers were founder members, who were taken as babies to the meetings. Over 90 years of inspiring women in the Ripple area!*

Carole - *I particularly enjoyed the coach trip to London/Greenwich. From the boat trip up the river, to walking round the historical buildings, and finally visiting the Fan Museum, which was fascinating. A great day out.*

Diane - *My pre-conceived ideas about the WI were swept away when I first came for a visit. The friendliness, speakers and trips have been first class.*

Shona - *Winning a bursary from my WI not only showed me how wonderful Denman is but I am now addicted to painting after the course I did.*

Di - *In the mid-Eighties some members of Ripple WI went on an exchange trip to Germany coming back with ideas for a Miming Circus Show that had been put on by their hosts. Props were made with much laughter and finally we had a cast. Ringmaster, Clowns, a Strong man, complete with leotard and droopy moustache. I also swept up escaping fleas after their performance!*

Jill - *I decided to join and phoned a member whom I did not know for some information. The next meeting was within a few days and I was told that I would be met and looked after. On arrival, I was met by the only two people in the room that I did in fact know! How weird was that?*

2011 Celebration of Ripple WI's 90 years

Rock

2018 sees Rock WI celebrating 86 years of friendship, sharing and laughter. The 1980's saw us meeting in a small, increasingly unsuitable village hall. Our WI included quite a number of younger members as well as some original founding members and we even had quite a few babies born during the 80's! The membership was around 32 with a good mix of different skills which enabled us to enter the County competitions and show the talents of our members. As the years have passed so a lot of members have moved away from the village and of course we have all got older! We now number 16, including one dual. Close friendships have been forged over the years which have endured the passage of time. We have not done anything truly remarkable but have had lots of social events which also included many WI husbands too.

2006 saw us moving to the new Village Hall which has been built nearer to the centre of the village. We are now endeavouring to bring our WI into the technological age by setting up an email account and possibly even a blog spot. Over the years we have attended Group, County and National events all of which we have thoroughly enjoyed. A former Worcestershire Federation County Chairman has been a longstanding member of our Institute.

To celebrate the Millennium we planted a black pear tree in the grounds of the church (see photo above) and have since then planted a flower bed in the grounds of the village hall. We also obtained a grant through NFWI to purchase a variety of different trees which were planted on the Millennium Green. Over the last few years, members of our WI have provided refreshments and other support at the annual Pound the Bounds sponsored walk which sees well over four hundred people supporting Midlands Air Ambulance which raised over seven thousand pounds in 2016.

We started a book club in 2010 which has gone from strength to strength and has certainly expanded the horizons of our reading experience. The NFWI triathlon challenge saw us all walking and swimming and some of us dusting off our old bikes in order to complete the required miles. We also contributed to the total number of miles it took to walk to the moon! Other WIs in our group joined us for strawberries, cakes and prosecco to celebrate 100 years of the WI in Britain in September 2015.

Although we don't know what the future holds, we are sure that the WI will continue to flourish with friends old and new.

Rubery

After having moved premises a couple of times, Rubery WI now meets at the Beacon Church Centre in Whetty Lane, Rubery. Previously, from formation in 1933 to about 1991, we met at St Chad's Church Hall and then had a brief sojourn at the Rubery Community Centre.

Throughout the years we have participated in Scrabble competitions, quizzes and skittles at Federation and Group levels and enjoyed short mat bowls, needlework, cookery and oil painting sessions on a weekly basis.

We also had members who provided the local community via the WI Markets with a wide variety of baking, garden produce and craft items for years until the markets ceased trading in Rubery.

We have talented ladies who sang in choirs, performed in drama groups, did voluntary work in hospitals, meals on wheels, WRVS and charity shops, served on committees and helped fundraise for ACWW and projects for Denman College for the WI and for local charities. Whether it be knitting for premature babies, or providing items for St. Basils (a Birmingham charity), our members are always enthusiastic and willing to give their time and so much the better if we can meet up in members' homes and enjoy tea and cake whilst we craft and work towards whatever project we are involved with. We are currently working on a new tablecloth in our crafts group and every member will have had some input.

At our monthly meetings we always have a competition which showcases the talents of our members be it collage, sugar craft, baking or photography, etc. At the end of the year the member with the most "wins" is awarded the Competitions Cup.

Over the years we have visited stately homes, beautiful gardens, various venues of historical, industrial and social interest, enjoyed taking holidays together and of course attended courses of wide and varied subjects at Denman College. We were lucky enough to win an "awards for all" grant and a group of us attended courses at Denman and were able to pass on our experiences and knowledge learned to the rest of the Institute and our community.

Our Institute has 26 members now, fewer than in earlier years but our commitment to the WI remains as strong as ever.

Rushwick in Bedwardine

People are at the centre of our WI, so we asked our 46 members to give us words that described our WI. The responses were 'friendship', 'fun', 'laughter' and 'participation'. This sums us up. Our history is not so much what we have done but what we are.

We have done many things over the years. The 1980's saw our 21st birthday party at the village hall in 1983. These were also the carnival years, with Rushwick taking part in the Worcester Carnival every year and winning several times with their imaginative and creative floats. There was one based on nursery rhymes and one based on 'a day at the races' among others. 'They involved lots of hard work but were great fun' commented one member.

We had strong ties with Saighton WI in Cheshire and visited Chester biennially throughout the years until they closed in 2005. They visited us in return. On one of the visits to Chester we all went to the town hall and met the Lady Mayor.

An annual party was given for senior citizens of the village until 2001. By then we had all become senior citizens ourselves and these parties were discontinued.

Visits and trips have always been popular and included Brighton in 1986, Lincoln in 1987, Bath in 1987, Pebble Mill in 1990 and Granada in 1995. There were visits to Oxford in 1997, Chatsworth in 2000, the Bull Ring in 2003. A highlight was a trip to Highgrove House in 2007. There were Christmas shopping trips to Cardiff and the Bull Ring in Birmingham.

Our WI had holidays abroad. There was Paris in 2001, Prague in 2005 and Seville in 2007. One member said of the visit to Prague – 'never stopped laughing from the moment we set off until we got back. A lovely city and we saw all the touristy things'.

Members take part in lots of varied activities including walking, singing, craft group, book group, skittles and lunch groups. There really is something for everyone. The picture was taken at a strawberry and cream tea when we had a spring bonnet competition.

There have also been strong ties in the community with us taking part in the St Johns Fair for many years and, in recent years, supporting the Rushwick May Fair as well as coffee mornings supporting local charities.

At our monthly meetings in Rushwick Village Hall, we have had memorable speakers who have talked to us about such diverse subjects as 'Textiles at the V&A', 'Work of the Air Ambulance', 'Belly Dancing', 'Rescue Dogs' and 'Working in a holiday camp'. A recent very memorable talk was about kidney transplants. It was an inspiring talk.

I would like to end with a quote from one of our long-standing members. 'Having lived in Rushwick all my life I can remember when it really was a village. It's only groups like the WI that unite us and keep us together, so we still feel we are a village and that Rushwick is still special.'

St Catherine's Blackwell

On 18th November 2004 a meeting was held at The Wheel in Blackwell. The idea was to introduce a new WI, in the evening, for ladies in Blackwell and the surrounding areas who were unable to attend a meeting during the day.

St Catherine's Blackwell was formed - the first meeting was 20th January 2005.

*Our Founder
Member*

*Visit to Chateau
Impney*

*Centenary at
Avoncroft*

Currently we have a programme of speakers and have extended our activities and interests within the local community and beyond. We support our local First School's annual fete and have knitted and sold poppies with the proceeds going to the British Legion. We have knitted blankets and hats for babies in Malawi and filled shoe boxes for The Samaritans Purse. We have also made donations to The Primrose Hospice and Bromsgrove Basement Project.

The group supports other WIs' activities as well as Federation events. We took part in passing on the Centenary Baton at Avoncroft Museum and also the Centenary Annual Meeting which was streamed to the Palace Theatre in Redditch in June 2015. Members also attend the annual Carol Services.

Many members have attended both residential and day courses at Denman College and we are already planning visits for 2018. Donations were made by our WI to the Denman Appeal.

We are a sociable group with a Culture Club for outings and lunches. There is a book club and a skittles group. Summer BBQs, afternoon teas and craft sales are also organised. We have annual trips; we have visited Buckingham Palace, Windsor Castle, Highgrove, Chatsworth, Highclere, Hampton Court Castle and Bletchley Park.

We have a reputation for being friendly and welcoming and are looking forward to the future with many more events in the planning.

At present we have 30 members and we meet on the third Thursday of every month at The Wheel St Catherine's Church, Linthurst Newtown, Blackwell, Bromsgrove B60 1BL.

St Gabriel's

In 1993 several senior members of Hanley Castle WI decided that they could no longer drive at night, but as long standing members of the WI they wished to continue to belong so Mrs Sheila Sivell investigated starting a new afternoon branch. The name St Gabriel's was chosen to avoid confusion with Hanley Castle WI who also met in Hanley Swan Memorial Hall.

Helen with the winning entry

Although not a very active group we did enjoy speakers and the friendship built up over many years, but our favourite activity was craft, and most years we entered the county craft show, which due to Helen Owens getting top marks for her beautiful beaded bag, helped to win the shield in 2004.

Latterly numbers have increased and the average age has dropped by 15 years. We are now an active group, with a skittles team, a book club, an eating group and still a craft group. Our varied and interesting meetings are still held at 2 pm. We now have an outing in August, a garden meeting in June and a Christmas meal in December.

We continue to support local, council and national meetings and have been proud to have the role of Group Co-ordinator filled by our WI for the past 18 years. Our WI now has 28 members (2016) and prides itself on being a happy and friendly group that is still growing.

Celebrating the Centenary Baton in 2014

St Michael's

St Michael's WI is situated in the market town of Tenbury Wells, Worcestershire and was formed as a result of two young married mothers taking their babies for a walk one sunny afternoon in 1954. In 2014 we celebrated our 60th anniversary with a celebratory lunch for members, family and friends.

We meet in our village hall and are a medium sized WI of approximately 32 members, having grown steadily since the fledgling beginning in 1954.

A plaque was made to commemorate this milestone and every member embroidered their initials, as shown on the photograph above.

Our WI is vibrant and sociable with a mixed age group. Our members enjoy having days out and lunch get togethers. We have a keen Book Club which meets once a month and an enthusiastic Craft Group (especially for beginners).

Over the years, St Michael's Women's Institute has taken part in many activities in the local community, carnivals, fetes and bring and buy sales to raise funds for the various groups.

Our professional crafters are amazing and have won the Horticultural Section Competition at the Tenbury Countryside Show every year for the last four years. The above photograph shows our president receiving the shield this year which was the play Macbeth, as shown in the picture below.

We have enjoyed a mixture of speakers over the years and look forward to organising many more speakers and outings over the years to come.

The last two years we have catered for the acts at the Tenbury Music Festival.

St. Peter's

Cotinus Bush

Members with the Mayor in the Mayor's Parlour after a conducted tour of the Guildhall in 2003

St. Peter's WI held its first meeting in May 1988 in St. Mark's Church Hall. Twenty-six members were enrolled and Mrs Julie Smith was elected as President.

The WI still meets in the Church Hall, Orchard Street on the 3rd Wednesday of each month at 7.30 pm. Mrs Maureen Matthews, Mrs Barbara Rowberry, Mrs Dilys Round and Mrs Diana Bethell are among those who joined in 1988 and are still active regular members today. Our membership in 2016 is still 26, although it has gone up and down over the years.

We are a very social group, with outings, theatre trips and meals out. We enter a team in the Skittles League every year and attend various County Federation events. Our birthday and Christmas meetings always include visitors from other Institutes in our Group. Social time in our meetings includes a competition every month where points are given not only for the winner, but for entering, the person with the most points at the end of the year wins £5 and a trophy to keep for the year. Quizzes are also very popular among the members.

To celebrate the Millenium, a Cotinus purple bush was planted in the garden of St. Mark's Church with a plaque to mark the occasion (see photo above).

New members are always made welcome.

Salwarpe

Welcome to Salwarpe WI. We meet on the second Monday monthly at 7.30 pm in Salwarpe Village Hall, Copcut Lane, Droitwich WR9 0AH.

We were formed on Monday 7th January 1918 with Mrs Sinker (the Vicar's wife) as President, Miss Lucy Hingley (the annual *Lucy Hingley Medical Lecture* benefactor) as Hon. Secretary, and Mrs Yates as Treasurer. Beginning at our up-market Salwarpe Court, time was spent at the local village school, then on to our local Pub (the Copcut Elm). It is finally residing in our wonderfully equipped Village Hall, for which we thank Mrs Anne Thomas, then of Salwarpe Court, for her land donation to the village and the assisted building of the hall in 1967.

Annually, in mid-August, we collaborate with the Village Fete Committee by organising and running the Teas in the Hall. As is expected of the WI, we bake cakes in vast quantities, and serve drinks of tea, coffee or squash. Much to the disappointment of many visitors, on a hot, sunny Saturday in August, none of the drinks are alcoholic! Proceeds go towards the repair and maintenance of our mediaeval St Michael's Church.

Meetings cover a wide range of subjects from *(naturally)* cookery, millinery, guide dogs, history, and theatre, to personal safety. Alternatively, we have demonstrators encouraging us to model clay, do T'ai Chi, draw and paint, etc. Other meetings may just be social fun nights while including discussions and voting on Annual Resolutions. We always have a competition item to raise funds for ACWW. At least once or twice a year we try to incorporate outings to Gardens, Stately Homes, or River Cruises, as well as Federation events, and once … to Highgrove.

In 2008, the County Federation twinned every WI within the County in the hope of extending the hand of friendship. Our twinning was with Wythall WI, and nine years on we are both proud to be the only two WIs continuing to be in close touch. Each year we alternate in hosting a special event or outing so we can get together, as well as meeting at other events during the year. We have made good and long-standing friends along the way and have a lot of fun.

We have various social groups including Book Group, Coffee, Skittles, UFOs … UnFinished Objects (craft, sewing, knitting etc), and Walkers.

One of our major achievements has been a needlework collage of our Village. It took four years, 1991-95, and 45 members to complete an 8x6 feet four-panelled screen. This screen now hangs in the hall, framed, as it was deemed too precious to leave as free-standing panels.

As we come up to our Centenary in 2018, the same year as the Federation, we are putting together a programme of events which we hope will do us proud as a WI, as well as pleasing our members. With a membership of 33, both long-standing and new, we have a good mix of tradition and fresh ideas.

Long may we continue to flourish!

web: salwarpewi.wordpress.com   *email: salwarpewi@gmail.com*

Sidemoor

Sidemoor WI started in 1956, by the wife of Godfrey Baisley (Archer Fame).

1980: Many members went to Holland to the bulb fields travelling by coach and ferry. The flowers were really beautiful. During this time, members were involved in a produce show making jams, cakes and knitted garments and flower arrangements. Several ladies won prizes!

1982: During the revival of the Carnival, Sidemoor WI entered a float named 'Past-present-future'. The float gained best in show for the non-commercial class. A certificate and money were the prizes. One member painted a picture of Noeroyfforeden for the Day Room at Bromsgrove General Hospital.

1983: For the Carnival the group had a Caribbean pirates' boat pulled by a car! This won the Silver cup which was very pleasing and helped raise money for the hospital. Other floats made by the group in subsequent years were: Postman Pat, Horse and Coach and George the Dragon.

There have been numerous successful trips over the years some of which are detailed below.

A visit to Highgrove walking round the gardens was very memorable with a stop in Tetbury to the Prince of Wales's shop. A ride on the wheel in London and a boat trip on the River Thames was another lovely trip! Our members particularly have enjoyed going on 'Mystery trips,' which ended up in Malvern, Astley and Stourport.

Members have visited Denman College to attend their courses which they loved. They were rather impressed by the high standard of accommodation, catering and tuition.

A few years ago the group were involved in Skittles matches at the D.D.S.S club in Bromsgrove which is no longer there. A very talented member wrote a St Trinian's play for members called 'Sylvia's Girls.' Our group has also had many social evenings with Rock WI, our twinning partners.

Overall, Sidemoor celebrates members' birthdays, Easter, Christmas and together has celebrated the Queen's Diamond Jubilee, and the 100 year celebration of the WI in 2015.

Locally, we are involved in donating Easter Eggs to Sunfield Children's Home whilst further afield we knit jumpers and blankets for babies in Uganda.

Sidemoor is an active member of Bromsgrove Group, and regularly attends its events and monthly walks.

Regular meetings are at Amphlett Hall. We continue to produce an interesting and fun-packed Programme for our 22 members, so that they can learn something, make friends and just have fun together!

Somerleyton

Our WI is unlike many of the Institutes in Worcestershire as we are based in a town. When formed 50 years ago this was quite unusual as The WI was usually synonymous with Village Life. Nowadays WIs are being formed in towns and cities across the country. And so it came to pass that Somerleyton on the east side of Kidderminster came into being!

Formed in 1967 with just over 50 members, meetings were held in St Chad's Church Hall, Somerleyton Avenue - hence our name.

Numbers were buoyant for a number of years but when membership began to decrease we moved to St Cecilia's Church Hall in Hoobrook.

The membership remained quite low, but members enjoyed the meetings and taking part in extra-curricular activities such as group meetings and outings. Despite these low numbers we were always active and some members looked beyond their own group and joined the wider circle of WI life.

In the 80's and 90's Somerleyton provided The Kidderminster Group with two Group Secretaries - Beryl Evans and Margaret Burbey. Both were very efficient in these roles with Beryl taking on the role of Group Treasurer when Margaret was Group Secretary. Beryl was indeed a very busy lady teaching Bridge classes across the county and was also the first Quiz setter for the County Quiz Competitions.

Another past president, Sue Jennings, also served on the County Executive Committee for a short time.

Over the last few years our membership has increased to around 50 members and we have now moved into the Church for our meetings in order to accommodate everyone.

Several of our members have shared their talents with fellow members at meetings: craft workshops; art workshops; speaking about their holidays. Walks have been organised for those who enjoy being active with several members participating in the Stepping Out Challenge to celebrate 90 years of the foundation of The WI.

To mark the centenary of the WI it was decided to create a new wall hanging, but rather than being made by a couple of our talented crafters, this time everyone would contribute!

Everyone was provided with a square of fabric and asked to complete a piece of needlework, which was to be a reflection of themselves. These included knitted pieces, applique, lace work, crochet, with hobbies and pastimes such as gardening, music and crafts being depicted. Each individual piece is individually signed.

The squares were then put together and quilted by Jane Inns, one of our newest members. The end result has been greatly admired and it is a lasting reminder of the ladies who were members of Somerleyton WI in 2015. Each piece is an individual time capsule, highlighting the diverse talents and interests that make up our WI.

SPArkles WI was formed on 6th December 2012. As a New Wave WI it was hoped that younger women would be encouraged to become members of Women's Institutes. We certainly have younger members, but not exclusively so. Our members have been aged from their 20s to their 70s, so we prefer to think of ourselves as young in heart and attitude.

We have a very varied programme of events including Morris dancing, crafting and talks from authors and screenwriters.

We also get involved in community events, holding a

stall at one of the Droitwich Festivals and judging jam for a local competition.

Outside of our monthly meetings we have many activities for our members to join in if they wish. We have a cookery group where members learn to cook anything from bread to profiteroles. There is a knit and natter group which meets in a local pub. There members can knit, crochet or just join in the conversation. Group projects have included yarn bombing with the items

being made into blankets for a local charity afterwards and twiddlemuffs. We also have a book group, skittles team and craft group. We enjoy theatre and cinema outings and we have a Bucket Club.

The Bucket Club invites members to tell others about things they would like to do but have no one to do it with. Other members then get involved. So far members have learned bee keeping, walked alpacas and participated in a Mud Run.

We are now five years old. We meet in the Old Library Centre and have grown to 40 members and are looking forward to the future.

Why SPArkles? Because we are in Droitwich Spa and were formed at Christmas.

Stone

1921 – 2010
Meeting on the first Monday of each month. Average attendance 45

Meetings were originally held at the old Land Army Hall at Harvington: damp and cold! When the hall was knocked down for redevelopment, we moved to Stone First School temporarily, warm at last. Our final move was to The Oaks Community Hall in Harvington, with all the modern facilities.

Stone WI had a very strong CRAFT following, which included Needlework, Art, Cooking and Flower Arranging. Craft lessons were held once a month, all presented by individual members.

We had lessons from our brilliant President Margaret Mills on "How To Make The Perfect Sandwich". It was military precision for group meetings and parties: they were always well attended.

Dorothy Bond was also fondly remembered as an excellent President, ensuring lots of fun at the Fancy Dress themed New Year party, where partners were also invited.

FUNDRAISING was always enjoyable with BBQs, coffee mornings and afternoon cream teas held at members' homes; wonderful jumble sales, car treasure hunts ending at a pub for drinks; skittles evenings with a fish and chip supper, and dog walking rambles.

OUTINGS were also very popular, visiting gardens, Denman College and tea at Peopleton WI. The highlight was a visit to Highgrove the home of HRH Prince Charles.

Time has moved on from when all members had to take a piece of coal for the fire at Stone Church Hall. We were like a family, our oldest member Edith Bell aged ninety years, was always happy to meet and greet new members. As the numbers dwindled, there was unwillingness to take office, and it eventually became financially impossible to continue. It was a very sad end after such happy times.

Stone WI Celebrating its 80th Birthday

Storridge

Our Millennium Year

The Parish Council produced a book containing details of all local organisations in which we were included. In May a plant sale was held for WI funds and in June we took part in a Flower Festival in Storridge Church with the theme 'Enigma Variations'.

What to do for the Millennium Project 'Celebrating our Communities'? It was decided to plant daffodils around the village signs and small shrubs around the village hall. In July a 'ragwort root-out' was undertaken and members spent several hours pulling up ragwort from the verges of the A4103. Dressed in luminous jackets and armed with signs warning the traffic, they filled a trailer with the five-foot tall weeds. Afterwards other members made tea and the ragwort was burnt. Ragwort is poisonous to grazing animals and they can die due to the build-up of toxins in their bodies.

In August we had a lovely visit to Hellen's, Much Marcle – a guided tour and supper made a splendid evening.

Storridge members entered the Group Craft Spectacular, where they won three first prizes and three thirds. The September meeting was unfortunately very poorly attended due to petrol shortages!

In October we hosted the Elgar Group autumn meeting, with the theme 'Music'. The speaker was William Boughton, conductor of the English String Orchestra, who spoke about Edward Elgar. The guests enjoyed a ploughman's, apple crumble and apple juice or cider, followed by a musical quiz. In November the President led a brainstorming session for ideas for Storridge's contribution to WFWI's 'Picture on Calico', to be part of one of three WFWI banners, and a sub-group was formed to produce this. In December the year was rounded off with mulled wine and ideas to celebrate Christmas.

We have a tradition, started in 1941, for the hostess to give a motto. This was an idea from a programme conference in Hereford, the federation Storridge belonged to at the time. The example we have chosen here sums up life today: 'If it wasn't for the last minute, nothing would get done!'

Storridge WI was formed in 1936 and, since 1956, we have met at Storridge Village Hall. Currently we have 17 members.

Stourton

Stourton WI is a thriving WI with a growing membership, meeting in Stourton Village Hall. We now have 69 members and 1 dual member.

We have several successful Clubs including a poetry group who read poems either on a certain topic or by a specific poet. They have made two poetry discs raising £400 for charity. Other groups include an art group and a craft group, who were responsible for making our superb table cloth between 1990 and 1992. We also have a book club, a family history group and a bridge group. We have run several very successful Bridge drives raising about £600 each. There are thriving Supper and Sunday Lunch groups. Our Choir sings every year at the Hagley Group Christmas Service and they have taken part with the Worcestershire WI choir's concerts at Kidderminster Town Hall and Worcester Cathedral.

We have also organised several outings including visits to the Melton Mowbery Pork Pie factory, Chester, Hunstanton, Llandudno, David Austin Roses, several museums including The Pen, The Jewellery, The Coffin and Kidderminster Carpet, The Back to Back Houses and several visits to the theatre.

In 2015 we had a party to celebrate our 600th meeting. It was a lively party with 60's and 70's music provided by Chris Rai. We had invited advisors from the Worcestershire Federation and several past Presidents. In this year we also organised the Autumn Group meeting for Hagley Group. It was a very successful meeting with David Heeley the blind marathon runner as our guest speaker. He was an inspiration to all.

Swanpool

A meeting was held on November 20th 1980, at the Scout Hall in Swanpool Walk, St Johns, Worcester, to discuss the formation of a Women's Institute. There was an attendance of 72 prospective members. It was agreed that it would meet on the 3rd Thursday of the month at 2.30 pm. There were suggestions to name it St Johns Institute or Swanpool, the old name for that part of Worcester. The area has underlying water and fed many springs which supported osier beds. Swanpool was voted for and it was noted that the name lent itself well to a design on its own tablecloth!

After a while the meetings moved to St Clement's Church Hall and then again to St John's Sports Centre. Later, meetings were held at the Parish Room in King Charles Place, where the 10th anniversary was celebrated whilst Betty Gardner was President. Once there was a trip to the Houses of Parliament as Peggy Brookes knew Peter Walker MP. Summer meetings often took the form of garden parties in Vera Barlow's garden.

The final move was to the present venue – the Methodist Church Hall in Bromyard Road. At some point the meetings changed to the 3rd Wednesday in the month. The meetings and visits have been many and varied. On our 25th anniversary, when Catherine Paterson was President, we were lucky enough to have James McDonald from the television news as our speaker (his mother Pat was and still is a member). We usually have a special meeting in July when we welcome visitors and have a jolly good tea. Since Catherine's Presidency we have had Joan Davies, Ruby Ruff and at present Kay Newman as our President.

We have a thriving Craft Club which meets once a month and has done so for thirty-four years. We also have a successful Book Club whose monthly meetings are held at our local library. Every two months we get together for lunch out. We usually visit the local theatre several times a year. This year, 2015, we were lucky enough to win the shield for skittles, in our second year of playing. Not all members do all things, but most do some of them. Last year we had an outing to Stratford and went on a backstage tour at the RSC. Other years have taken us to Ledbury, Hereford, Tewkesbury, Bromyard, Bourton on the Water and the lavender fields. A very memorable trip was to Prince Charles's home, Highgrove near Tetbury.

The numbers have not stayed at the heady heights of the initial group, but have risen again gradually to the present 44 and we feel optimistic that Swanpool WI has a happy and strong future.

Tenbury Wells

Tenbury Institute was formed in 1922 and since 1980 it has celebrated several anniversaries, the most recent being our 90th year. We had previously marked our 75th Anniversary by the planting of a flowering cherry tree in our park and also by planting spring bulbs in various areas of the town. The venue where we meet has not changed and it is still the Methodist Hall in Tenbury.

Left to right: Back Row - Mary Davison : Anita Green : Jan Kelly : Val Smith : Meg Rudd : Margaret Davis : Vicky Smith : Betty Boffey Front Row - Primrose Wallace : Treasurer Lynda Archer : 2016 President Maggie Downes : Secretary Monica Rees : Primrose Simpson.

The membership is not a large one, currently 21, but it has always been a friendly group which welcomes newcomers and which also takes part in community events such as the annual children's 'Party in the Park' organised by our local police, as well as the Tenbury Countryside Show which is organised annually in August by the local Agricultural Society.

Several of our members have attended Denman College and then returned to teach us the new skills that they have learnt.

In our present membership, we have several members who are keen knitters and we now have regular knitting sessions where we produce items for various organisations who work overseas, as well as here in Britain. Currently, many blankets, toys and children's wear have been produced for shipment to the refugee camps in Calais.

Other activities include some interesting outings to gardens and museums and libraries, the most recent being a visit to a local factory. Our members also like going to the theatre with an annual visit to a pantomime.

Members are encouraged to respond to the Resolutions – an important aspect of the WI that we try to act upon.

Meetings with other WIs in the Teme & Tenbury Group are held regularly and many long term friendships have been made over the years.

All of our members would agree that the WI has inspired us and given us lots of new experiences and friends.

Trimpley Green

Trimpley Green WI held its first meeting in Trimpley Village Hall on Wednesday 16th September 2009 and with the help of two WI Advisors and Elaine as our first President the new WI was born. The majority of our meetings have been held in the village hall, meeting on the 3rd Wednesday of each month.

Our core membership has remained the same people with our numbers varying between 28 and 35 as members have come and gone.

We have several small groups that meet once a month; our Art Group, hosted by Jane, is always a very therapeutic afternoon and always with copious amounts of yummy cake.

Over the years we have also enjoyed summer walks with the routes planned by Irene, plus winter games including darts, dominos and crib groups, meeting at a local pub, also organised by Irene with Paul trying to keep order and doing the maths for us.

In year three we hosted our first group WI meeting and our Craft group initially met to make a Trimpley Green WI cloth for this meeting. Since then we have continued to make a wide variety of craft items which we sell at various events to boost our funds so we can afford a special event every few years.

The first special event took place in year three when we enjoyed an evening cruise up the canal with Fish & Chips for supper and a 'sing along' on the way back.

The second was when we celebrated our 5th Anniversary with a meal and live music at a local restaurant with a cake made and decorated by Monica.

And in 2016 we invited Faith Sax to come along with her 'African Drums'. We all had a drum and were able to play an African tune together, quite an achievement. It was a really wonderful sound.

We are a very sociable and fun loving group that enjoys equally a simple 'catch up' evening with supper or a 'hands on' evening making something new or listening to a speaker giving us a talk on a new topic.

Each year brings new experiences, new ideas, new challenges and always new members and new cake recipes.

Our next goal is to reach our 10th Anniversary and celebrate it in a new fun way with of course a cake, we hope made and decorated by our own star baker, Monica.

Trotshill Totties

Trotshill Totties was set up by Louise Dorr who contacted WI House because she wanted to join the WI and they told her that there wasn't one in Warndon Villages and would she like to set one up? The name was Louise's idea. It was in an area called Trotshill on a new estate and, as we were a much younger group, Totties seemed to fit. It was probably about the end of 2007. We started off meeting at the Barn at St Nicholas church and probably had in excess of 30 members. As most were in their 20s and 30s they dropped out as they had kids and their priorities changed - we now have 17 members.

The venue has now changed and we meet at the Lyppard Hub which is much better for parking and we no longer have to walk through the graveyard.

This seems to be why most of our members have joined: "I joined the WI as I was looking for a way to broaden my horizons. I can say that this has certainly happened! I have attended many informative and interesting meetings as well as experiencing some very different and inspiring life stories, engaging in evenings of fun and games (Reindeer drive anyone?!) and exploring local attractions - all with a wonderful group of women, who themselves have been a real pleasure. I would definitely recommend the WI. "

We meet at the Lyppard Hub, Ankerage Green, Warndon Villages, Worcester, WR4 0DZ on 2nd Tuesday in the Month

trotshilltotties@gmail.com

Webheath

Our WI was reformed after a break of many years and re-instated on 22nd October 2009 with a new committee.

We have enjoyed a variety of social events and made lots of new friends along the way.

Experiences have included: Kurling, skin care advice, emergency First Aid, craft evenings, cooking hints and demonstrations, gardening tips, suggestions for keeping fit, calligraphy as well as historical information about The Land Army Girls and The Bournville Story.

Visits to The BBC studios and the David Austin Roses centre, shopping trips to Oxford and Cheltenham have also featured in our itinerary.

Each year we have had talks from charities such as: Air Ambulance, Admiral Nurses, St. Basil's homeless charity, Domestic abuse, Cinnamon Trust and the Redditch Nightstop. We select a charity to support every Christmas, so this year we donated food parcels to the Salvation Army to issue following referrals from Health visitors, Social Services, desperate appeals for help and doctors.

We have celebrated in party style the Queen's jubilee, her 90th birthday, WI's 100th birthday and hosted several Group meetings. Christmas is enjoyed with party food plus a quiz.

Three of our members joined in the event in Pershore this year, where the baton was received and passed on to celebrate 100 years of the founding of the WI.

This year, 2016, three of us set up a "Knit and Natter group". Ten of our members have knitted squares which were sewn together to create a colourful blanket. We donated our first two blankets to a local care home and the residents were delighted with them!

All in all, we are a friendly and sociable group who enjoy learning new skills and sharing fun, informative events. We have about 30 members and meet in Webheath Village Hall, Redditch.

Welland

In 2011, Welland and satellite villages were growing in density and the gap within the many activities hosted in the local village hall lent itself to the formation of a new activity - a new Branch of the WI. Welland has had a WI before and the fledgling committee was a combination of old hands and new. With the support of HQ and Patience Broad (WI Advisor), recruitment began. A feature in local newspapers helped highlight the event and in January 2012 Welland Village Hall opened the doors to welcome new members. Success - once again Welland had its own WI.

The first year's programme showed a diversity of interest to members and concluded in a rousing costumed Old Time Music Hall evening. A bright new logo for the branch was adopted - a good omen for the future. Welland WI was well and truly on the map!

Welland WI Members showing off their handiwork and new logo

Over the last four years Welland has run a diverse programme to hold the interest of a diverse group of ladies. Food themed evenings have always been popular: Burns night, Spanish night, pudding night and Wine Tasting to name but a few. Welland likes to keep active and the programme always includes the opportunity to have a go at something new, like Belly Dancing, Morris Dancing, Tai Chi and Biodanza.

Always keen to have a go at something crafty, Welland has done Arm Knitting, Willow Stars and Bird Feeders, Hand Painted Baubles, Pottery Making and Bag Decorating. Many of these activities have been led by Welland's own talented members. Sometimes it's good to have a chance to really connect with each other. Evenings of Desert Island Discs and Favourite Poetry Reading have provided a wonderful opportunity to share some of the things that bring joy into our lives. In August, Welland like to get out and about. We have had a number of BBQs, a National Trust picnic and visit, and a Vineyard Tour in our own village.

The Branch's competitive streak gets a chance to come through once a year at the County Annual Meeting Competition. We try to enter everything, living up to the motto "It's not the winning, it's the taking part". That said we usually come away with a smattering of certificates and commendations!

With 18 members, Welland WI is a very friendly group and certainly makes new members feel welcomed and involved. We are looking forward to welcoming more new members from several nearby new estates due to be completed soon. New recruits will find a broad range of activities to keep the membership interested and active over the coming years.

Wells & Wyche

Formed 1977

This is a small selection of activities enjoyed by our members:

Outings and Lunches; Craft Group; Bellringing Group; Book Group; Coffee with Books and an Annual Study Day.

Crafty Ladies

Bellringing Fun

Comput@bus

Ladies who Lunch

Outings

Coffee with Books

We also support the community by helping with The 'Let's Cook' Campaign; The Local Women's Refuge; The Food Bank; The Village War Memorial; The Village Fete; Malvern Civic Week and an Annual Tea Party for the Malvern Blind Club. We have 45 members and meet in Malvern Wells Village Hall.

West Malvern

During the 1980's West Malvern had a very active WI, with members enjoying various outings and events. Locally the group won the Malvern Horticultural Show WI cup no less than three times, 1984, 1989 and 1997. To win, members had to bake, flower arrange and produce a handicraft exhibition.

Annual events with Worcestershire Federation included train outings to Brighton, Portsmouth, Lincoln, Exeter and Winchester, so the group travelled far and wide, while still finding time for local mystery trips around Herefordshire & Worcestershire - these always ended at a pub for supper! Other activities included a visit to Madresfield Court, a tour of the Houses of Parliament and a trip to Blenheim Palace. So there was always plenty for members to do.

Members were also actively involved in Village life. They had a carnival float, and entered pancake races, while helping celebrate 150 years of West Malvern Village by holding a party for the older members of the community. The group kept afloat with fundraising activities, such as jumble sales, car boot sales and teas. Speaking to members who were part of the WI at that time, it is very clear that they had a wonderful time together, making lifetime friends while learning new things and being active. Sadly in 1997 the decision was made to disband, as there were too few members for the group to continue to be viable.

Happily, in 2010 a new WI was formed in West Malvern, and we now have about 40 members. The committee work hard to create a varied and interesting calendar of events for members. Our activities range from having a go at belly dancing and zumba to hearing talks on bee keeping and local history. Alongside this we support the West Malvern festival Westfest by running a tea and cake tent, our biggest fundraiser of the year. We are a fun and friendly group of ladies, and have members who live in the village and others who come from other places. Friendships have been forged, new skills learnt. A highlight of the past few years was making Christmas wreaths with a professional florist, when everyone took home a wreath worthy of any front door. These activities give us a chance to get to know one another and welcome new members. Working together at our fundraising activities gives us a chance to serve our community and to work together as a team. Our book and craft clubs, which have been running since 2011, give members the chance to read and discuss books they may not have considered reading before and to knit and natter at craft club while working on individual projects. More recently we have expanded our clubs in a more active way, through skittles and badminton. We play in the WI league and enjoy the chance to mix with other WI groups, and play badminton each week.

This cake was baked by one of our members in 2016 to celebrate 100 years of Jerusalem – we sang it twice during our meeting and then enjoyed eating the cake!

There is something for everyone in West Malvern WI, with friendship, fun, lots of laughter and a feeling of belonging.

Whitbourne

Whitbourne WI celebrated its 50th Anniversary in 1983, and at the time was at a peak with 40 or more members across the spectrum of ages. It made the most of the energy of younger members and the wisdom of seniors. Meetings were held in the Coronation Hall right in the centre of the village, and usually included a competition, as well as interesting speakers and demonstrations, along with a flourishing stall of members' creations which contributed 10% of proceeds towards WI funds.

A highlight of the year locally is the annual Bromyard Gala which, until increased insurance costs made this impractical, had a procession of decorated floats. Younger members decorated a lorry driven by a member's husband and dressed as characters from children's television programmes, drove through the town and out to the gala field. Many members entered the produce and craft sections both at the Gala and Whitbourne's own produce show, and there was strong competition for both the Silver Jubilee Trophy (baking and preserves) and the Clarissa Jones Challenge Cup for Flower Arranging.

For the millennium, it was decided to make extensive improvements to the village hall, and Whitbourne WI embarked upon a lovely project to make an appliqué map of the village. Tiny pictures of all the houses were worked by individual members using a variety of embroidery skills then carefully stitched into the final map. The work, completed in 2004, is about the size of a single bed cover and is protected by glass, neatly framed in oak, and greets all visitors to the new Whitbourne Village Hall.

Our Institute is now much reduced in number (15 members), but looks forward to gaining new members as new houses are built in the locality and new occupiers move into the older properties in our ancient village.

Wickhamford

A poem penned in 1980's by Betty Bowles for a competition which still sums us up today:

> If a stranger from Mars should ask me why
> I belong to Wickhamford WI
> I'd tell him a few of the things we have done.
> The wonderful friendship, the laughter and fun.
>
> I'd tell of the cakes we have learnt to bake
> The beautiful quilt we all helped to make.
> The speakers we have listened to – both good and bad!
> The footpaths we've trodden, the parties we've had.
>
> The sick members visited with flowers and cheer.
> The carols we sang when Christmas was near
> The evening we held a St. Trinian's Ball.
> When jelly and doughnuts were enjoyed by all.
>
> And I'd say to that man ere he returned to Mars.
> "Don't leave your poor wife alone with the stars
> The next time you come down to earth from the sky.
> Just bring her along to our WI."

The eighties saw us walk the Cotswold Way in both directions, complete a survey for the Domesday book project, walk our parish footpaths and the new Evesham by-pass prior to opening. Handicraft, produce and fashion shows were held and a splendid quilt was made and raffled. Many members also took part in a village concert.

Into the nineties we celebrated our 40th year helping with the village Flower Festival, taking part in the County Cavalcade, holidaying in the Yorkshire Dales and celebrating VE day.

The Millennium turned with Childswickham WI joining us whilst their Hall was undergoing refurbishment and the link between the two WIs is carried on today through joining together in Group activities and open meetings. The County Skittles competition was contested and won and we kept the village tidy with litter picking days. Whilst membership has had its ups and downs – we now have 15 members - we think we have adapted to the changing times and given the membership a wide range of talks and activities.

Wickhamford WI is proud to still have Peggy Hancock as a founder member and she still remembers the 3s 6d that she paid for her first year's membership!! Ladies lunches are enjoyed once a month, visits to gardens and days out run alongside our meetings with speakers held in the Memorial Hall. Social media has arrived and we have our own Facebook page for members, a website will follow and we hope that this will encourage more ladies to join the WI, having just celebrated our 65th year we look forward to our County Centenary Celebrations.

Witton

In 1980 Witton WI was 15 years old with a growing membership. By 1990 over 70 enthusiastic ladies attended meetings regularly and it was probably the largest WI in the County. Grace Atkins was County President at that time and she was also a commanding and encouraging presence among us. Always so smart and elegant, Grace embodied all the WI virtues of that time and fun and friendship, creativity and participation at all levels flourished. Grace was much missed after her unexpected death in 2001.

Looking through all the scrapbooks, meticulously kept over the years, provides an intimate and also emotional insight into our history. We meet again so many faces no longer with us. We realise too how fortunate we have been in our presidents over the years and in their committees. The scrapbooks log their influence so well.

What fun we had when we used bursary money for active learning for everyone! Tai Chi, Line Dancing, Pottery, Jewellery making, we tried them all. Clegg Lyster used her sugar craft expertise to lead us all in making cake decorations. The photographs are all there to remind us!!

Mavis Perks was a founder member of our WI and for years has led a weekly walking group along the footpaths of Worcestershire. So many people have benefitted from the exercise, the fresh air and the companionship, and say what a great help the walks have been for them when times were tough and life was not easy.

The sewing group, led by Anne Booker and producing so many beautiful examples of WI craft, has been meeting weekly for many years. Recently, our special tablecloth received additional ornament because 2015 was a special year for Witton WI. We were 50 years old in November.

Jenny Kerridge, our President, received a special certificate at the Council Meeting and she baked an anniversary cake, using the National Centenary Cake recipe. The cake was cut by five founder members to proud applause at our November meeting and a joyful anniversary lunch completed our celebrations.

From the start, we have always met in the Methodist Church Hall in Worcester Road, Droitwich. We now have 41 members, and although we are a smaller group than we once were, new members are still joining us to a warm welcome and to meetings that are lively, interesting and thought provoking. We are proud of our tradition.

Wolverley

Wolverley WI is a small WI which despite some dips in membership has continued to thrive over the last 40 years. We remain closely linked to the community in Wolverley, supporting and contributing to local events, including Wolverley Carnival, work that goes on in the village to raise money for charities and also for funds for the proposed new Memorial Hall. We have links with the church, supporting the flower show and we meet in the church hall, which is used by many local groups. We moved there in January 2016 from Wolverley Memorial Hall where we had met for a long time. We currently have 32 members.

2018 will be a very special year for us as we will be celebrating our own Centenary as well as the Worcestershire Federation's. A keystone of our WI is our speaker programme and over the years we have enjoyed talks on a vast range of topics, which have been truly educational, informative and entertaining and we have learnt a lot and had a lot of fun.

We have been keen to support group meetings and have organised many social events for our members ranging from garden parties, book clubs, craft afternoons, knit and natter sessions, fish and chip suppers, walks, games and quizzes. We have also engaged in many other activities.

We asked our members what most stuck in their minds during their membership. This is a selection of what they said:

'I joined WI after being persuaded to join the choir by a member – best thing I could have done, made so many friends, gained confidence and enjoyed doing so many things which I wouldn't have tried',
'Wolverley WI choir – taking part in Scene 80 at Warwick University and performing 'Come to the Fair' written by June Parkes',
'Taking part in the NFWI Choir Competition in 1990, winning the area round and being in the final in London',
'Taking part in various drama productions from Cinderella Revisited, Aladdin, Beauty & the Beast to The Owl & the Pussycat',
'I joined the WI following the birth of my first child, going to meetings with my Mum. There was a thriving drama group which enacted the Legend of Wolverley and through this I was hooked'
'The trips organised by Wolverley WI to local places of interest and further afield such as Kew Gardens',
'The main time I remember is the visit to the potteries in Stoke',
'Following the closure of my first WI, I transferred to Wolverley and was warmly welcomed. Everyone is always friendly and encouraging people to join in',
'Best place to gain friends and confidence'.
Long may it continue to be so as we look forward to the next 40 years.

Worcester Belles

Worcester Belles WI first meeting was on 10th December 2012, initially meeting in the café at Asda. Some of our early speakers had to contend with the tannoy calls for 'Cleaner to aisle five' or 'Supervisor to till three' so we moved to the store's training room, but as membership increased (we now have 36) we outgrew the space and, after much searching, moved to St Mary's Hall in the Arboretum.

In our first few years we have held two very successful swishing (clothes swapping) evenings, raising funds for local charities and enjoyed a variety of speakers, walks and social events. We've fielded a team in the Federation Skittles tournaments (and held a few much needed practice evenings!), taken part in the Commonwealth War Graves Living Memory Project and supported our local and broader environment, with links to our local wildlife trust, and have our own local Climate Change Ambassador.

We have also become an established part of the Worcester Festival Summer Fete, running a successful cake stall at the Swan Theatre which gives us an opportunity to chat to people about the WI, at the same time as raising funds by selling, amongst other things, cake - most definitely a staple ingredient of any successful WI.

Wychbury

Wychbury WI was formed in September 1965, Pedmore WI's membership having outgrown its accommodation. 50 ladies came to the inaugural meeting. Pedmore and Wychbury's joint choir became popular for raising funds for local good causes and achieved much success at music festivals as did Wychbury's Drama Group, in the early years, producing many enjoyable entertainments for members and friends.

Besides our lively monthly meetings, which open with the singing of Jerusalem, our 70+ members can join a variety of group activities, namely: Art, Handicraft, Produce, Reading (books and poetry), Walking (far and near!), Luncheon and Coffee & Chat each month, as well as Seasonal Gardening. One of our newest members has become a Climate Change Ambassador, thus keeping us up to date with this issue. She gave a short presentation at our October meeting inviting members to write their concerns on green heart cards which were displayed and photographed. Each member received a packet of seeds to sow at home.

Our talented Handicraft Group have items in the County Loan Collection and, with the Produce Group, have had great success in County competitions as well as staging exhibitions at the Three Counties Show. Afternoon Handicraft have knitted blankets and tiny clothes for children in hospital and for premature babies, and most recently hats for fishermen at sea.

Several of our members volunteer in various capacities at Mary Stevens Hospice. Hagley Group of WIs created a garden bed and border there to mark 90 years of Worcestershire Federation. Some of our members are part of a small group carrying out ongoing maintenance.

Being a member of Wychbury WI brings opportunities to learn new skills in a welcoming environment, to make new friends with whom to have fun and to be supported by these friends when times are difficult. Long may it continue to flourish!

Wyre Piddle

The name of our village comes from the Wyre Forest whose name is derived from the Celtic "gweyr" for winding, whilst the Piddle Brook which runs through the village is a tributary of the River Avon. Piddle in this regard has nothing to do with the nineteenth century slang term, but rather comes from the Old English "pidele" meaning marsh or fen. We are surrounded with plum orchards, which are very old, but still produce abundant crops, ideal for making jams. The WI was founded in December 1937, although there was a break between 1956 and 1960.

We have a letter from Jocelyn Halls who, in April 1984, went to Denmam on a course to discover bird life. The Tutor was Mr John Spencer, who was, as she put it, a bit accident prone. She says that the food was plain but plentiful and she stayed in a single room in "New Croft" block. She thanks the WI for paying for her course.

In December 1987 the WI celebrated 50 years with a party. The history of the group's past half century was compiled especially for the occasion and a hand embroidered table cloth, of the village main street, was donated by three local women. At that time Sue Taylor was the President and Siobhan Avery was the Secretary.

Since the 1980's we have held a Flower Show in August, which included produce, handcrafts and baking. This has been a very successful event and has been well supported by the village.

In December 2007 the President, Sylvia Fletcher, held a 70th birthday party. 14 ex members were invited together with 14 present members plus Grace Richardson, our Group Co-ordinator. We were entertained by the newly formed Wyred Up, with a selection of gospel, jazz and Christmas numbers. The birthday cake was cut by the past president, Joan Tudor and Sylvia Fletcher.

We meet in the village hall and currently have 17 members. Our latest project will be producing alternative Christmas trees. These will be displayed in our village church, St. Anne's, and any money raised will go towards the restoration of the fifteenth century window.

We have several outings during the year and a small group regularly meet up to see a film in either Evesham or Pershore. We also have a Christmas lunch or dinner, held in our pub in the Village.

This card was designed in 1997 by Norma Timms, a Wyre Piddle member, to commemorate 100 years of the WI

We have a Facebook site, www.facebook.com/wyrepiddlewi

Wythall

Wythall WI was formed by 45 ladies on 24th October 1934 at Silver Street School buildings. It moved to the Wythall Village hall in 1937 where it still meets on the first Thursday of every month. Our membership has fluctuated between 120 to the now more comfortable 60 in the 2000's. 1984 saw our 50th birthday when we celebrated by working a collage depicting WI activities. This now hangs in the village hall.

Keep fit classes commenced in 1992 on a weekly basis and are still "running". The Rambling club has celebrated its 10th anniversary and in 2015 accumulated over 3,500 miles in the University of Worcester Moon Mission challenge. For the past 30 years the Discussion group has monthly "put the world to rights". The Craft group are always learning new skills.

Having won the Worcestershire round of the Mary Pedley award in 1965 for producing a scrapbook depicting village life, members continued the tradition by producing similar scrapbooks in 1975, 1985, 1995 and 2005. These have been used by local schools to show the changes which have taken place in our village.

Members are always willing to take part in Group, County and National competitions. Our successes include first in the WFWI golf competition in 1999, first in several floral exhibitions at Perdiswell and Nationally. Stories and poems have been submitted to Home & Country in the past and there is an annual Denman Bursary award via a ballot box selection which is highly sought after.

Wythall members aim to move with the times, consequently we have a very flourishing web site which is updated on an ongoing basis. Looking to the future, in 1990 we buried a time capsule which contained a small WI scrapbook, our programme, craft items and a small survey of family life. Friendship is the aim of our meetings and to this end we have continued the 'twinning' of 2008 with Salwarpe WI near Droitwich.

We celebrated our 80th Birthday in October 2014 with a meal at a local restaurant.

In the National Centenary Year, our president acted as our delegate at the Royal Albert Hall and a member, Sheila O'Shaughnessy, won the WFWI and regional heats of the 'Centenary Rich Fruit Cake Competition'. She afterwards made sufficient cake for all members who attended the 'live streaming' of the AGM at a theatre in Redditch. In July 2015 we celebrated the WI Centenary with a garden party.

Wythall WI is the hub of friendship and we, the members, thank Presidents past and present for their warmth and comradeship.

The WIs of The Worcestershire Federation as at the start of the Centenary Year

Listed by year of formation

1916	Pershore	1933	Queenhill & District	1968	Catshill
1917	Bromsgrove		Rubery		Hampton
	Hadzor & Oddingley	1934	Leigh & Bransford		Hillside@Alvechurch
	Hanbury		Whitbourne	1969	Hollywood
	Mamble-cum-Bayton		Wythall	1971	Lower Broadheath
1918	Droitwich	1936	Storridge	1977	Wells & Wyche
	Malvern	1937	Finstall & Cofton Hackett	1978	Littleworth & District
	Salwarpe		Kington with Dormston	1981	Swanpool
	Wolverley	1938	Eckington	1984	Foley Park
1919	Feckenham	1940	Broome	1986	Lenches
	Holt	1941	Ashton Under Hill	1988	Kinver Village
1920	Blakedown		Crowle		St Peter's
	Chaddesley Corbett		Guarlford	1989	Link Top
	Hartlebury	1943	Hallow	1990	Powyke
	Hopwood	1946	Alfrick	1992	Brockencote
	Inkberrow		Frankley		Drakes Cross
	Kempsey	1947	Callow Hill	1993	St Gabriel's
1921	Abberley		Cropthorne with Charlton	1996	Oak Apple
	Callow End	1948	Far Forest	1998	Fernhill Heath
	Great Comberton		Little Witley	2000	Menith Wood
	Hagley	1949	Poolbrook	2005	Pump House
	Hanley Castle	1950	The Littletons		St Catherine's, Blackwell
	Martley	1951	Pebworth & District	2007	Trotshill Totties
	Ripple & Earls Croome	1952	Naunton Beauchamp	2009	Abberley Clockwatchers
	Tenbury Wells		Wickhamford		Finstall Cross
1923	Broadheath with Rushwick	1953	Broadwas-on-Teme		Trimpley Green
	Cookhill		North Claines		Webheath
1925	Astley	1954	St Michael's	2010	Ark Angels
1926	Areley Kings	1956	Dodford		West Malvern
1927	Badsey		Sidemoor	2011	Evesham Vale
1928	Childswickham	1960	Stourton		Welland
1929	Alvechurch		Wyre Piddle	2012	Chad's
	Clent	1962	Rushwick In Bedwardine		Sparkles
	Pedmore	1963	Bentley Pauncefoot		Worcester Belles
1930	Beoley	1964	Clifton upon Teme	2013	Hot Peppers
	Blackwell & Burcot		Lickey		Mitton
	Fladbury & Moor	1965	Witton	2014	Bewdley
	Peopleton		Wychbury	2015	Bromsgrove Belles
1931	Cutnall Green	1966	Bockleton	2016	Honeybees
	Himbleton		Ipsley	2017	Barnt Green
1932	Fairfield	1967	Franche		Pearls of Wythall
	Rock		Somerleyton		